COLLECTED PAPERS ON SOUTH ASIA NO. 10

INSTITUTIONS *and* IDEOLOGIES

A SOAS South Asia Reader

Edited by
DAVID ARNOLD
and
PETER ROBB

CURZON PRESS

First published in the United Kingdom in 1993 by
Curzon Press Ltd.
St John's Studios
Church Road
Richmond
Surrey TW9 2QA

ISBN 0 7007 0284 9 Paperback
ISBN 0 7007 0283 0 Hardback

Collected Papers on South Asia No. 10

British Library Cataloguing in Publication Data
A CIP record for this book is available from the British Library

CONTENTS

PREFACE

This volume was prompted by a felt need for an introduction to South Asia, and also to the Centre of South Asian Studies at the School of Oriental and African Studies (SOAS) in the University of London. The Centre is a body set up to help research, publications and interdisciplinary collaboration among its members, who include academic and library staff and graduate students at SOAS, in association with colleagues elsewhere in London and around the world. The volume has been edited by David Arnold, who is Professor of South Asian History at SOAS, and Peter Robb, the current Chairman of the Centre of South Asian Studies. The editors, helped by a wider committee, made a selection from among recent published works of internal staff-members of the Centre, of whom there are currently 47, their scholarship embracing languages and literatures, history, law and the social sciences. Further volumes of the same kind may follow.

The aims of this book are modest. We recognise that there is and can be no fully satisfactory introductory text on South Asia. Why should there be? We do not expect a single introduction to be able to encompass the richness and diversity of history and culture in the whole of Europe; and the Indian subcontinent is certainly not less complex than the European. This book therefore adopts an approach which will enable the newcomer to approach South Asia, as it were, little by little. It assumes that one has to give up any idea of 'understanding' it all, and think instead of building up and joining together small islands of information, isolated pieces of insight. That is why this volume presents a series of different and partial views on to South Asia, rather than a survey of it. This is one way, the collection suggests, in which the new student of South Asia can make a beginning, or in which old hands can refurbish their ideas. Here we focus on some institutions and ideologies—the state, an army, a political party, and religion, law, medicine, language, literature and political thought. Much is neglected here (in terms of what is studied at SOAS, let alone what can be found in South Asia), and not all that is included is 'representative' either; but then we are rather arguing against the notion of a single South Asia whose essence we could somehow capture.

Camera-ready copy has been prepared in SOAS. The editors are indebted, as ever, to Janet Marks, executive officer of the Centre, and to all colleagues who have helped in the work. Conventions of spelling and citation are not wholly standardised but reflect practice in different disciplines.We also gratefully acknowledge permissions granted by the first publishers of these papers, of whom details are given in notes to the individual chapters.

Peter Robb

INTRODUCTION
Institutions and Ideologies in South Asia

David Arnold

This reader has two main purposes. The first is to serve as a general introduction to the history, culture and politics of South Asia.[1] It reproduces a number of articles which have appeared in print separately elsewhere. Taken together, they give an overview of the region as well as providing a series of more detailed case studies, which serve as multiple points of entry into a vast and undeniably complex subject.

The reader's second aim is to illustrate the diverse ways in which the study of the region is currently being pursued by scholars of South Asia—through its religion and art, language and literature, legal institutions, history and politics. In part this represents the development of new disciplinary approaches to the region, such as women's studies, but it also reflects the critical reworking of some long-established subjects, such as law, medicine, art and literature, in the light of recent concerns and controversies. This multi-disciplinary and often cross-disciplinary perspective is a vital part of the current scholarship on South Asia. It recognises both the strengths and the frailties of individual disciplines when faced with particular problems of understanding and analysis, and the value of a combined or comparative approach to a region of this scale and diversity.

Although originally written for separate publication, the essays in this volume are linked by a common concern with institutions and ideologies. The essays can be read as individual pieces, each addressing its own specific issues, but they can also be seen as part of a common enterprise of scholarly exploration. It hardly needs to be said that many of the issues and conflicts that make the headlines in South Asia today—state violence, religious unrest, ethnic and communal clashes, rural insurrection, poverty, war and famine, to name but a few—are common to many other regions of the contemporary world, particularly eastern Europe, the Middle East and sub-Saharan Africa. As such they

[1] The term 'South Asia' has come to be widely used since the 1950s to describe the region covered by the present-day states of Pakistan, India, Nepal, Bhutan, Bangladesh, Sri Lanka and the Maldives. Afghanistan, Tibet and Burma, though they have important geographical, historical and cultural affinities with the region are now generally regarded as lying outside it. For two useful descriptive and illustrative accounts of the region, see especially Francis Robinson (ed.), *The Cambridge Encyclopedia of India, Pakistan, Bangladesh, Sri Lanka* (Cambridge, 1989); Joseph E. Schwartzberg (ed.), *A Historical Atlas of South Asia* (2nd impression, New York, 1992).

invite wider comparative study. But they also assume a distinctive character derived from the peculiar geographical, historical, cultural and political circumstances of South Asia.

It has often been suggested that one critical aspect of this distinctive regional identity is the tension, indeed the paradox, between unity and diversity in South Asia.[2] At least to the eyes of the outside observer, there seems to be much that unites the region and distinguishes it from its neighbours. This, by convention, is 'the subcontinent', a term that has, remarkably, been reserved almost exclusively for South Asia. If, on the one hand, it is suggestive of the almost continental scale and complexity of the region, it is also indicative on the other of the way in which it is seemingly walled off by the Himalayan mountains from the rest of the Asian land-mass and divided by sea from its nearest maritime neighbours. Historically, the region has known a succession of empires, which, while never quite holding the entire region in their sway, have exercised significant and often enduring influence over large parts of it. A home to Buddhists, Jains, Hindus, Muslims, Christians, Sikhs and Zoroastrians, South Asia has often been identified as having been deeply influenced by culturally distinctive social practices and religious beliefs. And the common experience of colonialism (almost entirely under a single power, the British, by contrast to the colonially-partitioned worlds of Africa and South-East Asia), has arguably left a common legacy of ideas and institutions, and even a lasting attachment to the English language.

But to what extent are these supposedly unifying factors merely superficial, more evident to the outsider than to those within South Asia who would define themselvesd by a host of other, even antagonistic, identities? One of the underlying issues of this volume is how far the kinds of institutions and ideologies discussed here serve to reinforce the idea of South Asia as a collectivity, how far they promote or express aspects of cultural, social and political unity, or, by contrast, how far they subvert such claims and suggest instead a deep-rooted plurality of perception and identity. For every aspect of South Asia's unity that scholars might adduce, it is possible to counter with at least as many expressions of division or diversity. There is the remarkable variety of climate and terrain, of agriculture and land-use; there is the rich profusion of languages and dialects, of sects and creeds. There is, no less strikingly in the present age, the great variety of political forms and institutions, even between the three original successors to British rule—India, Pakistan, and Sri Lanka—to say nothing of the idiosyncrasies of Nepal, Bhutan or Bangladesh.

One of the difficulties which South Asia constantly poses is that of

[2] For some earlier examinations of this theme, see Philip Mason (ed.), *India and Ceylon: Unity and Diversity. A Symposium* (London, 1967).

locating the appropriate form or level for analysis, and this is no less the case with a discussion of institutions and ideologies than it is for many other fields of enquiry. South Asia is far from being a homogeneous region: its people are, and long have been, subject to a complex scale of social hierarchies and overlapping identities. The region is heir to an immensely powerful and authoritative tradition—of formal religious precept and practice, of institutions of law and government, of education, arts and sciences. Some aspects of this 'classical' tradition are discussed and documented here. But the volume also acknowledges the importance of another tradition—that of peasant society. At times the two seem to stand in stark contrast; at others they seem happily to merge and mingle. Indeed, a great deal of the scholarship on South Asia—among historians, anthropologists, linguists and political scientists alike—has been devoted precisely to how these two broad traditions intersect or diverge, or need to be supplemented and refined by reference to other social and cultural categories. This problem—of relating form and practice, the orthodox and the eclectic, the classical and the vernacular—is far from being an exclusively South Asian phenomenon, but it is one which contributes to the difficulties and complexities of scholarly analysis of the region. The articles in this volume instructively present some alternative perspectives on this issue, even if they cannot presume to have finally resolved it.

No less at issue here, and more acutely represented in recent scholarship than in the work of earlier generations of South Asia scholars, is the question of how identities are formed, imposed and interpreted. Problems of agency, representation and intentionality are among the most perplexing of those currently under investigation. In some instances it would appear that the kinds of institutions and identities discussed here emerged through an almost effortless and barely conscious process of evolution. In other instances, most evidently during the period of colonial rule, identities seem often to have been imposed or constructed, whether wilfully in a deliberate attempt to categorise or to change certain aspects of South Asian society, or from want of adequate understanding. Again, there are situations in which identities and institutions were consciously changed or created for ideological reasons—through the reform of language, for instance, or through the introduction of new legal and political institutions—though not always with the effect intended. Likewise, it is easy enough to assume that certain groups almost automatically enjoy the perquisites of power—by virtue of their social status, their wealth, their bureaucratic position and so forth—and that other groups, by contrast, are by the same terms virtually powerless, mere 'victims' of others' whims or aggression. But such presumptions of domination and subordination, of authority and agency, need constantly to be re-examined, and not just from one side of the power equation alone. Often, as some of these essays suggest, the situation was far from clear-cut or monolithic. Ideologies and institutions could subvert as well as support systems of cultural hegemony and political authority, or throw up major contradictions within the exercise of state and social power.

One further concern informs a number of these essays. This is the relationship between South Asia and the West, especially as this was reflected in the nature of the British rule and its legacies for the post-colonial age. Here again is an essential but in many ways intractable theme. On the one hand it is possible to take a long-term view of South Asia which traces a basic continuity between the present and the more distant past and sees colonialism as a relatively shortlived and superficial event. Such a view would emphasise the durability and adaptability of pre-colonial political and legal institutions, the 'great continuities' in philosophy, art and social practice, and would indeed see these traditions as working to minimise or undermine the impact of colonial rule. It might finally see these traditions re-emergent and resurgent in contemporary South Asia. Certainly much of contemporary politics and polemic would seem to support this version, but so too would much serious and seemingly non-partisan scholarship. Those of this view might argue that to give much prominence to the West is to deny South Asians their own agency and to flatter the West with excessive notions of its own impact and capacity to transform a society so different from its own. But other writers would find this view too 'essentialist' or perhaps too 'Orientalist', giving insufficient attention to the vast scale of change in South Asia over recent centuries and recent decades, ignoring the profound impact colonialism and the West have had on many aspects of South Asian life and thought. To put it crudely, was it the Hindu tradition or was it colonialism which made India what it is today? Did the peculiar cultural and political circumstances of Islam in South Asia forge the identity of Pakistan and Bangladesh, or were British policies and practices of greater moment? Was colonialism a turning-point or just a hiatus?

The essays in this volume necessarily vary considerably in their emphases and conclusions, but they effectively suggest some of the ways in which the colonial experience and South Asia's on-going encounter with the West has been ignored, resisted or absorbed—or, indeed, has remained a constant dialogue or an unresolvable dilemma—across a broad swathe of human experience, reflected not just in the more obvious realms of history, politics and economics, but also in the arts, in language, and still more elusively, but perhaps most momentously, in understandings of the self.

Part I: Ideologies

The divide between institutions and ideologies is an artificial one, and it is offered here mainly as a convenient way of grouping papers which overlap conceptually and in subject-matter. Nonetheless, something of a collective view and some connected themes can be gleaned from the summaries which are given in a descriptive paragraph at the start of each paper. Some further suggestions will be made in this and one other introduction to the two main sections into which the book is divided.

First, there is a clear view that there are *distinctive* South Asian characteristics and conditions—from the classical traditions explained by Gelblum to the particular response to political ideology discussed by Byres. Secondly, it is clear that this 'South Asia' is thought of as plural and not uniform: we are shown different *kinds* and different *levels* of South Asian society (Anderson on Islamic law, Leslie on women, Stein on peasants, and so on). Thirdly, it is clear that this 'South Asia' is never unchanging (though distance of time or space may have made it seem so to some observers). It is a South Asia in constant dialogue with itself, and with external influences. Finally, though the West has provided the most powerful of recent influences, yet these are never seen as all-powerful. The most convincing pictures of South Asia show—as here by Tillotson, Radice, Snell, Shackle, Taylor and others—that it has created its own evolving forms out of a range of ingredients, equally with regard to language or culture, and to politics or government.

With all this in mind we should come to the first paper, by Chapman, with a keen appreciation of the difficulties which he faced in providing a broad overview. He traces the current political divisions of the subcontinent back over the millenia, arguing that the divisions are ancient and deep, but that they occur within a geographical unity. This is a valuable point at which to start, because it invites us to think about what we tend to take for granted: the 'nationhood' of the present nations, and the 'regionality' of the whole region. It also shows how difficult it is to tell large and general stories about South Asia. Of course, on South Asia, there will always be room for a range of different views; and some recent scholarship tends, in particular, to suggest that Indian culture was much less rigid, and that trade was much more advanced earlier on, than used to be thought.[1] Thus too, after

[1] Some of the complexity of culture can be pursued in such works as A.L. Basham, *The Wonder that was India* (third ed., London, 1967), Wendy O'Flaherty [Doniger], *Hindu Myths* (Harmondsworth, 1975), Peter Hardy, *The Muslims of British India* (Cambridge, 1972)—all written by one-time members of SOAS—and J.L. Brockington, *Righteous Rama* (Delhi, 1985); while an alternative and more detailed view of the economic past could start with the essays, especially by Irfan Habib and Burton Stein, in Tapan

Mughal decline in the eighteenth century, British rule, according to recent accounts, was not so much drawn into a vacuum as added gradually to a range of vigorous and competing local powers and interest groups, which the British co-opted, subverted or overwhelmed.[2] There are differences of view, finally, on whether or not Hindus and Muslims in South Asia did (or do) always inhabit such different worlds as the orthodox versions of the religions imply. The historian, Gyanendra Pandey, has written: 'Communalism in India'—that is, perceived and antagonistic socio-religious identity—'is another characteristic and paradoxical product of the age of Reason (and of Capital)': though religions and identities existed, religious groupings, he suggests, were not 'ready-made', and nor was religious identity necessarily 'primitive', or 'pathological', or merely 'nationalism gone awry'.[3]

Yet, to encounter India in any age, one must, of course, attend to religion. However recent their present forms and political implications, elements of religious difference are exceptionally old and exceptionally persistent—though never unchanging, they are possibly older and more continuous in South Asia than in any other civilisation. In this volume, the essays by Gelblum and Leslie take up the Hindu tradition, the first more briefly by explaining some of the ways in which its philosophical thought can be characterised and distinguished, and the second by examining a custom—*sati*, or suttee—something of which will be known to all, if only in terms of more or less colourful and fanciful descriptions such as in Jules Verne's *Around the World in Eighty Days*, which is based in turn on early European accounts (such as by Bernier).[4]

Raychaudhuri and Irfan Habib, eds, *Cambridge Economic History of India*, vol. 1 (1982): 'the economy of the Delhi Sultanate', claims Habib, 'seems to be marked by a considerable expansion of the money economy...' (p.82), resulting in a 'large inland commerce' (p.85). Then—that is, from the twelfth century A.D. if not before—the real costs of transportation, in time and risk, were not so great as to preclude specialisation and exchange, though not of course at levels achieved in more recent centuries.

[2] C.A. Bayly, *Rulers, Townsmen and Bazaars* (Cambridge, 1983).

[3] Gyanendra Pandey, *The Construction of Communalism in Colonial North India* (Delhi, 1990), pp.5, 10, 13-14.

[4] Bernier, who travelled in India in the late seventeenth century, contributed to a number of stereotypes later picked up by others, such as James Mill; though Bernier commented on Hindu tolerance (no doubt a fault to one who believed in a 'true' religion), he stressed caste, the lack of 'public spirit', the oppression of the poor and the lowly, and (apart from Brahman learning) the 'universal ignorance'; F. Bernier, *Travels in the Mogul Empire* (Oxford, 1914). See also James Mill, *The History of British India*, vol. I (5th ed., with notes by H.H. Wilson, London, 1858), especially pp.288-90, but also Wilson's attack on Mill's account as 'valueless' and 'unjust' (pp.368-76). On *sati* see Abbé Dubois, *Description of the Character,*

Gelblum begins from the assumption, which all would accept in one sense or another, that there are pan-Hindu sources; and he explains ways in which they differ from the texts of received religions such as Christianity and Islam, even though they have aspects of 'revelation' and of commentary or explanation which are analogous to the Bible, the Qur'an, the Talmud and the *shari'a*. One of the great differences between Hindu and much other religious thought lies in the value placed in the latter upon rule or authority, and hence upon singular, incontrovertible truth. The tradition described by Gelblum is difficult and complex (even once one has mastered the terms) because it is, by contrast, so multifarious, nuanced and ambiguous. Yet its great literature remains at the core of what it means to be Hindu.

Leslie, in writing of the sacrifice of Hindu widows on their husband's funeral pyres, reminds us of at least two great general principles. First, one needs always to try to approach other cultures (or other periods, or indeed other people) on their own terms, if one seeks to understand them. Second, one should be receptive to the likelihood that these different perspectives will have something of general importance to offer. In this case, Leslie is attempting to rescue the ideas of the *sati* herself, as part of what she calls a 'soteriological path' (a way to salvation, of giving life meaning). In doing so she contributes also to current efforts to see women as actors, even deciders, and not victims. South Asia in particular needs this kind of attention, and can offer such lessons.

Shackle and Snell provide consideration of the importance of language as a repository of ideas and an emblem of identity. Though South Asia contains many languages, their number and boundaries are ever a matter of debate. Yet, neither language nor identity remain constant over time, and in the Indian subcontinent there have been remarkable changes in recent centuries. In South Asia as elsewhere, political and other institutions, printing, and other 'modern' developments have encouraged orthography and standardisation of grammar and vocabulary, so as to define general languages out of less articulated dialects, both regional and specialised. Once a supposedly single language serves all purposes—conversation, formal and technical communication and record, and literature—so language can develop as an ideology: it can reflect or help create social and political identity. Shackle's essay plays upon the ambivalence, the paradoxes, the acts of will and the intrinsic preferences and tendencies which have formed choices about language. The discussion illustrates too the variety of approaches needed to examine such developments, the cross-fertilisation demanded between disci-

Manners, and Customs...of Hindus (Oxford, 1897), and, for a summary of such descriptions, V.P.S. Raghuvanshi, *Indian Society in the Eighteenth Century* (New Delhi, 1969), pp. 295-300.

plines, the challenges offered to the usual Western expectations. Snell offers a discussion—illustrated by linguistic examples but accessible to all—of the ways in which one language (English) can influence another (Hindi). Obviously this is important for literary analysis as well as for spoken Hindi; but it also has wider implications for our understanding of language as an expression of identity. Plainly in this case the borrowings from English are often unconscious, and should be contrasted with more contrived and politically-motivated sectarian preferences in language development, such as those of script and vocabulary which separated out a North Indian *lingua franca*, Hindustani, into various forms of Persian-influenced Urdu and Sanskrit-based Hindi.

Hutt broadens this discussion to consider not only the values attributed to particular kinds of language, but the reflection in literature of more general attitudes to identity. At one level the discussion concerns the meanings to be attributed to a single word, if such it be, 'Gurkha' or 'Gorkha'. Here literature as well as language is harnessed to the building of the 'nation', which has been the great enterprise of recent centuries in South Asia as elsewhere: in this case the issue is the attitude to be taken to the *lāhure*, the soldier who had served abroad.

Questions of mix and influence can be asked of literature (Radice) and architecture (Tillotson): now we may consider ideologies of art. Radice examines the influence of Milton on the Bengali poet Madhusudan Datta: the broader question is one of judging importance and quality, whether there are distinctive aesthetics and values whereby Bengali writing should be considered, or universal criteria which can readily be applied. A great deal of easy opinionating has surrounded this kind of question; South Asia demonstrates how difficult it really is, not just in terms of art but in terms of ethnic, social and political systems. Tillotson similarly makes explicit what must always be at issue in a volume of this kind—the character and validity of the point-of-view. He argues that European perceptions of Indian architecture reflected current ideas about architecture rather than distorted views of India: that is, that they were informed by particular systems of understanding and taste rather than by a general and political prejudice. This is *not* an argument that there are no distortions—*all* representations are affected by point-of-view. It is an argument against general or essentialist categorisations of art according to extraneous criteria (ethnicity, religion) or determinist assumptions about motivation. A current question in South Asian studies is whether there are particular South Asian modes of explanation which have been obscured by the intellectual paraphernalia of Western science and knowledge.

(PR)

RELIGIOUS VS. REGIONAL DETERMINISM: INDIA, PAKISTAN AND BANGLADESH AS INHERITORS OF EMPIRE[1]

Graham Chapman

For much of its history, South Asia has been divided into many different kingdoms and realms. At some periods it has been unified under a central imperial power—but whether or not politically unified it has a unity of geography and of culture, and to some degree of language, which marks it out as a well-defined subcontinental areas. To understand contemporary South Asia it is necessary to understand why, after the most recent period of imperial unity under the British, the subcontinent is again divided into different polities, and the role that religion has played in this fragmentation. Moreover it is necessary to understand that in many ways the current division is unusual, based on borders which have not occurred before when independent states have gone their own way. Despite the current fragmentation, there are forces which are compelling the countries to seek again some form of accommodation. These forces are not only those of trade complementarities, but of shares use of major resources such as the rivers of the Indus Basin and the Ganges and Brahmaputra. But improving relations between Pakistan and India can always be poisoned by one seemingly insoluble dispute, over the future of Kashmir.

Introduction

In the last 40 years, the two largest nations of South Asia, India and Pakistan, have been at war with each other three times. They are currently engaged in a covert nuclear arms race. For much of the 40 years, trade and other contacts between them have been almost completely severed. The region has been dogged by other conflicts, such as tribal problems on the Bangladesh-Indian border, and the communal dispute in Sri Lanka. Yet in 1985 the states of South Asia, that is to say Pakistan, India, Bangladesh, Nepal, Bhutan, Sri Lanka, and the Maldives, founded the South Asian Association for Regional Co-operation (SAARC). It is significant that these countries have found it in their interests to promote a new forum for the exchange of ideas and the development of new economic and cultural links, because the last decades have shown the extent to which opportunity costs have been

[1] First published in Michael Chisholm and David M. Smith (eds.), *Shared Space: Divided Space—essays on conflict and territorial organisation* (Unwin Hyman, London, 1990).

incurred by confrontation rather than co-operation. The theme of this essay is the extent to which communal divisions have been countered by regional forces of integration. It considers in particular the nature of the space shared by the big three—India, Pakistan and Bangladesh—and makes only passing reference to the mountain kingdoms of Nepal and Bhutan, and the island states of Sri Lanka and the Maldives.

The space that the big three occupy as separate and independent sovereign states has quite often in history been divided in different ways. There is little that is inherently 'natural' about the current arrangement: indeed, there are many questions which are raised by the current political map which command immediate attention. Why is it that the Punjab is divided between the Indian and the Pakistani Punjab—though both sides use the same language? Why is it that Bengal, throughout which there is a continuity of Bengali language and culture, is similarly divided? Why, if India can include Assam and Kerala within a federation, is Bangladesh a sovereign state and not part of the federation?

There are other questions which the map does not pose directly, but which seem curious given the proximities of the countries. Why do India and Pakistan trade so little with each other? Why do India's neighbours seem to fear that she meddles in their affairs, when India protests that she never does unless invited in or unless trouble spills over her borders? Why has India, such a large polyglot federation, survived as a democracy, when Pakistan and Bangladesh have not?

Behind all of these questions is the assumption that South Asia is in some sense a well-defined geographical region of the world, and that there are few obvious natural subdivisions within it. This is the starting point.

I. *South Asia as a geopolitical region*

Cohen (1963) divides the world deductively into, first, geostrategic regions, and then geopolitical regions. His geostrategic regions are multi-featured in cultural and economic terms, but are single-featured in trade orientation and are also distinct arenas within which power can be projected. His division of the world broadly follows Mackinder's views: there is the Maritime Dependent Trading world and the Eurasian Continental power. Between these two are the 'shatterbelts' of Southeast Asia and the Middle East. The geopolitical region is defined as a subdivision of the geostrategic:

> It expresses the unity of geographic features. Because it is derived directly from geographic regions, this unit can provide a framework for common political and economic actions. Contiguity of location and complementarity of resources are particularly distinguishing marks of the geopolitical region (Cohen, 1963, p.62).

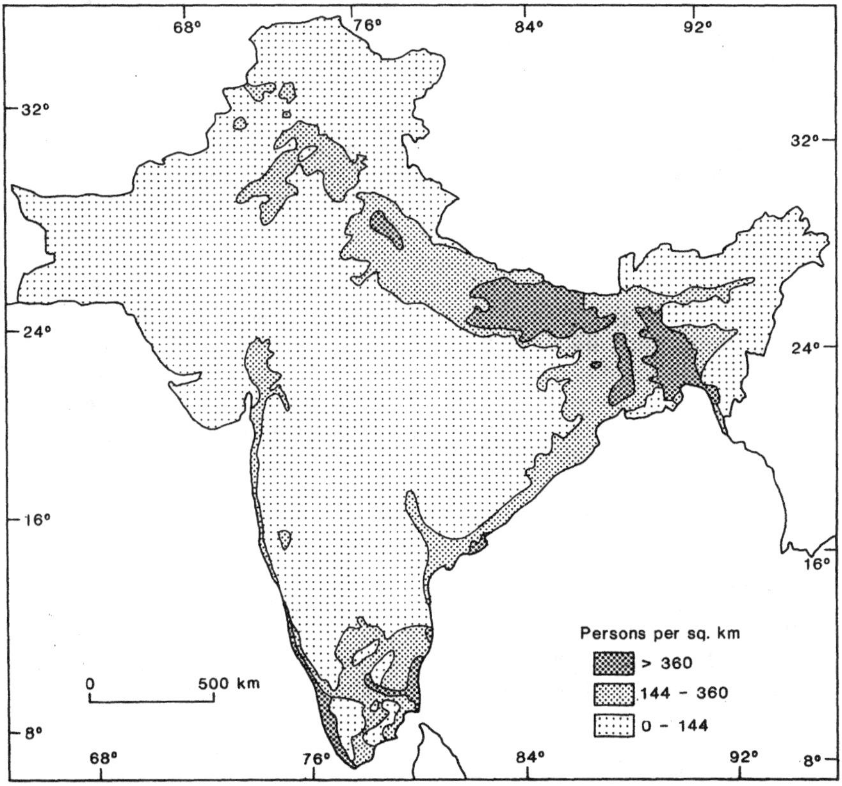

Figure 1. *Rural population density in South Asia*
Source: Spate and Learmouth, 1967, p.121.

So the Maritime Dependent Trading world is divided into Europe and the Mahgreb; Africa minus Egypt, Sudan and Ethiopia (part of the Middle East shatterbelt); North America; South America; and Australia with New Zealand and Oceania. The Eurasian Continental region is divided into the USSR and China. South Asia is distinctive: Cohen classifies it as an independent geopolitical region, not within a geostrategic region. It is big enough to be a subcontinent in its own right, it has been and is guarded from the Eurasian power(s) by the massive wall of the Himalayas, from the Middle East by the Hindu Kush and other mountains of the Northwest frontier, and from Burma and Indo-China by lower but heavily-forested jagged mountain ranges.

Like Gaul, this subcontinent can be divided into three parts: the high montane regions of the north, the depositional lowlands of the Indus and the Ganges, and the ancient Deccan block of peninsular India.

These three regions are of course subdivided: principally by moisture availability, either directly from rainfall or from littoral extraction from rivers. In the Ganges river, it is the lower or eastern parts which are wetter: the western parts and the Indus valley are much drier. In the Deccan, the extreme southwest coast (Kerala) is wet, and so are some of the coastal regions on the eastern side. But much of the interior is substantially drier, although not as dry as the Thar desert.

The map of the distribution of rural population (Figure 1, using 1961 data) shows little more differentiation from region to region than it would have shown centuries if not millennia ago. Perhaps the greatest change would be the higher relative densities now in the Punjab (between latitudes 26 and 30, and longitudes 71 and 76 on the map). It is a map which displays the agricultural potential of South Asia, defined principally by a combination of fertile riverine plains and higher and more reliable rainfall. There is one other factor. Movement in the plains has historically been much easier, whether using ox carts, or deploying armies, or using the river system. In the Deccan, navigation is more restricted seasonally, with shorter and smaller navigable reaches in the rivers; between the river basins where settlement may be possible are barren marchlands, or jagged ghat ranges, and forest areas.

Figure 2 shows the frequency with which boundaries between states have occurred in South Asia, and the fact that the northwestern, northern, and eastern mountains are the subcontinental frontier. (The northeastern frontier is historically more complicated—Assam has historically not often been incorporated by the powers of the Gangetic plains.) It also portrays quite clearly the threefold division of mountains, plains and Deccan.

The major variables to be considered in understanding the way in which this vast region has been divided and integrated over the centuries are linguistic, religious, cultural and economic. The arenas within which these variables have expressed differing kinds of forces and within which they have been manipulated are obviously political and military.

Language

As a result of its settlement history, South Asian linguistic geography is extremely complex. There are two major language groups: the Indo-Aryan group (derived from Sanskrit) of the North dominates the Indus and Ganges valleys, and includes Hindi (and the vernacular Hindustani), Punjabi, Sindhi, Bihari, and Bengali. This group also permeates the Thar desert and the northern parts of the Deccan—Rajasthani, Gujarati, Marathi, Oriya. All of these languages are within the Indo-European group, of which French and English are also a part. The northern languages are indeed closer to European languages than they

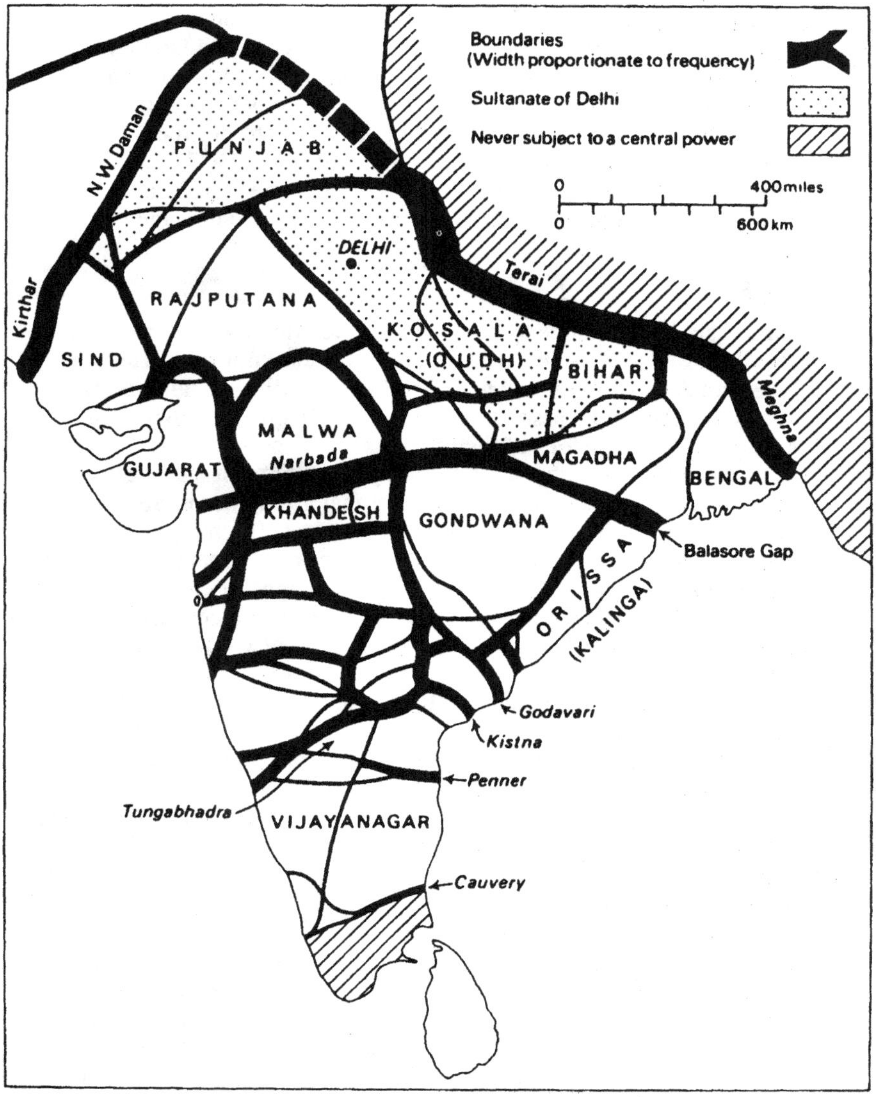

Figure 2. *Relative frequency of boundaries in South Asia from c.300 BC to c.AD 1750*
The map is suggestive: no absolute value is given to line widths.
Source: Spate and Learmouth, 1967, p.176.

are to the southern Dravidian group, comprising Malayalam, Kannada, Telugu and Tamil. In addition to these languages there are others, many associated with small tribal groups. There are also many scripts. In the contemporary Republic of India there are 14 recognised languages for constitutional purposes (plus Sanskrit, which is not in common use), and nearly as many scripts, and in addition, depending on the distinction between dialect and language, somewhere between 400 and 1000 others (*A Social and Economic Atlas of India*, 1987). In Pakistan there are four major languages, and a fifth of some significance. Even in uniform Bangladesh there are distinct tribal languages in the Chittagong Hill Tracts.

Religion

South Asia is pre-eminently the land of the Hindus—a word derived originally from the Indus. The country is often known as Hindustan. But South Asia is also home to 250 million Muslims—a number which dwarfs the numbers associated with the Muslim heartlands of the Middle East. The history of the relations of these two religious groups has had a significant impact on the varying patterns of state formation in South Asia. There are also many other major religions in South Asia: Jainism and Buddhism both have adherents (both are reformist offshoots from precursors of Hinduism); Sikhism commands the loyalty of a people small in number but significant in many fields and locally important in the Punjab. Zoroastrians, Christians and animists are also found. Table 1 shows the distribution of some of the communities in 1941.

To understand the relations between the two major religions, Hinduism and Islam, we need to understand the origins and theology of each. We can then see how they could relate at the popular everyday cultural level, and the grander political level.

Hinduism. Around the second millennium BC there started a series of periodic invasions by a pastoral and nomadic people from Central Asia, the Aryans, who were light-skinned, fair-haired, blue-eyed. They also penetrated northern Europe, and are presumed to be the ancestors of the Nordic people. They are in one sense the founders of Hinduism, though such a phrase will be heavily qualified below. They are the 'master race' that Hitler tried to refound, and from Hinduism Hitler took the everyday symbol of the swastika, a symbol of the sun and good fortune. Their language, in its most refined form, is known as Sanskrit, and when first encountered by European scholars was thought to be the original stem of all Indo-European languages, though now it is known that it is an offshoot of the lost stem as they are.

There clearly was considerable mixing between the various invading groups in India, and today there is some kind of colour gradient from the lighter and sometimes blue-eyed peoples of the Northwest, to the

Table 1. *Percentage distribution of communities in the Indian Empire 1941*

	Caste Hindu	Untouchable	Muslim	Sikh	Other
British provinces					
Madras	70.4	16.4	7.9	0.0	5.3
Bombay	70.5	8.9	9.2	0.0	11.4
Bengal	29.3	12.2	54.7	0.0	3.8
United Provinces	62.0	21.3	15.3	0.4	1.0
Punjab	22.2	4.4	57.1	13.2	3.1
Bihar	61.0	11.9	13.0	0.0	14.1
Central Provinces	58.8	18.1	4.7	0.1	18.3
Assam	34.7	6.6	33.7	0.0	25.0
NW Frontier Province	5.9	0.0	91.8	1.9	0.4
Orissa	64.1	14.2	1.7	0.0	20.0
Sind	22.9	4.2	70.7	0.7	1.5
Princely states					
Hyderabad	63.5	17.9	12.8	0.0	5.8
Mysore	72.1	10.2	6.6	0.0	2.1
Travancore	51.8	6.5	7.1	0.0	34.6
Kashmir	17.3	2.8	76.4	1.6	1.9
Gwalior	86.4	0.0	6.0	0.0	7.6
Baroda	68.8	8.1	7.8	0.0	15.3
Total of these and other states	59.3	9.5	13.6	1.6	16.0
Total	53.0	12.5	23.7	1.5	9.3

Source: Coupland, 1943, pt.2, p.339.

darker skinned and always dark-eyed peoples of the South. But there was also a limit to the mixing in an important sense. Imagine that in Britain there had been an apartheid that prevented the Roman-British from marrying the Celts (and language barriers and social stigma would certainly have made such a barrier for quite some time), that the Saxons never married the Celts, that in their turn the Danes and the Normans stayed aloof from the society which they had conquered (and to a large extent they did). Imagine society as frozen layers of serfs, and serfs of serfs. In Britain some would say we still have such a society, hidebound by class distinctions. But we have had since Roman times a dogmatic and egalitarian religious philosophy, which does not limit permissible marriages. The important qualification about India is this: the Aryans evolved their own religious philosophy before much homogenisation had taken place, and this philosophy in practice embraced a doctrine of the inequality of man, of the ritual hierarchy of caste. There is no space here to go into any detail about the immensely complex subject of Hinduism and caste (Cohn, 1971; Bougle, 1971; Dumont, 1970), so the following resumé is only a guide. Doctrinally, there are four grades of caste, the Brahmans (priests and pundits—guardians of knowledge), the Kshatriyas, or warriors, the Vaisyas, or merchants, the Sudras, or menials. Below them come groups of untouchables (now known as Harijans), and tribals, not normally embraced by Hinduism. The major groups are divided into 3000 sub-castes, and then into 90,000 endogamous marriage groups. Such groups have traditionally each had their own occupations, a ritual notion of which persists when caste-members have other jobs, and which in any one area are supposedly complementary. The untouchables carry out the most polluting jobs, such as cesspit cleaning, and labourers have always been Sudras of some type or other low-caste groups. The Brahmans traditionally eschew any manual work, but are the keepers of the *Vedas*, the sacred hymns of the Aryans, often recited by the Brahmans in their role as priests at important life ceremonies. Though such texts exist, Hinduism is not dogmatic. It does not claim a revealed truth, and does not prescribe one God. There is only one force in the universe, and it is in everything, but it has many faces and hence there are many gods. Different groups worship different deities, many will worship different deities for different purposes. One of the few common threads is that all groups traditionally believe in reincarnation, and that one's obligation in this life is to carry out one's duty according to one's rank at birth. Reward comes in the next incarnation. Other common features of Hinduism are a preference for vegetarianism, though lower classes may eat chicken or goat, and the untouchables frequently keep and eat pigs. The cow, the central pivot of agricultural life, is sacred to all, and in theory always allowed to die a natural death.

This complex society evolved with distinctive regional variations, and has bequeathed contemporary South Asia with the regional languages noted above. Hinduism, however, crossed the north/south linguistic divide, and Brahmanism is in many ways stronger in the South today than in the North. But within this umbrella of life philosophies, there are always, by caste and by region, a myriad of societies. Economically and culturally, until the advent of cities with populations of a million-plus, India can best be described as divided into numerous *pays*, as defined by Vidal de la Blache.

But there was a major difference. The *pays* of de la Blache existed within a well-defined and centrist state, whose laws were made centrally and recognised universally. In India there was no such centrist tradition—partly for reasons of scale. Given the early technologies, there was plenty of cost but little economic advantage in the integration of large areas of India. More significantly, it was because such functions as maintaining the social order were organised within castes, each having a tribunal (*panchayat*) for its own members. Inter-caste matters would be settled by the dominant caste of any one area, but by involving the *panchayat* of lesser castes to take action against its members where necessary. In such a society the concept of king or monarch had a very different connotation. The Raja, usually a Kshatriya and ritually inferior to the Brahmans, might be rich, but his wealth had, beside his own gratification, two major functions (Bayly 1983). One was for pomp and ceremony which were for public consumption; the other was that of a general, or minister of defence. In other words, the interpretation of customary law was the preserve of the Brahmans; the Raja's was the defence of the principality.

Islam. The establishment of Islam as a major political and military force occurred remarkably quickly after its foundation by the Prophet Muhammad. The Qur'an, or Koran, which he wrote is, according to Muslims, not his words but the direct dictation to Muhammad by God. This therefore is a revealed religion, with a dogmatic source, much as fundamentalist Christians believe the Bible to be The Word. But, unlike Christianity, Islam does not recognise the distinction of the secular and the religious in human affairs: it prescribes rules for nearly all contingencies in life, and sets the aim of introducing the comprehensive Islamic state on earth.

Muslim influences reached India through Arab traders in Sind and in Bengal, and through the teachings of wandering Muslim saints or mystics, known as Sufis, not unlike the wandering Christian monks who took Christianity to Ireland and Scotland. But when Islam came in force, literally, when the first of the successful Muslim invasions burst into India through the northwest in the twelfth century, it brought something radically different from anything India had encountered before. The Ghurids established in North India an empire (or more correctly a confederacy) acknowledged by the Khalif of Baghdad as the Sultanate of Delhi, and very rapidly after its establishment in India Islam was known to be precisely that—Islam in India, and not simply an extension of Islam in general. This was the beginning of 600 years of Muslim domination.

At times this Islam was iconoclastic, and brought destruction to many Hindu temples, and the forcible conversion of some subjects. Other subjects voluntarily chose the new religion, and this was particularly true of the untouchables and low-caste people, perhaps attracted by the doctrine of the equality of man. But one of the central tenets of Hinduism is that one cannot renounce one's birth; hence many, especially the higher castes, resisted conversion. Mass conversion of lower castes seems to have been greatest in East Bengal, for reasons which are not clear but may have been connected with Arab seafarers. Muslims were concentrated in the Indus valley, contiguous with the Middle East, and in East Bengal. These are roughly the areas of contemporary Pakistan and Bangladesh. In addition there were important Muslim populations in the imperial urban centres of the Ganges plain and in many imperial cities in the central Deccan.

Culture

Religion and culture may overlap, but cannot be seen as the same thing. In India, we have already noted the complexity of social groups that Hinduism spawned. When some of these groups were converted to Islam, they did not abandon their origins overnight, no more than someone today could expect to change his job tomorrow by proclaiming himself a Christian. Islam may prescribe the equality of man, but it does not command that people marry at random. Within Islam-in-India, therefore, caste persists in significant ways defined not so much by pollution rules as family marriage rules. It even persists to the extent that persons who were once distillers, who by being Muslim are not allowed to drink, nevertheless continue to make and market alcohol. In Pakistan, the network of families, each known as a *biradri*, is fundamental to all social and political life. Further, the acceptance of Islam and the recitation of the Qur'an in Arabic does not deprive a man of his native tongue—so that a Bengali Muslim is first and foremost a Bengali, yet also a Muslim.

In other words, within Islam as within Hinduism local regional cultures persisted. Usually the same regional culture pervaded both religions in one place. The major religious difference was that for Muslims the common and exact reference point of a revealed and egalitarian religion *could* be established with Muslims from different areas, whereas for Hindus such common references were much harder to establish and were always confounded by caste.

Economy

Economic variables enter into the question of integration from two viewpoints. One concerns the benefits that accrue from complementarities exploited, and the other the costs of integration.

The benefits argument is simply that of comparative advantage, that two regions linked together can each specialise to the ultimate advantage and increase in welfare of both. For this to happen, though, there have to be complementarities and there has to be a transport system whose operating costs are below the increased gains that trade engenders. Economic advantage must also obviously not be nullified by one-sided political power. In the case of South Asia, before the railways there were few complementarities that could be exploited. Those regions which could be connected by transport, primarily the northern plains, were fairly homogeneous. Indeed, if any complementarities could be established, they would be with regions outside India, not within—hence the interest of European traders once ocean transport became sufficiently advanced. The exploitation of internal complementarity, particularly linking regions in or across the Deccan, could only occur after the coming of the railways, and even then could only occur fully with a change in the political regime.

II. *Integration and empire*

We need to think of three forces of integration, and to consider their interplay at two social levels. The forces are identitive, utilitarian, and coercive. The two levels are those of the elites and the masses.

The bonds of identity are those mutually recognised by a people as the symbols of their community, and are usually associated with language and religion, but they may also be associated with territory. Where these are strong, utilitarian integration can also follow if the technology permits. Utilitarian bonds are those of economic self-interest. The British now know that they are bound economically to Europe and that to break away would be injurious, no matter if they do not 'feel' European. The only comment one needs to make about coercion is that it is expensive, and fundamentally its premise is the threat of destruction. So after the costs of an invasion, which may instantaneously be met by plunder, a period of accommodation and reconstruction has to occur.

The elite-mass distinction is useful in elaborating all three of these forces. An elite may have identitive bonds in common, although the subject peoples do not. These bonds can then form the cement of integration, and while the masses are divided they will not combine to eject the elite. In the case of utilitarian bonds, these may be perceived more easily by the elite than by the masses. In the case of the use of coercive force to achieve integration, this almost by definition has to be controlled by an elite. The use of force by the masses against other masses is more likely to lead (as we shall see) to anarchy, genocide and disintegration.

There were four major imperial periods in South Asia before the advent of the British (see Figure 3). They all had the following features in common. They were based on the agricultural and population heartland of the Gangetic plains, they projected power from this northern resource base into the Deccan, but none ever included the whole of peninsular India, and each decayed internally as much as collapsed because of external pressure. A major distinction between them was that the first two were Buddhist-Hindu or Hindu, whereas the third and fourth were formed by Muslim aristocracies which ruled over Hindu

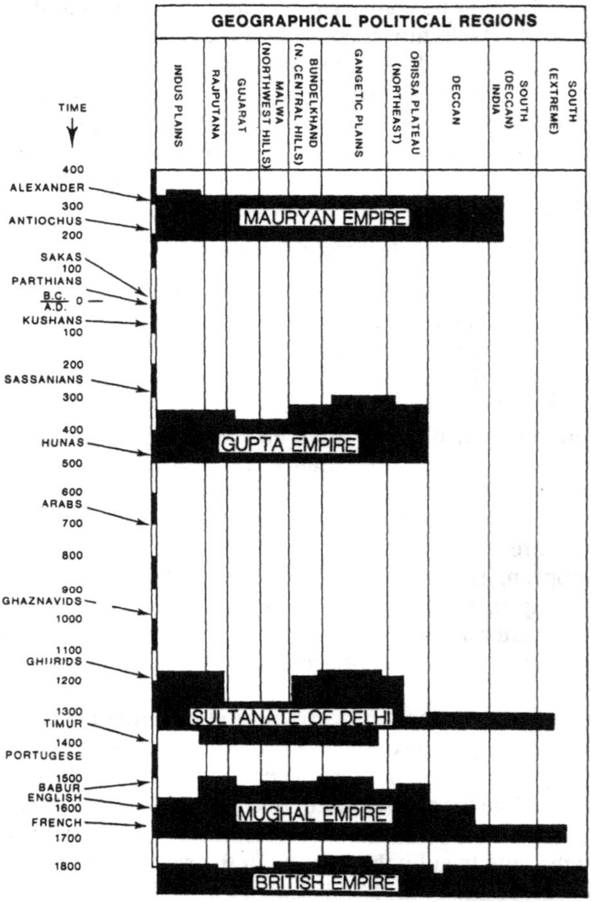

Figure 3. *The empires of South Asia in time and space*
(From a paper by S.C. Malik, to UNESCO/IGNA workshop, New Delhi, 1989)

India. The exact heartland of these empires did vary a little: the first two, the Mauryan and Gupta empires, were centred on East Uttar Pradesh and Bihar (modern names), whereas the Muslim empires of the sultanate and the Mughuls were based on Western Uttar Pradesh and the Punjab.

The Mauryan and Gupta empires

The Mauryan empire (Thapar, 1966) at its zenith was synonymous with one man—Asoka, who died about 232 BC. At the time that he forged the empire, by force, there were many differentiated local communities—the *pays* referred to above. There was therefore no mass identitive integration, and the empire relied on integration through fealty by subsidiary chiefs to the emperor. There was no, or very little, utilitarian integration—the transport technology did not allow it. Although it was a well-ordered empire, and order and stability were no doubt constructive, it was expensive to maintain. It went into decline after Asoka's death, many of its troubles blamed on inflation. Asoka in his lifetime tried to promulgate his own version of Buddhism as a state religion. Clearly, he perceived the need for a common identitive bond—but it did not take root. The next empire, that of the Guptas, in the fourth and fifth centuries AD, echoed in many ways the emergence and decline of the Mauryan. It, too, never penetrated far into the Deccan. It was, however, remarkable for its development of applied science, mathematics and astronomy, and much that Europe was thought to have learnt from the Arab world was in fact knowledge that had diffused to it from this Indian empire.

There is, however, a problem here in that it seems easy to put a line round an area on a map and say of an historical past 'here was an empire'. What does this mean? The exact tributary status of many of the component parts is often unknown to us: and the tributary status may be near to fiction, paid more in protocol than hard cash or armed levies. It may also involve more of a treaty alliance than acknowledgement of overlordship. Where documentary evidence is weak, we are left to surmise.

There is also a possibility that we may have introduced a North Indian bias. There were great empires in the South, which have left temples and ruins for us to marvel at. But there is one significant difference between them and the northern empires: their resource bases were neither as great nor as dense spatially as those of the North, and no southern empire ever threatened to take over the North. (This is true even of the Marathas, who could only have dominated the North by becoming an imperial power in, and the new aristocracy of, the North.)

The Sultanate and the Mughal empire

The Sultanate from the twelfth century and the Mughal empire between the sixteenth and the eighteenth, were different from the earlier empires, particularly, among many other reasons, because they were led and dominated by Muslims. The added complication of Hindu-Muslim relations could be used to work both for and against empire. These relations posed questions hitherto unknown in the Indian context. India is renowned for its syncretic civilisation, capable of absorbing and moulding a great many imported and invading cultures. Even the Huns were absorbed within Hinduism as the Rajputs of Rajasthan. But, despite having profound effects on the nature of Indian Islam, India and

Hinduism failed to absorb or dominate it. We may think of the relations between the two religions at theological, daily, and political levels.

Islam is the antithesis of Hinduism in nearly all ways. It is dogmatic, evangelical, egalitarian. The latter is inegalitarian, but tolerant of divergent views and practices, and is by definition not evangelical: you have to be born into a caste to be a Hindu. Where Hindus believe in reincarnation, Muslims believe in one life and heaven or hell afterwards. Where the Hindus believe all life is unitary, the Muslims, like the Christians, have their version of the Garden of Eden, in which Adam was placed last so that mankind could use the garden (the environment) as his birthright.

There are clear differences observable in daily life. Where Hindus worship idols, Islam prohibits all graven images—all ornamentation in a mosque is abstract. Muslim males go publicly to prayer as a congregation on a fixed day. Hindus usually go individually to a temple when they feel the need, and Hindu women, though not overtly the equal of men, are not debarred. They appear bare-faced in public where Muslim women appear veiled, if at all. Hindus are largely vegetarian, Muslims eat mutton and beef. No Muslim would eat pork, deeming it, as the Jews deem it, to be unclean. There are no pigs in Pakistan: there are many troughing in the rubbish dumps of India. Muslims bury their dead, the Hindus cremate theirs. Where differences are as great as these, though communities living alongside each other may normally be tolerant, small accidents or even contrived events can set off a riot, that may degenerate into long-lasting communal strife. In this there is the further problem that Indian culture stresses the family and the community more, and the individual less than in the West. The result is that a slight against one member of a community is more likely to be felt equally by his brethren. Thus riots may start when music is heard near a mosque at prayer time, when a cow is killed by a Muslim, when a pig is let loose in a mosque, when a roadside idol is vandalised.

At the grand political level Muslims could secure the political support of their Hindu subjects by minimising the discrimination against Hindus in public service, by reducing or eliminating the taxes levied on non-believers, by marrying into Hindu dynasties. But they could also close ranks by stressing their Muslim identity and persecuting Hindu idolaters.

The problem of maintaining the integration of these Muslim empires was essentially still the same as with previous ones: that though large areas could become incorporated by force, given that there were few utilitarian bonds that could develop because of inadequate transport, what was to prevent regional aristocracies breaking away, once established? So long as the empires were expanding and could therefore call on unification for the armed struggles, with the anticipation of reward after victory, mutual support provided the integrating impetus. In the case of the Sultanate, it became clear after the failure to dominate the Deccan that there were fissiparous tendencies which were suppressed by some sultans only at great cost (Thapar 1966). An aristocracy, once seated and landed, rapidly becomes more and more rooted in its own locale, seeing less and less interest in distant centres of taxation.

The Mughal empire (Spear, 1965) faced the same problems. But the manipulation of religious factors in seeking a solution is more in evidence. Different leaders pursued different policies towards their solution. Akbar (1542-1605), the greatest of the Mughals, who delineated the state most clearly, chose not to use Islam as the identitive bond of the ruling class, to keep it integrated by virtus of its opposition to the subservient masses. He indulged in patronage of Hindu nobles, took a Rajput princess as a wife, and went so far as to found a new religious cult centred around himself, in effect becoming an apostate. He also devised a system of appointments to the vice-royalties of the empire, which gave an incumbent wealth and tenure in his lifetime, but by which the state resumed all property and wealth at his death. The positions were not hereditary, and Akbar thus avoided the development of powerful locally-rooted aristocracies, and maintained the dependency on the emperor of the aristocracy as a class.

By the time of Aurangzeb (1618-1717), the fragility of the empire had been displayed. His solution was to unite the aristocracy by reasserting Islamic purity and domination; he became a zealot in the crusade against Hinduism, and reintroduced the discriminatory *jizya* tax. Conviction, confrontation, coercion and suppression were his guidelines. At its peak, the army directly or indirectly (through dependants and camp-followers) employed a quarter of the imperial population.

From the advent of Islam in India until the present day, there was always the possibility of local spontaneous conflict between Muslims and Hindus. The extent to which rulers and politicians may have played conflict up, or down, was always bound to vary, but none of them could ever rid India of this inherent communalism.

III. *The British raj*

The British came to India as traders, and their first territorial acquisition in Bengal in 1757 was largely an accidental result of self-defence. That Bengal was the first acquisition was, however, in a geographical sense not an accident: for here was the world's greatest delta, which ocean-going ships could penetrate far upstream, carrying with them their superior ordnance. It was here in the rivers that the problem of inland transport was solved.

The move in self-defence that caused the British to take Bengal had many indirect causes, one of which was the instability of the decaying

Mughal empire. This instability created a vacuum into which the British were drawn, as often as not in a proxy war with the French, both sides using local nobles and local feuds as surrogates in their own attempts to wrest the monopoly of trade, and as surrogates for inadequate manpower. The result of 80 years of such activity was that the 'British acquired India in a fit of absence of mind'. The lack of a clear policy and the use of a pragmatic approach are evident in the political map

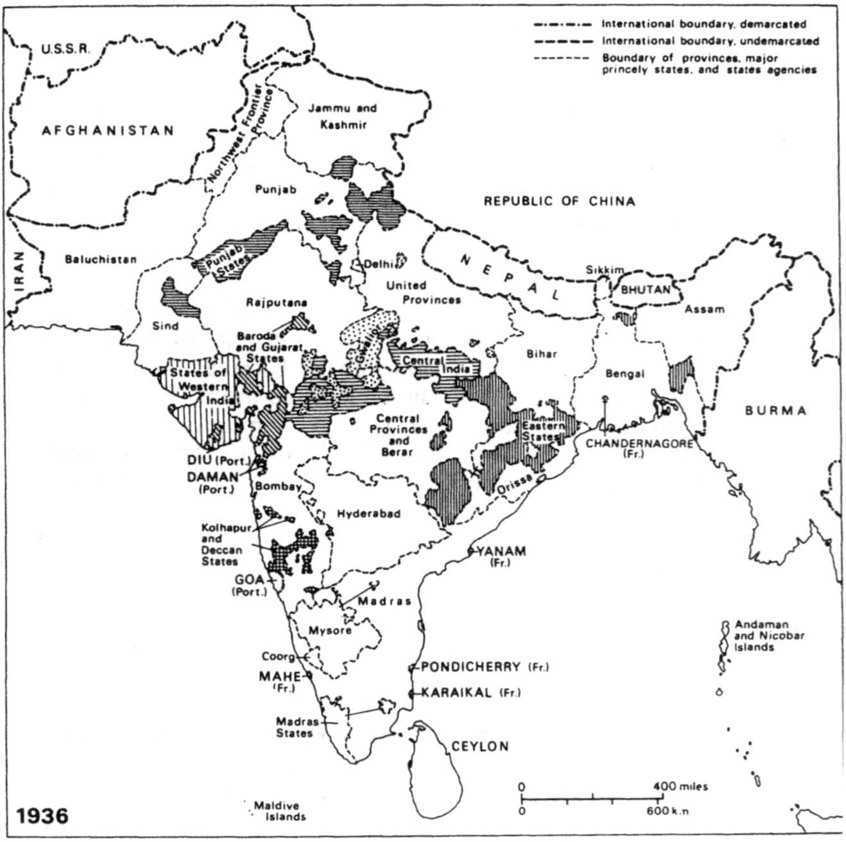

Figure 4. *Political divisions in South Asia, 1936*
Source: Schwartzenberg, 1976, and others.

which finally emerged in India (Figure 4). The British had built themselves three major port cities—Calcutta, Bombay and Madras, around which were territories they ruled directly themselves. But 40 per cent of Indian territory and 25 per cent of its population were encompassed in princely states (Coupland, 1943), the territories of major and minor nobles which emerged at the collapse of the previous empire, who had treaty obligations with the Crown in external affairs, but who were internally autonomous autocrats. In many ways the British fragmented India politically, dividing in order to rule. But it should also be clear by now that division both territorially and communally was by no means new to India. Under the British these divisions might have been shaped in new ways: but they were always there. As one independence leader observed: 'We divide, you rule'.

British integration relied on all aspects of the integrating forces we have mentioned, but not equally at elite and mass levels. They used superior technology as the basis of coercion where necessary. They relied on the bonds of British identity to cement the rulers of empire, and they too were forbidden to become landed gentry. The civil service was Europeanised at the highest level early on, and English instituted as the language of government, supplanting Persian. But the new rulers came from a country which had a rudimentary parliamentary democracy. At some stage they would have to confront questions about the legitimacy of their rule, and the exclusive proprietorship by their group of that right. Racialism was thus inevitable, not so much as an overt policy for future development, but as an explanation for what had happened. Conveniently, it also stressed and strengthened the adhesion of the rulers as a group. Although for the majority of the rural masses the British did nothing, they nevertheless fostered utilitarian integration by the development of the railways, and by the development in many areas of major irrigation schemes, incorporating millions of people within thecommand areas of thousands of miles of canals. They also founded new universities in which a new middle-class intelligentsia studied in English.

What they did not do was foster the identity of the Indian masses as 'Indians'. Partly it was not in their own self-interest to do so; partly they believed in their own propaganda, that India was a subcontinent of many races and tongues.

IV. *Independence and partition*

With the filtering of Western liberal ideas into India's small emergent middle class, demands for change were made, which were met gradually, starting with democratic elections on very small franchises to town boards. By the end of the nineteenth century, some elected representatives were allowed on provincial councils (Coupland, 1943), though outnumbered by appointees of the Governor ('official members'). But the power of veto remained at the centre, where the Governor-General (Viceroy) was answerable to London.

The growing demands in India for more representative government led to the founding of the Indian National Congress in 1885. This was above all a middle-class, urban, educated and English-speaking movement: the British had not only infused democratic ideas into India, they had given the slim new middle class the physical and linguistic means of communication on a pan-Indian basis. The adoption of the qualifier *Indian* was a propaganda ploy staking a claim on a perceived future (Rahmat Ali, 1942).

The realisation that there was a possibility of increasing democratisation on a Western pattern caused some alarm to farseeing members of the Muslim community. They realised that a simple first-past-the-post system of democracy, if ever entrenched in India, could lead to the interests of the minority community being permanently ignored. Representative democracy might work well in a culturally-homogeneous country such as Britain, where parties could express class interests, but it was doubtful that it could where such conditions did not exist. Because of pressure from the Muslims, the British adopted in 1909 the concept of separate electorates: one roll for the Muslims, one for the others. In legislative elections, there were to be blocks of seats allocated to these different electorates, the minority being given preferential treatment. The scheme, though well intended, wrote communalism into the constitution of India. Obviously the candidate who would appear most attractive was he who could claim to get the greatest concessions from the 'other side'. In the 1920s, Gandhi did not object to the idea of reserved seats *per se*, but he rightly pointed out that the electorate for reserved seats should be universal. In effect all electors could then vote twice, once for candidates for each of the blocks of seats. The effect would have been that though there would be a guaranteed number of Muslim or Hindus in the Councils the candidates would have to fight a campaign not on sectarian issues but on issues of wider appeal. Could such a system work in Ulster?

During and after the First World War the demands for Dominion status (independence within the Commonwealth like Australia or Canada) grew (Hodson, 1969; Philips and Wainwright, 1970; Moon, 1961). Gandhi and his philosophy were a key in the pattern assumed. He wanted a non-violent protest, which often involved non-co-operation. To do this he had to have the support of the masses, and in that lay his genius. Though not an official of the party, he transformed Congress from a small, middle-class clique to a much wider movement. Steadily the British conceded more—though always struggling with the contradictions inherent between ultimate responsibility held in London, and new representative institutions growing in India. The experience of these new institutions convinced more Muslims that their anxieties for the future were well-founded. Congress had always sought to be secular and multi-communal, but its behaviour locally was often more partisan. To understand this we need to refer back again to the idea of local community, so strong in India. The new leaders might well have been nationalistic: but the masses were sunk still in local perceptions. When they had to be enlisted in the struggle for power, they were told it was for self-determination. But who or what was 'self'? To a Tamil it is Tamils, or perhaps Tamil Brahmans or Tamil non-Brahmans. In Bengal, self meant one's own community, here very clearly either Hindu or Muslim. The Bengali part went unspoken—taken for granted as the starting point. With classic myopia, local differences seemed large, distant ones less important. Thus, later Jinnah could and did appeal to Muslim Bengalis to join his movement as Muslims.

In the 1930s, the Muslim League under Jinnah's leadership campaigned hard for more devolution of power from the centre to the provinces, with the aim of attaining more power locally for the Muslims of the Punjab and Bengal, two mixed provinces in which Muslims were in a majority (approximately 55 to 60 per cent in both: see Table 1). In 1935 the Government of India Act actually foresaw a federal future in which the princely states would be involved too. However, the Second World War intervened, and events ran rapidly beyond the ability of either the British or the Indian leaders to control them. Realising that Independence would follow soon after the war, the Muslims had in 1940 proclaimed their goal to be the creation of a separate state, to be known as Pakistan, to be founded in the Indus valley, and to embrace the whole of the Punjab, including eastern Hindu majority districts. The campaigners saw India in regional terms. Bengal was not part of the original Pakistan concept, but the Pakistani camp drew attention to the fact that Bengal, like Pakistan, ought to be able to claim its independence at the end of empire. The Congress leadership, seeing itself as the heir of the British raj, rejected the demands outright, and tense negotiations began in an attempt to reach a settlement. Basically, the only plans acceptable to the Muslims were based on a weak centre, and on reserving the right of secession to the provinces. But Congress wanted a strong centre, and rejected the right of secession.

Here we see the point behind the remark made above about coercion by the masses rather than the elites. Jinnah held very few cards, which was one of the reasons that he was given so little credit by Congress. The Muslim communities were the minority, and not strong in the institutions of the new society, nor strong in trade or banking, nor strong in the civil service. But the masses could be awakened, and what Jinnah could threaten was, simply, anarchy. The often fractious nature of the two communities was openly played upon by extremists on both sides, with the result that large-scale rioting broke out, particularly in Calcutta in August 1946, but it spread to other areas too. By 1947, the internal law and order situation had disintegrated to the point where it was possible that the British would have no effective government left to transfer to anybody. It was in this atmosphere that the last Viceroy, Mountbatten, reached an agreement with the Nehru and Jinnah for the partition of India, something which was acceptable to all only in so far as all could see each other equally miserable and disappointed by the conclusion. Jinnah was miserable, because the logic of partition had been applied within the provinces of the Punjab and Bengal—so he only got the Muslim parts—and hence East Pakistan (now Bangladesh) was formed from just the rural hinterland of Calcutta, but lost the city itself. Nehru was miserable, because he and Gandhi felt that India should never have been partitioned, and that the Muslim League's rejection of Congress's secularism was false. And the British were miserable because they saw the best defence arrangements for South Asia to be within a single state, itself defensible behind the boundaries of British India. They were right—after partition hostility between India and Pakistan has led to each turning to the outside for help—the USA supporting Pakistan and the USSR supporting India.

The real tragedy, however, was twofold. First, the partition of the Punjab and Bengal provoked some of the largest mass migrations ever known. At least 12 million people moved: some put the figure as high as 16 million. In the first few months the caravans and trains of refugees moved through a land where government, the armed forces, the police, the railway personnel, were being divided, and security was non-existent. In this atmosphere, extremists on both sides perpetrated the most ghastly atrocities (Collins and LaPierre, 1975). Whole trains arrived at their destinations with every passenger stabbed or hacked to death. The final death toll is not known, but was perhaps more than a million.

The second tragedy was due to a combination of decades of British procrastination and princely personality. The British had never unified South Asia. The existence of the myriad princely states was but one proof of that. In 1947, the paramount power was to be withdrawn, and from then on in theory the princes could proclaim their independence (which would have led to a Balkanisation of India like that at the collapse of the Mughal empire). In practice, they were persuaded that their communications and economies were bound up with the states of India and Pakistan, and that their only real option was to be absorbed into those states. All but three duly aligned themselves on the basis of majority community and contiguity. The most significant of the dissenting three was the state of Kashmir, where a Hindu raja ruled a largely Muslim population. The maharaja wanted independence, and dragged his feet. In October 1947, a force of invading Pathan tribesmen crossed from the Northwest frontier and invaded the state. The maharaja signed a temporary deed of accession with India to gain India's help in repelling the invaders. Within a short time this action had escalated into open warfare between Pakistan and India. On 1 January 1949 a ceasefire, which should have been followed by a plebiscite (which has never taken place), effectively established the line which has partitioned the state ever since, between Azad Kashmir, nominally still independent of Pakistan, and Kashmir in India, which the Indians have incorporated within their republic's constitution. This issue, more than any other, has continued to bedevil Indo-Pakistani relations since 1947.

It is thus quite clear that by the end of empire in 1947 pan-Indian identitive bonds were not strong enough to maintain the integration of South Asia. For this the Indians may blame the British who divided to rule, keeping princely states apart, and devising separate electorates for the Muslims. But the Muslims blamed Congress, for not in truth being secular at local levels. Casting blame to one side, it is clear now that to expect this subcontinent of creeds and castes, still largely illiterate, and a veritable linguistic Tower of Babel, to have formed a national identity at that time in history was to expect the impossible. As an alternative to identity, coercion was not possible either—except at the fringe over issues like Kashmir. For independence was about self-determination and the rejection of imperial coercion, and in 1947 Congress had reluctantly concluded that negotiated independence for Pakistan was best. That way they inherited a strong centre in the new India, still the largest self-governing unit the subcontinent has ever seen. The real 'surprise' was the creation of the state of Pakistan in two 'wings', separated by thousands of miles of Indian territory, separated by language and script, economically unrelated to each other, and linked only by Islam.

There is plenty of evidence to support the contention that India saw Pakistan in 1947 as a temporary aberration of the political map. South Asia was seen by the government at that time to be the same geopolitical region that the British had dominated. Although the current government of India has stated publicly that it has no designs on Pakistan (Bradnock, 1990), there are still regional imperatives that interlock the destinies of the two countries. Both countries, and Bangladesh too, may well wish to keep internal matters to themselves and not to interfere in their neighbours' affairs, but precisely because many issues are regional in a pan-South Asian sense, it is impossible to isolate many issues as purely domestic. There are Sikhs in both Punjabs, who can offer trans-border support to their brethren. There are Bengali Muslims and

Bengali Hindus in both Bengals. The Indus river basin is shared by Pakistan and India, the Ganges-Brahmaputra by India and Bangladesh (as well as Nepal and China). And there are Tamils in both India and Sri Lanka, some of the latter being locked in a civil war with the Sinhala majority.

Despite these continuities within the partitioned provinces, new boundary lines were drawn. These could simply have been administrative borders, open to normal trade flows. But because there had been no identitive basis for integrating a new South Asia, utilitarian complementarities were broken in a remorseless hunt for that economic independence which would serve political demands for sovereignty.

Table 2. *Exports and imports for India and Pakistan, 1984-5*

	Exports to	Imports from
India, Rs.million[1]		
UK	6,701	10,188
USA	17,685	16,666
USSR	16,546	18,034
Pakistan	129	157
Bangladesh	932	445
Iran	1,340	4,849
Pakistan, Rs.million[2]		
UK	2,538	5,277
USA	3,965	11,006
USSR	951	438
India	498	261
Bangladesh	1,132	869
Iran	695	1,061

[1] Indian rupees. *Source: A Social and Economic Atlas of India*, 1987.
[2] Pakistani rupees. *Source: Pakistan Statistical Yearbook*, 1986.

There were compelling reasons for 'normal' trade to continue between the successor states. The jute industry of Calcutta needed the growers of East Pakistan, the cotton industry the farmers of Pakistani Punjab; Pakistan needed Indian coal, India needed Pakistani wheat. But both this 'logical' economic geography and the technical geography of the irrigation works were sacrificed in the struggles to achieve total independence (Vakil and Rao, n.d.). During the Kashmir crisis of 1948, India turned off the water which flowed from its territory, and some of Pakistan's prime lands went brown. This led to a prolonged crisis (Michel, 1967) which ended only in 1960 with the signing of the Indus Waters Treaty under the auspices of the World Bank, by which the unified scheme was completely divided, at great cost. Pakistan put an export tax on jute exported from East Bengal to Calcutta. India banned all imports of jute. In 1949, the Indian rupee was devalued along with the pound sterling; but Pakistan did not devalue its rupee. All trade between India and Pakistan ceased. The banks refused even to exchange the two currencies. (See Table 2 for the current trading position.)

V. *The secession of Bangladesh*

In an attempt to develop a new national identity for Pakistan, Jinnah had in 1948 proclaimed Urdu, a language used more by the aristocrats of the West than the peasants of the East, to be the national official language. Urdu is written in the Arabic script, as are all other regional languages of West Pakistan. Those Easterners who were literate mostly used the Bengali script, and hence were being asked both to use an alien script as well as an alien language. The first anti-Pakistan riots in Dacca in 1951, which generated the first 'Bangladesh Martyrs', were in protest against the imposition of Urdu.

The history of utilitarian bonding between the West and the East has several twists (Griffin and Khan, 1972; Chakravarty and Narain 1986; Wilson and Dalton, 1982). Because of the Pakistani-Indian trade war, East Pakistan became drawn into a trade system with West Pakistan, in which the East of the country exported to the rest of the world, the West imported industrial goods and materials, and the balance was completed by the West selling high-priced consumer goods to the East. While in a sense West Pakistan lifted India's blockade, the system that developed was not based so clearly on natural complementarities, and was dominated by Western interests. While the standard of living did slowly grow in the West of the country, it stagnated and declined in the East (Table 3). Given the ethnic and geographical difference between the wings, it was inevitable that this too would become a major regional political issue. Pakistan, and particularly its armed forces, was dominated by Punjabis, the largest and most prosperous group of the West. They watched with increasing apprehension the inevitable demands

Table 3. *West and East Pakistan: income disparity, 1949-70 (1959-60 prices)*

	GRP per caput		
	West	East	ratio
1949-50	345	287	1.20
1959-60	355	269	1.32
1969-70	504	314	1.61

Source: Ahmad, 1972, p.34.

from the East of the country for more equal power-sharing, and since the East had the large populace, if Pakistan remained a democracy under the constitution of the Independence Act (which was basically the 1935 Act) then the East, the Johnny-come-latelies of the Pakistan movement, might dictate to the West, the 'homeland' where Pakistan was first defined.

After a bungled attempt to write a new constitution in 1971, following an election allowed by the military (rather like the recent election that returned Benazir Bhutto), outright rebellion broke out in Bengal. A savage (Punjabi) army response which included large-scale massacres, particularly of intellectuals and of Hindus remaining in East Bengal, was followed by waves of refugees fleeing to India, which finally brought war between Pakistan and India (for the third time since 1947) and the proclamation of Bangladesh as a sovereign state in 1972.

Religion alone had not proved a strong enough bond between West and East Pakistan on which to build a polity. The utilitarian bonds were one-sided, leading to exploitation, not mutual benefit. The last recourse was coercion. But at that point the issues involved, particularly the persecution of Bengalis by Punjabis, literally spilt over the borders, and the issue became truly a South Asian, not merely a domestic affair.

By these twists of fate, one of India's *pays* has achieved nationhood.

VI. *Regionalism and holism in India and Pakistan*

The question is interminably raised: has the division of South Asia into three (Figure 5) terminated the process? Or will Indian Punjab achieve what the extremists demand, their new Khalistan? Is another insurrection likely in Pakistan's Baluchistan? Will the Tamil south ever divorce itself from Delhi?

In India, the most pressing regional problem has been language (Hardgrave, 1975; Farmer, 1983; Taylor and Yapp, 1979; Wilson and Dalton, 1982). After Independence in 1947, the demands for self-rule which had been stoked by the nationalist struggle had to be satisfied. These demands took the form of protests for the delimitation of linguistic areas in certain provinces, such as in northern Madras. Here the leaders of the Andhra movement adopted such tactics as fasts unto death, in the Gandhi mould. More than 300 people were killed in rioting. Nehru was at first strongly opposed to changing the administrative map—which was old provinces and larger princely states, with lesser princely states merged into neighbouring provinces on a pragmatic basis. His view was that to change would be to give way to the forces of communalism and regionalism. But after the events, significantly in the South, he and the government performed a volte-face. Now the argument was: if these forces can be accommodated within the constitution, they will have a stake in it: if not, then they will break it. Starting in 1956 in a massive administrative reform, India was

Figure 5. *Political divisions in South Asia, 1975*
Source: Schwartzberg, 1976, and others.

divided into approximately 16 roughly equal states, each with its own majority linguistic basis, and quite often its own script. In these units, the populace does not find itself unable to communicate with the administrators and educators as once it might have done. Although one should not blame the development exclusively for the subsequent shift in political behaviour, it is also true that the state governments have less and less often been formed of Congress legislators, and instead are more and more of local political groups, such as the DMK, or Dravidian Federalist Party of Tamil Nadu. Even in the central Parliament, the Lok Sabha, regional parties are taking more seats, and the Congress, the only major national party, seems to be withering away. The strong centre which Nehru wanted, and to some extent had, is melting. But in the Indian case this does not necessarily mean the demise of the Union. Many commentators have pointed out that India is still remarkably divided by caste and local factions. This means that in a state such as

Tamil Nadu or Andhra Pradesh there are constant struggles between different elements within the state. The state does not define a unity which will voice its demands for secession. Significantly, the most strident demands have come from the Punjab, where division by caste within Sikhism is weak, and the common identity, though riven by factions, stronger than elsewhere.

Utilitarian bonds have also grown. What India has is size, and the diversity of resources to go with it. Since Independence, successive governments have stressed the development of a comprehensive range of industries, and have pursued a policy of import substitution in a heavily-protected environment. There are critics of the efficiency and cost of this industrialisation: but India now has more than 200 million urban people, who are in the cash economy, in manufacturing and commerce, in government. There is a large new pan-Indian middle class, with pan-Indian vested interests to protect. They are increasingly proud of national achievements, and no custodians of the Gandhian past of non-violence. Few critics are heard of the cost or size of the armed forces, which now include one of the world's largest standing armies, a 'blue water' navy with two aircraft carriers and nuclear submarine(s), and a large and comprehensive arms industry.

It would appear that, at present, utilitarian and identitive bonds in India are stronger than before, and also more widely appreciated. Yet one cannot assume they will necessarily continue to grow, since a new trading liberalism and lower levels of central government financial support for state governments may both lead again to greater local economic independence and assertiveness.

Pakistan

Pakistan was born as an anti-Congress nation of Muslims. The Muslim League had not had the time that Congress had had to debate before Independence the policies it would pursue afterwards. Perhaps because of this it had drawn fundamentalist clerics and intellectual Marxists of Muslim descent into an unlikely coalition. In India, Nehru lived long enough to set his mould on the new nation and its policies: in Pakistan, Jinnah died soon after Independence with no powerful successor or widely accepted programme of action left behind him to steer the new nation. Regionalism and factionalism have plagued it ever since. Many of the regional problems have international dimensions:the Pathans straddle the border with Afghanistan, and the Baluchs the borders both with Afghanistan and Iran. The country was dominated by feudal landlords on the one hand, and a wave of new urban and educated immigrants (Jinnah was one of them) on the other (Hussain, 1979). It had no industry worth speaking of, and had to build new institutions, such as the army and civil service, from the pieces hacked off from the bigger Indian parts. It had no obvious unity except Islam. It has cohesion when exposed to external threat by India, but left to its own devices is riven by regional dissent. The most remarkable feat of its history is that, apart from the loss of Bangladesh, it has survived. It has not done so through indentitive bonds: though perhaps there is a new generation that accepts Pakistan as a natural sovereign state. It has done so partly by a policy similar to India's: protected industrialisation which has created a new middle class with vested interests. But this has been smaller and more concentrated than in India. It has done so also through coercion, through several periods of army rule, by an army supported hugely by outside funds from the USA. There is no space here to go into the international relations of India and Pakistan in depth (Bradnock, 1990; Chapman, forthcoming), but it is significant that India has found a true friend in the Soviet Union, and that Nehru's independent non-aligned movement, socialist rhetoric and state planning strained relations with the USA. The Pakistan-China-USA axis that developed fitted American designs for containment, and of course became highlighted during the Afghan war.

Though no one had ambitions to absorb Pakistan, if the country itself fell to pieces, the little bits could soon enter into different arrangements with neighbours. The most important of the bonds that have sustained it since 1947 is the armed forces, supported by external powers. Across the border, in the Punjab, American aircraft types face Russian models. The British desire to see South Asia remain unified—because therein lay its best defence—has been vindicated.

Besides defence the rationale of a unified South Asia had other merits. In 1946 the raj governed a subcontinent with a uniform currency, uniform external tariffs, unified postal service, and a commercial and civil legal code which had many common elements. In specified spheres, such as agriculture, considerable powers were delegated to provincial levels. The overall impression is of the kind of common market which Europe is current trying to achieve—except that at its core was the coercion of empire. Since 1947, South Asia has 'de-common-marketed' itself. But the regional imperative cannot simply go away, and recognition of this has resulted in the foundation of the South Asian Association for Regional Co-operation (SAARC). This is years, if not decades, away from rebuilding a common market: but if one day this is achieved it will, one hopes, be done without coercion from the centre.

Conclusions

The aphorism 'nature proposes, man disposes' is applicable to South Asia. Nature has proposed a geopolitical region. Within that region the time which has elapsed between external human shocks has resulted in a continuity of culture despite the detailed complexity of society. This detail is important, but it is the finely patterned cracks in the glaze of an old cracked plate—yet the plate has survived. The aggregation of this fine patterning into larger hierarchical assemblages portrays a subcontinent of *pays*, blurred only by the metropolitan cities. The only fissure of any real depth is that of religion. It is a tragedy for South Asia that this fissure actually cuts right through some of its strongest regional cultures, in the Punjab and Bengal. In terms of Figure 2 the current borders are 'infrequent'. They do violence to nearly every usual boundary principle except of course one—namely community.

There is a school of thought that says that this has been a history of reactionary politics: that the British gave the nationalists too little and too late—for had they been given Dominion status at the end of the First World War, there would have been no calls for Pakistan. The Congress is likewise accused of offering Jinnah too little, too late, and even in 1946 Pakistan was not inevitable even though the British no longer accepted the responsibility for foisting unity on India. And West Pakistan offered East Pakistan too little, too late. But this is a little simple: counterfactual history cannot prove that, had there been in 1919 a great Indian Federation, it would have survived.

There had been no spontaneous grass-roots movements for subcontinental integration until this century. Before that, the sheer scale and complexity of South Asia meant that only coercive empire could in any sense (usually slight) unite it. What the twentieth century has given the public at large is some conception of the right to self-determination. This 'self' has usually had fairly narrow confines, and regionalism remains a threat to both Pakistan and India. But wider nationalisms are emerging in the age of mass communication and industrialisation, although whether the concept of the strong centrist state survives long in the next century is open to question. But the scale of problems, and the advent of large-scale technologies, combine to propel whatever forms of state survive to negotiate with each other those common resource problems (particularly in river basin management) and trading complementarities which they must accommodate to mutual advantage. Apart from resource issues, there are few causes for continuing outright hostility between the current states. Nearly all boundary problems are resolved, and from the nadir of trade embargoes one assumes that things can only get better, except that the size of India so outweighs the other states that they must have their anxieties quietened by Indian diplomacy. The only really major unsolved issue is that legacy of the unfinished business of the British raj, the ultimate fate of Kashmir.

References

Ahmad, K.U., *The Break-up of Pakistan* (London, 1972).
A Social and Economic Atlas of India, 1987 (Delhi).
Bayly, C.A., *Rulers, Townsmen and Bazaars: North Indian society in the age of British expansion 1770-1880* (Cambridge, 1983, 1988).
Bouglé, Celestin, *Essays on the Caste System*, translated with an introduction by D.F. Pocock (Cambridge, 1971).
Bradnock, R.W., *India's Foreign Policy* (London, 1990).
Chakravarty, S.R. and Virendra Narain (eds.), *Bangladesh: History and culture* (Delhi, 1986).
Chapman, G.P., *One into three: the geopolitics of South Asia from British Raj to India, Pakistan and Bangladesh* (MSS, publication forthcoming).
Cohen, S.B., *Geography and Politics in a Divided World* (London, 1963).
Cohn, Bernard S., *India: the sociology of a civilization* (Englewood Cliffs, NJ, 1971).
Collins, Larry and Dominique LaPierre, *Freedom at Midnight* (New York, 1975).
Coupland, R., *Report on the Constitutional Problem in India*. Pt.1: *The Indian problem 1833-1935*, Pt.2: *Indian politics 1936-1942*, Pt.3: *The future of India* (London, 1943).
Day, W.M., 'Relative permanence of former boundaries in India', *Scottish Geographical Magazine*, 65 (1949), pp.113-22.
Dumont, Louis, *Homo hierarchicus: The caste system and its implications*, translated from the French by Mark Sainsbury (Chicago, 1970).
Farmer, B.H., *An Introduction to South Asia* (London, 1983).
Griffin, K. and A.R. Khan (eds.), *Growth and Inequality* (London, 1972).
Hardgrave, Robert L., *India: Government and politics in a developing nation* (2nd ed., New York, 1975).
Hodson, H.V., *The Great Divide: Britain-India-Pakistan* (London, 1969).
Hussain, Asaf, *Elite Politics in an Ideological State: the case of Pakistan* (Folkestone, 1979).
Michel, A.A., *The Indus Rivers: a study of the effects of partition* (New Haven, CT, 1967).
Moon, Sir Penderel, *Divide and Quit* (London, 1961).
Philips, C.H. and M.D. Wainwright, *The Partition of India: Policies and perspectives 1935-1947* (London, 1970).
Rahmat Ali, C., *What does the Pakistan Movement stand for?* (Cambridge, 1942).
Spate, O.H.K. and A.T.A. Learmouth, *India and Pakistan; a general and regional geography* (3rd ed., London, 1967).
Spear, Percival, *A History of India*, 2 (Harmondsworth, 1965, 1970).
Taylor, David, and Malcolm Yapp (eds.), *Political Identity in South Asia* (London, 1979).
Thapar, Romila, *A History of India*, 1 (Harmondsworth, 1966).
Vakil, C.N., *The Economic Consequences of Divided India* (Bombay, 1950).
Vakil, C.N. and D. Raghava Rao, *Economic Relations between India and Pakistan* (Bombay, n.d.).
Wilson, A.J. and D. Dalton (eds.), *The States of South Asia* (London, 1982).

Further reading

Bowman, Isaiah, *The New World: problems in political geography* (New York, 1921).

Brush, J.E., 'The distribution of religious communities in India', *Annals of the Association of American Geographers* 39 (1949), pp.81-98.

The Cambridge Economic History of India, Vol.1: *c.1200-c.1750*, edited by T. Raychaudhuri and I. Habib (Cambridge, 1982); Vol.2: *c.1757-1970*, edited by D. Kumar and M. Desai (Cambridge, 1983).

Charlesworth, N., *British Rule and the Indian Economy 1800-1914* (London, 1982).

Chatterjee, S.P., *The Partition of Bengal: a geographical study* (Calcutta, 1947).

Chaudri, M.A., *The Emergence of Pakistan* (New York, 1967).

Chen, Lincoln (ed.), *Disaster in Bangladesh: health crisis in a developing nation* (New York 1973).

Griffiths, Sir Percival, *The British Impact on India* (London, 1952).

Islam, M. Rafiqul, *Ganges Water Dispute* (Dhaka, 1987).

Kirk, W., 'The role of India in the diffusion of early cultures', *Geographical Journal*, 141 (1975), pp.19-34.

Lamb, A., *Asian Frontiers* (London, 1968).

Mansergh, N., *The Prelude to Partition: concepts and aims in Ireland and India*. The 1976 Commonwealth Lecture (Cambridge, 1978).

Menon, V.P., *The Story of the Integration of the Indian States* (Calcutta and London, 1956).

Noman, Omar, *The Political Economy of Pakistan 1947-1985* (London, 1988).

Owen, Sidney, *India on the Eve of the British Conquest* (1872; reprinted Calcutta).

Rahman, M.A., *East and West Pakistan: a problem in the political economy of regional planning*, Occasional Paper No.20 (Cambridge, MA, 1968).

Rudolph, L.I. and S.H., *The Regional Imperative* (Delhi, 1980).

Schwartzberg, Joseph E., *An Historical Atlas of South Asia* (Chicago, 1978).

—, 'Factors in the linguistic reorganization of Indian states', in Paul Wallace (ed.), *Region and Nation in India* (Oxford, 1985), pp.155-82.

Tomlinson, B.R., *The British Raj 1914-1947: the economics of decolonization in India* (London, 1979).

Wilcox, Wayne Ayres, *Pakistan: the consolidation of a nation* (New York, 1963).

Zaman, Munir, *et al.* (eds.), *River Basin Development* (Dublin, 1983).

CLASSICAL HINDU SCRIPTURES[1]

Tuvia Gelblum

This paper considers some of the great continuities of Hindu tradition, by describing categories of its ancient literature. This is a literature which contains mysticism, philosophy and laws, but also myths and dramatic legends. The works are divided by time and composition, just as there are divisions among Hindus—followers of Śiva, for example, or of Vishnu (including devotees of Krishna). But all relate back to ancient roots; and to the relatively few main currents of thought which have dominated 'Hinduism'. The survey in this paper is historical-analytical. It attempts to give a brief introduction to the vast body of texts that constitute the classical Hindu scriptures. Their distinctive features are brought out; and in particular the cleavage between their immutable core—the older classificatory category of 'revelation'—and the later open-ended 'tradition'. Their epistemological status is also considered. In conclusion illustrations are provided of some of the ingenious conceptual, theoretical-fictional and mythical devices which facilitated the bridging between the two categories, and the accommodation as goals of life of seemingly 'profane' subject-matter, concerned with the enhancement of pleasure and power—alongside (and regulated by) piety.

The literary monuments of the Hindu religion, namely those of its scriptural sources which are distinctly of universal, pan-Hindu, rather than sectarian relevance and influence, are traditionally classified into two broad categories: (1) *śruti*, commonly rendered as 'revelation', and (2) *smṛti*, commonly rendered as 'tradition'. *Śruti* means literally 'what has been heard', implying direct perception or discovery by the ancient sages. *Śruti* provides, at least formally, the foundation of Hindu beliefs. It is, in principle, revealed truth, the sole source of authority. The term *śruti* refers to the vast corpus of the oldest Indian literary documents known by the title *Veda* (literally, 'knowledge', that is, essentially sacrificial lore). In the strict sense the *Veda* or *śruti* comprises:

(1) the oldest documents—the four collections:
 (a) *Ṛgveda*: primarily hymns addressed to deities—dating from before 1200 BC;
 (b) *Atharvaveda*: primarily magic incantations or prayers of a

[1] First published in G.R. Hawting (ed.), *Sacred Writings in Oriental and African Religions*, Occasional Papers XII (External Services Division, School of Oriental and African Studies, London).

compelling purpose;

(c) *Sāmaveda*, and (d) *Yajurveda*: both exclusively liturgical; and (2) *Brāhmaṇas*: prose commentaries expounding the ritual or the verbal formulae accompanying it.

In a wider sense, the *Veda* or *śruti* includes the notable *Upaniṣads*, traditionally also known as *Vedānta* (literally, 'the end or culmination of the *Veda*), which consist of mystic and speculative tracts characterised by poetic symbolism. Among their salient features are a unity of theme or purpose (despite a variety of approaches leading to it), a sense of certitude of the experience conveyed, and a consideration of reality at various levels. There are thirteen principal *Upaniṣads*, their most ancient dating from the eighth century BC, the youngest from the third century BC. By external criteria they are deemed to fall into four groups: ancient prose, early metrical, later prose and later metrical. Apart from these principal *Upaniṣads*, there are others, which, however, are essentially sectarian in orientation (for example, Śaiva, Vaiṣṇava or Śākta) and date from the medieval period. (In the West the term *Vedānta* is better known as a cluster of philosophical schools which developed from an attempted systematisation of Upaniṣadic thought.) The *Veda* is accordingly treated as consisting of two layers: the *karmakāṇḍa* (the part whose subject matter is ritual acts which lead to heaven, and *jñanakāṇḍa*, the part dealing with mystic insightful knowledge which leads to liberation from rebirth.

Early exegetes (the Mīmāmsakas) distinguished three semantic or functional categories of expression in the wide corpus of the Vedic literature: injunction (*vidhi*)—the principal one—recital (*mantra*), and commentary (*arthavāda*). The latter derivative category is extended to include the esoteric mystic *Upaniṣads*, which were ostensibly concerned with the inner significance of the ritual. The term *upaniṣads* itself apparently signified microcosmic-macrocosmic 'equivalence' or identity of the real self with the essence or substratum of the universe (*ātman*=*brahman*). The realisation of this ultimate reality, which entails a rigorous ethical-mental discipline (*yoga*), is the subject matter and purpose of these tracts.

The early devoted interest in the study, preservation and interpretation of the *Veda* gave rise to a subsidiary literature embodying six sciences known as *vedāngas* ('auxiliary aids to the *Veda*'), established between the eighth and fourth centuries BC). These consist of phonetics, metrics, grammar, etymology-cum-exegesis, socio-religious practice, and astronomy. Strictly speaking the *vedāngas* are extraneous to the *Vedas* in the narrow sense, and hence form part of *smṛti* rather than *śruti*.

Since it refers to the fundamental canonical scriptures, the term *śruti* is quite commonly rendered by 'Revelation'. According to Hindu orthodox exegetes, however, there is no revealer; the *Veda* is by no means the word of God.[2] Nor is the *Veda* concerned with a new truth revealed at a specific time in history. Rather the *Veda* is considered to be eternally given, being co-eternal with the uncreated world. The guarantee of the *Veda's* absolute validity and infallibility lies paradoxically in its negative correlation with the belief in a Creator God.[3] 'For were it authored it would of necessity be flawed by the author's imperfections, and its authority diminished. It thus validated itself insofar as it was the sole source of knowledge about matters lying beyond the senses.'[4] The *Veda*, it may also be noted, is a far cry from being a 'Holy Writ', as it seems essentially to have been composed and preserved orally.[5] Unlike the Bible or the Qur'ān, the *Veda* does not consist of one specific book, as its scope is a vast corpus of literature, whose composition in various localities spread over many generations of poet-priests and thinkers.

Śruti, or the *Veda*, is promoted by all Hindu philosophical schools to the rank of an accredited instrument of knowledge not less reliable than perception or inference. Its acceptance, at least as a formula of legitima-

[2] This is despite the Concise Oxford Dictionary: 'Revelation—Disclosing of knowledge, knowledge disclosed, to man by divine or supernatural agency. Compare, for example, Āpadevī's *Mīmāmsānyāyaprakāśa* (trans. F. Edgerton, New Haven, 1929), p.41: 'And since the round of existences is beginningless according to the accepted law that each world-aeon is preceded by another world-aeon, and since God is omniscient, all that can be established [about the origin of the Veda] is that in this world-aeon God remembers the Veda from past world-aeons and makes it known; but there is no basis for a hypothesis that its essence was got at by any other means-of-knowledge and composed. And so, since there is no person (author of it, not even God, who is also a person), it (the Vedic injunctive force) is based only on the word...' However, unlike the orthodox traditionalists of the Mīmāmsā and of some related schools for whom the Vedic texts are timeless, the theistic traditions view the Vedas as the word of God, and as a phase in an open-ended process of revelation. Cf. Wilhelm Halbfass, *Tradition and Reflection—Explorations in Indian Thought* (New York, 1991), p.4.

[3] 'The history of classical Hinduism presents a strange phenomenon. While, on the one hand, Hinduism sought to substitute the impersonal absolute of the Upaniṣads with a personal god, the various philosophical systems, which it adopted as its own, were, by and large, basically atheistic', R.N. Dandekar, *Insights into Hinduism* (Delhi, 1979), p.120. Cf. also Shlomo Biderman, 'Scriptures, revelation and reason' in Ben-Ami Scharfstein (ed.), *Philosophy East/Philosophy West* (Oxford, 1978), p.137 seq. For a brief characterisation of *śruti* as well as *smṛti* texts see J.L. Brockington, *The Sacred Thread* (Edinburgh, 1981), passim.

[4] J.A.B. van Buitenen, *The Bhagavadgītā in the Mahābharāta* (Chicago, 1981), Introduction, p.7.

[5] Significantly the Sanskrit word *śabda* can mean 'word, verbal testimony or authority (i.e. *śruti*, the *Veda*)' as well as 'noise, sound'. Similarly, the word *svādhyāya* can mean 'study' as well as 'recitation'.

tion, serves as the criterion for separating mainstream Hinduism from heterodox denominations such as Buddhism or Jainism. The latter are disparagingly referred to as *nāstika*, that is, 'deny-ers' of the validity of the *Veda*. Throughout the development of Hindu religious thought seldom has an innovation been propounded without recourse to a quotation (often mere formal lip-service) from the Vedic literature as respectable and ultimate confirmation.

As for the term *smṛti*, it means literally 'memory, recollection', implying validity which is secondary, or 'at a remove'. Its authoritativeness depends, according to orthodox exegetes, on being in accord with, or derivable from, a corresponding *śruti* text, which exists or existed once (in theory). According to Kumārila's *Tantravārttika* 1.3.3. wherever *Smṛti* is found to be contradicted by *Śruti*, it ought to be rejected—'just as the counterfeit coin is to be rejected as soon as it is found to be counterfeit'. The *smṛti*, whose scope is less rigorously defined than that of the *śruti*, comprises a vast corpus of extra-Vedic and post-Vedic literature, notably the books on *Dharma* (concerned with the cosmic-moral order and the fulfilment of duties required for its maintenance) such as Manu-smṛti, the Great Epic (*Mahābhārata*) and the medieval *Purāṇas* (distinguished by their myths, theology and cosmology). The core of the *smṛti*, that is, *smṛti* proper, is formed by the *Dharmaśāstra*, a corpus of literature embodying in verses the doctrinal teachings whose subject matter is *dharma* (duty, religious and moral laws governing individual conduct). It has developed out of the ancient prose manuals on human conduct known as *dharma-sūtra* (essentially part of the above-mentioned *vedāngas*). The most influential text in this category is the compilation known as *Mānavadharmaśāstra* or *Manu-smṛti* (first century BC to second century AD). Its subject matter is descriptive (an account of the creation of the universe in Chapter I) as well as prescriptive, notably laying down the *varnāśrama-dharma*, the functional duties and responsibilities of a Hindu both as an individual and as a member of society, these being determined by his class and station in life. The concept of the individual's duty (*svadharma*) is so all-pervasive as apparently to exclude the concept of 'rights' (yet the latter concept is arguably implicit in the formulations of the former; for the rights of X with regard to Y are frequently expressed in terms of the duty of Y with regard to X). The emphasis on one's minutely defined duty is reflected in the dictum 'it is better to do one's own duty badly than another's well' (*Manu-smṛti* 10.97; *Bhagavadgītā* 18.47).

In keeping with the mainstream tradition, Manu acknowledges and accommodates, alongside *dharma* (duty/merit/piety) as the paramount goal of life, also the two goals known as *kāma* (pleasure; sensual, aesthetic fulfilment of desires) and *artha* (wealth/power/profit) which were fundamentally awkward elements within mainstream Hinduism. Traditional commentators displayed much ingenuity in systemising and correlating these three motivational categories (*trivarga*).[6] Thus implicitly and indirectly, some ethico-religious status was accorded also to the secular literatures known as *Kāma-sāstra* and *Artha-śāstra*, manuals concerned with the means for enhancing pleasure and material power respectively. (See *Bhagvadgītā* 7.11 where the god Kṛsna himself proclaims: 'I am the strength of the strong, providing it is not tainted with the passion of *kāma*; in beings I am *kāma* so far as it is not inconsistent with *dharma*'.) With *dharma* is also correlated the ultimate goal, transcendence (*mokṣa*—the escape from continuous rebirth), in which context *dharma* is conceived as an instrumental goal, a prelude to, or corollary of, *mokṣa* which is ultimately to be superseded by the latter. Thus all philosophical literature proclaiming *mokṣa* as its chief aim, that is, *mokṣa-śāstra*, is implicitly relevant to *dharma*, which is the subject matter of *smṛti*. The influence exerted by the text of Manu on law in Burma, Siam, Java and Bali indicates the extent of its reputation even outside the Indian subcontinent. Yet Manu's concern with jurisprudence does not occupy much more than a quarter of the whole compilation. Indeed, it is the didactic and literary characteristics of *Manu-smṛti* that enhanced its popular appeal.

Secondary to the *dharma-śāstra* in the *smṛti* category stand the three great repositories of devotional Hinduism: the two great Sanskrit epics, the *Mahābhārata* and the *Rāmāyaṇa*, as well as the *Purāṇas*. Though essentially secular, these literary compilations were gradually incorporated into the sphere of *smṛti* by virtue of their being conceived as narratives illustrating the application of *dharma*, or the norm of conduct, to concrete situations in life. In this function they exerted an immensely inspiring ethical influence, and, in their direct personal appeal to all classes, served as an auxiliary medium to that of the *Dharma-śāstra*.

The *Mahābhārata*, 'The great war of the Bhāratas', is probably the longest poem in world literature, nearly 100,000 couplets—about ten times the length of the Iliad and Odyssey combined. It evolved gradually over a few centuries, beginning in the second century BC, under-

[6] However, J.A.B. Buitenen appositely warns against 'a natural overestimation of the significance of the *trivarga* (*dharma, artha* and *kāma*) as classifying different sets of practices'. As he puts it: 'In principle, all three are *dharma*. It is no less important for a man to seek *artha*, achievement in his occupation in the largest sense of the word, or to gratify those desires that maintain the population of the earth, than to follow the precepts of religion and observe the canons of law...In other words, *dharma* is all that activity that a man, if he is to live fittingly, is required to contribute to the fixed order of things, to the norm of the universe, which is good and should not be altered', in his 'Dharma and Mokṣa', *Philosophy East and West*, 7 (1957), reproduced in his *Studies in Indian Literature and Philosophy* (ed. Ludo Rocher) (Delhi, 1988), cf. pp.114-5.

going modifications and absorbing accretions. Warlike narratives are mingled with mythology and ethical disquisitions. The main story is concerned with the feuds between the Pāṇḍavas and the Kauravas culminating in the great war in which the former were victorious by the good offices of the god Kṛṣṇa—their mentor, friend and philosopher. A most celebrated and deeply inspiring part of this epic is the lengthy dialogue, almost a monologue, known as the *Bhagavadgītā* (in 700 verses). In it, on the eve of the great battle, Kṛṣṇa delivers a theological and ethical sermon, exhorting one to act dutifully without regard to consequential reward. In its context, this exhortation meant discharging one's duty to face up to and fight an evil enemy, the Kauravas. In the *Bhagavadgītā* both the ancient cult of the ritual act on the one hand, and an unsocialised subversive ascetic movement on the other, were supplanted by a fresh alternative: salvation through inner renunciation of egotistic ambition, coupled with God-centred activity aiming at the fulfilment of one's pre-allocated duties for the welfare of the socio-cosmic order.[7] Among the characteristic ideas propounded here are theistic tolerance and a middle path of self-discipline (for example, 'let him pin-point his mind, so that the workings of mind and senses are under control. Yoga is neither for him who eats too much or not at all...'; 6.12-16). Mysticism was thus rendered accessible to ordinary laity. The universal appeal of this text to all Hindus, down to contemporary times, is unrivalled by any other Hindu scripture. In the tradition of the Vedāntic schools of philosophy this text has gained the status of being one of its three fundamental sources (alongside the *Upaniṣads* and the *Brahmasūtra*).

The *Rāmāyana* or the story of Rāma, consisting of about 24,000 couplets, probably dates from the same period as the *Mahābhārata*. It is shorter and more homogeneous than the latter. Drawing on another pan-Indian legend, it relates the adventures of Prince Rāma and his noble consort Sītā from the time of their exile up to their triumphant return to Ayodhyā (Oudh, Awadh), and concludes with the subsequent banishment of Sītā by Rāma's unjust subjects and her death. To the folkloristic core of the text were added digressions, whose subject matter is *dharma*, the code of propriety. The motif of the victory of good (symbolised by Rāma) over evil (symbolised by the demon Rāvaṇa), as well as the identification of Rāma with the god Viṣṇu (in the first and last chapters), help to account for the vast popularity of this epic. It is frequently recited, privately and publicly, and dramatically enacted, notably in the Rām-Līlā—an annual pageant celebrated throughout India, and in Kathākali dance-drama performances in Kerala, South India. The impact of the *Rāmāyana* story is evident in an episode in the

[7] Cf. Tuvia Gelblum, 'On "the meaning of life" and the *Bhagavadgītā*', *Asian Philosophy*, 2, 2 (1992), pp.121-30.

Mahābhārata (entitled *Rāmopākhyāna*), a Buddhist Jātaka story, Kālidāsa's *Raghuvamśa* and Bhavabhūti's *Uttararāmacarita*, and in many other literary and dramatic works. It has continuously provided inspiration to artists, as is evidenced in illuminated manuscripts and in Rajasthani and Pahari paintings of the seventeenth and eighteenth centuries. Among the adaptations of the original epic in the vernaculars are the Hindi version by Tulsīdās, the Tamil one by Kampaṇ and the Bengali one by Kṛittibās. Versions of the epic (or rather of the underlying folklore) were transmitted to various parts of South East Asia, China and Tibet. It features, together with motifs from the *Mahābhārata*, in the Javanese-Balinese dramatic dance and shadow plays.

The *Purāṇas* (literally, 'ancient lore, antiquities') are a further extensive storehouse of transmitted tradition. They contain a bewildering variety of subjects, their main thrust conceived to be the illustration of *dharma* and evocation of sentiments of religious devotion through myths and stories, hymns of praise, glorificatory description of holy places and miracles wrought there, as well as exposition of rules concerning rituals, human prehistory, philosophy, theology and various practical aspects of life (such as medicine, house-building and omens). The main *Purāṇas* were composed over the first millenium of our era, already betraying sectarian bias, for example, through the different versions of the same myth occurring in them. There are 18 principal *Purāṇas*, a great number of lesser ones (*upapurāṇas*) as well as comparatively recent *sthala-purāṇas* (local ones) aimed at the glorification of temples and holy locations. The best known *Puraṇas* are the *Viṣṇu-purāṇa* (relatively old), noted for its summary of the mythology of Viṣṇu and the *Bhāgavata-purāṇa*, '*Purāṇa* of the adepts of the Blessed One' (i.e. Kṛṣṇa), a relatively late (perhaps ninth-century AD) repository of popular Hindu philosophical speculation and beliefs. The popular appeal of the *Bhāgavata-purāṇa*, to this day, has been instrumental in the spread of Viṣṇuite emotional devotionalism (*bhakti*) with its emphasis on the grace of God, and has in particular become a rallying point for the passionate and erotic cult of Kṛṣṇaite sects.

Apart from the encyclopedic genre of the *Purāṇas*, which are fundamentally of pan-Hindu relevance (even though functioning as rallying points for given sects), there are more recent analogous compilations which are wholly and distinctly sectarian. These are traditionally classified respectively as *samhitas* ('collections') of the Vṣṇuites, *āgamas* ('traditions') of the Sivaits, and *tantras* (doctrinal texts) relating to the current of Hinduism known as Tantrism. The character of the latter three groups of texts, related to sectarian theories and ritualism, and their place in the wider context of pan-Hindu scriptures, is illuminated in the following observation by J. Gonda (originally in his 1969 Jordan Lectures at SOAS):

One of the arguments which could be adduced in favour of the usual division of Indian culture into an older period, Vedism, and a later period, called Hinduism, would be that the former, at least at first sight, presents itself as a unity, whereas the latter is a varied and, already in the *Mahābhārata*, a confused spectacle of beliefs and practices. On closer inspection it becomes clear however, first that many features of Hinduism have their roots in the Vedic past, and in the second place that it has been a few main currents which, from the very beginning up to the present day, have come into prominence and have largely determined the character of that many-sided and all-enfolding culture which we in the West have chosen to call Hinduism.[8]

Notwithstanding the theoretical cleavage or contradistinction between *śruti* and *smṛti*, recurrent attempts have been made to bridge the gap between the two categories. The ambiguous position of the *Bhagavadgītā* as an authoritative document is a case in point. It is clearly *smṛti*, being part of the post-Vedic *Mahābhārata*, yet it is called an *upaniṣad* (in some colophons)—a term originally reserved to the later layer of the Vedic literature. As van Buitenen observes: 'A quotation of the *Gītā* (= *Bhagavadgītā*) can never suffice to prove a point without the corroboration of *śruti*. But not seldom the meaning of *śruti* is made to agree with the *Gītā* so that the *Gītā* might agree with *śruti*'.[9] A further bridging attempt adduces textual evidence from *Bṛhadāraṇyaka Upaniṣad* 2.4.10 (making use of terminological ambiguities) for its claim of a common supra-mundane origin for both *śruti* and *smṛti*

[8] J. Gonda, *Viṣṇuism and Śivaism—A comparison* (London, 1970), p.1. For a differing assessment, cf. Wilhelm Halbfass, *Tradition and Reflections—Explorations in Indian Thought*, pp.1-2: 'The Vedic texts contain no Hindu dogma, no basis for a "creed" of Hinduism, no clear guidelines for the "hindu way of life". They offer only vague and questionable analogues to those ideas and ways of orientation and that become basic presuppositions of later Hinduism. It may suffice to recall here the cyclical world-view, the doctrine of karma and rebirth, the ethical principle of *ahiṃsā* and the soteriology of final liberation. For all of this, the oldest and most fundamental Vedic texts provide no clearly identifiable basis. The Hindu pantheon, the forms of worship and devotion, and the temple cult are not Vedic. The traditional "order of castes and stages of life" (*varṇāśramadharma*) is far removed from the Vedic beginnings. Regardless of all retrospective glorification of the Veda, even the "orthodox" core of the tradition, as represented by the exegetic Mīmāṃsā and the Dharmaśāstra, follows largely un-Vedic ways of thought and is oriented around a projection or fiction of the Veda. While proclaiming the sanctity of the Veda, the Hindu traditon seems to be turning away from the Vedic ways of thought and life. The preservation and glorification of the text seems to coincide with its neglect and the obscuration of its meaning.... Is this the final word on the role of the Veda in India? Are Vedism and Hinduism essentially different religions and world-views, held together only by an ideology of continuity and correspondence?'

[9] J.A.B. van Buitenen, *Rāmānuja on the Bhagavadgītā* (reprint, Delhi 1968), p.8.

works:

As, from a fire laid with damp fuel, clouds of smoke separately issue forth, so, lo, verily, from this great Being (*bhūta*) has been breathed forth that which is *Ṛgveda, Yajurveda, Sāmaveda, Atharvaveda, itihāsa* (legend), *purāṇa* (stories about things past), Sciences (*vidyā*), mystic tracts (*upaniṣads*), Verses, fundamental rules (*sūtra*), Explanations (*anuvyākhyāna*) and Commentaries (*vyākhyāna*).

More extreme is the attitude exemplified in Śankara's blatant claim that the *Purāṇas* form an integral part of the *Veda* (in his commentary on *Bṛhadāraṇyaka Upaniṣad*). Still more extreme is the following hyperbole clad in poetical-mythical garb:

Once the divine seers foregathered, and on one scale they hung the four *Vedas* in the balance, and on the other scale the *Bhārata*; and both in size and in weight it was the heavier. Therefore because of its size and its weight it is called the *Mahābhārata* (*mahā* 'great'; *bhāra* 'load')—he who knows his etymology is freed from all sin (Mbh.1.1.205, trans. J.A.B. van Buitenen).

These and other attempts at bridging over the two classificatory categories highlight at one and the same time both the already given paramount sanctity or importance of the *śruti*, and the later newly-acquired popularity or essential role of this or the other among the *smṛti* works.

Finally a note of caution on the use of translations of classical Hindu scriptures may be sounded. Despite their usefulness as aids in the exploration of the meaning of the original texts, and their significance in terms of comparative religion or comparative philosophy—in a minimal and responsible sense—available translations are not infrequently inadequate, or at best tentative. This may be accounted by the nature of the sources, which are embodied in terms of a very different language, a different culture, and by our state of research. As Wilhelm Halbfass recently observed:

In some central instances, the resolution of technical problems, and the attention of minute philological details, are indispensable in order to approach the broader issues. Philology and philosophical reflection cannot be separated in such cases.[10]

[10] Wilhelm Halbfass, *On Being and What There is—Classical Vaiśeṣika and the history of Indian ontology* (New York, 1992), p.viii. Also cf. J.F. Staal, *Universals—Studies in Indian Logic and Linguistics* (Chicago, 1988), p.160: '[i.e. classical Yoga] the attempt at accurate description and construction is present to the same extent as, for instance, in the chapter on affections in Spinoza's *Ethics*. The study of Indian philosophy in general loses much of its importance if the underlying methods are neglected. These methods are not only related to the language in which they are expressed, but they are often directly inspired by studies of this language by Indian grammarians. In the West, the recognition that linguistic structures play a decisive role in

Further reading

The following is a selective bibliography which will be found useful by the non-specialist reader who wishes to acquaint himself with some of the scriptures (in translation) referred to, or gather what they are like:

H.W. Bailey, 'Ancient Indian literature', in E.B. Ceadel, *Literatures on the East. An appreciation* (London, 1951).
W.T. de Bary (ed.), *Sources of Indian Tradition* (New York, 1958).
A.L. Basham, *The Wonder that was India* (London, 1954).
J.L. Brockington, *The Sacred Thread* (Edinburgh, 1981).
J.B. van Buitenen, *Rāmanuja on the Bhagavadgītā* (reprint Delhi, 1968)
— *The Mahābhārata* (trans.) (Chicago, 1971).
—, *The Bhagavadgītā in the Mahrābhārata* (Chicago, 1981).
R.D. Dandekar, *Insights into Hinduism* (Delhi, 1979).
E. Deutsch and A.B. van Buitenen, *A Source Book in Advaita Vedānta* (Honolulu, 1981).
F. Edgerton, *The Beginnings of Indian Philosophy* (London, 1965).
Ch. Eliot, *Hinduism and Buddhism*, (3 vols., London, 1921).
J. Gonda, *Vedic Literature* (Wiesbaden, 1975).
W. Halbfass, *Tradition and Reflection—explorations of Indian thought* (New York, 1991).
R.E. Hume, *The Thirteen Upanishads* (Oxford, 1934).
A.A. Macdonell, *Sanskrit Literature* (London, 1900).
—, *A Vedic Reader for Students* (Oxford, 1917).
B.K. Matilal (ed.), *Moral Dilemmas in the Mahābhārata* (Delhi, 1989).
W.D. O'Flaherty, *Hindu Myths* (Harmondsworth, 1975).
—, *The Rigveda* (Harmondsworth, 1981).
H. Oldenberg, *Ancient India* (Calcutta, 1962).
A. Radhakrishna and Ch,. A Moore (eds.), *A Source Book in Indian Philosophy* (Princeton, 1957).
A. Raghavan, *The Indian Heritage* (Bangalore, 1956).
L. Renou, *The Nature of Hinduism* (New York, 1951)
—, *Vedic India* (Calcutta, 1957).
—, *Hinduism* (New York, 1963).
—, *Indian Literature* (New York, 1964).
—, *The Destiny of the Veda in India* (Delhi, 1965).
R.C. Zaehner, *Hinduism* (Oxford, 1962).

---

philosophy is slowly gaining ground. In India, it has long been explicit. This recognition may be expected increasingly to affect, if not to undermine, our philosophic certainties'.

SUTTEE OR *SATĪ*: VICTIM OR VICTOR?[1]

Julia Leslie

The interest currently being expressed in women and religion throws down an important challenge: the need to see women not merely as the passive victims of an oppressive ideology but also, perhaps primarily, as the active agents of their own positive constructs. My paper on sati was written shortly after the much publicised death of Roop Kanwar on her husband's funeral pyre in Rajasthan in September 1987.[2] *It is an attempt to understand how the public spectacle of a woman being burnt alive could possibly make sense. Without suggesting that the practice of sati is in any way praiseworthy, and without trying to minimise the manipulative powers of the orthodox tradition, I try to look past the notion of women as passive victims to the painful fact that some women, in some circumstances, may create a positive construct for sati. My presentation of 'the discourse on sati' takes the form of two accounts (one from the eighteenth century and one from the twentieth) in which the woman concerned is portrayed entirely as a victim, juxtaposed with two accounts (again, one from the eighteenth century and one from the twentieth) in which she is portrayed as an active and heroic agent. I conclude that, for some women, the concept of the* sati *is simply the ideal of the* pativratā *or devoted wife taken to its logical conclusion. For such a woman, sati lacks both the gloss of oppression given to it by non-Hindus and the negative associations allotted to widowhood within the Hindu tradition. By transforming herself into a 'deified eternal wife', the* sati *finds a soteriological path that takes positive account of the demands made of the traditional Hindu woman.*

Introduction

Sati—the death of a woman on her husband's funeral pyre—is a difficult topic to discuss. There are even two respectable arguments for not discussing it. The first, derived from a fear of sensationalism, is often

[1] First published in Julia Leslie (ed.), *Roles and Rituals for Hindu Women* (Pinter Publishers, London, 1991).

[2] An earlier version of this paper was published in *Bulletin: Center for the Study of World Regions, Harvard University*, 14, 2 (1987-88). One of the changes is my choice of terminology. While I continue to emphasise the distinctions between the terms 'suttee', *satī* and *sahagamana*, I now use the modern term 'sati' (the common idiom both for English-speakers in India and for most contemporary scholars) to indicate the act of self-immolation in general discussion.

voiced by Indian friends and Indologist colleagues. the argument runs as follows: sati was never common; now that even those isolated cases are a thing of the past, we should not make too much of them; dwelling on them merely gives India a bad name. In response to this, I shall give a brief historical survey of the practice of sati in India,[3] and draw two conclusions.

First, what is the historical background? The earliest reference to the practice in a Sanskrit text may be found in the *Mahābhārata* (which evolved between 400 BCE and 200 CE, reaching its present form around 400 CE). An account is also given in the first century BCE by the Greek author Diodorus Siculus writing his history of the Punjab in the fourth century BCE. 'Sati stones' (memorials to women who died in this way) may be found all over India, dating from as early as 510 CE. In the Muslim period, the Rajputs practised a form of sati termed *jauhar*;[4] that is, it was customary for a wife to burn herself before her husband's expected death in battle (as, for example, at Chitorgarh in Rajasthan). In the medieval period in general, the hardships experienced by Hindu widows (such as severe restrictions on diet and dress, and the stigma of inauspiciousness) probably encouraged the spread of sati. The increase in the practice of sati among the brahmans of Bengal (especially during the period 1680-1830) was partly due to the fact that the system of law prevailing there gave inheritance rights to widows.[5] While some widows enjoyed the powers this conferred, others conformed to the increased pressure to die.

There have been several attempts to abolish the practice. Even within orthodox Hinduism, there has always been a faction for whom sati is abhorrent; hence the debates on the issue in Sanskrit and vernacular texts. The Mughal rulers Humayun and Akbar made some attempt to prohibit the practice. But it was not until the British period that it was finally declared illegal with the Suttee Regulation Act of 1829. When the British left, the independent government of India reaffirmed the illegality of sati. Despite the official abolition of sati, however, instances still occur, even in the 1980s, and the respect and devotion paid to the memories of women who have died in this way remain un-

[3] Outside India, sati was practised by the ancient Greeks, Germans, Slavs, Scandinavians, Egyptians and Chinese. There is also evidence of the custom among the Aryans in the Indo-European period, but by the time they reached India only traces of an archaic practice remain.

[4] *Jauhar* (Marwari, Gujarati, Hindi), from the (hypothetical) Sanskrit *jatughara*, 'house plastered with lac and other combustible materials for burning people alive in' (Turner, 1966, p.281).

[5] Ashis Nandy argues that the responsibility for this increase belongs more properly to the colonial presence in India (1980). For recent historical studies of the origin, abolition, and persistence of sati, see Datta 1988; Sharma *et al.* 1988; Thapar 1988.

changed (cf. Harlan, in press).

My conclusions are twofold. First, sati remains as an ideal. While the numbers of women who died in this way have always been statistically small, the ideal of such women and such a death is reverenced throughout traditional India today. Sati evidently needs to be practised sometimes in order to serve as a model, but it becomes irrelevant how many times it is actually practised because its social effect as a model of the good (that is, socially-valued) woman remains. Second, women still die in this way. The death of any woman simply to coincide with her husband's is depressing. Death by burning, burning alive in a public spectacle, is deeply shocking. That such a death has become an ideal worthy of worship and (sometimes) emulation demands explanation. Clearly, the topic is sensational enough without my help.

The other argument for not discussing sati takes the opposite tack: that trying to understand it is tantamount to explaining it away. What Mary Daly calls the 'language of understanding' (which scholars use without a second thought) often takes the edge off what they are trying to understand. Thus when we talk about sati as the 'Indian custom of widow-burning', we are in danger of reducing the appalling suffering of countless women to a mere 'custom' that we outsiders should strive to understand. As Daly explains, 'the term custom—a casual and neutral term—is often used by scholars to describe these barbarous rituals of female slaughter' (1978, p.188). My response is to insist that we need to do two things: understand and judge.

First, there is a real need for understanding. If we wish to argue at all persuasively for change, we must first of all understand what is going on. We must construct that pathway to the pyre brick by brick and stone by stone so that, finally, we know how to destroy it and bring the horror to an end. But while trying to understand the empowering aspects of sati, we must never forget the violent and degrading reality. Second, there is a place for outrage. Understanding why sati makes sense to so many women and men does not mean condoning it, or accepting the necessity for it, or even refusing to judge. There must be a place for outrage.

The difficulties encountered in the study of sati are reflected in the terminology used. For the discourse on sati reveals a significant dichotomy. 'Suttee' in its older Anglicised spelling is the term coined by the British in India to denote the practice (Yule and Burnell, 1985, p.878-83). The term carries with it associations of widowhood and victimisation. This represents the predominant view of the West. The same word in its original Sanskrit is *satī* (feminine), derived from *sat* meaning 'goodness' or 'virtue'. The term *satī* thus denotes not the practice but the practitioner: the 'virtuous woman' who joins her husband in death. The term carries with it associations of great virtue, personal strength and religious autonomy. This still represents the predominant attitude of traditional India. The most common Sanskrit terms for the practice are: *sahagamana* ('going with'), *anugamana* ('going after'), and *anumaraṇa* ('dying after'). In this chapter, the practice is denoted by the modern term 'sati' (and, occasionally, in the colonial context, by its earlier version, 'suttee'), while the Sanskrit word *satī* is reserved for the person.

My concern is to juxtapose two views: the notion of 'suttee' that defines the woman as victim; and the concept of the *satī*, the woman as victor. I do not wish to suggest that the practice of sati is something to be condoned, or encouraged, or glorified. But I have difficulty with a view of women that sees them only as victims. To an important extent, of course, they are victims: both of their religious and cultural ideology in general; and of their menfolk, who (consciously or unconsciously) perceive an investment in continuing these ideas. But what is significant for me—as a woman scholar interested in how women cope with oppressive ideologies—is how these same victims find a path through the maze of oppression, a path that to them spells dignity and power. I wish they did not have to do this; but they did and do. So I believe we should look at what they have done.

Plate 1. *A sati ceremony*
Frontispiece to James Peggs, *India's Cries to British Humanity* (London, 1830). Note the reaction of the foreign observers on the right.

I. *The victimisation of women*

Let us now turn to the discourse on sati. I shall begin by presenting two assessments of sati according to which the women concerned are portrayed as victims.

An eighteenth-century eyewitness account

The first is taken from the unpublished diary of Benjamin Crowninshield, the captain of the American ship, the *Henry*.[6] The entry for 28 November 1789 describes what Crowninshield saw on a funeral ghat in Calcutta. According to his own account, he watched from a distance of four or five feet.

His description is detailed. He notes that men prepared the pyre; that women washed the widow's feet; that brahman priests advised her on the order of the ritual and assisted her in carrying it out. When she failed to circumambulate the pyre for the third time, he supposes that she has been taking opium. He describes the 'persuasions and art' of the brahmans to make her take up the correct posture on the pyre alongside her husband, 'her right hand under his neck, his right arm over hers, his right leg over her'. He notes four men standing by 'with green bamboos to hold her down in case she should not be able to stand the flames'. Finally, he describes how her two sons lit the pyre and 'the natives made such a noise that [he] could not hear the last groan'.

While Crowninshield names no villains in the unfolding drama, he unquestioningly sees the widow as an object of pity. For example, he writes:

> ...the poor object sat on a cot frame alongside of her husband, a corpse, with her two little sons about her... The poor woman, looking around, saw her husband with his face towards her... The poor creature sat down on the couch... The poor object then got upon her feet... The unfortunate woman....

And so on. Crowninshield concludes: 'I did not think it was in the power of a human person to meet death in such a manner'. His admiration is that of the civilised man for what he regards as the victim of an inexplicable and barbaric foreign custom.[7]

A modern feminist view

My second example of a Western writer in the discourse on sati is the

[6] I am indebted to Paul Courtright (1987) for drawing my attention to Crowninshield's account. For further details of the episode described, and for information on Crowninshield himself, see also Courtright's forthcoming work on sati. All references in this chapter are to the transcript of the journal currently on display in the Peabody Museum in Salem.

[7] For important studies of the implications of sentiments such as these when employed in the colonial debate concerning the place of women in the Hindu tradition, see Mani (1987); Nandy (1980, 1983).

radical feminist, Mary Daly. She denounces the practice as a 'sado-ritual', evidence of patriarchal atrocities against women. Her description (markedly different in tone from Crowninshield's) also sees the widow as a victim. She writes:

> If the general situation of widowhood in India was not a sufficient inducement for the woman of higher caste to throw herself gratefully and ceremoniously into the fire, she was often pushed and poked in with long stakes after having been bathed, ritually attired, and drugged out of her mind.

Her analysis seeks to 'unmask' what she calls the 'deceptive legitimations' of sati by scholars and self-styled 'authorities'. In particular, she condemns the scholar's habit of using the active voice when describing the burning of a widow. When Benjamin Walker writes of widows who 'adopted the practice', Daly rejects the phrasing outright: 'The use of the active voice here suggests that the widows actively sought out, enforced, and accepted this "practice"'. Elsewhere, Walker writer of Rajput women who 'immolated themselves' and for whom 'it became customary...to burn themselves'. 'Again', Daly expostulates, 'the victims, through grammatical sleight of hand, are made to appear as the agents of their own destruction' (1978, p.117-19).

My response is as follows. I agree wholeheartedly with Daly's main argument: that the act of sati—whether physically enforced by men, or internalised and 'embraced' by the women themselves—is an act of violence against women that could only arise in a male-dominated and women-demeaning society. However, it is precisely this idea of the *satī* as the apparent agent of her own destruction that I believe we need to confront. This is the most disturbing question facing anyone who wishes to understand the practice of sati (cf. Nandy, 1987, 1988). Why would any woman 'choose' to take her own life in such a way? What kind of a choice could that be? In the words of Madhu Kishwar and Ruth Vanita,

> If a woman does not have the right to decide whether she wants to marry, and when, and whom, how far she wants to study, whether she wants to take a particular job or not, how is it that she suddenly gets the right to take such a major decision as whether she wants to die? (1987, p.21).

External, physical force was certainly used in a minority of ugly cases. Several historical examples are documented by Daly. The Indian press points at many more. But are we right to dismiss every case as murder? Are not some cases, most perhaps, in some sense 'voluntary'?

II. *The path of victory*

In partial answer to this question, I shall turn to the other side of the discourse on sati. I shall again present two voices: one from the eighteenth century, the other from the present day.

Traditional views on a twentieth-century death

The first takes the form of a recent case of sati in Rajasthan. On 4 September 1987, an 18-year-old Rajput woman, Roop Kanwar, described as 'a bride of just eight months', burned to death on the funeral pyre of her 24-year-old husband in a public spectacle. According to a later reconstruction of her death:

Thousands of people had gathered to witness her immolation... After taking a ritual bath, the woman dressed once more in her bright red bridal finery. Sitting atop the funeral pyre with her husband's corpse, his head on her lap, she asked her teenage brother-in-law to light the fire. Within moments, as the crowd's cries reached a climax, she was consumed by flames (*Time*, 28 September 1987).

She is said to have sat there, 'showering blessings and benedictions on the crowds while chanting the Gayatri mantra' even when 'the fire consumed her torso and flames enveloped her neck' (Badhwar, 1987a).

By all early press accounts, her death was voluntary, pledged and carried out in public with great resolve. Journalists reacted in horror. But the young couple's immediate family and their village community seemed united in their reverence for the new goddess (*devī*). Within weeks, more than $160,000 had been collected to build a shrine in her honour (*Time*, 28 September 1987).

For the Indian authorities, the issue was where to lay the blame. The local police registered a case of murder under section 302 of the Indian Penal Code—and, interestingly, one of abetment to suicide under section 306—against Roop Kanwar's father-in-law, her young brother-in-law, and three other male relatives. But the blame also fell back on them for not preventing the death in the first place: the district magistrate, the superintendent of police, and three policemen were transferred. The Rajasthan state government issued an ordinance that made the glorification of sati (through public rituals, processions, the collection of funds and so on) a criminal offence, whether the sati was voluntary or not. The death penalty has been decreed for those aiding or abetting the practice; and any woman who attempts sati and survives will be imprisoned (for 1 to 5 years) and fined (Rs.5,000-20,000).[8] Central legislation followed similar lines.[9]

The Indian women's groups blame the authorities. In particular, they blame all those—family members, community leaders, local officials and police—who must have known what was going on, but who did nothing to stop it. Clearly, these people either supported the act or were afraid to intervene. The women's groups organised an anti-sati rally.

[8] The Rajasthan Sati (Prevention) Ordinance 1987, later turned into an Act. Cf. Badhwar, 1987b, p.18; Kishwar and Vanita, 1987, p.23-4.

[9] The Commission of Sati (Prevention) Bill 1987 (Bill No.133).

Three thousand women marched in silence through the streets of Jaipur carrying banners proclaiming, 'A woman's murder is a challenge to the entire sex' (Badhwar, 1987b, p.20). For Indian feminists, sati is only one symptom of a deep-seated hatred for women throughout India. Links are drawn with dowry deaths, female infanticide, and the increasingly prevalent abortion of female foetuses. According to this view, sati is not an aberration; it is part of the fabric of Indian belief regarding women (cf. Bhasin and Menon, 1988; Shekhawat, 1987).

Soon afterwards, a pro-sati rally was held. Seventy thousand people (men, women and children) marched beneath saffron banners, chanting: 'We salute Roop Kanwar! Who will protect the faith? We will! We will!' Priests read from the scriptures[10] and speakers (led by prominent government officials) harangued the crowds, all beneath a massive painting of a beatific *satī*. It was estimated that about three million dollars were collected towards the proposed shrine (Badhwar, 1987b, p.18).

Meanwhile speculated, both in India and abroad. The *New York Times* raised the question of whether Roop Kanwar 'placed herself—or was placed—on the funeral pyre', and recalled the many recorded instances of force being used (19 September 1987). Some journalists described actual physical force in the Kanwar case (that she was drugged, for example, or held down by firewood), but the evidence is sparse, and always third- or fourth-hand (see, for example, Mangalwadi 1987). Many reports emphasised the (actual and probably) financial gains accruing to individuals, or to the community as a whole, as a direct result of Roop Kanwar's death (see, for example, Badhwar, 1987a, p.61; Subramaniam, 1988, p.1). But most reporters agreed that the pressure that caused Roop Kanwar to kill herself was not of this kind. It was the indirect, impersonal—but none the less powerful—force of Hindu religious ideology concerning women. One woman (described as a feminist) was reported as saying:

> In every Rajput family, it is something drilled into you from earliest childhood. Your husband is supposed to be a sort of godlike figure, and sati is the ultimate achievement for a girl. You're almost hypnotized into thinking this thing (*New York Times*, 19 September 1987).

However, while urban Indians and Westerners tried to apportion blame, or at least to shift the responsibility away from Roop Kanwar, her own family and rural community did not. More than 200,000 people are said to have defied the government to honour her death and

[10] Brahman orthodoxy has always been divided on this issue; hence the debates on the subject in Sanskrit and vernacular texts. The controversy continues today. For the confrontation between Niranjan Dev Teerth (the powerful pro-sati Shankaracharya of Puri) and Swami Agnivesh (the maverick leader of the Hindu reform movement, the Arya Samaj), see Dutt, 1988, and Singh, 1988.

deification (*The Times*, 17 September 1987). Women brought their own daughters to the ceremony. One woman was reported as saying: 'Sati is not possible for all women, only those who are very blessed. I have come here for the blessings of this holy place' (*New York Times*, 19 September 1987). A 30-year-old Rajput landowner explained: 'You cannot say when a woman will feel this way. People tried to prevent here, but she was very strong. She had faith. The people have come here to honor that faith' (*New York Times*, 19 September 1987). Even her own father was reported to have said, by way of explanation, that she was always deeply religious.[11]

For these people, who perhaps knew Roop Kanwar best, the responsibility of her death was hers alone. They are inspired and honoured by her example. For (according to this view) she had the courage to walk the sacred path extolled in so many teachings and myths: the path of sati.

An eighteenth-century Sanskrit manual

What is the religious ideology behind this powerful belief? I shall take as my exemplar Tryambakayajvan's treatise on women: the *Strīdharmapaddhati* (Sdhp.) or *Guide to the Religious Status and Duties of Women* (see Leslie, 1989). This unusual text was written in the eighteenth century by an orthodox pandit whose aim was to summarise the views of Sanskrit religious law relating to women. His arguments are traditional. His evidence takes the form of hundreds of detailed quotations drawn from older and more authoritative religious and legal texts. A digest of the superior type (like a lecture with supporting quotations), it falls into five natural divisions: an introductory framework; a detailed list of the daily duties of the Hindu wife (*strīṇām īhnikam*); an essay on the inherent nature of women (*strīsvabhāvaḥ*; see Leslie, 1986); the 'duties common to all women' (*strīṇāṃ sādhāraṇā dharmāḥ*); and a final section of stories and quotations. Tryambaka's conclusion is that a women's highest duty is to serve her husband.

The sections on widowhood and sati are to be found among the 'duties common to all women'. The injunction relating to sati or 'dying with one's husband' (*sahagamanavidhiḥ*) is discussed first; the duties of the widow (*vidhavādharmāḥ*) second. Despite his evident preference for sati (*sahagamana*), Tryambaka concludes that both options are open to the woman whose husband has died (Leslie, 1989, p.291-304).

As an orthodox pandit, Tryambaka is not interested in women as individuals but as parts that fit into and therefore strengthen the whole. That whole is 'righteousness' (*dharma*). For the basic assumption of Sanskrit religious law (*dharmaśāstra*) runs as follows: if every individ-

[11] *Indian Express*, 13 September 1987; later reports (e.g. Badhwar, 1987a) insist that Roop Kanwar's father was not informed of the sati until it was over.

ual performs his or her allotted role—allotted, that is by the precepts of religious law relating to the (male) individual (*svadharma*) and to women (*strīdharma*)—universal harmony will result. Reinforcing the proper role of women in society is thus the surest way to uphold the orthodox Hindu moral code and, by extension, the perfect world. For Tryambaka, the proper role of women includes the practice of sati; not for every woman, but for those who aspire to the highest ideal.

Let us look at some of his arguments in favour of sati.[12]

The prohibition on suicide. The standard objection to sati is that it is a form of suicide, and suicide is prohibited. Tryambaka produces two authoritative quotations to support this objection (*Śatapathabrāhmaṇa*, 10.2.6.7; *Īśopaniṣad*, 3). He then argues that this prohibition is not an absolute ruling, but a 'general rule' (*sāmānyavacana*). It is therefore open to modification by supplementary rules that give the exceptions to it. To prove his point, he takes another general rule—that one should not kill any living being—and shows that this too is modified by supplementary rules: for example, that in certain rituals an animal should be sacrificed. Similarly, he explains, the general prohibition on suicide is also modified by supplementary rules.

Tryambaka gives three such rules. The first excludes the religious suicide of the ascetic who kills himself at a sacred place.[13] The second excludes the courting of death in battle by the warrior. The third excludes the self-immolation of the widow. In effect, the argument runs, such acts are not really suicide at all.

The rewards awaiting the good wife. It is important to note that Tryambaka's stress on rewards constitutes an admission that sati is optional. For ritual actions may be divided into three categories. The term *nitya* ('obligatory') denotes rituals which must be performed every day, such as the bath taken every morning by the orthodox householder. The term *naimittika* ('occasional' or 'periodical') denotes rituals which

[12] All references to the *Strīdharmapaddhati* are to Leslie, 1989; Tryambaka's views on sati and widowhood are summarised on pp.291-304. All translations are mine.

[13] The religious suicide of men (whether ascetics or fanatical devotees) is often cited to demonstrate that the phenomenon is not unique to women, and thus that sati cannot be used as evidence of Indian misogyny. As the spokesman for the demonstration in favour of the Roop Kanwar sati is reported to have said: 'This is but one suicide...Jains are known to die by fasting. Buddhists are known to immolate themselves. So why apply this law only to us?' (Badhwar 1987c). There are various arguments against this view. First, the numbers of male religious suicides are far fewer than those of *satīs* (see, for example, note 18). Second, there is no comparable ideal of male religious suicide as a model for men. Third, while a man's choice not to perform religious suicide leaves him no worse off than before, the woman who chooses not to become a *satī* faces the hardships and indignity of life as a widow (see Leslie, 1991).

must be performed on certain occasions, such as the bath taken by the menstruating women on the fourth day of her cycle. The term *kāmya* ('optional') denotes rituals which may be performed if one wants the rewards accruing to them, such as the bath taken at a sacred river or crossing-place in order to obtain the benefits associated with that place.

The crucial issue is this: is sati a *naimittika* ritual and therefore in fact required by the occasion of a husband's death? Or is it optional (*kāmya*) in the sense that it need only be performed if the wife wants the rewards accruing to the *satī?* As Tryambaka's argument unfolds, it is evident that sati is optional. But his insistence that it is to be recommended, together with his daunting descriptions of the life of the widow, makes his own support of the custom clear.

So what are these 'great rewards'? From the many quotations that Tryambaka provides, I have selected only three.

> Just as the snake-catcher drags the snake from its hole by force, even so the virtuous wife (*satī*) snatches her husband from the demons of hell and takes him up to heaven.
>
> Yama's messengers recognise a virtuous wife (*satī*) from afar and take to flight: even if her husband has been an evil man, they let go of him at once, exclaiming, 'When we see a devoted wife (*pativratā*) hurtling towards us to rescue her husband, we messengers of Death are less afraid of fire and lightning than we are of her!'
>
> Even in the case of a husband who has entered into hell itself and who, seized by the servants of Death and bound with terrible bonds, has arrived at the very place of torment; even if he is already standing there, helpless and wretched, quivering with fear because of his evil deeds; even if he is a brahmin-killer or the murderer of a friend, or if he is ungrateful for some service done for him—even then a woman who refuses to become a widow can purify him: in dying, she takes him with her.[14]

Tryambaka concludes that when sati is put into practice by a devoted wife (*pativratā*), it confers great blessings on both wife and husband.

The case of the bad wife. Tryambaka argues that if a sinful woman dies with her husband in this way, her sin is destroyed. The theory of *karma* is modified here to support the practice of sati. Strictly speaking, no one joins a deceased relative in the other world simply by dying with him or her: their different *karmas* automatically take them to different places. Nor can that person's accumulated *karma* be obliterated by the

[14] *vyālagrāhī yathā vyāalaṃ balād uddharate bilāt/evam utkṛṣya daityebhyaḥ patiṃ svargaṃ nayet satī//*Sdhp.42v.6-7. *yamadūtāḥ palāyante satīm ālokya dūrataḥ/ api duṣkṛtakarmāṇaṃ samutsṛjya ca tatpatim// na tathā bibhimo vahner na tathā vidyuto yathā/ āpatantīṃ samālokya vayam dūtāḥ pativratām//* Sdhp.42v.7-9. *yadi praviṣṭo narakaṃ baddhaḥ pāśaiḥ sudāruṇaiḥ/ saṃprāpto yātanāsthānaṃ gṛhīto yamakiṅkaraiḥ/ tsṣṭhate vivaśo dīno vepamānaḥ svakarmabhiḥ//* Sdhp.43r.4-5.

kind of death they experience. But from about 700 CE, the merit bestowed by sati was so great that it cut across the usual implications of *karma* both for the woman and for her husband.

More important, this applied regardless of the feelings of the woman involved. The quotation that follows is unambiguous.

> Women who, due to their wicked minds, have always despised their husbands (while they were alive) and behaved disagreeably towards them, and who none the less perform the ritual act of dying with their husbands when the time comes—whether they do this of their own free will, or out of anger, or even out of fear—all of them are purified of sin.[15]

This is the scriptural justification for encouraging or even forcing women to burn themselves. Whatever their reasons for doing so, whatever the past deeds of either husband or wife, the sacrifice purifies both of them. As a result of this ruling, Tryambaka concludes:

> When sati (*sahagamana*) is performed by a woman who throughout her lifetime has done wrong—that is, what her husband did not like—then it is said to have the quality of a sufficient atonement (*prāyaścitta*).[16]

In this sense, sati is the ultimate (and only truly effective) atonement for the bad wife.

The special rulings for the modern era. According to these rulings, rituals of atonement that end in the practitioner's death are applicable only to the legendary period of ancient India. All of recorded history belongs to the degenerate (*kali*) era in which such heroic rulings no longer apply. Tryambaka sidesteps the problem. He remarks rather disarmingly that whether or not the bad wife should in fact perform sati to wipe out her sins is best left to great men to decide. That it certainly can wipe out sins he has no doubt. For Tryambaka, sati works.

There are two important issues here. First, is sati (as Tryambaka says it is) a 'sufficient atonement' (*prāyaścitta*) for the bad wife? Second, if it is, then should this particular atonement ritual ending in death be included among those that are prohibited in the current age? Tryambaka argues neither point well. Instead, he gives a lengthy explanation of why it is important for a wife to behave properly during her husband's lifetime. While his argument is blurred, however, his intention is clear. If, as a result of these rulings for the modern era, sati is prohibited, then there remains no effective ritual of atonement for the errant wife. It follows that such a wife can never escape the torments awaiting her in the next world. Tryambaka quotes several passages to support this

[15] *avamatya ca yāḥ pūrvaṃ patiṃ duṣṭena cetasā/ vartante yāś ca satataṃ bhartṝṇāṃ pratikūlagāḥ// bhartrānumaaraṇaṃ kāle yāḥ kurvanti tathāvidhāḥ/ kāmāt krodhād bhayād vāpi sarvāḥpūtā bhavanty uta//* Sdhp.43r.7-9.

[16] *jīvanadaśāyāṃ bhartṛvipriyaṃ pāpaṃ kṛtavatyāḥ sahagamanaṃ prāyaścittatvenoktam//* Sdhp.43r.9-10.

view. In the following example, an epic husband is speaking to his wife:

> The woman who even once does something that her husband does not like will first endure the hell of burning oil and then, in her next life, become a widow. For the ascetic practice (*tapas*) for women is the service of the husband by a devoted wife. [Therefore, if you serve me properly] while I am alive, the merit which is your path to heaven is taking effect. For it is through the merit of being a devoted wife (*pativratā*) that a woman attains the highest heaven. If she does not do this, then, even if she has bathed in all the sacred places, she will go to hell.[17]

Tryambaka's point is this. Since such passages make no reference to any ritual powerful enough to wipe out the effects of unwifely behaviour, we must assume there is none. In that case—without recourse to the ritual power of sati—the wife's only hope is to behave properly; that is, to worship and placate her husband at every turn. However, as Tryambaka points out, sati does work. It wipes out the otherwise inevitable karmic effects of unwifely behaviour, and thus secures both wife and husband a place in heaven. Despite all the arguments against the practice, therefore, sati remains the safest course of action for the less-than-perfect wife.

The case of brahman women. Another standard argument is that the practice of sati is prohibited to brahman women. Tryambaka finds a number of quotations to support this view, including the following:

> The brahman woman who does not die with her husband, even though she is distracted by grief, obtains the goal of renunciation (*pravrajyā*); whereas by dying she becomes (and therefore incurs the sin of) one who has committed suicide.[18]

Tryambaka defines 'renunciation' as 'the life of the celibate ascetic' (*brahmacarya*), a term that in this context is synonymous with the duties or lifestyle of the widow (*vidhāvadharma*).[19]

Historically, sati probably originated as a custom associated primarily with the warrior (*kṣatriya*) class, as exemplified by the Rajputs of Western India.[20] From about 1,000 CE, however, commentators

[17] *karoti vipriyaṃ bhartuḥ yā nārī sakṛd eva hi/ sā taptatailanarakaṃ bhuktvātha vidhavā bhavet// bhartuḥ śuśrūṣaṇaṃ bhaktyā nārīṇāṃ tapa ucyate/ mayi jīvati te puṇyaṃ ghaṭate svargasādhanam// pātivratyena puṇyena nārī vaikuṇṭham aśnute/ anyathā sarvatīrtheśu snātāpi narakaṃ vrajet//* Sdhp.44r.3-6.

[18] *na mriyeta samaṃ bhartrā brāhmaṇī śokamohitā/ pravrajyāgatim āpnoti maraṇād ātmaghātinī//* Sdhp.44v.9-45r.1.

[19] For an exploration of this definition in terms of a comparison between the life of the widow and that of the male renunciate, see Leslie 1991.

[20] Contrary to conventional belief, sati was never restricted to Rajputs or even to high-caste groups. For example, the official breakdown according to

began to explain away the prohibitions on its practice by brahman women. For example, the ruling that the brahman wife should not kill herself in a fit of grief is taken to mean that she should not kill herself out of grief as women of other classes do, but as the result of mature deliberation. Similarly, the ruling that sati (*anugamana*) is prohibited to the brahman woman means that she should not die after him (*anu*) but with him (*saha*); that is, she should not die on a separate pyre from the one on which her husband lies, but should join him on his pyre. Tryambaka follows this line of thought. The chief wife (ideally, a brahman woman) should die with her husband's body on his pyre, while the wives of the lower classes should burn on separate pyres. Thus sati is to be recommended for women, whether they are brahmans or not, whether they have been good wives or bad.

Three kinds of devoted wife. Tryambaka concludes that three kinds of wife merit the name of *pativratā* ('she who is devoted to her husband'), and so enjoy the rewards accruing to that name. The first of these is the woman who dies before her husband and waits patiently for him in heaven. She is the most auspicious wife, the ideal. But, if the man dies first, inauspiciousness and misfortune may be warded off by either of the two options open to his wife. She may—like Mādrī, the epic prototype of the wife who expiates her guilt for her husband's death by dying with him—follow him onto the pyre. Or she may—like Kuntī the epic prototype of the wife who chooses to stay alive to care for household and children—live an ascetic and celibate life for the rest of her days (*Mahābhārata*, 1.90.63-76; 1.116; 1.117.25-32). Given the supposed nature of women, however, and (consequent upon that) the difficulties of leading the ascetic life of the widow, sati is both far easier and far safer than the path of the celibate widow.

Conclusion

So what conclusions may we draw from Tryambaka's views? Four concepts or categories concern us here: 'woman', 'wife', 'widow', and *satī*. The distinctions between these four concepts are important.

In Sanskrit religious law (*dharmaśāstra*), the concept 'woman'—*strī* as in *strīsvabhāva* ('the inherent nature of women')—is almost invariably negative (see Leslie, 1986). In religious terms, the only answer to being female is to become the perfect wife (see Leslie, 1989). Hence, as Tryambaka explains, 'the ascetic or religious practice (*tapas*) for a woman is to be a devoted wife (*patrivratā*). In the orthodox view, this is the only religious path open to a woman. But the future does hold some choices for the wife.

---

class (*varṇa*) of the 575 cases reported in the Bengal Presidency in 1823 was: 41 per cent brahmans; 6 per cent warrior (*kṣatriya*) class; 2 per cent merchant (*vaiśya*) class; and 51 per cent servant (*śūdra*) class (Yang, 1987, p.28).

The concept 'wife'—*strī* as in *strīdharma* (the religious duties of women or wives)—is often defined as 'a married woman, that is, one whose husband is still alive'. But if this is so, then the wife becomes a widow the moment her husband dies; and the *satī* is a kind of widow. But neither is the case. For not until the husband's body is consumed in flames and he is thereby deemed to have departed this world alone, without his wife, may she be called a 'widow'.

The concept 'widow' denotes the woman who has chosen to remain in this world without her husband. More important, it implies that such a woman has chosen to follow the difficult ascetic path of the widow-renunciate (*pravrajyā*, *vidhavādharma*; see Leslie, 1991). The religious path of wifehood (*strīdharma*) is now closed to her; and she has chosen not to follow the path of the *satī*.[21]

The concept *satī* therefore does not carry with it any of the associations of widowhood. In fact, Tryambaka never calls the *satī* a 'widow'. Thus when the practice is described as 'widow-burning', or 'the self-immolation of the widow', an important point has been missed. For the *satī* is the wife who has in fact chosen not to become a widow. The two terms are mutually exclusive. The widow can never be a *satī*; and the *satī* has never been a widow.

What we have here is a clear religious progression: from 'woman' to 'wife', and from 'wife' to either 'widow' or *satī*. Better still, in orthodox eyes, the concept of 'woman' should be suppressed altogether: before the onset of 'womanhood', the girl should become a 'wife'. While her husband is alive, her religious path and duties are clear. When he dies, she is faced with a choice: not simply life or death as we might see it, but a choice between two religious paths. This is how Tryambaka describes it. His entire argument is geared to deciding which of these two religious paths she should take. Either may be recommended on positive grounds. For they both enable her to demonstrate the essential power of the good woman for the salvation of her husband. Tryambaka's point is simply this: sati is both easier in terms of gaining merit (for oneself and, most important, for one's husband and family), and also safer for all concerned, than the alternative path of the widow. The *satī* is thus seen as making a conscious choice, both for her own sake and for the sake of her family, a choice that is grounded in the soteriological power of the good woman.

If we return to the death of Roop Kanwar, we find that she has done precisely what Tryambaka might have told her to do. The crude montage photograph, bought by thousands of devotees for private worship, says it all. (See Plate 2.) Roop Kanwar is shown seated amidst the flames of the funeral pyre, her husband's dead body across her lap. She

[21] In the ideal world of Sanskrit religious law, remarriage is out of the question, as indeed it still is for most high-caste groups.

wears her wedding finery and an enigmatic half-smile. This is the iconography of a modern legend. As the legend spreads the new sati myth takes shape, we shall probably never know the true circumstances surrounding her death. But what the iconography tells us is important. It tells us that Roop Kanwar has made a conscious choice not to become a widow. It tells us that—as a *satī*, a 'truly virtuous woman'—she ceases to be a woman at all. For she has become endowed with stupendous powers: she will bring salvation to her husband and to generations of their two families, regardless of their actual behaviour in the world; she will be worshipped in her own community for ever. According to the iconography, Roop Kanwar has chosen to become a goddess (*devī*), a deified eternal wife. For, as the leader of the Rajasthan Janata Party put it, 'Rajput culture...believes that sati and shakti [*śakti*] ([feminine divine] power) are identical' (Badhwar, 1987c). This is the empowerment of sati: a strategy for dignity in a demeaning world. The tragedy is that Roop Kanwar could find no other. For in such a world, for most women choice itself is a fiction.

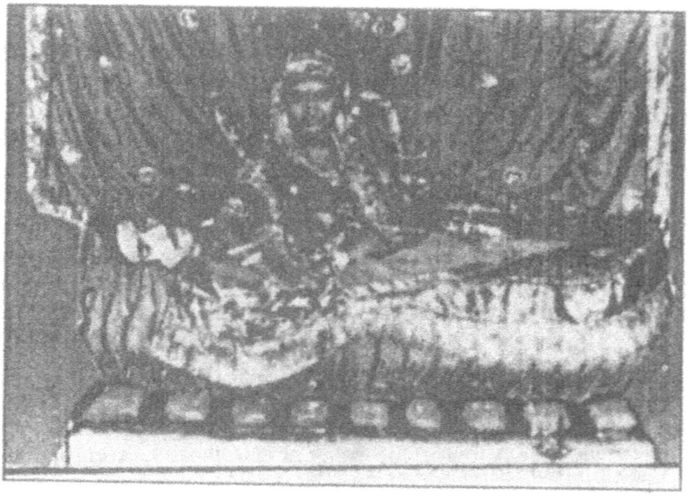

Plate 2. *A popular souvenir* (superimposed photographs)
This was on sale in Deorala in Rajasthan after the death of Roop Kanwar. She is shown wearing her bridal clothes and holding her husband's head on her lap as the flames begin to consume the funeral pyre beneath them both.

References

Badhwar, Inderjit, 1987a, 'Sati: a pagan sacrifice', *India Today* (Delhi), 15 October 1987, pp.58-61.

—, 1987b, 'Rajasthan: militant defiance', *India Today* (Delhi), 31 October 1987, pp.18-20.

—, 1987c, 'Kalyan Singh Kalvi: beliefs cannot be repressed' *India Today* (Delhi), 31 October 1987, p.20.

Bhasin, Kamla, and Ritu Menon, 'The problem'; see *Seminar*, 1988, pp.12-13.

Courtright, Paul B., 'Western perspectives on Suttee in the eighteenth and nineteenth centuries'. Paper presented at the Centre for Cross-Cultural Research on Women workshop on 'Women in Indian Religions', Oxford University, June 1987.

—, *The Goddess and the Dreadful Practice* (New York, forthcoming).

Crowninshield, Benjamin, 'Description of a Suttee: excerpt from the Journal of the *Henry*, November 18, 1789, by Benjamin Crowninshield'. Transcript of part of the *Journal of the* Henry, *1788-89, kept by Benhamin Crowninshield* (Salem, Mass.)

Daly, Mary, *Gyn/Ecology: the metaphysics of radical feminism* (Boston, 1978; London, 1979).

Datta, V.N., *Sati: a historical, social and philosophical enquiry into the Hindu rite of widow burning* (Delhi, 1988).

Dutt, Anuradha, 'The weekly debate (Niranjan Dev Teerth and Swami Agnivesh)', *Illustrated Weekly of India* (Bombay), 1 May 1988.

Harlan, Lindsey, *The Ethic of Protection among Rajput Women: mediations of caste and gender duties* (Berkeley, in press).

—, 'The ideology of sati among Rajput women', in John Stratton Hawley (ed.), *New Light on Sati* (New York, forthcoming).

Indian Express (Delhi), 'No remorse or fear in the land of satis', unattributed report, 13 September 1987.

Kishwar, Madhu, and Ruth Vanita, *In Search of Answers: Indian women's voices from Manushi* (London, 1984).

—, 'The burning of Roop Kanwar'; see *Manushi*, 1987, pp.15-25.

Leslie, Julia, 'Essence and existence: women and religion in ancient Indian texts', in Pat Holden (ed.), *Women's Religious Lives* (London, 1983), pp.89-112.

—, '*Strīsvabhāva*: the inherent nature of women', in N.J. Allen, R.F. Gombrich, T. Raychaudhuri and G. Rizvi, *Oxford University Papers on India*, vol.1, part 1 (Delhi, 1986), pp.28-58.

—, *The Perfect Wife: the orthodox Hindu woman according to the Strīdharmapaddhati of Tryambakayajvan* (Delhi, 1989).

—, 'A problem of choice: The heroic *satī* or the widow-ascetic', in Julia Leslie (ed.), *Rules and Remedies in Classical Indian Law* (Leiden, 1991).

—, (ed.) *Roles and Rituals for Hindu Women* (London and USA, 1991; Delhi 1992).

—, 'The significance of dress for the orthodox Hindu woman', in Ruth Barnes and Joanne Eicher (eds.), *Dress and Gender: the making and meaning in cultural contexts* (Oxford and New York, 1992), pp.198-213.

Mangalwadi, Vishal, 'Making a carnival of murder', *Indian Express* (Madras), 19 September 1987.

Mani, Lata, 'Contentious traditions: the debate on sati in colonial India', *Cultural Critique* (Fall 1987).

Manushi (Delhi), double issue 42-3 (September-December 1987) [devoted to sati].

Nandy, Ashis, 'Sati: a nineteenth-century tale of women, violence and protest' (1975). Reprinted in *At the Edge of Psychology: essays in politics and culture* (Delhi, 1980), pp.1-31.

—, *The Intimate Enemy: loss and recovery of self under colonialism* (Delhi, 1983).

—, 'The sociology of sati', *Indian Express* (Delhi), 5 October 1987.

—, 'The human factor', *Illustrated Weekly of India* (Bombay), 17 January 1988, pp.20-3.

New York Times, 'Indian widow's death at pyre creates a shrine', unattributed report, 19 September 1987, p.1.

Peggs, James, *India's Cries to British Humanity, relative to the Suttee, Infanticide, British Connexion with Idolatry, Ghaut Murders, and Slavery in India; to which is added Humane Hints for the Melioration of the State of Society in British India* (2nd ed., revised and enlarged, London, 1830).

Seminar: The Monthly Symposium, issue 342 (February 1988), entitled 'Sati: A symposium on widow immolation and its social context' (Delhi).

Sharma, Arvind, with Ajit Ray, Alaka Hejib and Katherine K. Young, *Sati: historical and phenomenological essays* (Delhi, 1988).

Shekhawat, Prahlad Singh, 'The culture of sati in Rajasthan', see *Manushi* 1987, pp.30-4.

Singh, Ramindar, 'Sati debate: polemics postponed', *India Today* (Delhi), 30 April 1988, p.71.

Strīdharmapaddhati, see Leslie, 1989.

Subramaniam, V., *The Sacred and the Secular in India's Performing Arts* (Delhi, 1980).

Thapar, Romila, 'In history', see *Seminar*, 1988, pp.14-19.

Time, 'Fire and faith: Out of immolation, a goddess', unattributed report, 28 September 1987.

The Times, unattributed and untitled report, 17 September 1987.

Turner, Ralph, L., *A Comparative Dictionary of Indo-Aryan Languages* (London, 1966).

Weinberger-Thomas, Catherine, 'Cendres d'immortalité: la crémation des veuves en Inde', *Archives de Sciences Sociales et des Religions*, 67.1 (January-March 1989), pp.9-51.

—, *Cendres d'immortalité: la crémation des veuves en Inde* (Paris, forthcoming).

Yang, Anand, 'The many faces of sati in the early nineteenth century'; see *Manushi*, 1987, pp.26-9.

Yule, Henry and A.C. Burnell, *Hobson-Jobson: a glossary of colloquial Anglo-Indian words and phrases* (1886; reprinted London, 1985).

Further reading

Altekar, Anant Sadashiv, *The Position of Women in Hindu Civilization: from prehistoric times to the present day* (Delhi, 1938, 1959, 1962; rep.1978).
Bennett, Lynn, *Dangerous Wives and Sacred Sisters: social and symbolic roles of high-caste women in Nepal* (New York, 1983).
Falk, Nancy A. and Rita M. Gross (eds.), *Unspoken Worlds: women's religious lives in non-Western cultures* (San Francisco, 1980).
Haddad, Yvonne Yazbeck, and Ellison Banks Findly (eds.), *Women, Religion and Social Change* (Albany, 1985).
Hawley, John Stratton, and Donna Marie Wulff (eds.), *The Divine Consort: Rādhā and the Goddesses of India* (Berkeley, 1982: Boston, 1986).
Jacobson, Doranne, and Susan Wadley (eds.), *Women in India: two perspectives* (New Delhi, 1977).

SOME OBSERVATIONS ON THE EVOLUTION OF MODERN STANDARD PUNJABI[1]

Christopher Shackle

The paper suggests that contemporary issues of identity in South Asia, which are so often self-defined in terms of linguistic as well as religious allegiance, can generally only hope to be properly understood if the linguistic evidence is examined in its own right. It examines the part played in the formation of the contemporary Sikh identity by Modern Standard Punjabi, itself an important token of that identity. The conscious forging of this standard language by the Sikh reformers is briefly explained, with particular reference to the linguistic choices which they made. Observations on the subsequent changes in the character of Modern Standard Punjabi are shown to have often paradoxical implications, too easily passed over in attempts to understand the Sikh identity without an examination of these linguistic patterns.

One of the most striking features of contemporary South Asia is the degree to which religion on the one hand, and language on the other, have come to determine social, political and cultural identities with ever sharper emphasis. Even now, of course, there is seldom a perfect congruence between these two factors, given the inherent complexity and variety of South Asian societies. Nevertheless, when there is a considerable measure of overlap between religious and linguistic boundaries, the results are liable to escape the full control of central governments, all committed to more or less open pursuit of the centralising ideals of the former imperial regimes. The most obvious current instances of this rule are provided by the civil war in Sri Lanka between Buddhist Sinhalas and Hindu Tamils, the long-running tension in Assam between Assamese-speaking Hindus and Bengali-speaking Muslims, and of course the seemingly insoluble crisis in Punjab, the state brought into being in 1966 as the result of the long Sikh campaign for the creation of a state in which Punjabi would have undisputed official status.

These and similar conflicts involve so many complex and interlinked factors that they are hardly easier to analyse fully than they have been to resolve satisfactorily. It is, moreover, a striking common feature of the analyses of all these situations and of their historical antecedents in the colonial period that they tend to concentrate primarily upon poli-

[1] First published in Joseph T. O'Connell, Milton Israel, Willard G. Oxtoby with W.H. McLeod and J.S. Grewal (eds.), *Sikh History and Religion in the Twentieth Century* (S. Asian Studies Papers, 3; University of Toronto, 1988).

tical, social and economic factors, and only secondarily upon identifiably religious phenomena, with language issues tending to receive only cursory reference. There thus results a rather curious imbalance between the situations on the ground, where issues of religion and language are so prominently articulated, and the emphases of the analytical literature upon other factors presumed to underlie these rallying cries.

This imbalance is to be attributed to several factors. On the one hand relatively greater prominence has come to be given to social-science-based studies of South Asia in Western universities, as compared. with the meagre funding generally available for those based on language and literature. In South Asia, too, there is a comparable imbalance, if for rather different reasons, notably the greater pressure upon academics in departments of language and literature to conform to or, still better, to enhance local linguistic chauvinisms in their published work, rather than to analyse them. And finally, it is simply rather difficult to give a meaningful picture of what is going on in one or other South Asian language through the medium of English.

Since the emphasis of the majority of the papers included in the Toronto collection (in which this essay was first published) conforms to the characteristic pattern outlined above, it was thought worthwhile to offer some reflections on the development of modern standard Punjabi (MSP), from the point of view of a linguist. The creation of this literary language as the prime vehicle for Sikh thought and culture is after all one of the most striking achievements of the Sikh community in the twentieth century. It is hoped that the preliminary observations offered here, which in no way aspire to the status of the substantial paper the subject deserves, may serve to stimulate the development of long-overdue research in this branch of Sikh studies, still very much the Cinderella in the descriptive literature available in English.

The crude tripartite division of South Asian history into its ancient, mediaeval and modern periods is open to many sensible objections; but it serves well enough to establish rough parameters within which to outline characteristic changes in the currency of written languages in northern India, historically peopled by largely illiterate speakers of the endless varieties of the closely related group of Indo-Aryan languages.

The need for an unlocalised standard language to record administrative, religious and secular materials was met during the ancient period by the prolonged use of Sanskrit, carefully preserved for some 1,500 years in the archaic mould established by Panini. The Muslim conquests resulted in the establishment of Persian in the place of Sanskrit, except in a restricted religious-intellectual sphere. During the Mughal period, many local Indo-Aryan languages began to be used for limited types of writing, typically religious poetry: but only Braj, jointly fostered by the huge spread of the Krishna cult and the casual patronage of the Agra court, was seriously to emerge as a widely used extra-local standard *bhasha*.

The imposition of British colonial rule gradually resulted, by the later nineteenth century, in major changes to this previous pattern of written-language use. English replaced Persian as an imperially imposed standard, but both the more meticulously applied administration of the new rulers and their related encouragement of 'vernacular education' demanded the development of selected varieties of Indo-Aryan as standardised written languages. That segment of the role previously played by Persian which was not annexed by English was accorded to Urdu, the Persianised form of the *lingua franca* based on the Khari Boli dialect of Delhi, spoken to the immediate north of Braj; and thus it was that Urdu replaced Persian in the Punjab after the Anglo-Sikh wars of the 1840s. The great spread of Urdu over northern India, though generally welcome to the Muslim population, came under increasing challenge, however, from its Sanskritised variant, Hindi, promoted by the enthusiasts for this newly-formed medium from Benares and Allahabad in increasingly successful measure against the Urdu norms of Lucknow and Delhi. As the two great religious communities of northern India came into increasing conflict during the later years of the Raj, the Urdu-Hindi controversy—hardly affected by Gandhi's muddled flotation of that elusive middle ground, 'Hindustani'—was eventually to be enshrined in the constitutions of the successor states, with Hindi ensconced as the *rashtra-bhasha* (national language) of India, and Urdu pushed back to the west as the *qaumi zaban* (national language) of Pakistan.

Although the outlines of this process are generally familiar, it is important to remember that the evolution of both Urdu and Hindi towards their present status as 'national languages' has been accompanied and indeed effected throughout by a whole series of often hotly debated creative decisions by writers of those languages as to standards of correct usage, the account to be taken of the norms of everyday speech *vis-à-vis* those of formal niceties, and the extent to which the rival classical exemplars of Perso-Arabic on the one hand or of Sanskrit on the other should be more or less carefully followed.[2] While the continuing role of English as the carefully fostered language of the elite in both India and Pakistan has encouraged committed protagonists of both Hindi and Urdu to push for the excision of obvious anglicisms from correct usage in either language, both have been equally oblivious of the insidious influence of the world's currently dominant international language. This influence appears not simply in the coinage of neologisms at the

[2] The process is both surveyed in general and examined in detail in C. Shackle and R. Snell, *Hindi and Urdu since 1800: a common reader* (London, 1990).

familiar level of *dur-darshan* for 'television' in Hindi or *havai jahaz* for 'aeroplane' in Urdu, but in so many apparently unperceived syntactic patterns in everyday usage, e.g., *saval/prashn uthta hai*, 'the question arises'.

Thus it is that much formal writing in contemporary Urdu or Hindi gives the impression to the objective reader that it is composed in a sort of elaborately Persianised or Sanskritised translationese calqued on the same underlying English patterns, which is only remotely indebted to the classic styles of earlier writers. By the same token, modern formal Urdu and Hindi are often rather remote in syntax and style of expression, as well as in their mutually divergent vocabulary, from the natural patterns of everyday speech. But it is of course precisely this remoteness that has helped to ensure their establishment as standard languages over such a vast speech-area.

The Indo-Aryan languages outside this huge Hindi-Urdu zone, for example, Bengali, Marathi or Gujarati, underwent a broadly similar process of standardisation during the nineteenth century, as they were transformed to meet the requirements of contemporary expression by the efforts of grammarians and lexicographers continually enticed by the inexhaustible capacity of Sanskrit to produce all manner of neologisms. In each case, the process was aided by the prior existence of substantial quantities of pre-modern literature, usually recorded in a distinctive script.

The strong regional identification of these languages did, however, entail a much livelier debate as to the proper adjustment to be reached in written styles between classical standards and colloquial usage than was required in the evolution of Hindi and Urdu as non-local standards of a different type. Immediately related to this issue was the question of the most appropriate choice of dialect upon which the regional standard should be based, a choice inevitably determined as much by the location of major urban centres in the region as by cultural tradition. Obvious examples of both these issues are provided by the historic Bengali differentiation of the everyday *chalit bhasha* style from the Sanskritised *sadhu bhasha*, and by the modern replacement of Calcutta-based norms in favour of those of Dhaka in the contemporary Bengali of Bangladesh.[3]

What makes the evolution of modern Sikh Punjabi so strikingly interesting is that it represents the creation of a standard regional language not on the periphery of the Hindi-Urdu area, but one ensconced in its very heart. The map of contemporary official-language use would vividly show Indian Punjab as a small Punjabi zone between the Urdu

[3] Cf. J.V. Boulton, 'Bengali', besides the short surveys of other languages presented in C. Shackle (ed.), *South Asian Languages: a handbook* (London, 1985).

territory of Pakistan and Jammu and Kashmir to its west and north, and the vast bloc of Hindi states to the south and east in India.

Since the institutional process by which this intrinsically rather remarkable situation was brought about, culminating in the success of the long Sikh campaign for a 'Punjabi Suba', has been amply dealt with elsewhere,[4] the following observations relate to more strictly linguistic and cultural aspects of the language's evolution.

The conscious forging of modern standard Punjabi as the distinctive vehicle for the expression of a revitalised Sikhism was the achievement of a quite small number of outstandingly industrious and talented literary figures associated with the Singh Sabha movement around the turn of the century. The magnitude of their achievement is best appreciated against the background of the essentially quite unpromising linguistic and cultural situation that they faced. The intrinsic contrasts, with Urdu and Hindi on the one hand and with the regional languages of the Bengali type on the other, are worth underlining.

The transfer of the imperial crown from the Mughals to the British had permitted Urdu to enjoy an unbroken pattern of evolution as a literary language, and this firmly established heritage provided a solid linguistic base for the Sanskritising proponents of the new Hindi to work from, to such effect as soon to be able to claim the very different idioms used by Kabir, Tulsidas and Surdas as mediaeval Hindi. On any objective criterion, Punjabi is quite as close to the Khari Boli dialect, which underlies both Urdu and Hindi, as Surdas's Braj, and is indeed far closer to it than the eastern Avadhi of the *Ramcharitmanas*.[5]

Then, again as compared with the independent peripheral Indo-Aryan languages, Punjabi lacked the intrinsic advantages not only of recognisably sharp distinction from the norms of Hindi-Urdu grammar and vocabulary, but also the institutional patronage provided by the provincial governments in Calcutta or Bombay. Lahore was, after all, the seat of an administration which conducted its business in English and in Urdu until Partition (as it indeed still remains, although without direct impact on the Sikhs).

Finally, the pre-existent literary heritage in Punjabi was more than usually ambiguous in identifiable linguistic character. Although some form of Punjabi had always been the spoken language of the vast majority of the Sikh community, and although the distinctive Gurmukhi script had always been used to record the vast bulk of its sacred and other literary heritage, the triple Punjabi-Gurmukhi-Sikh equation that

[4] Most notably in part 3 of Paul R. Brass, *Language, Religion and Politics in North India* (Cambridge, 1974).

[5] Although the traditional taxonomy of the Indo-Aryan languages effected by Grierson in the classic *Linguistic Survey of India* is open to all sorts of objections, these are hardly to be levelled against his alignment of Punjabi with Western Hindi and assignment of Eastern Hindi to a separate volume.

has come to be taken for granted by so many Sikhs in India and abroad today hardly existed before the creation of modern standard Punjabi (MSP) in the period around 1900.

The idiom which Guru Nanak, as a poet of utterly superb originality and power, evolved for the matchless expression of his universal message certainly owed much to his native Shekhupuri speech. But the very requirements of the universality of his teachings, not to speak of then pre-existent norms of literary expression and his own wide travels, involved his drawing upon a far wider range of available linguistic resources. The composite idiom he thus created was expended by his successors, most notably by the prolific and linguistically versatile Guru Arjan, and was also transferred to prose by the humbler compilers of the *janam-sakhis*. This scriptural language, which I have termed the 'sacred language of the Sikhs', is certainly not 'Old Punjabi', though many of its elements are drawn from that local source.[6]

Although modernised versions of this composite Punjabi-based sacred language of the Sikhs survived in some post-scriptural Sikh texts, it was Braj and Persian, the great North Indian literary languages of the later Mughal period, that came to dominate Sikh writing after the time of Guru Arjan. Those parts of the Dasam Granth that can plausibly be attributed to the pen of Guru Gobind Singh himself indicate that, while he was equally at home in Persian, his preferred medium was Braj, as it had been his father's. And Braj, written in the Gurmukhi script, was thereafter to be the prevalent medium for the production of most later Sikh writings throughout the heroic *gurbilas* period down to the colossally effective final synthesis of pre-modern Sikh tradition composed by Bhai Santokh Singh.

By one of those paradoxes with which the linguistic and cultural history of South Asia so abounds, it was precisely during this period of the eighteenth and early nineteenth centuries, when the Sikhs were writing in Braj, a now discarded language claimed by Hindu enthusiasts as one of the major 'ancestors' of modern Hindi, that Punjabi was being developed as a literary medium for the creation of superb verse by Muslim poets. Drawing extensively upon their Persian heritage, and writing in the Persian script, such masters of the Sufi *kafi* as Bullhe Shah (1680-1758) were joined by such glorious exponents of the narrative *kissa* as Varis Shah, whose *Hir* (1766) is the universally acknowledged masterpiece of Punjabi literature,[7] and the later Hasham Shah (1753-1823).

[6] The picture given in my teaching manual, *An Introduction to the Sacred Language of the Sikhs* (London, 1983), should be supplemented by reference to the preface of my earlier *A Guru Nanak Glossary* (London and Vancouver, 1981), and the listings of more specialist treatments of the sacred language of the Sikhs appended thereto.

[7] A treatment of the poem, with rather full references to sources in English for the related Muslim literature, has been attempted in my paper 'Transitions

The universal appeal of this literature, generated from within the Muslim community, which has for so long constituted the majority of Punjabi-speakers, is attested to by the number of nineteenth-century manuscripts recording its compositions in Gurmukhi.[8]

Although literary histories and bibliographic listings record the names of many Sikh authors of *kissa*-narratives, they were latecomers to this well-established poetic tradition and are hardly to be resurrected as major contributors to it, except within the context of a careful examination from the linguistic viewpoint of that heterogeneous mass of Punjabi books put out by the publishers of Lahore and lesser centres during the formative years of the period c.1870-1914.[9] A necessary prerequisite of this urgently needed examination would be a carefully judged distancing from that prevalent Sikh-Punjabi chauvinist perspective which would view almost anything written in Punjabi as a part of the 'Sikh literary heritage', however imperfectly understood.

As the preceding remarks should have served to show, 'Punjabi' is one thing and 'Sikkhi' is quite another, and the contemporary perception of a virtually complete overlap between the two is quite something else again. The following observations are offered in a deliberately disjointed fashion, in the hope of suggesting that the contemporary Sikh identification with the Punjabi language is quite as much in need of sympathetic but rigorous academic investigation as are rather more generously covered aspects of contemporary Sikhism.

These observations are loosely presented in ascending order of complexity of the phenomena involved. Their collective purpose is less to offer definitive answers than to raise questions which may some day receive an adequate explanation.

At the simplest visual level, the equation between script and separate linguistic identity is one inevitably seized upon by linguistic protagonists in the amazingly multi-alphabetic environment of South Asia. The early proponents of the MSP had the Gurmukhi script to hand as an immediate weapon to support their cause. But the contemporary spelling norms of MSP are rather different from those of the sacred language of the Sikhs (although continuing to reflect these in the orthography of many words). When was it, for instance, that the mod-

---

and transformations in Varis Shah's *Hir*', in C. Shackle and R. Snell (eds.), *The Indian Narrative Tradition* (Wiesbaden, 1993).

[8] Cf. the summary suggestions made in my 'Some observations on the London collections of Panjabi and Gurmukhi Manuscripts', *IAVRI Bulletin* 13 (1986), pp.5-8.

[9] E.g., the listings provided in the invaluable specialist bibliography of N.G. Barrier, *The Sikhs and Their Literature: a guide to tracts, books and periodicals 1849-1919* (New Delhi, 1970), as well as the more general, also more casual, coverage of the catalogues of Punjabi holdings in the British (Museum) Library and the India Office Library.

ern conventions of the use of dotted letters to distinguish *sh*, *z*, *f* from *s*, *j*, *ph* became established? Here the prior influence of Hindi norms seems to be indicated; but on the other hand, the modern convention of indicating the doubled consonants so intrinsic to Punjabi by the use of the symbol *addhik* is hardly to be explained without reference to the convenient *tashdid* of the Perso-Urdu script. But how? And when?

These may seem very drily technical questions, but a much greater range of linguistic issues was involved in the successful creation of MSP. This, after all, had on the one hand to be created in explicit rivalry with the well-established norms of Urdu, the officially established medium of provincial administration and education, and its Hindi variant increasingly employed by the anti-Sikh Arya Samaji polemicists. On the other hand the very imperfectly established norms for the appropriately selected use of one or other of the many spoken dialects of Punjabi provided at best a shifting base from which to confront these major challenges to the carving out of the sort of linguistically-based community identity the Singh Sabha activists and the wider circle of associated Sikh writers so actively pursued.

Three broad stages may be distinguished in the evolution of MSP as an increasingly standardised medium of formal expression, and in the range of uses to which it has been put. Both these aspects, i.e., the linguistic and the literary,[10] naturally correspond in turn to the contemporary evolution of the Sikh community itself and to wider changes in its South Asian social and political environment.

In the formative first stage, the dominance of specifically religious concerns is symbolised by the enormously copious and influential output of Bhai Vir Singh (1872-1957). Linguistically, this stage is characterised by the strong influence of the earlier sacred language of the scriptures which provided the reformers with their spiritual inspiration. The location of Guru Nanak's birth and upbringing had given the sacred language of the Sikhs an equal heritage, deriving both from the Majhi dialect of the central Punjab, many of whose features are rather close to Hindi-Urdu norms, and from the so-called 'Lahndi' dialects of the western Punjab, which are much more distinctive in linguistic character (e.g., the formation of the future tense as in *jasi* 'he will go' or the use of suffixed pronouns as in *akhius* 'he said'). This distinctive Lahndi component was sustained in much post-scriptural writing in the sacred language of the Sikhs originating from the non-Jat Sikh communities of the north-west. Drawing upon this heritage, the early creators of MSP

[10] Neither aspect is very adequately treated in English, but some possibilities are suggested in my 'Problems of classification in Pakistan Punjab', *Transactions of the Philological Society* (London, 1979), pp.191-210, or from a quite different perspective in M.P. Kohli, *The Influence of the West on Panjabi Literature* (Ludhiana, 1969).

preserved this Lahndi colouring in their writings, even if they themselves came from further east, as in the case of Bhai Vir Singh himself, born and bred in Amritsar.

The overlapping second stage may be dated from soon after the First World War and is characterised by the extension of MSP from an overwhelmingly religious emphasis to its use for the creation of a secular literature by Sikh authors. The exposure of most of these writers to Urdu and to English brought a new sophistication and suppleness to the language, and it is from this period that the classics of modern Punjabi date. Many of the most prominent authors of the period themselves came from the western regions, thus encouraging the continuance of the Lahndi influence on dominantly Majhi-based norms. This classic mix is to be seen, in varying degrees, in the elegant essays of Teja Singh (1894-1958), the immensely popular novels of Nanak Singh (b.1897), the poems of Mohan Singh (b.1905), or the short stories of Kartar Singh Suggal (b.1917) and Kulvant Singh Virk (b.1921).

Although many of these writers, of course, developed their careers in India after 1947, the post-Independence third phase in the evolution of MSP has been dominated by other factors. The wholesale eastward shift of the Sikh population was soon accompanied by a massively increased emphasis on the development and use of MSP as a medium of education and administration, thus extending it far beyond its already established functions as a medium for religious debate and literary expression. With the establishment of the Language Department in Patiala, MSP had for the first time something approaching an official academy, whose influence on the standardisation of the language was soon to be augmented by the proliferation of Punjabi departments in universities and colleges and the recognition of Punjabi as the state language of Punjab in 1966.

This great enhancement of the status of MSP has been accompanied by very noticeable changes in the character of its linguistic erlements. The drawing of the Radcliffe line right through central Punjab left the Lahndi areas in Pakistan and split the Majhi area in two. Contemporary standard Punjabi has therefore tended to incorporate a greater colouring from the eastern dialects of Doabi and Malwai, which are intrinsically often closer to Hindi. At the same time, the abrupt termination of the previous official dominance of Urdu on the eastern side of the Partition line has resulted in a rapid loss of awareness of the historically influential Perso-Urdu component in the vocabulary of MSP, which is naturally still very prominent in the much less altered Punjabi of Pakistan.[11]

[11] My earliest personal observations of the Punjabi scene in Pakistan are recorded in 'Punjabi in Lahore', *Modern Asian Studies* 4, 3 (1970), pp.239-69; my most recent ones, in 'Language, dialect and local identity in Northern Pakistan' in W.P. Zingel and S. Lallemant (eds.), *Pakistan in Its Fourth Decade*

It is true that some attempt has been made to preserve the distinctiveness of MSP by looking to indigenous sources to express new concepts: thus, while the English 'researcher' is expressed in Urdu by the Arabic *muhaqqiq* or in Hindi by the Sanskritic *shodh-karta*, MSP has developed a new sense for the homely Punjabi word *khoji*, originally 'tracker'. But the intrinsic preference of all Indo-Aryan languages for coining neologisms from classical languages has usually proved too strong to resist, and the most formal registers of MSP are becoming quite as Sanskritised as Hindi.

As is so often the case when the attempt is made to examine the linguistic underpinnings of religious and cultural identities in South Asia, there are therefore a number of apparent paradoxes suggested by the modern evolution of Punjabi. It is, after all, somewhat extraordinary that while so much emphasis should be laid on the separate identity of the Sikhs and on the closeness of the identification with the Punjabi heritage, the formal expression of this position should increasingly be couched in a Sanskritised MSP divorced from the vital idiom of spoken Punjabi,[12] which is far less intelligible to educated Punjabi-speakers from Pakistan than it is to the Hindi protagonists so often viewed as the bitterest critics of the Sikhs and their language. But then no one involved with the scholarly investigation of Sikh religion and history in the twentieth century is going to expect simple answers to any serious issue in the field. These preliminary observations will have served their purpose if they suggest that this general rule is quite as true of language as of any other area.

Further reading

Brass, Paul R., *Language, Religion and Politics in North India* (Cambridge, 1974).
Fox, Richard G., *Lions of the Punjab: culture in the making* (Berkeley and Los Angeles, 1985).
Masica, Colin P., *The Indo-Aryan Languages* (Cambridge, 1991).
McLeod, W.H., *The Sikhs: history, religion and society* (New York, 1989).
—, *Who is a Sikh? The problem of Sikh identity* (Oxford, 1989).
Mizokami Tomio, *Language Contact in Panjab* (New Delhi, 1987).
Nayar, Baldev Raj, *Minority Politics in the Punjab* (Princeton, 1966).
Shackle, C.. (ed.), *South Asian Languages: a handbook* (London, 1985).
—, *The Sikhs* (2nd ed., London, 1986).
— and R. Snell (eds.), *Hindi and Urdu since 1800: a common reader* (London, 1990).

(Hamburg, 1983), pp.175-87.

[12] Although it is precisely to his exploitation of the vigorous resources of the spoken idiom that Bhindranwale's message has owed so much of its appeal, it is important to remember that this was primarily disseminated by cassettes, not by the printed page, where formalised MSP dominates.

THE HIDDEN HAND: ENGLISH LEXIS, SYNTAX AND IDIOM AS DETERMINANTS OF MODERN HINDI USAGE[1]

Rupert Snell

The English presence in the Indian subcontinent over the last two centuries or so has had a profound influence on the development of spoken and written Hindi. The process of influence begins with the mere borrowing of words for obvious historical imports such as 'train', 'motor', etc.; it then continues with the use of loan-translations in which neologisms and other English phrases wearing Indian dress are incorporated into Hindi. At a more deep-seated and perhaps more pernicious level, influence is even felt in the composition of sentence patterns and the conventions of idiom. Drawing on examples from a wide range of written and oral sources, this paper looks at the part that English has played in the development of modern Hindi style.

During a public speech in the 1989 election campaign, Rajiv Gandhi found himself saying *cāhe ham jītẽ yā lūzẽ...yānī hārẽ*[2] ('whether we win or lose'), in which the spontaneous coining of *lūznā* from English 'to lose' was hurriedly substituted by *hārnā*, a verb of more conventional pedigree. Rajiv's howler illustrates both the gulf separating a Doon School alumnus from the real lives of India's less-privileged electorate and the extent to which English has permeated certain registers of modern Hindi—with important implications for the perceptions of Hindi-speakers, -readers, and -writers as to their view of themselves and of the world they inhabit. This paper, whose starting point is a recent analysis of the constituents of modern Hindi/Urdu prose,[3] assesses in broad terms some of the linguistic and social factors involved in the development of 'Anglo-Hindi'.

The paper does not aim to analyse the situationally determined choices and interactions which characterise all types of language use, nor does it seek to locate the position of specific examples of English influence in terms of such clines as formal/informal or written/spoken. Rather it attempts, in defining the parameters of that influence, to clear the ground for discussion of aspects of identity within the Hindi speech community and within the smaller inner circle of producers and

[1] First published in *South Asia Research* 10, 1 (May 1990), pp.53-68.

[2] *India Today*, 15 December 1989, p.8.

[3] C. Shackle and R. Snell, *Hindi and Urdu since 1800: a common reader* (London, 1990). I am grateful to C. Shackle for his comments on the present paper.

consumers of Hindi literature.[4]

Loanwords in Hindi: 'Merā jūtā hai jāpānī'

Indian languages are well known for their ability to assimilate loanwords—a necessary and natural process, made relatively complex by the various possible sources of loans available to expand the vernacular lexicon. The eleventh and final volume of the standard dictionary *Hindī śabd-sāgar* embraces words in the alphabetical sequence *skaṁk* to *hvel*; and a large proportion of English loans relate similarly to items as far removed from first-hand Indian experience as these skunks and whales.

The most obvious level at which English has taken root in Hindi is that of the individual loanword, usually a noun: words like *kriket* (or metathetical *kirkeṭ*), *film* (or *filam*), *kampanī, sāikil* etc. are assimilated into the language to the extent that many Hindi speakers would hardly think of them as 'loans' at all. English is merely another loan language, to be added to the already broad range of vocabulary sources such as the tatsama and tadbhava, Perso-Arabic, and Portuguese lexicon. The necessity for a spontaneous choice between these various possible sources tends to cause an instability of lexis, in which the existence of a choice between, say, *pustak* and *kitāb* ('book'), readily admits the possibility of *buk* as a (third) loan.

Even assimilated loanwords mostly remain readily recognisable as the Indianised offspring of their European parents. Only in certain specific social situations has the need for a basic communicability led to a kind of pidginisation at the level of the phrase. Thus nineteenth-century Indian army usage included such assimilations as *aj-vār* from 'as you were', *hukamdār* from 'who comes there?', and even *āpkā sulūk* from 'half-cock fire lock',[5] while conversely, memsahibs allegedly gained their first (and perhaps final) initiation into Hindustani through such cute assimilations as 'there was a banker' (for *darvāzā band kar*, 'close the door'), 'banker dear' (for *band kar diyā*, 'I've closed it'), and 'there was a cold day' (for *darvāzā khol de*, 'open the door').

The extent to which English loanwords show phonetic assimilation to Indo-Aryan patterns varies with register and also with time. Words which have gained widespread currency are obviously more prone to becoming naturalised than words whose use is confined to Westernised

[4] Recent parallel discussions of other languages include: Christopher Shackle, 'Some observations on the evolution of modern standard Punjabi', in Joseph T. O'Connell *et al.*, (eds.), *Sikh History and Religion in the Twentieth Century* (Toronto, 1988), pp. 101-109; Gabriella Eichinger Ferro-Luzzi, 'The influence of English on serious and humorous Tamil speech', *Zeitschrift der Deutschen Morgenländischen Gesellschaft* 140, 1 (1990), pp. 80-95.

[5] Tej K. Bhatia [quoting Gilchrist], *A History of the Hindi Grammatical Tradition* (Leiden, 1987), p. 87.

bureaucracies. London, usually known as *laṇḍan* in nineteenth-century sources, has with increasing familiarity acquired the dentalised spelling *landan* (though dissimilation from *laṇḍ*, 'penis'—or rather 'prick'—may be involved here). Rāmcandra Varmmā, author of an influential manual of Hindi usage first published fifty years ago, advocates the use of such disingenuously assimilated words as *atlāntak, avalā̃ś, antimetham* for 'atlantic, avalanche, ultimatum';[6] translators are skilled in finding Indian names for Shakespearian characters, rendering Antonio as 'Anant' and Solanio as 'Salone';[7] in spoken Hindi one sometimes hears such delights as *paramānand* for 'permanent' or *aṭak-maṭak* for 'automatic' (but with the sense 'immediate(ly)'), while further examples such as *vṛkhabhān* for 'brake-van', *rāy-barelī* for 'library', the ingenious *ras-bharī* for 'raspberry' and the ingenuous *prayogrām* for 'programme' are also reported.[8] Folk etymologies may play their part here, as in a fanciful derivation of *kaṃkrīṭ* 'concrete' from *kaṃkaṛ* 'pebble' + *ī̃ṭ* 'brick'. Conversely, the conscious Anglicisation of Indian words underlies some contemporary Hindi slang—especially where Westernisation suggests raciness, as in the nickname of Shatrughna 'Shotgun' Sinha, archetypal baddie of the Hindi movies.

Some once-current loans have become rare since 1947: *hāthīcok*,[9] *kvekar-oṭ* and *jāmpap*[10] (artichoke, Quaker Oats, jam-puff) have probably disappeared from the Anglo-Indian menu, but *ḍabal roṭī* ('fat bread', i.e. the English loaf) is still available, whether as *ṭosṭ* or (*i-*) *slāis*. Some loans have been borrowed into Hindi with Indian English meanings at deviance from standard English usage: *śifṭ karnā* 'to move house', *riḍyūs karnā* 'to lose weight, slim'. And as British English examplars recede into history, Indian English pronunciations may take over: Gilchrist was referred to as *gilkrisṭ* by his Fort William contemporary Lallūlāl, but now appears in Hindi sources as *gilkrāisṭ*. V. R. Jagannāthan (whose pioneering work provides Hindi with its first Fowler or Partridge) reports an unusual orthographic dissimilation of meaning in the Hindi uses of English 'pound', allegedly spelt as *paũḍ* when meaning 'pound sterling' but as *pāũḍ* for 'pound imperial'.[11]

In certain loanwords, dental consonants derive from contact with

[6] Rāmcandra Varmmā, *Acchī hindī* (6th ed., Banaras, 1950), p.354.

[7] Viśvanāth Miśra, *Hindī bhāṣā aur sāhitya par aṅgrezī prabhāv (1890-1920)* (Dehradun, 1963), p. 272.

[8] Kailāścandra Bhāṭiyā, *Hindī mẽ ãgrejī ke āgat śabdõ kā bhāṣā-tāttvik adhyayan* (Allahabad, 1967), p. 345.

[9] T. Grahame Bailey, 'The development of English *t, d*, in North Indian languages', *Bulletin of the School of Oriental Studies* [*BSOS*] IV-V (1926-8), pp. 325-9.

[10] T. Grahame Bailey, 'English words in Panjabi', *BSOS* IV-V (1926-8), pp. 783-90.

[11] V. R. Jagannāthan, *Prayog aur prayog* (Delhi, 1981), p. 209.

Portuguese rather than English originals: thus *agast* 'August', *sitambar* 'September', *kaptān* 'captain', *tauliyā* 'towel', *patlūn* 'trousers', *pādrī* 'priest', *botal* 'bottle'. Loans from languages other than English regularly show dental consonants: *bāstīl, vietnām, perestroikā,* (even though English may have played a part in the process of transmission).

Though loanwords will normally follow Hindi inflexional patterns, forming obliques such as *sineme mẽ* and plurals like *lāibreriyā̃,* they are not productive of a wide range of derived forms; occasional spontaneous coinings such as *lūznā* and *boriyat* ('boredom') hardly represent a major trend, and are slow to gain formal acceptance. The possibilities of phrase verb combinations with *karnā—ḍisṭarb/fiṭ/risarc/ṭāip karnā* etc.—are, however, more or less infinite, as are intransitive combinations with *honā,* based on either intransitive or transitive English verbs: *pās/fel/bor honā*, 'to pass, to fail, to become bored'. The common usage *ḍīpẽḍ karnā* 'to depend' shows a rather surprising transitivity. Genders either follow final vowels (*lāibrerī* 'library' f.; *baksā* 'box' m.), or assume the gender of a Hindi synonym, as in *baccõ kī luk-āfṭar karnā* 'to look after the children' (cf. *dekhbhāl* f.).

Compounds with Indian words, such as *nem-ṭem*[12] 'calendrical observances' (Sanskrit *niyam* + English 'time') are few and far between; the example approximates to the type of the generalising reduplication which produces such jingle-compounds as *mīṭiṅg-śīṭiṅg, biskuṭ-viskuṭ,* and, with inverted echo, *amanelā-samanelā* (*aṇḍõ mẽ bhī yah sab amanelā-samanelā hai* 'and eggs are full of salmonella and God knows what'); cf. the phrase *sāikil kā pamp aur lamp*[13] 'bicycle pump and lamp'. Adjectives and abstract nouns are often formed with suffixed *-ī,* e.g. *fimlī* 'from the films', *līḍarī* 'politics'. Postpositions such as *ke thrū* 'through [the agency of]' and *ke aṇḍar* 'under [the supervision or authority of]' have some currency in the bureaucratic contexts which form the natural breeding-ground for function-specific words of this sort. Sometimes an English loan substitutes a Sanskritic loan which has itself substituted a Perso-Arabic loan, as in the progression *ke khilāf* > *ke viruddh* > *ke agẽsṭ.*

Sanskritisation

This last example is part of a general pattern in which Sanskrit loans take the cuckoo's role in ousting Perso-Arabic loans from their long-inhabited nest, achieving for Hindi a deliberately chosen Sanskritic identity. In terms of this process and of the equally common 'upgrading' of tadbhava words in the direction of real or imagined tatsama etymons, the tendency towards Sanskritisation (here meant in its pre-Srinivas linguistic sense) is a conspicuous feature of modern

[12] Phaṇīśvarnāth Reṇu, *Pratinidhi kahāniyā̃* (2nd ed., Delhi, 1985), p. 41.
[13] Amṛt Rāy, *Sargam* (Allahabad, 1977), p. 145.

Hindi usage. But here too English has been an important catalyst for change, for in helping to neutralise the Persian element in Hindi it has opened the door to wholesale importation of Sanskrit loans and neologisms. It is significant that while an educated Hindi-speaker would readily recognise a word such as *buk* or *kitāb* as a loanword, a Sanskrit loan such as *pustak* is granted full and unconditional membership of the 'Hindi' lexicon; in terms of traditional values, *śuddha* or 'pure' Hindi is that from which 'foreign' (i.e. Perso-Arabic, English, Portuguese etc.) loans have been excluded, necessarily to be replaced either by real Sanskrit words or by Sanskrit-based neologisms. The concept of *ṭheṭh hindī*—the unadulterated vernacular, unmixed with artificially introduced loans and neologisms from whatever source—can hardly compete in terms of prestige with that of *śuddha hindī* with its allusive, sonorous and grandiloquent Sanskritic register. Unsurprisingly perhaps, linguistic pedigree is perceived in terms of a simple vertical hierarchy. And Hindi is now causing its own neologisms to oust earlier ones from their currency in other Indian languages: in Maharashtra, Sanskrit-based Marathi *pant-pradhān* for 'prime minister' is being or has been replaced by Sanskrit-based Hindi *pradhān mantrī*.[14]

Words which can genuinely be described as 'loans' from Sanskrit are those with attestation in Sanskrit usage. The lower ordinal numbers are a good example, and are common in the higher registers as attributive adjectives (though their take-up as predicatives is less certain). A Sanskrit loan may form a doublet with a Hindi derivative, as in the example of Hindi *khet* 'field' and its Sanskrit etymon *kṣetra* whose Hindi use as 'field' is restricted to the metaphorical sense, and which otherwise means 'area'. Another type of loan is that on to which a completely new application has been imposed, such as *upanyās* 'setting down', used for 'the novel' (vs. Urdu *nāval*), or whose sphere of reference has been made to match an English equivalent, e.g. *sāhitya* 'literature', *prakāśak* 'publisher', *saṅgīt* 'music', *dharma* 'religion', *kalpanā* 'imagination'.

Vast numbers of Sanskrit-based neologisms are coined in imitation of English words. Prefixes such as *an-*, *up-*, provide convenient parallels for English un-, sub- etc.; and the suffix *-(ī)karaṇ* translates '-isation' in words such as 'modernisation' (*ādhunikīkaraṇ*). But familiarity with the Sanskrit lexicon is no guarantee that neologisms will be automatically comprehensible, unless the underlying English model can be perceived: thus it may only be clear from context that *yantrasth* means 'in the press', said of a book before it is *prakāśit*, 'published'.[15] A Sanskritised register often necessitates a direct or indirect gloss in English: *kuch prādhyāpak bandhuõ ne mujhse kahā ki 'aṃgrejī haṭāo' mẽ se*

[14] Madhav M. Deshpande, *Sociolinguistic Attitudes in India: an historical reconstruction* (Ann Arbor, 1979), p. 98.

[15] Cf. the extended sense of the Hindi verb *nikalnā* 'to come out'.

niṣedhātmaktā kī gaṃdh ātī hai. yah 'nigeṭiv' nārā hai. [16] 'Some academic colleagues said to me that "Get rid of English" has a whiff of prohibitionism about it; it is a "negative" slogan'.

The fundamental point here is that though Sanskrit and English may seem odd bedfellows in the context of modern Hindi, their illicit relationship is proving extremely productive to an extent which would have been unthinkable for either one of the pair acting alone. Given the absolute requirement for the coining of countless new words if Hindi is even partially to replace English in all technical registers, this partnership has no real alternative; for though existing words may be given new meanings, the insatiable demand for neologisms calls for tatsama roots.

Loan-translations

There is of course much variation in the take-up rate of neologisms: *dūrbhāṣ* has made little headway against the preferred *(ṭelī-)fon,* but *dūrdarśan* and *ākāśvāṇī* are enjoying some success as 'television' and 'radio' respectively, largely through being adopted as the name of the Indian broadcasting channels; and the Indian press, with its *stambh-lekhak* ('columnists') so often dependent on English models for their copy, have played a major part in the establishing of loan-translations in the accepted style of modern prose.

The process of borrowing extends beyond the level of the individual word, and is at its most creative at the level of the phrase and/or idiom. If both parties in a conversation are familiar with English, there is little restriction on the degree to which idioms can be calqued in a kind of coded language; and gradually the calques become established loans. At one end of the scale there are such self-consciously calqued expressions as the tongue-in-cheek euphemistic request *kyā maĩ āpke ghar ke sabse choṭe kamre kā istemāl kar saktā hū̃?* [17] 'Can I use the smallest room in your house?'—whereas less self-conscious, if equally transparent, usages are exemplified by the following (in which references are given for literary sources):

kāvya sandhyā	'poetry evening' (cf. Urdu's analytical *faiz kī śām*, 'Faiz evening')
adhohastākṣarī	'the undersigned'
viśeṣ ākarṣaṇ kā kendra [18]	'a special centre of attraction'
śuruāt	'starters, entrées' (restaurant menu)
cīthṛā [19]	'rag' ('cheap newspaper')
śubh rātri	'Good night'
safed jhūṭh	'white lie'

[16] Vedpratāp Vaidik, *Aṃgrejī haṭāo: kyõ aur kaise* (Delhi, 1973), p. 1.
[17] See below for a discussion of this new usage of *saknā.*
[18] COI Training Commission Leaflet (London, 1988).
[19] Śrīlāl Śukla, *Rāg darbārī,* (2nd ed., New Delhi, 1985), p. 336.

indirā gāndhī rāṣṭrīy khulā viśvavidyālay	'Indira Gandhi National Open University'
apnī zindagī kā sarvaśreṣṭha bhāg	'the best [better?] part of my life'[20]
pūrva-niścit hatyā[21]	'premeditated murder'
ek taklīfdeh saccāī[22]	'an uncomfortable truth'
gāṛī pakaṛnā	'to catch a train'
maĩ dillī se ātā hū̃	'I come from Delhi'
māf kījie	'Excuse me' (conversation opener)
itihās apne ko dohrāyegā[23]	'history will repeat itself'
prem mẽ girnā[24]	'to fall in love'
rikārḍ bajānā[25]	'to play a record'
lāṛ se bigaṛā huā laṛkā[26]	'a boy spoiled by affection'
tathyõ ko jhuṭhlānā[27]	'to falsify the facts'
apnī kursī majbūt karne ke lie[28]	'to strengthen his [parliamentary] seat'
kauve uṛnevālī lakīr ko pakaṛe[29]	'going as the crow flies'
naye khūn ko protsāhit karnā[30]	'to encourage new blood'
maĩ apne mahattva se bharā thā[31]	'I was full of my own importance'
pitājī munśī-ḍesk ke fāyde batāte na thakte the[32]	'Father never tired of telling us of the advantages of a clerk's desk'
bhāṣā ke sāth majhab ko joṛ kar bhārtīy rājnītijña ghṛṇā kā ek nayā adhyāy śurū kar rahe haĩ[33]	'by linking language and religion, Indian politicians are starting a new chapter of hatred'
unke yugal-band rikārḍ...garam samose kī tarah bikte haĩ; bhārat ne āp ko padmabhūṣaṇ padvī se ābhūṣit kiyā[34]	'his duet records...sell like hot cakes; India decorated him with the Padma Bhushan award'
cunāv kitne niṣphal hote haĩ yah to bhaviṣya hī batāegā[35]	'history alone will tell how ineffective the elections are'

[20] Nirmal Varmā, *Dūsrī duniyā* (Hapur, 1978), p. 215.

[21] Śrīlāl Śukla, *Sīmāẽ ṭūṭtī haĩ* (Delhi, 1983), p. 41.

[22] Ravīndra Tripāṭhī, '*Hindī ke lie ek aur pahal*', in *Dinmān*, 31 December 1988, pp. 75-6.

[23] Śrīlāl Śukla, *Rāg darbārī*, p. 139.

[24] Varmā, *Dūsrī duniyā*, p. 259.

[25] Nirmal Varmā, *Merī priya kahāniyā̃* (3rd ed., Delhi, 1977), p. 14.

[26] Amṛt Rāy, *Sargam*, p. 142.

[27] V. P. Vaidik, *Aṃgrejī haṭāo*, p. 5.

[28] Anil Ṭhākur, '*Aur ab urdū kā lālīpāp*', *Ravivār*, 1-7 October 1989, p. 69.

[29] Śukla, *Rāg darbārī*, p. 333.

[30] Śukla, *Rāg darbārī*, p. 37.

[31] Jainendra Kumār, *Tyāg-patra* (Bombay, 1954), p. 58.

[32] Harivaṃśrāy Baccan, *Kyā bhūlū̃ kyā yād karū̃* (Delhi, 1973), p. 171.

[33] Anil Ṭhākur, '*Aur ab...*', p. 69.

[34] Īśvardatt Nandlāl, *Bhārat kī saṃgīt kalā* (Vakoas [Mauritius], 1972), pp. 83, 85.

[35] Candraśekhar, *Merī jel ḍāyrī* (Delhi, 1978), p. 721.

The tendency is hardly a new one. Examples reported from the Hindi press in the first half of this century include:

jhagṛe kī haḍḍī[36]	'bone of contention'
is pāgalpan ke pīche ek paddhati hai[37]	''there is (a) method in this madness'
nissandeh yah līg ke pākistānī kaphan kī dūsrī kīl hai[38]	'indubitably this is another nail in the shroud [sic] of the League's Pakistan'
ānand-ratan[39]	'Gladstone'

...and so on. Forced as these calqued idioms may seem, not all such correspondences between Hindi and English idiom are to be dismissed so lightly. An expression such as *kām karnā* 'to work', when meaning 'to function' as in *yah maśīn ṭhīk se kām nahī̃ kartī* 'this machine does not work properly', is hard to assess in terms of its dependence on an English model. Many usages are genuinely parallel, the verb *cunnā*, for example, extending over a similar semantic range to that of 'to choose, pick', including the sense 'to pick a flower'; *hāth ānā* 'to come to hand' is a long-attested Indian idiom; *jhukāv* has long had the range of metaphorical senses that apply with English 'leaning, inclination, bent'; *ghaṛiyāl ke ā̃sū nikālnā* 'to shed crocodile tears', an expression which earns Varmmā's scorn, may well derive from English idiom, but overlays the Persian *aśk-i-temsah* (itself based on an Arabic usage of ancient pedigree); and the expression *safed-poś* for 'white-collar worker', though a calque in its idiomatic application, is also an established Persian compound. Conversely, the translator has to beware the *faux amis* in idiomatic expressions such as *parīkṣā/imtahān denā* literally 'to give an exam', i.e. 'to take an exam' (versus ~ *lenā* 'to set an exam, examine'), *dā̃t dikhānā* 'to smile ingratiatingly' (not 'to bare the teeth'); and *bāl kī khāl khī̃cnā/nikālnā* 'to go into fine details' does not have the derogatory implication of pedantry implicit in the English 'to split hairs'. Some authors are all too aware of the extent to which idiom is culture-bound: Kailāścandra Bhāṭiā notes that the expression 'to kill two birds with one stone' typifies the violent tendencies of the English, whereas non-violent India prefers the more emollient *ek panth do kāj* ('one path, two tasks').[40]

Even though second-hand, loan expressions such as the ones listed above can be said to enrich the language after a fashion; and the process is, after all, parallel to that by which European languages have passed

36 Rāmcandra Varmmā, *Acchī hindī,* p. 185.

37 Ibid.

38 Ibid., p. 184.

39 Viśvanāth Miśra, *Hindī bhāṣā ...* , p. 160.

40 Kailāścandra Bhāṭiyā, *Hindī mẽ aṃgrejī ke āgat śabdõ kā bhāṣā-tāttvik adhyayan* (Allahabad, 1967), p.239.

expressions to and fro for centuries. Yet the process of translation from English to Hindi may tend to overlook the culturally distinct natures of the two languages, resulting in infelicities of style: *bas sevā* seems inappropriate for a mundane 'bus service'; *sajjan kī sāikil* implies 'the bicycle of a gentleman' rather than the intended 'gent's bicycle'; *pratinidhi kahāniyā̃*, a noun-compound title adopted for a series of 'representative short stories' by the Delhi publisher Rājkamal Prakāśan, suggests rather the literary career of a 'representative'; and *hṛday parivartan*, title of a short story by Śāntipriya Dvivedī, evokes images of a transplant operation rather than the intended metaphorical 'change of heart'. Compare also the confusingly recycled usage of the word *paṇḍit*, used in Hindi journalism in the English sense 'expert'—*rājnītik paṇḍitõ kā yah kahnā galat nahī̃ hai*[41] 'the political pundits are not wrong in saying...'.

Considerations such as these have led Hindi stylists to avoid excessive blind copying from English. Varmmā, writing in 1946, was impatient with the perpetrators of the more banal examples, and accurately anticipated worse to come with the continuing development of the language. He pointed out the inappropriateness, in the Indian context, of such Eurocentric terms as *nikaṭ/madhya/sudūr pūrva* ('Near/Middle/Far East'), preferring instead *paścimī/madhya/pūrvī eśiyā* ('Western/Central/Eastern Asia'). But the incursions of English influence are insidious to a degree, and even such cautious linguists as Varmmā cannot escape the irony that the conceptual perspective from which they view their material, the linguistic analysis with which they approach it, the terminology with which they discuss it, and even the institutional structures in which their ideas are postulated, are all irreversibly imbued with European conceptions and attitudes. Consider the vocabulary used recently in *Dinmān* in discussing Hindi-medium science teaching: *yah ek* mith *hai ki vijñān ke viṣayõ se saṁbaṁdhit ucc śikṣā hindī ke mādhyam mẽ nahī̃ kī jā saktī hai. lekin...*miśan *kī bhāvnā jarūrī hai*[42] 'it is a *myth* that higher education in scientific subjects cannot be given in Hindi medium...but an attitude of *mission* is necessary'. The attempted replacement of English with Hindi generates many such ironies; the Hindi term for 'loan translation', *udhār anuvād*, is after all an example of its own class.[43] Expressions such as *ṭāip-rāiṭar kī dṛṣṭi se vicār kījie*[44] (lit. 'consider from the view of [i.e. the question of] the typewriter', betray the thinness of the Hindi overlay in much technical writing; and the syntax of Varmmā's statement *[is] prakār kī racnā*

[41] '*Kā̃gres banām kā̃gres*', in *Ravivār*, 1-7 October 1989, p. 11.

[42] Ravīndra Tripāṭhī, '*Hindī ke lie ek aur pahal*', *Dinmān*, 31 December 1988, pp. 75-6.

[43] V. R. Jagannāthan, *Prayog*, p. 63.

[44] Varmmā, *Acchī hindī*, p. 369.

param parakīya aur phalataḥ tyājya hai,[45] with its paired Sanskritised predicates, is a transparent calque of the syntax of an English construction on the lines of 'this kind of construction is wholly alien and accordingly to be abandoned'.

Code-mixing and code-switching

Code-switching is endemic in Indian languages, and we are all familiar with such virtuoso performances as the following:

> *maĩ to* pure *hindī hī bolnā* like *kartī hũ*, mix *karne kā to* question *hī nahĩ uṭhtā. apnī* daughter *aur* sons *ko bhī* pure *hindī bolne ko* encourage *kartī hũ.*[46]

Similar examples may be found in any Indian language, even from considerably earlier parts of the century. In the 1920s Grahame Bailey recorded the Panjabi sentence *merā fādarinlā merī vāif nũ baṛā bædlī ṭarīṭ kardā e*, noting laconically that 'such Panjābī does not help us'.[47] Hindi-English code-switching and -mixing is only one aspect of a complex pattern of language use which may also involve, for example, pairs such as Hindi with Panjabi, standard Khaṛī Bolī Hindi with a dialect such as Bhojpuri, Sanskritised Hindi with Persianised Hindi-Urdu, etc. The brief discussion here considers only the Hindi-English phenomenon.

Much of the literature on code-switching is concerned to analyse motivations for the phenomenon and the constraints on its use. Braj Kachru considers there to be three motivations: 'role identification, register identification, and desire for elucidation and interpretation',[48] and notes that 'the available studies seem to confirm that in India, and in other multilingual areas, the devices of code-mixing and code-switching are being used as essential communicative strategies with clear functional and stylistic goals in view'.[49] A fourth function of code-switching, noted elsewhere by Kachru is that of 'neutralisation',[50] in which speakers wish to conceal clues as to social and regional identity.[51] In an examination of perceptions of identity, it is this fourth

[45] Ibid., p. 238.

[46] Ira Pandit, *Hindi English Code Switching: Mixed Hindi English* (Delhi, 1986), p. 22. (Transcription standardised.)

[47] Bailey, 'English words in Panjābī', pp. 783-90.

[48] Braj B. Kachru, 'Towards structuring code-mixing: an Indian perspective', in Braj B. Kachru and S.N.Sridhar (eds.), *Aspects of Sociolinguistics in South Asia. [International Journal of the Sociology of Language*, 16] (The Hague, 1978), pp. 27-46.

[49] Braj B. Kachru, *The Indianization of English: the English language in India* (Delhi, 1983), p. 205.

[50] Ibid., p. 198.

[51] A similar function in Tamil is described by Ferro-Luzzi, 'The Influence of English', pp. 86-7.

function which is the most revealing, and it is equally in evidence in both the 'communalist' context of modern India and in its moderated form as reproduced in the diaspora. Simply put, the English lexicon is seen as culturally neutral, being free of the cultural and religious associations of (Hindu) Hindi and (Islamic) Urdu. An interviewee on Channel 4's *Bandung File*, speaking about the *Satanic Verses* affair, was able to say *kisī holī parsan ko gālī na denā* 'Do not abuse any holy person', in which the English component perfectly caught the necessary ecumenical register. Other more mundane examples are the names of artifacts, qualities, concepts or social constructs whose Indian and Western manifestations are similar in function but distinct in style: thus words like 'kitchen', 'family', 'friend', 'husband', 'office', 'classical', though readily expressible in either vernacular or Sanskritised or Persianised Hindi, are often subjects for English code-mixing because of the obvious or subtle distinctions of meaning implied by the various Indian and English terms.[52]

The function of trigger-words such as *ki* is an important aspect of code-switching, especially given the importance of parataxis in Hindi grammar: when clauses are autonomous, switching is facilitated. Conjunctions therefore represent positions of extreme instability. The results are plain to see both in Hindi-governed code-mixed sentences and also in Indian English, which may maintain a superfluous English or Hindi conjunction. The sentence 'I asked him where Saral was' may be represented as follows:

maĩne usse pūchā ki saral kahā̃ hai.
I asked him that/*ki saral kahā̃ hai*
maĩne usse pūchā ki where is Saral
I asked him that/*ki* where is Saral.

Grammatical influences

While examples of loans, calques, and code-switching tend to be fairly conspicuous, more deep-seated English influences are also to be detected in the actual syntax of certain styles of modern Hindi, particularly in journalism.

(1) Changes of word or phrase or clause order following English norms, especially with subordinate clauses: *maĩ hī piche kyõ rahtā yadi*

[52] At the other end of the scale it is precisely the culture-bound nature of a concept which requires a switch of code, whether within a Hindi-governed sentence involving switches to English, or an English-governed one involving switches to Hindi. A friend recently relating some problematic marriage negotiations epitomised the situation in a sublime synthesis of North India and South London, with 'I tell you, yār, our izzat's down the f****** drain'.

uske lie apne ko mānsik rūp se taiyār kar pātā[53] ('I myself would hardly have lagged behind if I had managed to prepare myself for it mentally'), in which the subordinate 'if' clause follows the main clause (and the conjunction *to* is dispensed with altogether).

(2) A tendency for relative-correlative constructions to imitate the English pattern: *laṛkā jo dillī se āyā hai vah merā bhāī hai*[54] 'the boy who has come from Delhi is my brother'.

(3) A growing preference for shifted tenses in reported speech: the sense of 'I asked him what he wanted' is increasingly likely to be rendered by *maĩne usse pūchā ki use kyā cāhie thā* rather than by *maĩne usse pūchā ki tumhẽ kyā cāhie*, with its embedded original question 'What do you want?' (As noted earlier, the Hindi pattern commonly governs Indian English sentences: 'It was Savitri who told him that "take this hundred rupees" '.)

(4) Increased use of abstract nouns as 'countables', admitting plural forms, e.g. *śaktiyā̃, sundartāẽ* 'powers, beauties'.

(5) Increased use of continuous tenses, especially on the model of the English progressive; e.g. expressions such as *hindī āndolan kā svarūp bhī badalne jā rahā hai* 'the form of the Hindi movement too is going to change'.[55]

(6) Use of English loans as determined by borrowed English syntax: *maĩ bahut leṭ hū̃* 'I am very late' (vs. periphrastic expressions such as *mujhe bahut derī ho rahī hai*).

(7) Encroachment of the postposition *ke sāth* into contexts generally covered by *se*: *bhāratīya saṃskṛti...kā unhõne gaharāī ke sāth adhyayan kiyā hai*[56] 'he has studied Indian culture...with depth'; *maĩ ek din śānti ke sāth so rahā thā*[57] 'I was sleeping peacefully one day' (and not 'I was sleeping with Shanti', as it first appears).

(8) Supplanting of active intransitives with passive transitives; and the specifying of an agent (with the postposition *ke dvārā*) in passive constructions.

(9) As pointed out by Nicole Balbir,[58] deductive reasoning on the Western model has led to an increased use of concessive and other

[53] Candraśekhar, *Merī jel ḍayrī* (Delhi, 1977), p. 293.

[54] Prem Sagar Bhargava, 'Linguistic interference from Hindi: Urdu and Punjabi and internal analogy in the grammar of Indian English' (PhD thesis, Cornell University, 1968), p. 118.

[55] Hazārī Prasād Dvivedī, *'Hindī kā varttmān aur bhaviṣya'*, in *Kuṭaj evaṃ anya nibandh* (Varanasi, 1964), p. 143.

[56] Publisher's preface to H. P. Dvivedī, *Aśok ke phūl* (9th ed., Varanasi, 1968), p. 3.

[57] Varmmā, *Acchī hindī*, p. 202.

[58] Nicole Balbir, 'La modernisation du Hindi', in István Fodor and Claude Hadège (eds.), *Language Reform: History and Future*, Vol. I (Hamburg, 1983), p. 122.

subordinate clauses, typically introduced by such words as *yadyapi/ hālā̃ki* 'although', *tāki* 'in order that', etc.

(10) A range of new idiomatic usages of Hindi words (particularly verbs):

lenā, 'to take': this has proved very productive in the calquing of phrase verbs. Examples are: *phoṭo lenā* (vs. ~ *khī̃cnā*); *bhāg/hissā lenā* (a usage much disapproved of by Varmmā, but now widespread); *kā rūp lenā* ;[59] *klās lenā* ;[60] *lenā* as 'to take X amount of time' (supplanting *lagnā* expressions);[61] *lenā* as to react/respond', e.g. *na jāne vah use kis rūp mẽ lẽ* 'there was no knowing how she might take it';[62] *cāy lenā* etc. Varmmā is critical of the expansion of this verb, citing numerous examples, but later declares *ab muhāvare lījie* 'now take idioms...'.[63]

dekhnā 'to see' *ham dekhẽge (hamẽ dekhna hai/hogā)* 'We'll see (We'll have to see)'; these are expressions which, though long-established, seem to have derived support from parallel English usages. There are also examples of *dekhnā* being used as 'to visit' (English 'come and see me'), supplanting *milnā*.

saknā 'to be able to', encroaching on the use of a subjunctive verb to suggest possibility. Thus *kyā maī̃ āpkī madad kar saktā hū̃?* 'Can I help you?'—a question which, logically, the questioner alone isqualified to answer. Also *saknā* + negative, or equivalents such as *asamarth honā* 'to be incapable of', are taking over the role ofnegative passive with agent in privative sense.[64]

ek 'one, (a)': increasingly used superfluously as an equivalent for the English indefinite article. The statement *maī̃ ek ṭīcar hū̃* 'I am a/one teacher' seems to raise questions as to how many teachers one might reasonably expect to be.

(11) Use of pre-modifying adjectival phrases in place of relative-correlative constructions (in written registers): *aṃgrezī ke mādhyam se kām karnā cāhne vālõ ke lie*[65] 'for people wishing to work in the English medium'; *aṃtarrāṣṭrīy kūṭnīti ke ām taur par śānt māhaul mẽ bhī*[66] 'even in the usually calm atmosphere of international diplomacy'. (Constructions of this type are popular in newspaper headlines, because of space restraints.[67]) Sanskrit participial adjectives, typically in *-it*,

[59] Kṛṣṇa Baldev Vaid, *Merī priy kahāniyā̃* (Delhi, 1978), p. 56.

[60] Śrīlāl Śukla , *Rāg darbārī*, p. 27.

[61] Mohan Rākeś, *Kvārṭar tathā any kahāniyā̃* (Delhi, 1972), p. 173.

[62] Ilā Dālmiā, *Chat par aparṇā* (Delhi, 1988), p. 19.

[63] Rāmcandra Varmmā, *Acchī hindī*, p. 198.

[64] Balbir, 'La modernisation du Hindi', pp.101-26.

[65] Jagannāthan, *Prayog*, p. 7.

[66] *'Kūṭnītik kauśal kī kamī'* [editorial], *Iṃḍiyā Ṭuḍe* [Hindi ed. of *India Today*], 15 August 1989, p. 9.

[67] B. Lakshmi Bai, 'Syntactic innovations in newspaper Hindi', in Bh.

(*likhit, sthit, sthagit*) form convenient translations for the English equivalents in '-en', '-ed' etc. ('written', 'situated' 'postponed'), to which they approximate more closely than Hindi constructions using participle plus auxiliary—*likhā huā* etc.

Orthographic conventions

(1) Hindi has long since adopted many of the conventions of English typography, including the full range of punctuation (though the colon is little used because of potential confusion with *visarga*), the use of italic and other stylised fonts (including some imitating the shapes of the Perso-Arabic script, e.g. in Devanagari cover designs for books of Urdu verse), and so on.The Roman full stop is now increasingly replacing the Devanagari *khaṛī pāī*. A usage which falls headlong into the conceptual gulf between the Roman and Devanagari scripts is that in which a sequence of dots indicating an incomplete sentence is set at the level of the Devanagari headline, and immediatedly followed by a fullstop aligned with the base of the character, thus—

न जाने क्या होगा . . . .

Limitations imposed by the restricted mechanics of the typewriter are now being visited upon typeset Devanagari, so that *buddhi* (बुद्धि) for example is sometimes printed as बुद्‌धि, and *tra* and *tta* (त्र, त्त) as त्‌र, त्‌त.

(2) The replacement of Devanagari numerals with the Arabic set has official sanction; and English numbers are very commonly used in speech, particularly in the quoting of telephone numbers, year dates, and the like.

(3) Devanagari characters on the model of English '(a) (b) (c)' are used to designate successive paragraph headings, etc. A sequence may start with the consonants, (क) (ख) (ग), or with the vowels, (अ) (आ) (इ).

(4) Usages such as १ला for '1st' are occasionally found.

(5) The pronounced and written values of some Indian names indicate their status as re-imports: 'Tagore' is *ṭaigor* rather than original *ṭhākur*, and in conversation 'India' is more commonly *iṇḍiyā*[68] than either *bhārat* or *hindustān*. The short vowel following a final conjunct consonant in a name such as 'Gupta' (गुप्त) becomes lengthened to a (feminine!) -*ā* in the spelling *guptā*.

(6) The Hindi press is increasingly coining acronyms (which Jagannāthan calls *praś*, itself an acronym for *prathamākṣarik śabd*),[69] mostly in the names of organisations and institutions: *iṃkā* (for *indirā kāṅgres*,

Krishna Murti and Aditi Mukherjee (eds.), *Modernization of Indian Languages in News Media* (Hyderabad, 1984), pp. 20-28.

[68] This usage is an example of the 'neutralising' function of code-mixing discussed below, avoiding as it does the various implications of Sanskrit *bhārat* and Persian *hindustān*.

[69] Jagannāthan, *Prayog*, p.219.

'Congress I'), *bhālod* (*bhāratīy lok dal*), etc.

(7) The Hindi convention for abbreviations, using the first syllable of the word, is inexorably yielding to a transcription of the pronounced value of the English initial letters: thus वि॰ प्र॰ for *vi(śvanāth) pra(tāp)* becomes वी॰ पी॰ *'vī. pī.'* (and serves as a spoken as well as a written convention). The small circle which follows the Devanagari abbreviation is now often dropped in Hindi journalism, as in the headline वी पी सिंह सी आइ ए के एजेंट हैं.[70]

Literary and journalistic Hindi

Earlier this century, Tagore noted that 'the foundation of all modern Indian literature is absolutely European—in fact, none of its literary genres, e.g. fiction, poetry, drama, is orientated by the Ars Poetica of the ancient Orient.'[71] While Indian literature has established its own credentials very substantially since Tagore's day, it has continued to feel the influence of English language and literature, as for example in the appearance of new sub-genres such as Candraśekhar's 'jail diary' quoted elsewhere in this paper. Some writers freely admit that 'we Indians of today think in English and then coin words in Sanskrit'.[72] The results of this process are to be seen in some of the examples already quoted above, and are commonplace in the works of many authors such as Premcand, whose writing is thick with examples of calqued English.[73]

Yet it is in the columns (*stambh*) of Hindi newspapers that Anglo-Hindi really comes into its own. The extent to which it influences also the mass media is an enormous and as yet unanswered question. Journalism depends largely on English-language sources; small wonder, then, that much of the Hindi press seems so hurried a calque of its English exemplars. A joke syndicated through various local papers provides a useful example:

adhyāpak:	*'rājū, bure bacce kahā̃ jāte haĩ?'*
rājū:	*'mandir ke pīche.'*
Teacher:	'Raju, Where do naughty boys go?'
Raju:	'Behind the temple.'

The 'temple' here is surely the 'gym' transmogrified, and though the joke deals with universals, its 'Scripture class' context (not to mention

[70] Headline in *Ravivār*, 1-7 October 1989, p. 43.

[71] Quoted by Lothar Lutze, *Hindi Writing in Post-colonial Literature: a study in the aesthetics of literary production* (Delhi, 1985), p. 24.

[72] Kākāsāheb Kālelkar, *'Viśva-bhāṣā ke sandarbh mẽ hindī'*, in Sarojinī Mahiṣī, (ed.), *Viśva hindī darśan* (Nagpur, 1975), p. 117.

[73] For example, one may wonder what if anything is Indian about a clause such as *jab parīkṣā-phal nikalā aur prakāś pratham āyā* 'when the examination result came out and Prakash came first' ('Mā̃', in *Mānsarovar* I (Allahabad, 1980), p. 59.) [Some editions read plural *nikale* for singular *nikalā*.]

its eschatology) is imported.

The survival of Hindi: '...phir bhī dil hai hindustānī...'

The question of style and lexis in Hindi is largely the preserve of those already committed to a process of Sanskritisation on an English-influenced base. The generation of scholarship equally at home with the Persian and the Sanskrit components of Hindi is gradually disappearing[74], and as Hindi becomes more and more narrowly defined as a Hindu language, Perso-Arabic vocabulary is increasingly regarded as alien to its character. F. S. Growse, in an 1866 article entitled 'Some objections to the modern style of official Hindustáni',[75] criticised the Persianising tendency of the bureaucratic register; his arguments apply with reference to Hindi today, reading 'Sanskritising' for 'Persianising'. Some Hindi writers are themselves vocal in their criticisms of current trends in language use: S. H. Vātsyāyan 'Ajñeya' has bemoaned the fate of Hindi as India's new sacred cow, coralled but not nourished by its keepers, for whom sanctity rather than function is a priority;[76] and he laments an accompanying change amongst the constituency of modern India 'from the illiterate educated audiences of yesterday to the literate uneducated public of today and tomorrow'.[77]

The Constitution of India makes a specific recommendation as to the development of Hindi:

> It shall be the duty of the Union to promote the spread of the Hindi language, to develop it so that it may serve as a medium of expression for all the elements of the composite culture of India and to secure its enrichment by assimilating without interfering with its genius, the forms, style and expressions used in Hindustani and in the other languages of India specified in the Eighth Schedule, and by drawing, whenever necessary or desirable, for its vocabulary, primarily on Sanskrit and secondarily on other languages. [78]

[74] Awareness of Persian norms of word order is similarly in decline. That it was once very much stronger is evident from Grierson's discussion: 'The subject [in Hindi prose] *must* precede the predicate, the governed word *must* precede the governing (*us ke bād,*—never *ba'ad us ke,* which is Urdū), the adjective *must* precede the substantive with which it agrees and, most fixed of all, the verb *must* be the last word in the sentence. If these rules are broken a Hindū says that the sentence ceases to be Hindī, it has got the Persian infection and has become a Muḥammadan. It is Urdū, even though it may not contain a single Arabic or Persian word.' G. A. Grierson (ed.), *The Satsaiya of Bihari* (Calcutta, 1896), p.13.

[75] *Journal of the Asiatic Society of Bengal* XXXV, I, pp.172-181.

[76] Ajñeya, *Ātmanepada* (Banaras, 1960) p.130. I owe the reference to the Rev. Roger Hooker.

[77] Lutze, *Hindi writing,* p. 15.

[78] C.L. Anand, *The Constitution of India,* (2nd ed., Allahabad, 1966 [with 1974 supplement]), p. 534; discussed by Alfred Pietrzyk, 'Problems

The apparently increasing dependence of Hindi on the English model, not simply as a source of loans but more importantly as an influence on the deeper levels of syntax and idiom, infringes this cautious stipulation that assimilation should not interfere with the 'genius' of the language. While it is obviously the case that the modernisation of Hindi calls for a substantial amount of borrowing (primarily from English and Sanskrit), the pell-mell urgency of this process has led to a situation in which the criterion of appropriateness is in danger of being lost, and the true sense of 'enrichment' obscured. In many registers of modern Hindi usage the diaphanousness of the Indian veneer reveals more than it conceals of underlying English thought-patterns; such language, coined by the small élite of English-educated Hindi-speakers, is of little use as a means of communication for the majority of the Hindi-speaking population, whose world is remote from the sources of allusion and reference underlying Anglo-Hindi. Furthermore, the willingness of Hindi writers to Westernise their language appears to set little store by the notion that attitudes and beliefs are themselves linguistic constructs, and that many questions are begged by the ready adoption of a foreign idiom. There is a need to consider the cultural implications for the character of Hindi once the Trojan horse of English becomes an accepted part of its heritage.

Further reading

Balbir, Nicole, 'La modernisation du Hindi', in István Fodor and Claude Hadège (eds.), *Language Reform: history and future*, 1 (Hamburg, 1983).

Bhatia, Tej K., *A History of the Hindi Grammatical Tradition* (Leiden, 1987).

Kachru, Braj B. and S.N.Sridhar (eds.), *Aspects of Sociolinguistics in South Asia* [International Journal of the Sociology of Language 16] (The Hague, 1978).

Pandit, Ira, *Hindi English Code Switching: mixed Hindi English* (Delhi, 1986).

Shackle, C. and R. Snell, *Hindi and Urdu since 1800: a common reader* (London, 1990).

in language planning: the case of Hindi', in Baidya Nath Varma (ed.), *Contemporary India* (London, 1964), pp. 247-70.

A HERO OR A TRAITOR? THE GURKHA SOLDIER IN NEPALI LITERATURE[1]

Michael Hutt

The self-image of a people and the narrative of their past exploits are an important part of the creation of a national identity in South Asia, as elsewhere. In this sense the attempt to form a Nepali identity from a variety of people and localities has several strands, including the projection of the nation as a Hindu kingdom. One obvious complication in recent years has been the relationship with India as a very much larger neighbour; but arguably that difficulty has a history in Nepal's relationship with India under British rule. In that period, frontiers, external relations and internal political structures were defined; and also a particular connexion was established between Gurkhas from Nepal and the British army. The connexion survives to complicate questions of Nepali identity today. The Gurkha soldier is lionised in a large body of writing in English, most of it written by British ex-officers of the Brigade of Gurkhas. Such authors tend to assume that British Gurkhas are admired or even envied by their Nepali compatriots. To some extent this is probably the case, but a thorough analysis of the ways in which Gurkhas are perceived should not omit some reference to writings in Nepali, as well as in English. The aim of this article is to present a brief survey of the ways in which Nepali writers have represented the Gurkha, and to suggest some reasons for their attitude to him. It concludes that some negative portrayals of Gurkhas reflect a nationalist sentiment, but also an urban/rural divide in attitudes, between writers and intellectuals, and the peoples from the hills, among whom the Gurkha soldiers are recruited. The article grew out of a more far-ranging scheme of research between 1987 and 1990 which resulted in the publication of a book on Nepali literature, Himalayan Voices, *in 1991.*

Some years ago, *The Times* carried a special report on the kingdom of Nepal which quite naturally included a short article on the subject of the fabled Gurkha soldier. This began with the following words:

> The first Gurkha regiment was formed in 1815 because the British, sent on a punitive expedition against rampaging Nepalese tribesmen, found the enemy so difficult to beat. After a lot of blood, sweat and tears, victors and vanquished looked dazedly at each other over the foothills of the Himalayas and decided there was only one solution—if you cannot beat them, join

[1] First published in *South Asia Research* 9, 1 (May 1989); reprinted in *Kukri* (the journal of the Brigade of Gurkhas) in January 1991.

them.

Britain's recruitment of soldiers from Nepal began in 1815 during two minor wars between Nepal and the British East India Company which had been provoked by Gorkhali expansion and a consequent clash of territorial ambitions. After the British victory in these wars, a treaty was imposed upon the Nepalis, signed at Segauli (now in Bihar), and ratified in 1816. This drastically reduced the size of the Gorkhali kingdom and installed a British resident in Kathmandu. The Segauli Treaty did not stipulate that Nepal should allow Britain to recruit its citizens for army service: this arrangement dates back to an agreement made in May 1815 between Amar Singh Thapa, Gorkha's western commander, and his British adversary in the field:

> All the troops in the service of Nepal, with the exception of those granted to the personal honour of Kagjees Ummersing and Rangor Sing, will be at liberty to enter into the services of the British Government if agreeable to themselves and the British Government choose to accept their services (Smith, 1973, p.9).

Three Gurkha regiments (the 1st Nasiri Battalion, the Sirmoor Battalion and the Kumaon Battalion) were formed in 1815, and later became known as the 1st, 2nd and 3rd Gurkha rifles. Greatly impressed by the quality of their Nepalese recruits, the British became anxious to enlist the hillmen in greater numbers. The Nepal Government, however, opposed all moves to reach a formal agreement on the issue until 1884. Until this time, the British were obliged to recruit outside the borders of Nepal, although clandestine recruiting drives were made from time to time within the kingdom (Mojumdar, 1973, p.157-69).

Today, the most widespread conception of the nature of the relationship between Britain and Nepal which has led to the recruitment of men from that kingdom is one of equality and mutual respect. Books about the Gurkha regiments of the British Army are usually glowing accounts of the roles their men have played in various campaigns during the past 170 years.[2] Such books pay little attention to the factors which encourage Nepalis to fight in foreign armies, or to the image which the general populace at home holds of those who do so. Writers such as Smith tend to dismiss the concerns of Nepali nationalists and intellectuals:

> intrigues at the Royal Court and the feelings of the upper classes in Kathmandu were of little concern to the Gurkha hillmen in their mountain villages. Volunteers flocked down to the plains to enlist in the new corps. For over 150 years the Gurkhas' desire to serve as soldiers has transcended the

[2] A plethora of quasi-historical accounts is available. See, for instance, Forbes 1964, Bolt 1967, James and Shiels-Small 1975, Bishop 1976, Farwell 1984, as well as Marks' novel, published in 1971.

whims of politicians (Smith, 1973, p.9).

It is certainly true that young men from particular ethnic groups and regions of Nepal, who have little prospect of anything other than lives as subsistence farmers in the rigorous Himalayan environment, have been exceedingly enthusiastic to enlist in the Gurkha regiments of the British and, latterly, Indian armies since they were formed in the early nineteenth century.[3] Indeed, competition is fierce, since only a small proportion of those who present themselves at recruiting centres is actually selected. Primarily, these men have been Gurungs, Magars and Tamangs from western and central Nepal, and Limbus and Rais from the east—'Gurkha' is meaningless as an ethnic denotation. British writers on this subject have tended to ascribe the phenomenon more to 'pull' factors—the mystique and prestige of the British Army—than to 'push' factors: limited choice in employment, and the arduous nature of rural life in the hills. A fair picture of these 'push' factors can be drawn on the basis of several recent studies of Nepali rural economy. (See, for instance, Blaikie, Cameron and Seddon, 1980, or Seddon, 1987.) Here I propose to demonstrate that the enlistment of Nepalis in foreign armies does cause disquiet among certain sectors of the educated classes of Nepal. For the purposes of this discussion, I shall present a sample of twentieth-century writings in Nepali on the subject of the 'Gurkha' soldier, identify some views of the Gurkha soldier which are apparent from this literature, and attempt to analyse and explain the attitudes of the writers concerned.

It is important to point out that the term 'Gurkha' is nowadays used mainly by outsiders to refer to Nepalis enlisted in foreign regiments. Inside Nepal, its proper form, Gorkha, is the name of a small town to the west of the capital whose kings conquered and annexed neighbouring petty states to form the modern nation of Nepal during the eighteenth century. When applied to a group of people, the term *Gorkhā* or, more properly, *Gorkhālī*, usually refers fairly loosely to the Indo-European Hindu group which has achieved ascendancy over the other races of Nepal. The members of this dominant group are not by and large recruited by the British Army. Since 1815, the most sought-after recruits have been men from the so-called 'martial tribes' (see Hodgson, 1833) of central Nepal: the Gurung and the Magar. The British Army's continued use of the words 'Gurkha' for Nepali recruits and 'Gurkhali' for their language is a legacy from the earliest Anglo-Nepalese contacts, when the newly-unified state was more commonly known by the name of the small principality which had contrived to unite it. In modern

[3] Before 1947, there were ten Gurkha regiments in the British Army. After Indian independence, six of these were retained by India. In 1963, the British Brigade of Gurkhas comprised a total of 14,600 soldiers. Farwell, 1984, pp.276 and 296-9.

Nepali, the word for soldier is *sipāhī* (the same word appears in Hindi, and has been corrupted into the English word 'sepoy'), whereas the term most commonly used for a Nepali soldier who serves or who has served in a foreign army is *lāhure*. This word is derived from the name of the city, Lahore, where the Sikhs began the recruitment of Nepalis for service in their army in 1839. By association, *lāhurmā āunu*, 'to come into Lahore' means 'to be enlisted' (Turner, 1980, p.555).

The lāhure *in Nepali fiction*

The examples presented here have all been drawn from twentieth-century Nepali literature. Although the national literacy rate has yet to exceed 40 per cent, a substantial body of published Nepali poetry and prose has developed in recent decades. This serves as an important reflection of educated opinion in Nepal which has attracted only limited attention from foreign scholars to date. Polemical or political texts on the subject of Gurkha recruitment may well have been published from time to time, and Gurkha soldiers certainly feature in the rich oral literature of the region, particularly in the songs of the minstrels *(gāine)*, but this discussion is restricted to the realms of published 'creative' literature—to fiction and to poetry.

The earliest publication in Nepali concerning Gurkha soldiers seems to have been a story entitled *Ratan Singh Gurungko Outpostko Kathā, (The Tale of Ratan Singh Gurung at the Outpost)*, first published in Banaras in 1914, which had actually been translated from an article in an English magazine. It recounted the valorous deeds of its hero in the Tiraha campaign of 1897-98, and is now regarded by some literary historians, rather tendentiously since it is a translation, as an early example of the modern short story in Nepali. Its popularity at the time is evident from the number of editions which emanated in subsequent years from Indian military centres such as Dehra Dun. A verse narrative by one Yoga Bikram Jang Rāṇā, entitled *Vajiristhānko Yātrā*, was published from Bombay in 1918. This relates the experiences of the two Gurkha platoons which joined the Field Force expedition to Waziristhan in 1917, and is again a similar tale of derring-do.

A more considered portrait of the *lāhure* is to be found in one of the finest Nepali short stories, *Sipāhī* (*The Soldier*, 1938) by Bishweshwar Prasād Koirālā. Koirālā was a writer and politician who later became Nepal's first elected prime minister. The story's protagonist is a young student returning on foot to his home in Ilam. On the way, he meets up with a soldier, stationed at Quetta, who is returning to Nepal to select new recruits. They walk for a day together, and the soldier tells the student all about his life. The student is nervous of him at first, but gradually warms to him because of his entertaining conversation. The main characteristic which Koirālā attributes to the soldier is his complete freedom from responsibility: this, he seems to imply, is something to be envied. But is it to be admired?

I'm stationed at Quetta. I've been there for a long time. I do have a wife, but she's sickly and good-for-nothing. But we've had two children, all the same. I haven't been home for ages, and I don't want to go either. She'll have gone off with someone else by now, and my sons will have turned into rogues. Well, the little one seemed bright enough and I really hoped to educate him. But who could be bothered? My father didn't have me educated, and I'm content. I found myself a wife in Quetta too. Wherever you go you should have what you want (Koirālā, 1938, p.95).

The serious young student is mildly shocked by his friend's attitudes, and particularly by the fact that the soldier claims to enjoy himself in battle. But he also finds him great fun, particularly when he teases all the young women who pass them on the path. The most telling passage comes at the end of the story, when the pair part company after a night in a lodging-house:

'Little master', said the soldier, 'I bid you farewell. We go different ways from here'.... I felt quite sorry: I had begun to grow fond of him, but he cared for no-one. He strode off down the path, and I stood there watching him go. Many times I have seen stone memorials to soldiers killed in battle. But this was the only chance I had to meet a soldier in the flesh (ibid., p.100).

A more jaundiced view is taken of the mercenary soldier in one of the more successful Nepali novels of the 1960s. This was Pārijāt's *Shirīshko Phūl* (*The Mimosa Flower*) first published in 1964. Although it was awarded the Madan Puraskār, a prestigious literary prize, it caused considerable controversy since Pārijāt's depiction of Nepali life was totally without precedent. The central character of *The Mimosa Flower* is Suyog Bir Singh, an ex-Gurkha soldier who spends his life aimlessly drinking in the bars of Kathmandu. Singh becomes friendly with another drunkard, Shivrāj, and makes the acquaintance of his friend's sister, Sakambarī. Sakambarī is a highly unorthodox heroine: she wears her hair cropped short, smokes continually and takes a negative, cynical view of life. Yet Singh becomes infatuated with her, despite her scornful attitude towards him:

After that, our conversation took its usual course. But I spoke warily and irritably, fearing that a bullet would explode beside me. As we talked, Shivrāj turned to Sakambari and said,

'Have you noticed, Bari, how distracted Suyogji becomes when the subject of war comes up? How he tries to elude us!'

Bari blew smoke from her mouth, 'Perhaps he's afraid,' she said.

'What does a soldier fear?' retorted Shivrāj, then Bari said, 'War is a crime, Shiva. The war we fight on somebody's command is a crime one person has to perpetrate against another, a crime which every killer should have to write on his own forehead. The crime can't be seen from outside.'

In all the years that had passed since I came back from the war, no-one had judged me like this. I did not know what Bari meant—but what did she know, anyway? We die for the sake of heroism: we sacrifice and we are sacrificed. What crime is that? (Pārijāt, 1965, p.25-6).

The psychological background to Singh's meaningless existence is his memory of his maltreatment and sexual exploitation of tribal women during service for the British army in Burma. One memory causes him particular remorse:

The British captain comes to slap me on the back, but he doesn't know what a worthless man I am. In two days' time, Matinchi will be waiting for me, with a glass filled with liquor. The bruises on her breasts will still hurt her, but still she will love the boots her brave Gurkha wears. She will be waiting for the time when she can live in his house as his wife. But I will already be far from these orchid jungles, far from the longings of life, far from its very meaning. When Matinchi finds out that her Gurkha has fled, she can hang herself or take poison: a cheap, facile death. I felt like laughing—what had I done? I had plucked an orchid flower and crushed it under my boot (ibid., p.60).

At last, Singh is overcome by his feelings for Sakambarī and, finding her alone on the lawn of her house one day, he impulsively kisses her just once on the mouth. But she simply turns away and walks back into the house. They never meet again: first Singh hears that Sakambarī is sick, and then that she has died. Pārijāt's message seems to be that he is a man who is polluted by death and exploitation, and that he is incapable of giving genuine love. The sole attempt he makes to express sincere emotion proves to be fatal for the object of his desire. Pārijāt's story is not primarily a portrait of a Gurkha soldier. It is a novel about social alienation which is deeply influenced by Freudian psychology and existentialist thought. But the author has admitted to a secondary motive:

Before I began the novel, I felt a small desire to give Gurkha soldiers a bad name, because I had heard many stories during my childhood about the terrors they inflicted. Such unpleasant things were always happening in Darjeeling that later it seemed to me that those Gurkhas who gave their lives so pointlessly for others must surely be rogues. Then I interviewed my brother and his friends, all experienced soldiers from the World War, and wrote the novel while I was at Kathmandu campus (Pārijāt, 1987, p.33).

Another supposed characteristic of the returned *lāhure* is his feeling of guilt. A short story by Shivakumār Rāī, a Darjeeling writer, entitled *Jyānamārā?* (*A Murderer?*) addresses this theme in the tale of an old man, Ujīr Mān, who has returned to his village after long years of service overseas. He takes a young wife and settles down to live quietly on his savings and his army pension. Ujīr Mān is well-known in the village for his hunting skills and marksmanship, but one night he accidentally shoots a young policeman in the forest, mistaking him for a bear in the darkness. He confesses to his mistake immediately, and is taken into custody pending trial. It then transpires that the dead policeman had actually been conducting an affair with Ujīr Mān's young wife: her old husband seems to have been the only villager who was ignorant of this fact. Thus widespread suspicion exists that the old Gurkha has shot the policeman in anger and jealousy, although he is in fact quite innocent. At the trial, witness after witness affirms that the policeman had indeed been carrying on with the wife of the accused, and it becomes increasingly obvious that he is going to be found guilty of murder. Perhaps recognising this, Ujīr Mān astonishes the court by suddenly changing his plea and confessing to the crime he has not committed:

> 'I am guilty, my lord, I did put an end to that adulterer. I did fire the gun simply to kill that wretch. I am prepared to go to prison.'
>
> For a moment, the whole court was stunned. His lawyer turned to the judge and said, 'My lord, I request a few days' adjournment. Because of what his wife has gone through, the prisoner is not in his right mind.'
>
> But Ujīr Mān interrupted, 'I have not gone mad, my lord. I certainly did kill him, and I've no regrets. Ha ha ha.'
>
> He began to laugh out loud (Rāī in Aryāl (ed.), 1979, p.98).

What Rāī wishes to convey, it seems, is that the old Gurkha has decided to accept imprisonment honourably, not for the crime of which he stands accused, but for the life of killing and violence he led before his retirement. Although the judgment of character inherent in this representation is basically critical, the author does credit the soldier with a kind of moral integrity.

The three examples described above are of course not the only works of fiction in Nepali in which the Gurkha soldier appears, but their representations of his character are quite typical of the way in which he is depicted in the genre. The soldiers in the stories by Koirālā and Rāī are neither evil nor immoral: they are, in a sense, somewhat romantic figures, set apart from the ordinary people of their communities by the nature of their experience. Pārijāt, on the other hand, seeks to depict the ex-soldier in a much less favourable light, but again he is represented more as a victim of circumstance than as someone whose behaviour is morally reprehensible. Thus it seems that the Gurkha in Nepali fiction tends to be a figure who attracts some criticism but is also deserving of sympathy and a certain amount of grudging admiration. The supposed guilt and pollution of the Gurkha which is hinted at in these works are characteristics which have been stressed more heavily in recent Nepali poetry.

The lāhure *in Nepali poetry*

Since the latter years of the Rāṇā regime, verse genres have remained the primary medium for the expression of social and political dissent in

Nepali literature, and the figure of the Gurkha soldier has appeared in several works by well-known poets. Perhaps the most thorough treatment of the theme of mercenary service in foreign armies is a minor epic by the Darjeeling poet Agam Singh Girī entitled *Yuddha ra Yoddhā (War and the Warrior,* 1970). Pradhan has suggested that this poem was inspired by a statement which he attributes to Subhas Chandra Bose: 'you can perhaps force a man to shoulder a rifle, but you can never make him fight to give his life for a cause which is not his own' (Pradhan, 1984, p.123). In this vein, Girī urges the departing soldiers,

Turn back, do not approach
The dreadfulness of war,
Turn back, do not uselessly sacrifice
Yourselves in its fires,
Your bravery graces your own land,
Your sacrifice is needed here (quoted in Pradhān, 1977, p.8).

The same sentiments are expressed by Bhūpi Sherchan in a poem entitled *To the Children of Partridges, Quails and Sacrificial Oxen* (*Tītarā, Baṭṭāī ra Bhakkūko Rāngokā Santānharūprati*). First, Sherchan characterises the soldiers as oxen offering themselves in a pointless sacrifice: he puns *Gorkhālī* with *goru khālī,* 'mere oxen':

Unselfishly they died,
Meaninglessly, quite pointlessly,
Partridges, quails, oxen to slaughter,
Adding their 'yes' to strangers' agreements,
Awaking to strangers' applause and slogans,
Drunk on the dregs of strangers' beer,
Crying 'the Gorkhalis have come'
But becoming merely oxen,
Tumbling headfirst into war (Sherchan, 1983, p.62).

Nepali poets also describe the returning soldier as unclean. This conception may hark back in part to the traditional belief that a man will lose his caste status if he crosses the 'black waters' to Europe. After his celebrated visit to Britain and France in 1850, even the great Jang Bahādur was obliged to undergo formal purification (Whelpton, 1983, p.289). On the other hand, it may reflect a pacifistic belief that war is in itself polluting, or a nationalistic view of men who fight for causes in which Nepal has no real interest. Mohan Himānshu Thāpā addresses a soldier returning to his home in Pokharā:

I wonder, brother *lāhure,*
Is there a speck of poison
In the food you are bringing,
Some noxious gas
In the cool breaths you breathe? (Thāpā, 1973, p.28).

In the concluding lines of the poem cited above, Sherchan suggests that the economic benefits which dead soldiers' families enjoy are also tainted and unclean:

It is lovely as it adorns your breast,
This decoration, this Victoria Cross,
But does it not emit sometimes
The rising stench of the corpse of your kin? (Sherchan, 1983, p.63).

Girī, too, urges the returning *lāhure* to leave his memories behind:

Do not tinge the dreaming moments,
Do not adorn the sacred memories
Of the pure Himalaya's steep slopes
With hot mud and blood
Shed in vengeance and murder,
With the stink of dead bodies:
Your memories are bloody, polluted (Pradhan, 1984, p.123).

This pollution is not only moral: by spending so long away from their homeland, soldiers serving in foreign armies are sometimes described as corrupted in a cultural sense. Some writers have conveyed this by sprinkling their military characters' speech with Hindi or Urdu vocabulary. A clear example of an ironic use of this device is found in a recent and celebrated poem by Mīnbahādur Bishtha:

So there's nothing in the hills
On which to pen a poem,
You could even say there's nothing there
For anyone to write.
It's like the soldiers always say,
Home for a few months' leave:
Sālā pahāḍmeṃ kyā hai?—
'What's in the bastard hills?' (Sharmā (ed.), 1983, p.323).

The soldiers' question, which is also the title of the poem, is phrased in a vulgar kind of Hindi, despised by modern nationalists for whom the purity of Nepali is an important marker of cultural identity, particularly since it sets them apart from India. Bishtha's poem also describes the degradation of the mountain environment which is forcing hillpeople to migrate to the plains. He suggests that young men who leave their homes to serve in foreign armies will always return with a contemptuous attitude toward their homeland.

Furthermore, there may be solid medical reasons, for which one might find parallels in many other cultures, for regarding the returning mercenaries as unclean or polluted. It is clear from two reports by the Sanitary Commissioner for the Government of India, filed in 1895 and 1900,[4] that Gurkhas serving in the British Indian Army were particu-

[4] My thanks to David Arnold for drawing my attention to these sources.

larly susceptible to venereal diseases, tuberculosis and typhoid.[5] The 1895 report notes a high incidence of secondary syphilis among Gurkhas: 'Those native troops that are serving in regions furthest away from their homes appear to be the most affected by venereal disease. The Gurkhas are the most conspicuous example of this' (p.66). Whatever the reasons may be, it is clear from this sample, which includes the most famous poems on this theme, that Nepali poets tend to pity, despise and resent the men of their country who enlist in foreign armies. Their treatments of this subject evince a more clear-cut and aggressive attitude to the *lāhure* than is apparent in Nepali fiction.

Context and motives

On the basis of the works to which I have referred above, it can be established that Nepali writers have attributed several distinct characteristics to the *lāhure*. Although often portrayed as a romantic figure, and envied for his freedom, he is also considered unpatriotic, because he fights in 'strangers'' wars (Sherchan), and socially irresponsible because he deserts his homeland (Koirālā). During his term of service abroad, he gains valuable experience of the outside world, and broadens his horizons immeasurably. But he may also become morally corrupt through possessing the power of life and death over weaker civilians (Pārijāt), or culturally alienated because he has forgotten his homeland and, to some extent, his language (Bishtha). When he returns home, he is feared and respected (Koirālā). But he may come bearing a burden of guilt (Rāī) or with an attitude of arrogance and contempt (Bishtha), and several writers consider him unclean or polluted (Girī, Sherchan, Thāpā).

Here we are confronted by an important question: of what relevance are the views of an intellectual elite, of which these writers may be said to be members, to mass public opinion in Nepal or, indeed, in any other country? Do the negative aspects of these portrayals of the *lāhure* reflect a view of him which is held by any significant proportion of the kingdom's population? One supposes not, since, if the issue of Gurkha recruitment has a controversial aspect nowadays it stems from the fact that Britain plans to *reduce* the number of men from Nepal employed in the British Army, and not because Nepal is felt to resent the continuation of the arrangement. On a recent visit to Nepal, the Queen sought to reassure the Nepal government that recruitment would not cease. Clearly, her words were not addressed to the writers and intellectual elite of the country, but to the central authorities, for whom the Gurkhas represent an important source of revenue, and to public opinion in the hill regions where service in the British army is seen as a grand old tra-

[5] The 1895 Report (p.63) compares the incidence of T.B. in Gurkha regiments (8.4 cases and 4.07 deaths per 1,000), with its incidence in the Bengal and Punjab commands (3.2 cases and 0.93 deaths.)

dition and an important opportunity for overseas experience and the improvement of one's economic status.

It is notable that none of these works attacks the validity or morality of the political arrangement which exists between Britain and Nepal; rather they address themselves to the consciences of the individuals who make use of it. There are no references to official policy here: the focus is on personal ethics. Furthermore, the view which is taken of the socially irresponsible character of the returning *lāhure* is not wholly borne out by the historical record. After both world wars, returning soldiers were in the vanguard of the emergent anti-Rāṇā movement, and Höfer (1978) has described a situation in the Dhading district of central Nepal where a group of ex-Gurkhas has achieved considerable success in the education and social emancipation of local Tamang communities.

What axes, then, do Nepali writers have to grind when they portray the *lāhure* in an unfavourable light? One suspects that a number of factors are at work. First, since the Nepali language and its literature have in recent years become important elements of an integrated national culture, Nepali writers are inherently nationalistic. Several of those quoted above, notably Bhūpi, Sherchan and Pārijāt, combine their instinctive nationalism with an avowedly Marxist approach which is at odds with national ideology. Second, they are all city-dwellers: indeed, all of the writers whose works have been cited here are residents of either Kathmandu or Darjeeling, although several have migrated to those towns from more remote regions. Their links with village Nepal, from which Gurkha recruits emanate, are therefore tenuous at best. One also suspects that a kind of prejudice might influence these writers' portrayals. If so, this is a prejudice based less on caste/ethnic differences (those quoted above include a Tamang, a Rai and a Thakali) than on an urban-rural class divide.

In general, nationalism and leftwing ideology probably grow more readily in a climate of literacy and relative prosperity. In rural areas, where life is an unremitting struggle, patriotic feeling may be outweighed by economic imperatives. One wonders whether the average *lāhure* would recognise himself in these descriptions. It seems unlikely that the Gurungs and Magars of the central hills, or the Rais and Limbus of the east, perceive any conflict between their Nepali patriotism and the tradition of service in foreign armies which has become an unquestioned way of life in many of their mountain villages.

If the difference between the views of the educated urban nationalist and those of the rural farmer's son is as great as one supposes it might be, what conclusions might be drawn from the somewhat censorious attitude adopted by most established writers to the returning *lāhure?* In a society which is primarily agrarian, it is inevitable that most 'modern' literature will be produced by intellectual groupings in urban centres, and that the philosophical attitudes apparent in much of this literature will not always reflect public opinion in rural areas. Since Nepali is the national language of Nepal, Nepali literature might justifiably be considered to be the kingdom's national literature. Of course, this literature contains much that is politically neutral: rhapsodic descriptions of natural beauty, love poetry and so on. But the process of development and modernisation which has occurred has inevitably resulted in a number of important writers adopting standpoints which are implicitly at odds with national ideology.

References

Annual Report of the Sanitary Commissioner with the Government of India, 1895 (Calcutta, 1896).

Annual Report of the Sanitary Commissioner with the Government of India, 1900 (Simla, 1902).

Aryāl, Bhairav (ed.), *Sājhā Kathā* (Kathmandu, 1979, 3rd ed.).

Bishop, Edward, *Better to Die. The story of the Gurkhas* (London, 1976).

Blaikie, Cameron, Seddon, *Nepal in Crisis* (Oxford, 1980).

Bolt, David, *Gurkhas* (London, 1967).

Farwell, Byron, *The Gurkhas* (London, 1984)

Forbes, Duncan, *Johnny Gurkha* (London, 1964).

Hodgson, Brian Houghton, 'Origin and classification of the military tribes of Nepal', *Journal of the Asiatic Society of Bengal* vol. 17 (1833).

Höfer, Andras, 'A new rural elite in central Nepal', in Fisher (ed.), *Himalayan Anthropology* (Paris and the Hague, 1978).

James, Harold and Shiel-Small, Denis, *A Pride of Gurkhas* ((London, 1975).

Koirālā, Bishweshwar Prasād, 'Sipāhī' in *Kathā Kusum* (Darjeeling, 1938).

Marks, J.M., *Ayo Gurkha!* (London, 1971).

Mojumdar, Kanchanmoy, *Anglo-Nepalese Relations in the Nineteenth Century* (Calcutta, 1973).

Pārijāt, *Shirīshko Phūl* (2nd ed., Biratnagar, 1965).

Pārijāt, Interview in *Vedanā* , 15, 3/4 (Kathmandu, 1987).

Pradhan, Kumar, *A History of Nepali Literature* (New Delhi, 1984).

Pradhān, Shiva, *Girīko Bhāvabhūmi 'Yuddha ra Yoddhā'* (Kathmandu, 1977).

Rāī, Shivakumār, 'Jyānamārā?' in Bhairava Aryāl (ed.), *Sājhā Kathā* (Kathmandu, 1979; 1st ed. 1968).

Rāṇā, Yoga Bikram Jang, *Vajiristhānko Yātrā* (Bombay, 1918).

Seddon, David, *Nepal—a state of poverty* (New Delhi, 1987).

Sharmā, Tārānāth, *Samasāmayik Sājhā Kavitā* (Kathmandu, 1983).

Sherchan, Bhūpi, *Ghumne Mechmāthi Andho Mānchhe* (Kathmandu, 1983; 1st ed. 1969).

Smith, E.D., *Britain's Brigade of Gurkhas* (London, 1973).

Thāpā, Amar Singh and Sardār Bahādur (trans.), *Ratan Singh Gurungko Outpostko Kathā* (Banaras, 1914).

Thāpā, Mohan Himānshu, *Khukurimāthi Ek Chauṭā Bādal* (Kathmandu, 1973).
The Times: 'Nepal: a special report', 14 April 1973.
Turner, Ralph Lilley, *A Comparative and Etymological Dictionary of the Nepali Language* (New Delhi, 1980; 1st ed. 1931).
Whelpton, John, *Jang Bahadur in Europe* (Kathmandu, 1983).

Further Reading

Caplan, Lionel, 'Bravest of the brave: representations of "the Gurkha" in British military writings', *Modern Asian Studies* 25 (1991), pp.571-97.
Hutt, Michael, *Himalayan Voices. An introduction to modern Nepali literature* (Berkeley, 1991).

MILTON AND MADHUSUDAN[1]

William Radice

Michael Madhusudan Datta (1824-73) is regarded as the founder of modern Bengali poetry and drama. As a student at Hindu College in Calcutta, he converted to Christianity, and had ambitions as a poet in English. Ostracised by his family, he worked as a teacher and journalist in Madras, and married a woman of English parentage. He deserted her for another English woman, Henrietta White, the daughter of a colleague, and returned with her to Calcutta, achieving eminence as a Bengali writer in the 1860s. His major work, the epic poem Meghnād-badh Kābya, *is based on the* Rāmāyaṇa *but influenced by Homer, Virgil, Dante and Milton. Later Madhusudan spent six years in Europe, qualifying as a barrister at Gray's Inn. Alcoholism and extravagance, however, got the better of him when he returned to Calcutta, and he died a broken man. This essay considers whether Madhusudan indeed deserves to be known as 'the Milton of Bengal'.*

Michael Madhusudan Datta (1824-73) was not as great a poet as John Milton. As an Englishman, I can say this without fear of apparent condescension, for Madhusudan himself would have agreed. In his flamboyant English letters, we find that the only limit to his ambition and self-confidence was set by Milton. After the publication, in 1861, of the first two books of *Meghnād-badh Kābya,* he wrote to his friend Rajnarayan Basu:

> The Poem is rising into splendid popularity. Some say it is better than Milton—but that is all bosh—nothing can be better than Milton; many say it licks Kalidasa; I have no objection to that. I don't think it impossible to equal Virgil, Kalidasa and Tasso. Though glorious, still they are mortal poets; Milton is divine.[2]

Anyone making a careful comparison between *Meghnād-badh Kābya* and *Paradise Lost* will find as much to divide the two poems as to unite them. Madhusudan is, for a start, much easier to read than Milton. Younger readers in Bengal find him taxing: the narrator of Tagore's story *Kaṅkāl* ('Skeleton'), for example, recalls with distaste 'studying *Meghnād-badh Kābya* with a Pandit, and anatomy with a student from the Campbell Medical School. Our guardian wanted us to become

[1] First published in G.R. Taneja (ed.), *R.K. Das Gupta Festschrift* (New Delhi, 1993).

[2] Kshetra Gupta, *Kabi Madhusūdan o tā̃r Patrābalī* (Calcutta, 1963), p. 146. Hereafter 'KG'.

instant experts in all fields of learning'. But once one is used to Madhusudan's idiosyncratic, Sanskritic vocabulary, or his famous fondness for making verbs out of nouns, his Bengali verse is as racy as his English prose. There is no Miltonic intricacy or ambiguity of syntax; no allusions beyond what the most basic knowledge of the *Mahābhārata* and *Rāmāyaṇa* will supply; no abstruse dependence on geography, history, astronomy or theology.

In what sense, then, is Madhusudan justifiably known as 'the Milton of Bengal', other than for writing a literary epic influenced by Western classical models, for inventing Bengali *amitrākṣar* (blank verse), and for admiring Milton so much that he named his son by Henrietta White after him?[3] Many of the qualities admired by readers as Miltonic—grandeur of style, elevation of sentiment, cosmic breadth—derive as much from the Indian epic tradition as the European. The 'Milton of Bengal' label may reflect no more than a nineteenth-century Bengali desire to match up to English writers: so that Bankimchandra Chatterjee is 'the Scott of Bengal', Mukundaram Chakravarti is 'the Chaucer of Bengal' and so on.

Madhusudan is thought of as a learned poet, *bahu-pāṭhī,* as opposed to the *svabhāb-kabi* ('natural poet') Rabindranath. Undoubtedly he had a tremendous appetite for languages, grappling with Sanskrit, Greek, Latin and Italian epic poetry in the original. He learnt French very well: contemporaries attest that he and Henrietta often spoke French to each other in their house in Calcutta after five years in Europe. With regard to some of his other linguistic claims (Tamil and Telegu when he was in Madras, German when he was in Europe), one feels a little sceptical: but rather than guessing at how well he actually knew all these languages, it is important to define the kind of relationship he had with the poems he read. He was not learned as Milton was learned. His mind was not replete with the exact and disciplined command of Scripture and the Classics that Milton possessed. Whereas Milton explored the Aonian mount with extraordinary patience and thoroughness before allowing his Christian inspiration to soar above it, Madhusudan, one feels, rushed up its slopes with reckless zest. He loved Milton's poetry rather as Keats fell for Chapman's Homer; *Paradise Lost* was a 'new planet' to him, an object of wonder, never a world that he charted with precision.

I propose, in this essay, to look at *Meghnād-badh Kābya* for indications as to why Madhusudan loved Milton so much. My assumption is that if one poet loves another, this is bound to be reflected in his writing in ways both vaguer and more subtle than any obvious influence or imitation.

[3] Henrietta's name and parentage have now been conclusively established. See Ghulam Murshid's article in *Deś* 56, 17 (25 February 1989).

1. *Mazes intricate*

For those who can respond to it, the best description of the beauty of Milton's blank verse is found in Raphael's lines on the music of the spheres:

> mazes intricate,
> Eccentric, intervolved, yet regular
> Then most, when most irregular they seem.[4]

Madhusudan's verse sentences are seldom as long or complex as Milton's, and his lines have a lighter, faster movement. But as in Milton, an intoxicating music emerges from constant variation and irregularity. Regularity is provided by a fixed number of syllables in the line—fourteen, as in medieval Bengali *payār*; but unlike Milton's blank verse, it is very difficult to divide Madhusudan's line into metrical feet. I do not believe that this is because Bengali is more lightly stressed than English, for the *payār* line falls very easily into eight trochaic feet. Nor is his verse quantitative. Madhusudan writes in a letter of how 'the melody of a line is improved when the 8th syllable is made long', preferring *sucārutārā* to *tārākuntalā* 'because the double syllable *-nta-* mars the strength of *-lā*';[5] but I am not convinced that he was clear in his mind about the (elusive) distinction between short and long syllables in Bengali. The phrasing of the verse—the placing of pauses—was far more important to him than its metre. He wrote to Rajnarayan:

> You want me to explain my system of versification for the conversion of your sceptical friends. I am sure there is very little in the system to explain; our language, as regards the doctrine of accent and quantity, is an 'apostate', that is to say, it cares as much for them as I do for the blessing of our Family-Priest! If your friends know English, let them read the Paradise-Lost, and they will find how the verse in which the Bengali poetaster writes is constructed. Let your friends guide their voices by the pause (as in the English blank verse) and they will soon swear that this is the noblest measure in the language.[6]

In another letter he gives examples of how the *yati* (caesura) 'instead of being confined to the eighth syllable' (as in *payār*) can come almost anywhere in the line.[7]

In his second, recantatory essay on Milton, T. S. Eliot spoke of 'the peculiar feeling, almost a physical sensation of a breathless leap, communicated by Milton's long periods'.[8] I am sure that Madhusudan responded to this: in the Invocation that opens *Meghnād-badh Kābya*,

[4] *Paradise Lost*, V. 622-4.
[5] KG, p.155.
[6] KG, pp. 133-4.
[7] KG, p.143.
[8] 'Milton II', *On Poetry and Poets* (1957), quoted by Christopher Ricks in *Milton's Grand Style* (Oxford, 1963), p.28.

the imperative '*kaha, he debi*' falls with something of the same emphasis in his third line as Milton's 'Sing heavenly Muse' in his sixth. But the grammar of Madhusudan's style does not permit much complexity of syntax, and I suspect that it was sheer *enjambement*, the running over of a line to a punctuation point somewhere in the next, that thrilled him. He disliked end-stopped rhymed verse, writing to Keshabchandra Gangopadhyay: 'A *true* poet will always succeed best in Blank verse as a bad one in Rhyme. In China, they confine the feet of their women in iron-shoes. What is the result? Lameness!'[9] This echoes Milton's strictures on 'the troublesome and modern bondage of rhyming', and a sonnet on the subject ends with the same image of foot-binding in China. The sonnet is, of course, rhymed, but the lines run on in a way that was second nature to Madhusudan:

baṛai niṣṭhur āmi bhābi tāre mane,
lo bhāṣā, pīṛite tomā gaṛila ye āge
mitrākṣar-rūp beṛi! [10]

The sensitive reader of Madhusudan has to feel the *frisson* that he himself would have felt in writing, say, the opening of Book IV of *Meghnād-badh Kābya*:

nami āmi, kabi-guru, taba padāmbuje,
bālmīki![11]

The placing of '*bālmīki*', after a sequence of phrases that 'ascend' both in length and idea, matches the *élan* of Madhusudan's recollection and invocation of Valmiki here. The 'breathless leaps' of Madhusudan's verse are not over such wide gulfs as Milton's: they have a *tablā*-like energy, a boisterous virtuosity that inspires the reader to gasp '*vāḥ! vāḥ!*' rather than suspend his breath in wonder. But their musical irregularity amply indicates why Madhusudan revelled so in Milton's blank verse.

2. *e mor sundarī purī*

Never was a long poem summed up more completely in its title than *Paradise Lost*. Its central image, springing to mind whenever one thinks of the poem, is 'delicious Paradise' herself, which Satan gazes on with such envy; and its central tragic event is the loss of that Paradise. At the centre of *Meghnād-badh Kābya* is an equally haunting image of beauty:

mari! yathā sur-pure!—
laṅkār bibhab yata, ke pāre barṇite—

[9] KG, pp. 161-2.
[10] *Caturddaśpadī Kabitābalī*, No. 97. ('I think of his mind as very cruel, O Language, he who distresses you by first making shackles of rhyme.')
[11] 'I bow, Master Poet, to your lotus-feet, Valmiki!'

deb-lobh, daityakul-mātsarya? ke pāre
gaṇite sāgare ratna, nakṣatra ākāśe?[12]

These lines from Book VI not only emphasise the beauties described immediately before—Lanka's golden palaces, her temples, gardens, lakes and fountains, her stables and armouries, her 'fire-coloured chariots' and theatres 'studded with jewels'; they also resonate with all the other descriptions of Lanka in the poem. When I first started reading *Meghnād-badh Kābya* more than fifteen years ago, it was lines like these from Book I that won my heart, and which I tried to translate:

Captivating Lanka,
Crowned with golden palaces, sparkled all around: rows of gleaming mansions,
Set amidst flower-groves; lotus-spread lakes; brilliant silver fountains;
Trees, blooms as gorgeous to the eye as a girl's youthfulness; diamond-towered temples;
Multi-coloured shops, laden with many gems: as if the world had gathered,
As a divine offering, its varied treasures, and placed them at your feet,
O lovely Lanka, world's desire, you abode of joy.[13]

Lanka is not 'a happy rural seat of various view': her irridescent beauties are in some ways closer to Milton's Heaven than to Eden, to the 'opal towers and battlements adorned/Of living sapphire' seen from afar by Satan at the end of Book II of *Paradise Lost.* But just as Milton had to build up an image of the beauties of Paradise so as to emphasise the tragedy of their loss, it is equally essential to Madhusudan's purpose that 'golden Lanka' should be powerfully evoked in his readers' minds, and be poignantly associated with loss. The lines from Book I above come when Ravana, grief-stricken at the death of his son Birbahu, climbs on to the battlements of his palace to survey the city; the lines from Book VI come as Lakshman and Bibhishan enter Lanka by stealth, on their way to kill Meghnad.

Is it mere coincidence that they should be compared several times to a snake? Rendered invisible by Mayadevi, they are compared, as they circumvent the Rakshasa guards, to 'a snake entering flowers by trickery' (*kauśale*).[14] When Meghnad, interrupted while at worship, faces Lakshman and realises with horror who he is and what he intends, he is 'like a wayfarer, when he suddenly sees a serpent on the path with raised hood, and is paralysed with fear'.[15] When he defies Lakshman and fights with him, he cries, 'If a snake enters Garuda's nest, does it

[12] *Meghnād-badh Kābya,* VI. 337-340. ('Ah! What a heavenly city! Who can describe all Lanka's glories, the desire of the gods, the envy of the demons? Who can count the jewels in the sea, the stars in the sky?')

[13] Ibid., I. 207-17.

[14] Ibid., VI. 315.

[15] Ibid., VI. 434-6.

ever return to its own hole, O sinner?' (*pāmar*).[16] Bibhishan, shamed by his own treachery, is 'like a snake brought low' (*namraśiraḥ*).[17] There is no Eve, no Tree of Knowledge, no 'guileful tempter'; but there is most assuredly a Fall, Meghnad's fall, leading to Lanka's fall. When Eve eats the apple:

Earth felt the wound, and nature from her seat
Sighing through all her works gave signs of woe,
That all was lost.

When Meghnad falls:

tharathari kā̃pilā basudhā;
garjjilā uthali sindhu; bhairab-ārabe
sahasā pūrila biśva! [18]

Ravana's golden crown slips from his head; Pramila (Meghnad's wife), forgetting herself, commits the deeply inauspicious act of rubbing her *sindur-bindu* from her forehead. All in all, *Paradise Lost* would not be inappropriate as a subtitle to *Meghnad-badh Kābya.*

3. *pāp-pūrṇa svarṇa laṅkā*

When Bibhishan, 'pale-faced with shame', answers Meghnad's charges of betrayal, he uses arguments that the reader of *Meghnād-badh Kābya* encounters frequently throughout the poem:

It is not my fault, *batas*; you are wrong to berate me.
The King of Golden Lanka is sinking through his own sinful actions, alas, sinking by himself!
The gods are always opposed to sin; and now the city of Lanka is full of sin; like the earth at the time of its destruction,
Lanka is drowning in a sea of death![19]

'*phal*' is as much a key-word in *Meghnaḍ-badh Kābya* as 'fruit' in *Paradise Lost;* but whereas the 'fruit' of Eve's sin comes with the plucking and eating of the forbidden fruit itself, Meghnad's fall is the inevitable fruit of Ravana's sinful abduction of Sita. One by one, the gods withdraw their protection, bowing to the inevitability of *karmaphal.* Kamaladevi, *rāj-lakṣmī* of the Rakshasas is the first: in Book I she announces to the sea-nymph Murala that she is leaving Lanka and returning to heaven: the King of Lanka has brought his downfall on to himself: *nij-doṣe maje rājā laṅkā-adhipati...pāpe pūrṇa svarṇa-laṅkāprāktaner phal tvarā phalibe e pure.*[20] The important thing

[16] Ibid., VI. 499-501.
[17] Ibid., VI. 568.
[18] Ibid., VI. 625-7. ('The earth trembled; the sea surged and roared; the world was suddenly filled with an awesome sound!')
[19] Ibid., VI.. 571-6.
[20] Ibid., I. 604, 607, 612. ('The King of Lanka is drowning through his own

is to save Rama from the might of Meghnad. Indra in Book II needs no persuading: he is himself terrified of 'Indrajit' (Meghnad), having once been vanquished by him. Indra and Shachi go to mount Kailasa to enlist the support of Shiva, who is currently engaged in *tapas*. Durga at first says that Shiva is too attached to Ravana to be persuaded, but she quickly accepts the moral argument, wakes up Shiva with the help of Madana, and tells him that he too must bow to the inevitable: *nij karma-phale maje duṣṭamati...hāy, debi, debe ki mānabe, kothā hena sādhya rodhe prāktaner gati?* [21] Despite his attachment to Ravana, Shiva gives in at once; Indra is dispatched to Maya, who gives him the weapons that Shiva gave Kartikeya to kill the demon Taraka. The charioteer Chitaratha delivers the weapons to Rama and Lakshman.

Adam and Eve were given freedom to obey or not, but the gods have not 'left free' Meghnad's will: he never has a chance. In the battle in Book VII, Shiva, out of sympathy for Ravana, gives him specially powerful *rudra-tej* , so that Lakshman is slain; but persuaded by Durga, he arranges for Rama (in the famously Virgilian Book VIII) to descend to *yama-purī* to receive from his dead father Dasharatha instructions for finding the magic herb that will revive Lakshman. Shiva's sympathy for Meghnad and Ravana never leaves him totally: Mount Kailasa trembles with his anger as he watches Ravana grieving over Meghnad's funeral pyre. 'You know how I loved Meghnad,' he says to Durga, but he accepts her insistence that Meghnad died *bidhir bidhāne* ('through the edict of fate'), and he forgives Rama and Lakshman for killing him.

Truly, *Meghnād-badh Kābya* is driven by a relentless moral mechanism, derived partly from the Indian conception of *karma-phal*, but also perhaps from Christianity. Madhusudan was never a devout Christian; his conversion in 1843 was influenced primarily by a desire to evade an orthodox arranged marriage and to improve his chances of visiting 'Albion's distant shore'.[22] But he cannot have emerged from four years at Bishop's College (which was essentially a seminary for Anglican priests) entirely unaffected: and the Christianity he was taught there was far more steeped in notions of sin, guilt, hell, and divine retribution than is customary today. The lurid descriptions of the sinners in Hell in Book VIII are not there just as conventional trappings: they stem from the same feelings as are found in his autobiographical poem *ātma-bilāp*, or in *paralok* , one of the hundred or so sonnets that Madhusudan wrote during his sojourn in Europe:

---

fault...Golden Lanka is full of sin.... The fruits of past actions will ripen in this city.')

[21] Ibid., II. 431, 433-4. ('The wicked one is drowning as a result of his actions.... Alas, goddess, where is there the power in gods or men to stop the workings of fate?')

[22] English poem No. 8, *Madhusūdan Racanābalī* (Sahitya Samsad, Calcutta, 1965), p.438.

Into the dawn sun's radiant sea of light
The star of morning sinks her smiling fire;
And flowers there are whose swelling buds desire,
And greet with blooming love, approaching Night;
And eager are the streams that rush to reach
Joyous Nirvana at the ocean's feet—
Likewise mortality receives the sweet
Jewel of immortal life (the Scriptures teach)
If we have faith. Ah Faith, to what false gain
Does man forget you, choose the path of sin?
What lures prevail on him to sever
Your golden boat, to let the windswept main
Of the world drag her down? Willing to win
Two paltry days of life, to die forever?[23]

In *Meghnād-badh Kābya* Madhusudan certainly never set out 'to justify the ways of God to men', but his strong sense of a morally driven *bidhi* is a further link with Milton. When he wrote to Rajnarayan, 'Good Blank Verse should be sonorous and the best writer of Blank Verse in English is the *toughest* of poets—I mean old John Milton!'[24] I suspect he was referring not only to Milton's syntactic intricacy but to his moral toughness. For all his wit and exuberance, there is an element of 'toughness' in Madhusudan too.

4. *Tremendous literary rebel*

But what *is* the essential morality of *Meghnād-badh Kābya*? Any serious reader of the poem must wrestle with this question, and it is part of Madhusudan's greatness and complexity as an epic poet that the question is not easy to answer. An initial answer might be: the morality of the poem is that of *karmaphal*. Ravana commits a sin by abducting Sita, and pays the price for it. Madhusudan's sympathies, on the other hand, are with the Rakshasas. Lanka is an image of power and glory; her destruction is tragic; Meghnad is the hero. Like Shiva at the end of the poem, Madhusudan may accept the moral justice of what has happened, but he never lets us forget *kata bhālabāsi naikaṣeya-śūre āmi*,[25] and famous comments in the letters convey the same:

He was a noble fellow, and but for that scoundrel Bivishan, would have kicked the monkey-army into the sea.[26]

People here grumble and say that the heart of the Poet in *Meghnad* is with the

[23] *Caturddaśpadī Kabitābalī*, No. 45. (My translation. 'Faith' may not be an exact translation of '*dharma*', but '*pāp*' is definitely 'sin'.)

[24] KG, p.129.

[25] *Meghnād-badh Kābya*, IX. 417-18. ('How I love the valiant son of Nikasha [Ravana]!')

[26] KG, pp.136-7.

Rakhasas. And that is the real truth. I despise Ram and his rabble; but the idea of Ravan, elevates and kindles my imagination; he was a grand fellow.[27]

This simple analysis, however, is inadequate in both its aspects: *karmaphal* is not the only morality; Madhusudan's sympathies are not confined to the Rakshasas.

Ravana, like the gods, often uses the word for sin (*pāp*), but unlike them he does not know what sin he has committed: to him, *bidhi* is inexplicable Fate, not a moral law. Thus, grieving over Birbahu's death in Book I, he cries:

ki pāpe hārānu āmi tomā-hena dhane?
ki pāp dekhiyā mor, re dārun bidhi,
harili e dhan tui? [28]

Similarly, when Meghnad faces death in Book VI, he cries:

ki pāpe bidhātā
dilen e tāp dāse, bujhiba kemane?[29]

Dinanath Sanyal, editor of *Meghnād-badh Kābya,* comments: 'Meghnad has no conception that Ravana's abduction of Sita was a grievous sin, because abducting others' wives is not contrary to Rakshasa *dharma*'.[30] When Lakshman is revived at the beginning of Book IX, Ravana is still entirely unaware of any personal fault: 'Who can analyse the edicts of Fate (*bidhir bidhi*),' he says. 'It is because my fortune is at fault (*mama bhāgya-doṣe*) that Death has forgotten his proper *dharma* today.'[31]

When Meghnad is killed by Lakshman in Book VI, it is Lakshman who stands condemned morally, not only by Meghnad, but also, surely, by the poet: for killing him *kauśale* ('by a trick'), *anyāy samare* ('in unfair combat'); for being a *bīr-kul-glāni* ('defiler of the warrior race'). Bibhishan, too, has mortally offended against the *kṣatriya* warrior-code, the *dharma* of the Rakshasas, by betraying his kin and associating with *adham* ('low-born') Rama.

Madhusudan was a self-confessed 'tremendous literary rebel',[32] who broke all the conventions of medieval Bengali verse, who in his free use of Sanskrit diction and sources deliberately set out to 'turn away those beggars or pretenders, whom they call Pandits but whom I call

[27] KG, p.153.

[28] *Meghnād-badh Kābya,* I. 86-8. ('For what sin have I lost treasure such as you? Seeing what sin in me, O harsh Fate, have you taken this treasure?')

[29] Ibid., VI. 650-1. ('For what sin has God given his servant this torment—how shall I understand?')

[30] Dinanath Sanyal, (ed.), *Meghnād-badh Kābya* (2nd ed., Calcutta, 1929), pp.434-5.

[31] *Meghnād-badh Kābya,* IX. 29,32-3.

[32] KG, p.135.

barren rascals!'[33] But nothing he did in literature or life was more audacious than his presentation of Meghnad's death, the centre-piece of the poem. The *kauśal* by which he is killed is not to be found in either Valmiki or the medieval Bengali *Rāmāyaṇa* of Krittibas. In both, Lakshman has to attack Meghnad before he completes his sacrifice to Agni, as this will make him invincible; but there is no suggestion that he is unarmed or unaccompanied. When Lakshman fights with him, their respective armies join in, and a tremendous battle develops. In *Meghnād-badh Kābya*, Meghnad is entirely alone in the *nikumbhilā-yajñāgār.* In resisting Lakshman, he is forced to use sacred *pūjā-* vessels as weapons. The dastardly tactics of Lakshman and Bibhishan, aided by Mayadevi and the other gods, not only engage sympathy for the Rakshasas, they run counter to the entire morality of *karmaphal.*

It seems to me impossible to resolve this contradiction. When Rama agrees to Ravana's request, in Book IX, for seven days respite from battle so that Meghnad's funeral rites can be performed, the reason he gives—given the way Meghnad was killed—is breathtaking: *dharma-karme rata jane kabhu nā prahāre dhārmik* ('The righteous man never strikes people engaged in righteous acts').[34]

If Rama were consistently unappealing as a character, we could take this as nauseating hypocrisy; but in his sympathies, too, Madhusudan is tantalizingly complex. Rama is not unattractive: he has a very human capacity for doubt and uncertainty, and constantly depends on encouragement from Lakshman and Bibhishan. One of the finest passages of *bilāp* ('lament') is at the beginning of Book VIII, when Rama grieves over the lifeless body of Lakshman. When Madhusudan, in desperate financial straits, wrote to Ishvarchandra Vidyasagar from France in 1864, it was Rama he quoted:

> I hope I shall not have to cry out with Ram in my poem of Meghanada,
> *bṛthā, he jaladhi, āmi bā̃dhinu tomāre.*
> My heart is full of bitterness, rage and despair.[35]

In all this complexity and ambiguity of attitude, is Milton again a subtle model? Madhusudan did not, of course, have access to the researches of Chistopher Hill and others on Milton's heresies, and there is no evidence that he was interested in Milton's involvement in the English Revolution. But I think he perceived the revolutionary audacity of Milton's 'vast design', the contradictions that arose from so personal a treatment of sacred material:

> Like his own Satan, he is full of the loftiest thoughts, but has little or nothing that may be called amiable. He elevates the mind of the reader to a most

33 KG, p.136.
34 *Meghnād-badh Kābya*, IX. 101-2.
35 KG, p.208: 'In vain, O ocean, I bound you'.

astonishing height, but he never touches the heart. And what is the consquence? He has a glorious name but few readers. He is Satan himself. We acknowledge him to belong to a far superior order of brings; but we never feel for him. We hear the sound of his ethereal voice with awe and trembling. His is the roar of a lion in the silent forest.[36]

This is not professional criticism, and only embraces a fraction of the ways in which *Meghnād-badh Kābya* connects with *Paradise Lost*. But I sense in these remarks, on the one hand admiration that Milton could take the basics of Christian tradition and present them in so complex and ambiguous a way that readers never cease to argue about his attitude to his protagonists; on the other anguished awareness that the poet who does this, as Madhusudan himself did in his epic, sets himself apart, limits his audience, condemns himself to being 'a proud, silent, lonely man of song',[37] who must live in hope that his inspiration will, in the future, 'fit audience find, though few'.

5. *Adventurous Eve*

The line most often quoted from *Paradise Lost* when referring to Adam and Eve's marriage and Milton's own attitude to marriage is: 'He for God only, she for God in him'.[38] In fact, of course, serious biographical research and careful reading of Milton's divorce pamphlets reveal that he was far from advocating the total subordination of women, seeing marriage as a contract based on mutual consent, whose purpose was mutual solace. The most moving aspect of *Paradise Lost* is the relationship between Adam and Eve. Her freedom to stray, her intelligence, her remorse, Adam's 'comiseration'—none of these would be possible without the underlying morality of reasonableness and compassion expressed by Raphael in his advice to Adam at the end of Book VIII:

What higher in her society thou find'st
Attractive, human, rational, love still;
In loving thou dost well, in passion not,
Wherein true love consists not; love refines
The thoughts, and heart enlarges, hath his seat
In reason, and is judicious, is the scale
By which to heavenly love thou mayst ascend,
Not sunk in carnal pleasyre, for which cause
Among the beasts no mate for thee was found.[39]

In orthodox theological and matrimonial terms, Adam is blamed for not exerting sufficient control over Eve ('Thus is shall befall/Him who to

[36] KG, p.151.
[37] KG, p.139.
[38] *Paradise Lost,* IV. 299.
[39] Ibid., VIII. 586-92.

worth in women overtrusting/Lets her will rule...'[40]); but had he done so, he would surely have lacked the humanity to forgive her and share her penitence.

A wife who followed to the letter the principle 'He for God only, she for God in him' would be a Sita, not an Eve. Sita features in Book IV of *Meghnād-badh Kābya*, where, confined to the *aśok-kānan*, she tells her tale of woe to Bibhishan's wife Sarama. This is somewhat extraneous to the main action, but clearly Madhusudan could not resist the opportunity to wallow in tender *karuṇ-rasa*, writing to Rajnarayan: 'Perhaps the episode of Sita's abduction (Fourth Book) should not have been admitted since it is scarcely connected with the progress of the Fable. But would you willingly part with it?'[41] Sita is portrayed in wholly conventional terms. When Ravana fights with Jatayu, she faints and dreams of her rescue by Rama: she sees him before her like the rising sun and rushes to embrace his feet—at which moment she wakes. Dinanath Syanal approvingly comments that this is a mark of her beautiful nature ('*iha ati sundar svabhābokti*').[42]

Other types of conventional womanhood appear in *meghnād-badh kābya* : Ravana's distraught wife Chitrangada in Book I; Meghnad's anxious mother Mandadari in Book V; Sarama the devoted *sakhi* in Book IV. But the heroine of the poem, the character who comes closest to Madhusudan's ideal of heroic womanhood, is Meghnad's wife Pramila.

She is not 'adventurous' as Eve is; but the adjective could nonetheless be fittingly applied to her. One of the most splendid passages in the poem is in Book III, when she arrives at Rama's camp with her Amazon army, and challenges him to let her through so that she can find Meghnad in Lanka. Her beauty and defiance amaze Rama and his allies, and she passes through their ranks with magnificent *éclat* to make a tumultuous and triumphant entry into the city. Madhusudan builds up his effect not only by describing Parmila herself, but by giving her companions such as her messenger Nrimundalani, who in forging through Rama's army is compared to a ship:

yathā garutmatī tarī
taraṅga-nikāre raṅge kari abahelā,
akūl-sāgar-jale bhāse ekākinī![43]

The simile is reminiscent of Madhusudan's sonnet No. 77, *sāgare tari*, where the waves part to applaud a dream-ship progressing through them like a noblewoman through a crowd. The power and eroticism of

[40] Ibid., IX. 1182-4.
[41] KG, p.148.
[42] Sanyal, *Meghnād-badh Kābya*, p.304.
[43] *Meghnād-badh Kābya*, III. 250-2. ('As a winged ship, spurning the enmity of the waves, floats alone on the waters of the boundless sea!')

his portrait of Pramila is developed further in Book V, where Meghnad's beautiful dawn song to her as they wake is profoundly reminiscent of the opening of Book V of *Paradise Lost.* If one were to pick out a place where the seventeenth-century English epic and the nineteenth-century Bengali epic 'touch', it would be here. The same ecstasy and lyricism are there, and the same irony, too, as Meghnad and Pramila are woken by the birdsong that celebrates Mayadevi's fatal instructions to Lakshman, while Adam and Eve's joy is overshadowed by their imminent Fall. In *Paradise Lost*, we have:

then with voice
Mild, as when Zephysrus on Flora breathes,
Her hand soft touching, whispered thus. Awake
My fairest, my espoused, my latest found,
Heaven's last best gift, my ever new delight,
Awake, the morning shines, and the fresh field
Calls us.[44]

In *Meghnād-badh Kābya* :

Taking Pramila's lotus-hand in his lotus hand, the warrior, with soft voice,
Ah! like a bee buzzing in the ear of a lily its mysterious message of love, spoke
(Lovingly kissing her closed eyes)—'The birds are gently calling you, O lovely one,
Because you are like the golden dawn! Open, my love,
Your closed eyes! Awake, my eternal joy!
My heart is a jewel that only glitters in sunlight, dear wife, and you are an image of the sun....?[45]

The poems touch, then draw apart, for Pramila's role in the epic is not equivalent to Eve's in any precise sense. It might be more apposite to look to Madhusudan's contemporary Wagner than to Milton: to compare her *sati* with Brünnhilde's immolation at the end of *Götterdämmerung*. But there is more than enough in her unsubmissive nature to suggest that Madhusudan would have appreciated Milton's Eve.

He would also, in his personal life, have sympathized with Milton's doctrines on divorce. The biographical record is too scanty for us to form impressions of the personalities of his wife Rebecca or his *sahacārinī* Henrietta; but in basing his relationships on courtship, and in looking to Englishwomen for a companionship better educated than could be found in Bengali society, he allied himself with Milton. The opinions he expressed in a student prize essay 'On the Importance of Educating Hindu Females' (1842) are not so different from Raphael's:

The happiness of a man who has an enlightened partner is quite complete. In India, I may say in all the Oriental countries, women are looked upon as created

[44] *Paradise Lost,* V. 15-21.
[45] *Meghnād-badh Kābya,* V. 373-81.

merely to contribute to the gratification of the animal appetites of men. This brutal misconception of the design of the Almighty is the source of much misery to the fair sex, because it not only makes them appear as of inferior mental endowments, but no better than a sort of speaking brute. The people of this country do not know the pleasures of domestic life, and indeed they cannot know, until civilization shows them the way to it.[46]

Madhusudan, like Milton, was as 'adventurous' in his personal life as in his song, preferring Pramila to Sita every time.

6. *Farewell hope*

Paradise Lost is a Christian poem, but unlike the *Divina Commedia* of Dante it does not seem to demand Christian conviction in its readers for its glories to be fully appreciated. This is because its dominant mode is tragic, not ecstatic. Although Milton assures his readers, through the words of the archangel Michael to Adam, that God 'to his own a Comforter will send,/The promise of the Father',[47] it is the tragedy of the Fall, of Adam and Eve leaving Paradise to take their solitary way in the real, fallen world, that stays with us at the end. Madhusudan set out in *Meghnād-badh Kābya* to write an epic tragedy: he looked to Western epic and dramatic models not only for their formal disciplines and dramatic shape, but for their tragic power, which he valued for being essentially true to life. His own life had tragic, self-destructive aspects to it, as he himself lamented in his *ātma-bilāp*. He responded with delight to the romance and lyricism of Indian literature, but found it lacking in tragic realism. He wrote to Keshab Gangopadhyay:

> I must tell you, my dear G., what, I dare say you will allow at least to some extent, *viz,* that we Asiatics are of a more romantic turn of mind than our European neighbours. Look at the splendid Shakespearean Drama. If you leave out the Midsummer Night's Dream, Romeo and Juliet and perhaps one or two more, what play would deserve the name of *Romantic*? Romantic in the sense in which Sacoontala is Romantic? In the great European Drama you have the stern realities of life, lofty passion, and heroism of sentiment. With us it is all softness, all romance. We forget the world of reality and dream of Fairylands.[48]

In a letter to Rajnarayan Basu he berates the poet Rangalal Banerjee for his taste in poetry:

> Byron, Moore and Scott form the highest Heaven of poetry in his estimation. I wish he would travel further. He would then find what 'hills peep o'er hills'— what 'Alps on Alps arise!' As for me, I never read any poetry except that of Valmiki, Homer, Vyasa, Virgil, Kalidas, Dante (in translation), Tasso (Ditto) and Milton.[49]

[46] *Madhusūdan Racanābalī,* pp.623-4.
[47] *Paradise Lost,* XII. 486-7.
[48] KG, p.166.
[49] KG, p.134.

I cannot prove it, but I suspect that it was Milton's ability to change his notes to tragic that took Madhusudan to the highest peaks, and that Satan's tragedy moved him as well as Adam and Eve's. In Ravana's great lament over the corpse of Meghnad at the end of the poem, we should sense not only Adam's exile from happiness, but Satan's. Like Satan, Ravana has to bid farewell to hope—and his pain is all the greater because, as we have seen, he has no understanding of the wrong he has done. Ravana the 'innocent evil-doer' is an original creation in literature, but by no means uncommon in life:

> It was my hope, Meghnad, that I would finally close these two eyes of mine in your presence!
> Resigning the burdens of rule on to you, son, I would make my great journey
> But Fate—how shall I understand her wiles?—has robbed me of that joy!
> It was my hope, my child, that I would soothe my eyes by seeing you on the throne of the Rakshasas;
> And my son's wife would be on your left, like Lakshmi in the form of guardian of the Rakshasa race! What vain hope!
> Because of the sins of past lives, I behold you today on this fell throne. The glorious sun of the Rakshasa race is permanently eclipsed!
> Did I worship Shiva with such devotion, to deserve this? How shall I return—
> Alas, who will tell me—how shall I return again to the empty palace of Lanka?
> What deceiving consolation can I offer your mother, who will tell me? 'Where is my son,
> Where is my daughter-in-law?' Queeen Mandadari will ask. 'To what joy have you left them,
> Lord of the Rakshasas, on the sea-shore?' What shall I tell her then?
> What, alas? O son,
> O finest of warriors! Ever-victorious in battle! O Mother Lakshmi of the Rakshasas!
> For what sin has harsh Fate written this torment on Ravana's forehead?[50]

At the behest of Shiva, Meghnad and Pramila are swept up to Heaven in Agni's fiery chariot; the gods rain down flowers; the world fills with the sound of joy. But Madhusudan's heart remains, one feels, with his tragically human conception of Ravana grieving for his son.

Would Milton himself have understood any of the links and comparisons I have tried to make in this essay? I doubt it—if only because Madhusudan is allied—by his lack of faith in anything other than his own genius and his creation of a lasting monument—to pre-Christian pagan writers, or to post-Christian writers of the twentieth century. The most interesting of Madhusudan's early English poems is a fragmentary and obscure piece in blank verse called *Visions of the Past* (published with *The Captive Ladie* in 1849). It is a kind of dream vision of Par-

[50] *Meghnād-badh Kābya*, IX. 378-400.

adise, Fall and Redemption. It begins with a description of primeval Man and Woman lying in a bower of bliss attended by a choir of angels. Then Satan comes along, and all is plunged into darkness, with the Angels replaced by Devils. Then comes a 'fulgent vision bright', which at first seems to offer Redemption; but it does not restore Paradise—far from it. The bower of beauty is sadly 'changed alas! from primal loveliness'; the 'gentle beings and fair' flee guiltily, and in the closing section we see them 'wander in dim solitude'. Redemption and Mercy are possibilities at the end, but are not the essential message of the poem:

I woke—that vision of ethereal ray
Had melted—and 'twas night again and dark,
With stars of sickly smile and pallid brow: —
I look'd toward that fair bow'r and as I look'd
I saw a sword of flame and fiery gleam
Wav'd round it by some viewless hand and fierce!
And on the silent plain that gentle pair—
Its tenants—wandered in dim solitude.
They wept—but were those tears which gently flow'd,
Oh! were they tears which dark despair will wake
T'embalm the memory of our blasted hopes?
They wept—but not in dark despair—they wept
As Guilt—all penitent—when, Mercy! thou
Dost plead—nor plead in vain— in gentle strains
To justice stern to win redeeming grace![51]

Madhusudan was Christian—or Christian-influenced—enough to aspire to Mercy and Grace, even if he lacked any sure conviction of it. Perhaps it was because he found in *Paradise Lost* both the tragedy he knew and the faith he lacked, that he reserved for Milton alone the epithet 'divine'.

Further reading

Ghosh, J.C., *Bengali Literature* (London, 1948).
Zbavitel, Dušan, *Bengali Literature* (Wiesbaden, 1976).

[51] *Madhusūdan Racanābalī*, pp.477-8.

INDIAN ARCHITECTURE AND THE ENGLISH VISION[1]

G.H.R. Tillotson

Arguments about how Europeans perceive and describe Asia have, in recent years, been extended into the realm of the visual arts. It is asked how, for example, British artists and architects portrayed South Asia and its past, and what can be deduced from their results. For some art historians, the starting point in this debate (as in others) is Edward Said's polemical book Orientalism *(1978), which sought to locate Western misunderstandings and misrepresentations of the East within the framework of colonial relationships. So, to some, a British visual image of India both reflects and contributes to political realities. The present article questions whether the transfer of Said's argument to the visual arts can be effected so easily as some suppose. While it argues that much remains to be explored in the field of visual representations and misrepresentations of South Asia, it also insists that there can be no facile equation between the artistic representation and the preceding perception. Works of art can be powerful expressions of ideologies, but whatever else they are they remain imaginative constructions, and they attain special qualities by virtue of the processes by which they are made. Any analysis of them must take into account their properties as art.*

There is a paradox in the work of Thomas and William Daniell. Their pictures of Indian buildings are rich with accurate detail and information, but they are also suffused by a picturesque vision. Both aspects are recognised by art historians and it has been noted that the picturesque treatment can involve a wilful distortion or re-arrangement of the subject (e.g. Archer, 1980, no.123). This peculiarly English aesthetic is in many cases quite opposed to the Indian aesthetic of the building depicted, and so its use undermines the picture's factual value, in which the details urge us to believe.

Their aquatint showing *An Antient Hindoo Temple in the Fort of Rotas, Bahar* (Fig.1) may be taken as an example. It shows the proportions and some details of the building clearly, and recently it was even used as a guide by those restoring the temple (Sutton, 1954, p.64). But the choice and treatment of this subject—one of the very few north Indian temples depicted in the volumes of *Oriental Scenery* (1795-1808)—reveal a very English interpretation. To a Hindu, typically, a temple is the terrestrial residence of a god, and a place of worship. To

[1] First published in *South Asian Studies* 7 (1991), pp.59-74.

Figure 1. Thomas and William Daniell, *An Antient Hindoo Temple in the Fort of Rotas, Bahar.*
(Aquatint, 1796; India Office Library and Records)

the Daniells, apparently, a temple was a ruin and had no use except as an object for conversation among leisured peasants.

Among a temple's physical features, a Hindu might consider to be of special importance those which express its main symbolic meanings: the plan, the elevation and the images of the gods. Indian artists depicting temples tend to emphasise these features and even contrive to represent them all at once (Fig. 2). The Daniells emphasised none of them: the deity and the plan are not shown at all, and the elevation is obscured by foliage and the oblique perspective. These devices were employed to integrate the building into the scenery, in accordance with English artistic norms. This does not mean that Indian pictures are more objective or any less suffused by an aesthetic, but rather that their aesthetic is more in harmony with that of the subject. By overriding the intrinsic aesthetic with a different and alien one, the Daniells' interpretation of the temple misrepresents it.

Figure 2. Indian artist c.1800, *View of a Southern Indian Temple*
(Gouache; British Architectural Library Drawings Collection, RIBA F3/20)

A similar exercise could be undertaken with regard to any work by the Daniells, or indeed the work of any British landscape painter who visited India during the period in which the Picturesque was a dominant force in English art, from William Hodges in the 1780s to Edward Lear in the 1870s. To describe examples of misrepresentation is not the purpose of this paper (cf. Tillotson, 1990, 1991); the aim here is to examine how such misrepresentations arose and what end, if any, they served.

Indian architecture was represented by Britons in other media besides landscape painting. One of these was architecture itself, as British architects attempted to design in Indian styles. This occurred first at home in Britain, in the early nineteenth century, the most famous examples being Sezincote in Gloucestershire (1805-11) and the remodelled Royal Pavilion at Brighton (1815-18). Later, more sustained attempts were made by British architects working in India, resulting in what is known as 'Indo-Saracenic' architecture. Of this, the work of Charles Mant and R.F. Chisholm is typical (see Figs. 5, 6 below). In all these buildings, the interpretation of Indian architecture is a misrepresentation, since they do not follow faithfully the principles of Indian design. For all the domes and minarets on the surface, Sezincote and the Royal Pavilion are unmistakably European buildings underneath; and likewise we stand at no risk of mistaking an Indo-Saracenic building for the Mughal architecture that ostensibly provided the model. Both movements have been the subject of much excellent recent research (Conner 1979, Stamp 1981, Davies 1985, Head 1986), and a recitation of their details would be superfluous; the purpose here is to focus on what lies behind the misrepresentation in terms of inspiration and possible motive.

Along with painting and architecture, the third medium to be considered is writing, specifically writing on Indian architecture in the eighteenth and nineteenth centuries by travellers, such as Lord Valentia and the travel artists, and by early art historians such as James Fergusson and Alexander Cunningham. Even without a detailed review of the extensive literature, it will not be contentious to assert that the interpretation of Indian architecture offered by such writers frequently contains misrepresentations. William Hodges, for example, though adamant that the architectural traditions of India were distinct from others and just as admirable, was also on occasion tempted to see affinities between Indian and European buildings—especially between Indo-Islamic and Gothic buildings—which led him to exaggerate their historical connections.[2] But again, the concern here is not to enumerate

[2] Especially striking in this context are Hodges's comments accompanying the aquatint version of the oil reproduced here at Fig.4; see Hodges, 1785-8, pl.19. For a further instance, see Hodges, 1794, pp.62-3. For his views on the disparities between, and equal excellences of, architectural

errors, but to investigate how the various kinds of error arose, and whether they reveal anything of the authors' motives for their study.

It must be recognised that in all three fields under review, those involved claimed to be aiming at a faithful representation of their subjects; their declared aim was objectivity. Thomas Daniell, for example, compared his work with the investigations of scientists (Daniell, 1810, Preface); his intention was to produce a reliable record of Indian architecture. Hodges insisted that fact was preferable to fancy, and even went so far as to describe the inappropriateness of applying a Western aesthetic to Eastern subjects (Hodges, 1794, p.153). Fidelity to the subject was a standard criterion of art criticism until well into the nineteenth century, and artists frequently gave assurances as to the authenticity of their views.[3]

Similarly, the Indo-Saracenic architects claimed to be working in Indian styles, not ones of their own devising. The very name 'Indo-Saracenic' indicates their intention. This name had been given by art historians to India's Islamic architecture, and since it was this that the architects claimed to be reviving they used the same term to describe their own work—they did not call it 'Neo-Indo-Saracenic' or 'Anglo-Indian', for they saw no fundamental distinction to be made between their work and its models. Commentators such as Lord Napier hailed their work as a 'revival in native art'.[4]

The claim of objectivity is perhaps implicit among the writers. Unlike the painters and architects, they rarely made overt declarations of objectivity, but this is because the reader was expected to take it on trust. Whatever it actually achieves, the very writing of travelogue or art history involves the implicit claim to be describing things as they are. But with the writers as with the painters and architects (as already selectively shown) the claim to objectivity is not sustainable; in all three fields the alleged quest for truth delivers misrepresentation, and we may reasonably wonder why this should be so.

The subject of European representations of the East has, of course, been greatly influenced by the publication in 1978 of Edward Said's polemical work *Orientalism*. Said there advanced the thesis that European writing on the East was never politically neutral, indeed that it could not be since the author could not escape being party to a colonial relationship. Whether consciously or otherwise, Said argued, European scholarship on the East served the purposes of colonialism. *Orientalism*

---

traditions, see ibid. pp.64-5, 69.

[3] For some examples, including William Daniell's criticism of the work of Hodges, see Tillotson, 1990, pp.146, 151 n.6. See also Elliot, 1833, Preface.

[4] For further discussion of the claim to authenticity among Indo-Saracenic architects see Tillotson, 1989, pp.46, 52, 60.

examines the motives for such work, but since these are taken to be political, the argument also concerns misrepresentation: it examines the misunderstandings and distortions that arose from the partiality of the observer.

Responses to Said have been mixed. In fact, the validity of his argument is not crucial in the present discussion. Said was concerned primarily with writing in the fields of history and sociology, with reference to Arab countries—disciplines and regions not here under consideration. But whatever the merits of his case, his argument raises the question whether an analogous case could be made with reference to other disciplines and other colonial regions that he did not examine closely. These might include representations of Indian architecture in the various media described above.

The possibility of transferring Said's thesis to India and to art has been noticed before, and again the response has been mixed. Some who are sceptical of the original thesis, such as John Sweetman, have apparently supposed that the extension or transfer will also be doubtful, and they have been content to dismiss the matter perfunctorily (Sweetman, 1988, p.246), while those who assume the original thesis to be unassailable have assumed also that the extension of it must be valid, and they have scarcely troubled to rehearse the argument. Neither therefore has acknowledged that whether a Saidian case can be made for artistic and art-historical representations of India depends not on the truth or falsehood of Said's original claims about a different context, but on the historical circumstances in India. At the very least, it is worth investigating those circumstances. In a preliminary way, that is what is attempted below. The enquiry is limited to the field of Indian architecture, with representations in the three media mentioned being taken in turn.[5]

The pictorial image

The aesthetic that we call the Picturesque arose in English art in the mid-eighteenth century and it affected many media including architecture and gardening. In landscape painting its immediate sources lay in continental art of the seventeenth century, especially the classical landscapes of Claude Lorrain and Gaspard Dughet Poussin, and the more animated work of Salvator Rosa and Jacob van Ruisdael. These somewhat contradictory influences were combined in the work of English painters such

[5] The argument presented here, that British views of Indian architecture are generally interpretations, is not intended as an argument for an extreme relativism. It does not mean, for example, that an objective reality about Indian architecture does not exist or is unimportant—nor even that the reality is unknowable. It is an argument about the divide between the reality and the vision (each of which is taken to be knowable) and about what caused the divide.

as Richard Wilson and Thomas Gainsborough to create a new vision. This vision was subsequently codified by theorists such as William Gilpin, who laid down precise prescriptions about how it could be achieved, and so helped to disseminate it (Gilpin, 1792).

The Picturesque was enormously pervasive. It was not simply one style of landscape painting in Britain, but an aesthetic that shaped the very formation of the English landscape school. Christopher Hussey's list of artists who were affected by it is, as Hussey acknowledged, a list of every English painter from Wilson until the Pre-Raphaelites (Hussey, 1927, pp.251-73). Hussey, in fact, was the first writer in modern times to distinguish the Picturesque as a particular movement, for it had previously been considered synonymous with English art; and it is still recognised as the major contribution made by Britain to European aesthetics (Watkin, 1982, p.vii). To an English artist working around 1800, the Picturesque was almost unavoidable, for it was the overwhelmingly dominant manner of seeing and depicting the world.

In the work by Daniell already cited (Fig.1), many aspects of the treatment are derived from this stylistic tradition as codified by Gilpin. The dark mass in the foreground that throws the eye into the main picture plane, the bushy foliage and broken masonry that create variety, the general roughness or irregularity of the detail, and the few figures that lend animation without dominating the scene, are all standard motifs of the period. They all appear again in other works by the Daniells, in spite of the differences in the subject-matter: Islamic subjects are treated in just the same way (Fig.3). The motifs amount, in other words, to a formulaic treatment that can be applied to any subject.

Any work of art is in some sense an interpretation of its subject; but where the subject is itself the product of design then it has its own aesthetic; and this is a constituent part of the subject, with which the artist's interpretation can be in sympathy to a greater or lesser degree. The pictures of artists such as the Daniells disregard the intrinsic aesthetics of their subjects, make them conform to a set of norms developed elsewhere, and so misrepresent them.[6]

Does that misrepresentation relate to India's position as a former colony? Did it serve colonial purposes, and reflect the Daniells' status as members of a ruling race? The extent to which it might have served British rule practically is probably limited, but it might be seen as an attempt—unconscious, perhaps—to tame Indian civilisation, to force India to conform to European norms. Clearly it relates to the Daniells' Englishness, but does being English in this context signify a particular

[6] This is not an argument for the priority of indigenous as opposed to foreign interpretations, but for the priority of the intrinsic aesthetic of the architectural subject. The latter is taken to be an objective reality (see note 5).

Figure 3. Thomas and William Daniell, *Remains of an Ancient Building near Firoz Shah's Cotilla, Delhi*
(Aquatint, 1795; India Office Library and Records)

kind of power status, as some have been inclined to suppose (Pal and Dehejia, 1986, p.16), or a particular kind of artistic training?

In answering these questions, the first thing to note is that the Picturesque has no peculiar connection with India. Originating in Britain, it was a treatment applied by British artists to landscapes all over the world—not only in other part of the East and in the British Isles themselves but throughout parts of Europe, such as Italy, Germany and Switzerland, over which Britons could not even pretend to exert political control.[7] The treatment can have no colonial meaning in those contexts. So the putative Saidian case would have to suppose that the extension of the Picturesque to Indian subjects involved a fundamental change in significance; that far from there having been a continuity of treatment between other regions and India, the artists were using the

[7] For studies of European pictorial representations of other non-European regions see Stevens (1984), Smith (1985), Tillotson (1987) and Llewellyn (1989).

same method to achieve something different.

This raises the question of the artists' intentions. A Saidian case would be that there was a conscious or unconscious will to misrepresent and that the Picturesque was adopted as a suitable instrument to that end. The artists' stated intention, as already shown, was to represent Indian architecture accurately, to convey information about it objectively. If we accept that such indeed was their aim then we must recognise that they failed: their method was such as to render their task impossible. Alternatively we may suppose that in declaring such an aim they were deceiving us (or themselves); that there was a hidden agenda to distort the truth—an end which the Picturesque served.

It would be difficult to amass evidence against a supposition about unstated intentions, but if such an assumption cannot definitely be disproved it can be shown to be irrelevant. The Picturesque, as already suggested, was not only widespread but the dominant aesthetic in British art in the period in question. For a British artist trained either at professional or amateur level around 1800, it was not a chosen instrument but an unquestioned norm. Of course there were some, like Samuel Palmer, who transcended it to forge a personal vision, but even for them the Picturesque was the starting point. For most it was simply synonymous with art. Art is the only instrument available to artists. And so the misrepresentation was the consequence of the unavoidable use of the current pictorial style. It would have occurred whichever way the artists' intentions lay, and so those intentions are unimportant. They were not decisive, for they were over-ruled by the medium itself, at which level no choice was made.

The answer so far, then, is that the misrepresentation of Indian architecture by British artists arose not from any undeclared (or even unrecognised) political programme but from an inescapable aesthetic vision. It remains to be shown that these two are genuinely distinct alternatives, that the aesthetic is not simply an expression of the political. The emphasis here placed on the force of stylistic influence, that is taken to operate independently of political factors, invites scorn particularly from a currently vigorous school of thought within the field of art history, namely the Marxist school. A detailed critique of Marxist art history is not necessary here, but it is important to examine the objections of that school to assumptions about style such as those made here, because some who have been inclined to apply Saidian theories to art in a colonial context have seemingly also been much impressed by Marxist approaches.

The major achievement of Marxist art history, according to one of its most energetic proponents, Janet Wolff, has been to expose the ideological nature of art. Any alternative view—such as the one followed here—that art is not wholly socially determined since the development of style is independent—is regarded by the Marxists to be itself the reflection of an ideology, and one to which they object. By the Marxist account, an artist is not a creative individual working within a stylistic tradition, but the agent or representative of a social group, expressing that group's ideology. Thus Wolff declared:

> Works of art...are not closed, self-contained and transcendant entities, but are the product of specific historical practices on the part of identifiable social groups in given conditions, and therefore bear the imprint of the ideas, values and conditions of existence of those groups and their representatives in particular artists (Wolff, 1981, p.49).

The present argument may pass over the bludgeon against individuality that this view entails, and ignore the echo of popular horoscopes in the assumption that all members of a particular group must share certain characteristics. Janet Wolff has been taken as an example of the Marxist school—rather than a more exuberant figure such as John Berger (1972)—because, being more sophisticated, she recognised that the relation between an ideology and its supposed expression in art might not be crude, but problematical. To cope with the problem, she introduced the concept of 'aesthetic mediation'. A work of arı is not sımply and literally a reflection of an ideology, according to Wolf:

> The way in which the ideology of a class or other group is expressed in...painting will be affected, or mediated, by...existing aesthetic conventions...This is not to deny...that the artist is in some sense the agent of ideology, through whom the views and beliefs of a group find expression. It is to insist, however, that this does not take place in any simple fashion...The ideas and values of the artist, themselves socially formed, are mediated by...cultural conventions of style, language, genre and aesthetic vocabulary...He or she works with the available material of aesthetic convention (Wolff, 1981, pp.61-5).

This refinement is perceptive, but also destructive of the main theory. It proposes the existence of an element within a work of art that is distinct from the ideology that the work expresses. Wolff did not go on to examine the nature of that element—the 'aesthetic conventions'—too closely, perhaps for fear that it might turn out not to be ideological.

And this is indeed the case. In a later, seemingly casual remark, she conceded that:

> a symphony, a quartet or any music without lyrics is hard to assimilate to ideology of any sort...It is not as simple a matter to detect the ideological nature of abstract art as it is with Gainsborough's paintings (Wolff, 1981, p.72).

That she should have encountered difficulties in just the cases mentioned is significant. Music without words and abstract art are both art forms that are empty of subject-matter—at least as far as is possible.

To some degree, no doubt, they may suggest subjects to our imaginations, but as far as can be achieved we are presented not with representations but only with aesthetic form. And in such cases Wolff found it hard to 'detect the ideological nature'.

Now of course figurative paintings have aesthetic form, or style, quite as much as abstract art, even if it is not in those cases presented alone. What follows from Wolff's difficulty is that the ideology of a work of art resides in its subject-matter (including its treatment in a thematic or literary sense), and that aesthetic form expresses no ideology. Where the form exists alone no ideology can be detected. Since music without words and even abstract painting can be counted as art, it follows that an essential distinctive quality of works of art—their aesthetic form—is not ideological, not socially formed.

Any such argument proposing the autonomy of art from social forces is anathema to the Marxists; but while it is clear that there are frequently causal links between social forces and choices of subject-matter, we should not assume that there are causal links between social forces and pictorial styles.[8]

It will be noticed that this argument has not challenged the Marxist belief that the ideology of an artist is necessarily that of the social group to which he belongs. It has not needed to. For even if the Marxists were right about that, the artist would still express that ideology through the medium of an 'aesthetic convention' which, as shown, is not socially formed. For this argument, it is only the artist's style and not his ideology that needs to be autonomous from the group's ideology. The argument began by showing that the misrepresentation of Indian architecture in British landscape painting was due not to an undeclared political programme of the artists, but to their inheritance of a potent style, the Picturesque. It has now shown that such styles are themselves apolitical, and so we may conclude that the mistrepresentation was not a political matter at any level.

Returning from theory to the pictures, William Hodges's view of *A Gateway leading to a Mosque in Chunargarh* (Fig.4) may serve as an example.[9] In depicting this building, Hodges was obliged to work with what Wolff called 'the available material of aesthetic convention'. For Hodges as for others of his period, this meant the English landscape style as formulated by Gainsborough and Wilson, a style communicated

[8] Of interest in this context is David Solkin's interpretation of the work of Richard Wilson (Solkin, 1982), which included the suggestion of political motives for the misrepresentation of the English countryside. There have been hostile responses to Solkin (McWilliam and Potts, 1986), but these somewhat exaggerate his position since Solkin also took pains to explain Wilson's style in terms of an art-historical inheritance (p.14).

[9] Private Collection, London; see Stuebe, 1979, no.257. Photograph by courtesy of Dr Mildred Archer.

Figure 4. William Hodges, *A Gateway leading to a Mosque in Chunargarh*
(Oil on canvas, c.1790; Private collection)

even more directly to him than to other British painters in India since Wilson was his teacher. This aesthetic inheritance led him to treat the subject in particular ways: to place the main subject eccentrically on the canvas; to frame the composition with trees and use their foliage to maximise the variety of outline; and to employ a loose painterly technique that creates further irregularity of tone and form. It is not that he strived to fulfil a particular programme; he simply shared the dominant mode of seeing and representing that amounted in his time to art. And it is this necessary use of artistic convention that prevented him from giving an objective account of the mosque's gateway. Its own salient design features are negated, as the intricate decoration on its façade disappears in the hasty brushstrokes, and the strict symmetry of its form is disrupted by the foliage.

In such a manner, the use of the Picturesque by British artists tended to understate local particularities and make India converge towards a European ideal. Their images of Indian architecture are certainly therefore 'constructions' or mythical statements; but their inspiration was artistic.

This discussion has dealt exclusively with images of architecture, in adherence to a general theme. Other subjects, of course, were treated by British artists in India, and the argument is not meant to imply that all British painting in India is apolitical. In some cases a political content is both obvious and intended. History paintings especially, in which artists depicted current or recent events judged to be of historical significance, tend to focus on moments of British triumph and are unambiguous celebrations of them. Another favourite subject was Indian people, whether represented as individuals, or as representatives of trade or caste groups, or as the performers of certain customs. Within this large category there is room for a variety of different kinds of treatment, and although most are in some sense misrepresentations the degree of political content varies.

Architectural Imitations

Unlike the landscape paintings, the British architectural projects under review were connected to an overt political programme. In the later Victorian period a debate took place within India about the adoption of an architectural style that would be appropriate for the buildings of the Raj. Politicians, journalists and architects all contributed to this debate, which has often been described (e.g. Stamp, 1981, p.358; Davies, 1985, p.192). Though some of the issues discussed concerned the relative merits of different styles with regard to climate and utility, the essential division of the field was political. Those who wished to impose a Western style—and preferably classicism—on India, as an element in the wider process of Westernisation inaugurated in the Bentinck era, were opposed by those who sought local relevance and a reflection of the Indian environment. Indo-Saracenic architecture was developed largely in response to the latter demand; it was an attempt to apply the vocabulary of India's own architectural heritage to the building requirements of the Raj.

A cautious approach in this process was made in the work of F.W. Stevens in Bombay. His Victoria Terminus (1878) and Municipal Building (1888) are basically Gothic buildings but they are spiced with Indian details. Bolder experimenters included R.F. Chisholm who worked in Madras, for example on the Revenue Board Offices in the 1870s (Fig.5), and was later commissioned by the Maharaja of Baroda to design a University Senate House (c.1880). His work in Baroda continued that of Charles Mant: Mant had begun his contribution to the movement with Mayo College in Ajmer (1875) and subsequently designed numerous palaces and other buildings for maharajas including

Above: Figure 5. *Revenue Board Office, Madras*
Designed by R.F. Chisholm, 1870s; India Office Library and Records.
Below: Figure 6. *Laxmi Vilas, Baroda*
Designed by Charles Mant, 1878.

Figure 7. *The Gateway of India*; designed by George Wittet, 1911

Laxmi Vilas at Baroda (1878, Fig.6). The movement was still flourishing in the early twentieth century. Henry Irwin followed Chisholm in Madras with, among other buildings, the Art Gallery, in 1909. Vincent Esch designed a group of Indo-Saracenic public buildings for the Nizam of Hyderabad (1914-18); while George Wittet added the Prince of Wales Museum (1905) and the Gateway of India (1911) to Bombay (Fig.7).

Much as they made use of various regional historical styles, no example of the movement is in fact an authentic exercise in Indian design. Although Wittet's Gateway of India, for instance, has been described as entirely in the style of the architecture of Gujarat of the fifteenth and sixteenth centuries (Morris, 1986, p.194), and though it is clear that Wittet had studied that tradition, the general form of his building is based not on an Ahmedabad mosque but on classical triumphal arches such as that of Septimius Severus. The *chajja* has significantly become an entablature.

As in the paintings, so in the Indo-Saracenic buildings, the Indian architectural material has been pressed into a Western mould and has come out distorted. Again we may reasonably ask why this should be so. Did the force of artistic habit prevent the architects from achieving accurate representation, or were they inspired by a political programme?

The latter explanation has recently been urged by Thomas Metcalf, in his book *An Imperial Vision* (1989). Metcalf sees the Indo-Saracenic movement as an exercise in British dominance over India's cultural past, as a declaration of cultural mastery. Following a Saidian formula, he harnesses the wish to know the past with the wish to control the present. Undoubtedly it helps to know a place if you wish to rule it, but the Saidian theory perhaps mistakes a necessary for a sufficient condition by supposing that academic knowledge confers power. By accepting this assumption, Metcalf can represent the British use of traditional Indian architecture as primarily a political gesture (e.g. Metcalf, 1989, pp.24, 75).

Does this interpretation fit with the art-historical facts? In the first place it must be recognised that, like the Picturesque, the use of historical styles in architecture was not confined to India. During the period in question, and for some decades before, architecture in Britain was in the grip of the Gothic Revival, as architects such as Sir George Gilbert Scott and Alfred Waterhouse redeployed the styles of medieval Europe for modern purposes. Here too, however ardent individual architects were in their study of the sources, however anxious about the fidelity of their revival, their designs are adaptations in which elements or tokens of the historical style are re-assembled into a new language.

Earlier in the century, British architecture had been dominated by the revival of Greek and Roman forms. There was also at this time an occasional spirit of pluralism that encouraged the most eclectic of revivals, leading to those exercises in Indian styles within Britain such as the Royal Pavilion. Thus, whether as long-term movements or as passing fashions, the use of historical styles was a constant feature of British architectural design. Indeed it could even be claimed with reason that (excluding only vernacular traditions) all major European architecture from the Renaissance to the inception of the Modern Movement involves some sort of revival, and that the theory of its design includes issues of authenticity and licence in adaptation.

The Indo-Saracenic movement seen in this context is no more than the application to India of the method universally (or at least very widely) followed in Europe. British architects and engineers trained in Europe were accustomed to being surrounded by re-creations of the classical world, and accustomed to the Victorians' easy handling of Europe's Middle Ages; and it is scarcely surprising that they should have experimented in similar ways with India's past when working there. They were following an established artistic practice.

That this was how Indo-Saracenic architecture was generally perceived at the time is apparent from the analysis of one of its most hostile and outspoken critics. E.B. Havell pointed out that it was in essence no different from other British architecture: his complaint against it was that the British architect used the Indian tradition as another set of historical garments to add to the established repertoire of classic and Gothic (Havell, 1913, pp.222, 230-1). If a declaration of control were intended, it would have had to be unambiguous to British eyes. But Britons of the period saw in the use of the past merely the standard procedure of architecture.

It must be acknowledged that the uses by British architects of classical and medieval styles do contain political statements. But those statements are not declarations of dominance over the classical and medieval worlds; rather they are claims of descent—cultural or spiritual—from distinguished ancestry. It is therefore not at all obvious that the analogous use of Inidan styles can safely be read as delivering a different message, one of control. Similarly, Indo-Saracenic architecture has much in common with the use by Indian architects of Western styles—for example the use of classicism in Lucknow and of Gothic in Junagadh. These works indicate an Indian attempt at cultural alignment or association with the West, not a claim of colonial authority over it; we cannot therefore invert the meaning for the corresponding British examples, unless we have prejudged what message we must find in them.

It was argued above that the work of the Picturesque painter was apolitical. The case of the architecture is different since, as acknowledged, the Indo-Saracenic movement arose in part from an attempt to establish an architectural imagery that could represent a political entity, the Raj. Just as the use of classicism could mark a claim of descent from the Roman Empire, so the Indo-Saracenic style might be interpreted as a claim of descent from the Mughals, and thus far a claim of imperial power; but it would be power achieved through assimilation and identification with India. And so it could also be seen—and undoubtedly was by both supporters and opponents—as a gesture of concession to India.

The argument against Metcalf's interpretation therefore is not that Indo-Saracenic architecture had no political meaning, but that its meanings were complex and not those that Metcalf identifies, and that politics were not its only inspiration. Metcalf's adaptation of the Said thesis ignores entirely the processes and influence of British architecture outside India, and thus the movement's art-historical context. Metcalf concedes that he is not an art historian, but his oversight is due also to certain assumptions about art that have much in common with those of the Marxist art historians; in particular his assumption that art is essentially ideological, and that a design can therefore be fully explained by reference to the supposed shared ideology of the social group to which the artist belongs, and without reference to the individual's aesthetic preferences or artistic training.

What then are we to make of the architects' misrepresentation of India's traditions if their motives were not political? The distortions are primarily the consequence of the necessary adaptation of the styles to new functions. If Wittet's Gateway of India looks more like a triumphal arch than a mosque then this is largely because it is indeed a triumphal arch, celebrating the visit of the Emperor. And Stevens and Mant could scarcely have built an authentically Mughal railway station and a Rajput public school. The distortions of Indian architectural grammar were as unavoidable as the distortions of Gothic styles in Victorian Britain; and if they are more extreme that is because of the greater divide between the needs served by the modern architects and those served by their sources.

But function was not the only cause. Many of Mant's designs, for example, are characterised by asymmetry in planning and irregularity in the massing of parts—a treatment that was central to the Picturesque method in architecture, and was reconfirmed by the Gothic Revival. So that Mant's misrepresentation of the traditions he used was due also in part, again, to the force of stylistic habit.

The written accounts

While picturesque paintings and Indo-Saracenic buildings each form fairly homogeneous groups, the writing of the period is very varied. It must be acknowledged that comment on Indian art and architecture by Britons was frequently a form of political comment. Rosie Llewellyn-Jones has shown that some (though not all) nineteenth-century criticism of the architecture of Lucknow was intended as criticism of the Nawabs, as the bad design was seen as a reflection of dissolute rule (Llewellyn-Jones, 1985, p.239). In the year after the Mutiny, John Ruskin similarly disparaged Indian art, explaining that it must be understood as the product of wicked minds (Ruskin, 1903-12, vol.16, pp.262-6). The insistence of Sir George Birdwood, later echoed by Vincent Smith, that Indian painting and sculpture are too ugly to be reckoned fine art, belittles the civilisation in general by suggesting India to be incapable of faculties taken for granted in Europe (see Tillotson, 1989, p.38). The persistent attempts to attribute the Taj Mahal to Western architects was even more cynical: in this case the excellence of the work could not be denied, but Britons did not have to believe that Indians achieved it if they could claim the credit for the West.

Responses such as these have been examined at length by Partha Mitter (1977). But, as Mitter showed, not all British writing on Indian art and architecture was of such crude kinds. There exists a large body of serious and enthusiastic writing and comment by art historians and travellers. The present argument must consider what inspired their study and, when they misrepresented their subject, what caused their mistakes.

Misrepresentation in this field was of many types. One type arose when the writer, like the artists described earlier, while regarding his subject, overlooked or depreciated the aesthetic of the building because his vision was tinged by an aesthetic that he had brought with him. This is apparent in the frequent description of buildings—and especially ruins— as 'picturesque' or 'romantic' even where such an effect may have been at the furthest remove from the building's intrinsic aesthetic. The use of such terms again reflects aesthetic habits or universal modes of vision. Accustomed to looking at English pictures, the writers tended to see the world in their terms, and were not always successful in subduing that obstacle to understanding.

A further type of misrepresentation arose from a different mental habit. Faced with something unfamiliar, people frequently attempt to understand or rationalise it by comparing it with something that is familiar; but the thing that happens to be familiar to the viewer may be quite irrelevant to the new object, and so misleading as a key to understanding it. This pattern is common in the journals of travellers, who most assiduously recorded their reactions to strange objects. Lord Valentia in 1804, for example, was amazed by the *gopura* of the temple at Rameswaram, but it did strike him as reminiscent of the Egyptian architecture that he also inspected on his travels. The comparison is unhelpful: though pyramidal, a *gopura* is in important respects unlike an Egyptian pylon, and there is no historical connection between the two. Valentia thought of the Egyptian type only because that was what he knew, so the comparison tells us more about Valentia's itinerary than about either of the objects he was discussing (Valentia, 1809, vol. I, p.340).

James Tod tended to come to terms with Indian buildings by relating them to classical ones. Visiting Kumbhalgarh in 1819, he thought the fort's battlements to be strongly reminiscent of Etruscan types. On an eminence within the fort, he found a temple that 'is truly classic'. Admittedly its plan is almost like that of a classical dipteral temple, but the building is scarcely, as Tod has it, 'our temple of Theseus in Mewar'. From its supposedly Greek form, Tod deduced it must have been built in the seond century BC, and represent a late flowering of the influence of Greek Bactria. He contemplated 'the possibility, nay the probability' that this temple 'may have been designed by Grecian artists, or that the taste of the artists among the Rajputs may have been modelled after the Grecian'. Both the date and source proposed are highly implausible; but Tod was enraptured by his discovery and was soon scrambling down the hill having glimpsed in the distance 'the Sybilline Temple of Tivoli in miniature' (Tod, 1972, vol.I, pp.531-3).

It should be noted that Tod was here mistaking an Indian building for a Greek one; he was not applying classical criteria in the criticism of a building accepted to be Indian. This latter approach others were to adopt later—as Ruskin and Birdwood, in the remarks already referred to, chastised Indian art for failing to conform to the canon of Western classicism. Neither was Tod attempting to construct a theory that all Indian art and architecture owes its design to foreign influence; this too was an approach that others were later to pursue, in varying degrees from Vincent Smith (1930) to Nirad Chaudhuri (1966). Both such arguments might reasonably be called Orientalist in a Saidian sense: the inappropriate application of classical criteria because it assume a status for Western art as a superior form or norm from which deviation is deformity; and theories of foreign origin because they depreciate the inventiveness of indigenous art and by implication seek to justify Western cultural domination by reference to precedent.

These Orientalist approaches are certainly to be found in writing on art. But Tod's remarks have been quoted to show that every time a Briton compared Indian and Western architecture he was not necessarily engaging in such a discourse. He may, like Tod, have been suffering from a common traveller's affliction: the need for points of reference, the need to relate new scenes to old ones in an attempt to understand them—an attempt that is doomed since, as with the artists, the very method defeats the purpose. Again the affliction was not confined to India. In 1793, Sir George Staunton travelled through Soochow on China's Grand Canal, with the artist William Alexander, and both men independently were reminded of Venice (see Tillotson, 1987, pp.110-1). And indeed the problem continues unabated; for it is only in such terms that we can account, for example, for Sten Nilsson's view that the plan of the city of Jaipur was based on European models—a view followed by some, but now conclusively disproved by Susan Gole (Nilsson, 1987, p.17; Davies, 1989, pp.371-2; Gole, 1989, p.144).

The most notorious type of misrepresentation of Indian architecture by scholars is the classification of Indian buildings by ethnic or religious criteria. In the late nineteenth century, a system of ethnic categories was established by James Fergusson and Alexander Cunningham, a system which assumed that the salient determining factor in any architectural design was the racial origin of the patron. A sample absurdity of this system is Cunningham's treatment of the buildings of Sher Shah Sur. These were designated 'Afghan', in a reference to the birthplace of Sher Shah's grandfather, and thus they were distinguished both from earlier Indo-Islamic architecture and from the buildings of Akbar that followed (Cunningham, 1873, p.2). A stylistic analysis, by contrast, reveals continuities and changes that are unrelated to dynastic changes.

Was this system innocent or political? Chris Pinney has argued that the categorisation of Indian society by Victorian anthropologists was related to administrators' attempts to organise and so control Indian people (Pinney, 1990). Can the ethnic categorisation of Indian architecture be seen as part of an attempt to dominate Indian civilisation? Saying that it can, like other Saidian cases, would ignore the wider context. The desire to organise material by classifying it in neat compartments, to construct systems that label specimens in an ordered manner, was typical of the Victorian period. The system described was used by art historians to explain artistic traditions throughout the world—notably by Fergusson in his wide-ranging studies. Like the picturesque artists and the Indo-Saracenic architects, the art historians were not developing or choosing an instrument for a local purpose but following a universal pattern that was assumed to be viable. However fallacious it turned out to be, their adoption of it need not suggest an attempt to achieve particular ends, but a failure to question the received method.

This returns us to the question not of error but of underlying motive, the purpose for which the scholarship was undertaken in the first place. Tapati Guha-Thakurta has suggested recently that Fergusson and his contemporaries 'felt it a part of their wider imperial commitments to weave their theories about Indian art' (Guha-Thakurta, 1988, p.111). The nature of these 'imperial commitments' is not defined, and no evidence is adduced in support of the assertion, which is therefore based only on a Saidian assumption about what the case must have been.[10]

The difficulty of investigating a scholar's motives is sharply revealed by a recent study by O.P. Kejariwal (1988). Kejariwal is concerned with the founders and early members of the Asiatic Society of Bengal rather than with the art historians mentioned here, but the problems are analogous. He is anxious to defend figures such as Sir William Jones, Charles Wilkins, H.T. Colebrooke, H.H. Wilson and James Prinsep against the charge that their work was essentially imperialist, and therefore by implication untrustworthy—a charge that has been made increasingly by historians in India, Kejariwal points out, since the publication of Said's *Orientalism.*

Kejariwal's main chapters on the activities of these scholars are well researched hagiography, but when he turns to the question of motive he

[10] Guha-Thakurta goes on to describe the reforming work of E.B. Havell and A.K. Coomaraswamy as a 'new Orientalism'. While stressing that these scholars 'consciously stood outside the existing mainstream of European and official thought' (p.110), she insists that an 'implicit "cultural hegemony"' remains 'manifest in the very authority [their writing] commands...in its ability to...fix the image of Indian art'. They sought, she suggests, to construct notions of 'tradition' and Indian-ness' (pp.111-2). But for Havell especially (regarding art as an expression of life) change was central to his view of art (Havell, 1913, p.vii). If 'authority' alone is an indication of Orientalist 'cultural hegemony' then—Guha-Thakurta's view implies—any Western writing on the East must be Orientalist so long as its claims to know its subject-matter. This echoes the universality of Said's thesis (see below).

advances no argument that could persuade his opponents. He claims, for example, that the scholars' writings contain no mention of intended benefit to the Government; but the Saidian could reply that this merely shows that the benefit was not given barefacedly. He points to the frequent lack of sympathy between the scholars and those in government; but lack of sympathy is not evidence of fundamentally different aims rather than means. And again, the scholars, he claims, received little patronage from the Government, and though in many cases were themselves civil servants, pursued research in areas unrelated to their professional duties; but no one had suggested that the strategy was applied efficiently. For the same reason it would be fruitless to show that the information gathered was not all actually useful for colonial purposes (Kejariwal, 1988, pp.39, 167, 226).

In the attempt to recover the motives of a scholar we cannot rely on his own writings, since he may have misrepresented his motives, or even deluded himself about them. If we wish to examine whether a writer has a concealed purpose, then we cannot admit as evidence his own plea of innocence.

Kejariwal's last gasp is to suggest that the motives must have been as numerous and varied as the individuals involved (Kejariwal, 1988, p.227). This appeal to common sense ignores the central assumption of the Saidian view: that the individual will operates only a level that is situated in, or determined by, its political context.

At this point it becomes clear that the Saidian view, in its stronger and general version, is one which does not admit of argument. If the individual is always situated politically then the actions and intentions of any Briton in colonial India must inevitably derive from that political matrix. Anything that looks like evidence against the general rule—such as an individual's plea of innocence—can be dismissed as evidence and regarded as a fraud, precisely because it contradicts the general rule, which is taken to be true by necessity. The Saidian view in its strong version is not the view that some or much British scholarship on the East was distinctively colonial in character, but the view that all of it had to be since individuals cannot detach themselves from their political context. Membership of the colonial culture, by this view, necessarily entailed having certain political intentions.

This is why even Kejariwal's assaults fail to upset the theory. But Kejariwal may take comfort from the reflection that his very failure reveals the weakness of the assertion, not of his attack: he fails because the theory cannot admit of argument, and this is a serious flaw. By denying the possibility of exception, the Saidian view ceases to be an empirical theory based on investigation, and becomes an *a priori* assertion. It prejudges the very issue that we wish to investigate, and is therefore not a helpful instrument in the investigation. If we wish to

Figure 8. William Simpson, *The Palace at Amber*
(Watercolour, c.1861; India Office Libary and Records, WD 3951)

discover whether the facts of a case are one thing or another, it does not help to start from the assumption that they have to be one.

Conclusion

This last criticism is aimed at what is here called the 'strong' or 'general' version of the theory and not at the whole content of *Orientalism*. If the theory were presented in an empirical version then it might be helpful. In such a version it would not be the claim that Western scholarship of the Orient must be colonial, but the claim that in some cases it was. The use of that empirical observation should be apparent from the discussion above. In this investigation of British representations of Indian architecture, it has been shown that the picture is a mixed one: that some representations (and particularly some written ones) are indeed colonial in a political sense, but that others are not.

The debate over Said's book has often been polarised, and this conclusion may find disfavour with both extremes. The Saidians can dismiss the argument on political grounds, while their opponents may wonder why the matter requires more attention. It is hoped that this discussion shows that the British misrepresentation of India is a subject that merits serious attention, and especially from positions other than the extremes of the Saidian polarity.

In addition to suggesting that the empirical picture is a mixed one, this discussion has shown that there can be other kinds of inspiration for British 'constructions' of India besides political ones. With respect to the works of art described here, the inspiration was largely or wholly aesthetic. A British image of an Indian building—such as William Simpson's view of the Amber palace (Fig.8)—is not an objective documentary record; something intruded between the artist and his subject to make him misrepresent it. The picture is consequently a construction, a kind of myth. But we need not assume because the artist was British that it was his nationality that was the intruder; more relevant to art was his being an artist.

Bibliography and further reading

Archer, M. 1980, *Early Views of India: The Picturesque Journeys of Thomas and William Daniell 1786-1794*, London

Berger, J., 1972, *Ways of Seeing*, Harmondsworth.

Chaudhuri, N.C., 1966, *The Continent of Circe*, Bombay.

Conner, P., 1979, *Oriental Architecture in the West*, London.

Cunningham, A., 1873, *Archaeological Survey of India: Report for the Year 1871-2*, Calcutta.

Daniell, T., 1810, *A Picturesque Voyage to India by the Way of China*, London.

Davies, P., 1985, *Splendours of the Raj: British Architecture in India 1660 to 1947*, London.

—, *Monuments of India*, vol.2, *Islamic, Rajput, European*, London.

Elliott, R., 1833, *Views of the East*, 2 vols., London.

Gilpin, W., 1792, *Three Essays: On Picturesque Beauty: On Picturesque Travel: and On Sketching Landscape*, London.

Gole, S., 1989, *Indian Maps and Plans: From Earliest Times to the Advent of European Surveys*, New Delhi.

Guha-Thakurta, T., 1988, 'Art, Artists and Aesthetics in Bengal, c.1850-1920: Westernizing Trends and Nationalist Concerns in the Making of a New Indian Art', DPhil thesis, Oxford.

—, 1992, *The Making of a New 'Indian' Art*, Cambridge.

Havell, E.B., 1913, *Indian Architecture*, London.

Head, R., 1986, *The Indian Style*, London.

Hodges, W., 1785-8, *Select Views in India*, London.

—, 1794, *Travels in India*, 2nd ed., London.

Hussey, C., 1927, *the Picturesque: Studies in a Point of View*, London.

Kejariwal, O.P., 1988, *The Asiatic Society of Bengal and the Discovery of India's Past 1784-1838*, Delhi.

Llewellyn, B., 1989, *The Orient Observed: Images of the Middle East from the Searight Collection*, Victoria and Albert Museum, London.

Llewellyn-Jones, R., 1985, *A Fatal Friendship: The Nawabs, the British and the City of Lucknow*, Oxford University Press, Delhi.

McWilliam, N. and A. Potts, 1986, 'The Landscape of Reaction: Richard Wilson (1713?-1782) and His Critics', in A.L. Rees and F. Borzello (eds.), *The New Art History*, pp.106-19, London.

Metcalf, T.R., 1989, *An Imperial Vision: Indian Architecture and Britain's Raj*, London.

Mitter, P., 1977, *Much Maligned Monsters: History of European Reactions to Indian Art*, Oxford.

Morris, J., 1986, *Stones of Empire: The Buildings of the Raj*, 2nd ed., Oxford.

Nilsson, S., 1987, 'Jaipur, in the Sign of Leo', *Magazin Tessin*, no.1.

Pal, P. and Vidya Dehejia, 1986, *From Merchants to Emperors: British Artists and India 1757-1930*, New York and London.

Pinney, C.,1990, 'Colonial Anthropology in the "Laboratory of Mankind"', in C.A. Bayly (ed.), *The Raj: India and the British 1600-1947*, pp.252-63, National Portrait Gallery, London.

Ruskin, J.,1903-12, 'The Two Paths', in E.T. Cook and A. Wedderburn (eds.), *The Works of John Ruskin*, vol.16, pp.260-310, London.

Said, E.W. 1978, *Orientalism*, London.

Smith, B., 1985, *European Vision and the South Pacific*, 2nd ed., New Haven and London.

Smith, V., 1930, *A History of Fine Art in India and Ceylon*, 2nd ed., Oxford.

Solkin, D.H., 1982, *Richard Wilson: The Landscape of Reaction*, Tate Gallery, London.

Stamp, G., 1981, 'British Architecture in India 1857-1947', *Journal of the Royal Society of Arts*, cxxxix, pp.357-79.

Stevens, M. (ed.), 1984, *The Orientalists: Delacroix to Matisse*, Royal Academy of Arts.

Stuebe, I.C., 1979, *The Life and Works of William Hodges*, New York.

Sutton, T., 1954, *The Daniells: Artists and Travellers*, London.

Sweetman, J., 1988, *The Oriental Obsession: Islamic Inspiration in British and American Art and Architecture 1500-1920*, Cambridge.

Tillotson, G.H.R., 1987, *Fan Kwae Pictures*, London.

—, 1989, *The Tradition of Indian Architecture: Continuity, Controversy and Change since 1850*, New Haven and London.

—, 1990, 'The Indian Picturesque: Images of India in British Landscape Painting, 1780-1800', in C.A. Bayly (ed.), *The Raj: India and the British 1600-1947*, National Portrait Gallery, London.

—, 1991, 'The Paths of Glory: Representations of Sher Shah's Tomb', *Oriental Art*, xxxvii, 1, pp.4-16.

Tod, J., 1972, *Annals and Antiquities of Rajasthan*, 2 vols, London (first edition 1829/32).

Valentia, G., 1809, *Voyages and Travels to India*, 3 vols, London.

Watkin, D., 1982, *the English Vision: The Picturesque in Architecture, Landscape and Garden Design*, London.

Wolff, J., 1981, *The Social Production of Art*, London.

Part II. Institutions

The second part of this book is concerned more particularly with institutions of law, government and politics, and also once again with the ways in which South Asian experience may be placed in a wider world. With Menski, writing on Hindus in Britain, we come to another dimension of cross-cultural or cross-civilisational influence. What happens within South Asia must be the key to understanding it; but increasingly nowadays those events also have an international dimension, not just (as before) in the impact from outside, but also in contributions from South Asians overseas. There is a comparative and theoretical value in studies of culture in a situation of diaspora; and the presence of South Asians abroad, and the different experiences they have had, are arguably of special concern and interest to scholars of South Asia who themselves are based outside the sub-continent. Migration has cast into relief the question of what is a South Asian, an Indian, a Hindu, and of the extent of overlap between these categories, each of which is itself imprecise. The example taken by Menski is of marriage, an institution which exists in parallel in both religious practice and legal provisions.[1] In Western societies—and also for a long time in South Asia—marriage has had both a public and a private profile, and the balance between the two is an obvious pointer to identity among the migrant population. Migration produces its own peculiar tensions. Thus this paper raises questions about ideas and institutions which are repeatedly being examined in this book.

Anderson's paper, at the start of a historical section concerned with the period of colonial rule, introduces two great influences, from Islam and Britain, influences which may be seen to have taken particular forms in South Asia, and also to have become integral parts *of* South Asia, even while at some levels and by some persons being thought still distinct from a mainstream ('Hinduism'). Anderson combines the two by showing that the effect of the West was partly to encourage a separate and orthodox Muslim identity. Indeed, generally, this may be seen to be a feature of the impact of law during the colonial period. Next—on chronological and theoretical grounds—comes Stein's discussion of peasant society and insurgency in Mysore. Departing from an old consensus about the quietism and stagnation of Indian rural

[1] The story is taken further (for British Muslims, but with general impact) by recent Scottish Court of Sessions' decisions to annul the arranged marriages of Nasreen Akmal (October 1992) and of Shahid Mahmood (June 1993) on the grounds of young age or emotional or physical coercion at the time of marriage—the rulings will probably influence courts elsewhere, including England; see Cameron Fyfe, 'Till Scottish law do us part', *Independent*, 21 June 1993.

society, Stein here represents a new emphasis among historians upon opposition at all levels in South Asia, perhaps especially from 'peasants', not only to colonial rule, but to other forms of higher or rival authority. (This view is shared by all the papers here dealing with the so-called colonial period.) Stein describes, in effect, rival political structures—including a long 'peasant' history—upon which colonial polity encroached. The paper by Robb draws the same moral as Anderson, about harder and broader categorisations, after discussing the impact of law and another important locus of Western influence, land revenue policies and agrarian administration. Implicit in this analysis is a contrast between different ways of conceptualising and ordering society, a partial misfit between what British rulers applied and what Indians expected. Arnold makes explicit this contrast between different kinds of rationale and organisation. His paper contributes to awareness of another of the points at which influence was felt: that of technical knowledge and professional expertise. It discusses the mix of practices and beliefs, in India and among Western-trained medical officers, whereby smallpox was confronted and understood. This too was a frontier along which Western influence advanced and was contested.

Such papers as those by Stein and Arnold, and to some extent Anderson and Robb, seek to widen the spheres within which confrontations and exchanges between South Asia and outside influences are perceived. The result is to make our understanding of those processes far more complex. A sphere in which these questions have always been raised is the political one encountered indirectly in Part I: the attempt by South Asians to build 'nations' in the modern sense of sovereign, territorial states with a right to 'self'-government. Taylor tells the story of the Indian National Congress, formed in 1885, and the varying ways in which it has been understood. The independence struggle was a means whereby many Indians opposed colonial rule, though it was also a process in which they took over parts of its legacy: in state boundaries, political institutions, law, administration, education, technology and so on. The ways of discussing the political revolution—and the matters relevant to it—are still under active discussion among scholars of South Asia.

Byres also is concerned with the sources of the ideologies which inform political institutions and the practice of politics. He claims that Charan Singh, sometime Chief Minister of Uttar Pradesh and Home and Finance Minister of India, leader of the Lok Dal, evolved his own personal theories: the paper traces their origins in his social background, and in Indian and Western, especially socialist, thought. The paper is also valuable for its report on issues important in independent India, and its portrait of political life. Though ostensibly about ideology, it reveals much about the institutions and process of Indian government, economy and society. The paper provides, by the device of assessing the ideas and career of one man, a kind of overview of recent conditions in one, very important part of South Asia. It is a very different overview from the one offered at the outset of this book, by Chapman, but it sums up the journey into and beyond the minutiae which we hope the reader will have experienced.

At least one general lesson can be drawn from all these papers. If language needs to be studied to answer questions about politics, if law can tell us something of religion, medicine something of colonial impact, and so on, then the conventional division of disciplines may be an obstacle rather than an aid to understanding South Asia. Again and again, the fascination of South Asian studies is to be found in their complexities. It is a matter of conjecture whether or not these too are peculiarly South Asian. It used to be thought by some Europeans that society there was somehow organic, growing and reproducing itself without rational thought or higher structures of organisation. This idea is now properly discredited, but like many common and persistent notions, it surely had a kernel of observation behind its mask of pre-assumptions; and that kernel may have been a heightened interdependence between different social elements in South Asia, the lack of a linear idea of worldly progress for individuals or civilisation, and a reluctance to posit wholly distinct categories of being or analysis. It is not least in these possibilities that South Asia requires its students in the West constantly to rethink their assumptions. To do so generally was the advice of the great Scottish philosopher, David Hume, and it has become a motto for much modern scholarship. There are few studies in which it is more necessary or challenging than those on South Asia.

(PR)

LEGAL PLURALISM IN THE HINDU MARRIAGE[1]

Werner Menski

This paper explores how Hindus in Britain match the requirements of English law and South Asian customs when it comes to marriage solemnisation. The discussion is placed in the context of legal pluralism, seen as a central element of South Asian legal culture. But the practices observable among British Asians are not simply a continuation of customary legal pluralities. Fieldwork in 1987 clearly shows that Hindu marriage solemnisation is even more plural in Britain than in India because the English legal system requires an act of administration, the official registration of every marriage—which is not mandatory in India—as the means of ensuring the legal validity of the marriage. British Asians have largely learnt to follow the English law. But, this does not mean that Hindus abandon their customary marriage rituals. In the eyes of the community, the registered marriage ceremony is treated more like an engagement. The 'real' wedding remains the Hindu marriage; only when this public form of registration has been completed will the couple cohabit. Subsequent fieldwork shows that British Hindus have become concerned to reduce the stress and the potential for abuse connected with this plurality, by amalgamating the English legal ceremonies and the South Asian customary procedures. Not surprisingly, the South Asian elements are proving dominant: the new trend is to incorporate the English registered marriage ritually into the Hindu marriage ceremonies. The English law finds itself 'orientalised'.

While the topic of arranged marriages among South Asians has generated some interest among researchers (Ballard, 1977-8; Brah, 1977-8), is often taken up by the media, and remains of tremendous importance to the South Asian communities in Britain themselves, nothing has, to my knowledge, so far been written about the effects of the British legal system and its requirements on South Asian customs and practices with particular reference to the solemnisation of Hindu marriages.

The presence of large communities of South Asian Hindus in British cities has imported into this country interesting elements of legal pluralism (Hooker, 1975); indeed, the perceptive observer can detect numerous instances of competition between conflicting obligation systems. We are not concerned here with the implications of this situation

[1] First published in R. Burghart (ed.), *Hinduism in Great Britain* (Tavistock Publications, London, 1987), pp.180-200.

for the English legal system (the prevailing view seems to be, at any rate, that little if anything has changed as a result of the presence of Hindus, Muslims, and Sikhs in the UK; see Bromley, 1981); we are concerned with the effects of legal pluralism in a British context on the institution of Hindu marriage and on the Hindu spouses themselves, who as parents of the next generation of South Asians in this country will have a decisive role to play in the maintenance or abandonment of Hindu culture in Britain. So our considerations of past and present patterns of marriage solemnisation among Hindus naturally have implications for the question whether and how Hindus in Britain can maintain their culture in an alien socio-legal context.

This essay, then, describes elements of legal pluralism, with particular reference to marriage solemnisation, within Hindu culture in South Asia. It discusses the effects of the transfer of this plurality to the British social context, and it tries to analyse the present rather confused situation with regard to marriage solemnisation among Hindus in the UK.

While we find an abundance of material on Hindu marriage in India, written both in India and abroad (see Kapadia, 1966; Mayer, 1960), we have very little published information about Hindu marriage in Britain. Kanitkar and Jackson (1982, p.17-19) give a general description of a Hindu marriage ritual in Britain, but do not make it clear enough that there are tremendous variations between different regional and social groups in the UK; Khera (1981, p.105-7) puts forward some comments on Hindu marriage, but is exclusively concerned with the topic of arranged marriage. Our lack of information is, of course, partly due to the fact that the phenomenon of Hindu residence in the UK is a fairly recent one. Hindu marriage does not appear to be a topic that interests the English lawyer. The assumption is that immigrants and their descendants are governed by English law, which is clear and familiar. That there may be problems of adjustment for Hindus, Muslims, and other immigrants is conveniently overlooked; the prerogative of the rule of English law is assumed without a clear understanding of the legal background of immigrant cultures. More dangerously, there is a general assumption that South Asian laws themselves are largely, if not exclusively, the same as English law, so that there is no need to teach, study, or research into such laws with special reference to Hindus, Muslims and other members of communities. Such attitudes are utterly wrong: India's Hindu law, though much reformed on Western lines, is alive and constantly developing, also on traditional lines.[2] Much better

[2] In the area of marriage solemnisation, customary law has recently won a major victory. In *Baby* v. *Jayant Mahadeo Jagtap* (*All India Reporter* 1981 Bombay 283) the High Court of Bombay accepted that new customs can indeed develop and that the modern law will eventually have to recognise them if

known is the fact that the Muslim laws of South Asia form vigorous legal systems with much control over the Islamic population.

The fact that modern legislation dominates Indian family law does not mean that traditional Hindu law is dead (but see Derrett, 1978). True, much of it is abrogated or reformed beyond recognition, but the majority of Hindus do not appear to be aware of modern laws issued from Delhi or some state capital, and the further one goes away from the capital, the less people appear to know that there exists something like the Hindu Code, a conglomerate of four Acts of Hindu Law.[3] Many aspects of traditional Hindu law have been codified in those Acts, which are not just a wholesale import from the West, as is often believed. The Hindu Marriage Act (HMA) has left absolute scope for custom in the field of marriage solemnisation and has not even tried to reform this area of the law on Western lines. Registration of marriages, the crucial legal component in the West, is not a requirement under Hindu law, and so a uniform demand of the state's law at the point of solemnisation of a marriage does not exist and the customary plurality of solemnisation patterns is maintained in full strength. We shall see below how the demands of a Western legal system, with its emphasis on certainty and written, documentary evidence designed to facilitate administrative processes, not only change patterns of behaviour relating to the solemnisation of marriage itself, but may have wider repercussions on culture and its maintenance in a fast-changing environment.

Legal pluralism in Hindu marriage in India

The aim of this section is to describe the relationship between the different sources of legal authority in Hindu India—that is, customary, Brahmanical, and state law—and to show how they tolerate and legitimate different forms of marriage. We shall then examine how relevant these sources of authority have remained in contemporary Britain.

We have to emphasise the importance of the well-known concept of Hindu 'unity in diversity' (see Derrett, 1979). Hindus in Tamil Nadu, Gujarat, the Punjab, or Kashmir may be governed by totally different customary rules, but we would refer to them as 'Hindu law'. Regional and local diversity has always been of enormous importance in the subcontinent as a parameter in defining rules of law. Apart from that, social class, whether measured in terms of ritual purity and caste membership, or less traditionally, in terms of socio-economic status, adds to the plurality of customary legal rules and concepts.

The crucial and central notion of Hindu *dharma*, a set of duties and

---

many people are involved.

[3] They are the *Hindu Marriage Act* of 1955 (HMA), the *Hindu Succession Act* of 1956, the *Hindu Adoptions and Maintenance Act* of 1956, and the *Hindu Minority and Guardianship Act* of 1956.

rights, whether pertaining to a particular individual (*svadharma*), as a global notion of affecting the whole universe, or at any of the intermediary stages (the *dharma* of the family, the clan, a particular profession, a whole state, or human society), leads by definition to a system of law not characterised by uniformity. What is 'right' and 'wrong', in a Western sense, appropriate behaviour in different life situations, is determined from case to case and varies according to circumstances. Traditional Hindu law, therefore, being largely customary, is not a legal system that can prescribe identical behaviour in many different situations and for many people. It is highly localised and particularised. Facts and circumstances of a particular case weigh more heavily than any abstract rule, so that in theory no two situations are completely alike. On the other hand, identical life situations, like marriage, constantly arise, and certain repeated patterns of behaviour evolve, acquiring a superior status when it comes to laying down rules of appropriate conduct.

At such a crucial point as the rite of passage of marriage, then, quite apart from Sanskritic rules of a ritual nature, the position of the individual Hindu as a member of a certain family, clan, caste, or any other social group, will largely determine how a particular marriage is solemnised. It also matters, for example, whether the bride is presumed to be a virgin or not, and whether a spouse is widowed or not. The basic pattern that we find in Hindu India is an immense variety of customary forms of marriage solemnisation, locally and socially determined and observed.

In a complicated relationship of mutual dependence with the customary Hindu law we find what may be called the Sanskritic Hindu law. This adds to the customary 'unity in diversity' rather than acting as a unifying force, at least in the realm of marriage solemnisation. In the literature, the impression has been created that Sanskritic models of marriage solemnisation among Hindus have provided an element of unity and of cultural continuity. While this is no doubt true to a certain extent (see also Kanitkar and Jackson, 1982, p.18), statements of social scientists to the effect that contemporary Hindu marriage rituals are nothing but true copies of their ancient Vedic models have not proved right (for details, see Menski, 1984). In reality, Sanskritic Hindu law is based on an enormous variety of written sources, some of them unknown to the present day, others like the famous *Manusmrti* (also referred to as the *dharmasastra* or handbook of *dharma* by Manu) overvalued and over-interpreted as a 'code of Hindu law', implying uniformity where even the text itself does not warrant that kind of interpretation. Thus the *Manusmrti*, for example, says almost nothing at all about ritual details of marriage solemnisation. It merely lays down (8.227) that a particular ritual, the *saptapadi*, when completed with the seventh step, signifies legal validity of the marriage. This means, in particular, that from that point onwards the bride/wife would be classified as a widow should her husband die.

The rite of *saptapadi* appears to have a special position even in present-day India (Mayer, 1966, p.229) and also in British Hindu marriages (Kanitkar and Jackson, 1982, p.18), but the Sanskrit texts that deal with marriage solemnisation in great detail are by no means uniform. There is an abundance of such texts, and they tend to differ in points of detail when it comes to the various rites that make up a complete marriage ritual. Some of the texts expressly state that the local variations in marriage solemnisation should be given preference, while others merely state what appears to be common to all.[4]

The evolving pattern seems to have been that of an age-old continuous competition between local customary traditions, developed and controlled by the family and clan elders, and more or less localised Sanskritic traditions propagated and interpreted by the Hindu priests. This seems to have led to two developments: the professional priests, with an interest in the performance of elaborate marriage rituals designed to give maximum profit to all participants, supported a trend to perform long and complicated rituals lasting for days rather than hours (see also Mayer, 1966, p.228). This practice was justified and legitimised by the Hindu theory of marriage as a sacrament (*samskara*), which means that the performance of elaborate rituals is deemed to have a beneficial effect on the spouses and their environment, and creates, in fact, some awareness in the minds of the spouses that they are getting married. This theory was apparently readily accepted by the higher sections of the highly-stratified Hindu society. On the other hand, many communities that were not so highly placed in the ritual hierarchy of Hindu society and the caste system (and they seem to have maintained that lowly position), appear to have abandoned Sanskritic rituals of marriage altogether and have developed customary forms of marriage which may stress the acceptance of the bride and the union of the couple, adding at times some rudimentary forms of dramatisation of crucial marital expectations, such as progeny, which would be expressed through fertility symbols. It is thus not correct to assume that all Hindus marry in elaborate Sanskritic fashion, but we appear to know very little about the simpler forms of marriage.

For the average Hindu, however, solemnisation of marriage as a crucial step in an individual's life is an occasion on which to call a priest and to celebrate with elaborate rituals. While the ritual aspects of marriage are largely delegated to the priest, the social functions of the event seem of crucial importance to the families and individuals involved. Considerations of whom to invite, what presents to give, and what to

[4] See, for example *Asvalayana-Grhyasutra* 1.7.1-2 as translated by Hermann Oldenberg, *The Grihya-Sutras*, pt. I (reprint, Delhi, 1973).

expect from others seem prominent rather than concern over the ritual aspects of the marriage, though the latter are by no means unimportant (see Mayer, 1966, p.227ff.).

In conclusion, we see a largely harmonious coexistence between the customary and the Sanskritic laws of marriage solemnisation in traditional India, both supporting and supplementing each other, thus creating the confusing plurality with which we are concerned here.

As far as the state law is concerned, one must note that there was no legislative interference with the Hindu patterns of marriage solemnisation until the HMA of 1955. Legal validity of a particular Hindu marriage was determined socially on the basis of community recognition (hence the importance of the publicity of rituals) and depended, if at all framed in ritual terms, on the performance of the rituals customary to particular communities. This position was not disturbed by the HMA of 1955. Section 7 of that Act reads:

(1) A Hindu marriage may be solemnised in accordance with the customary rites and ceremonies of either party thereto.
(2) Where such rites and ceremonies include the *saptapadi* (that is, the taking of seven steps by the bridegroom and the bride jointly before the sacred fire), the marriage becomes complete and binding when the seventh step is taken.

Thus, also under contemporary Indian law, any customary form of Hindu marriage solemnisation leads to a lawful union. The definition of 'customary' is found in section 3 of the HMA of 1955:

(a) The expressions 'custom' and 'usage' signify any rule which, having been continuously and uniformly observed for a long time, has obtained the force of law among Hindus in any local area, tribe, community, group or family: Provided that the rule is certain and not unreasonable or opposed to public policy; and Provided further that in the case of a rule applicable only to a family it has not been discontinued by the family.

Thus even a family custom, under the conditions described, may be employed to solemnise a valid Hindu marriage. This rule gives tremendous discretion to Hindu spouses and their parents, but has created many problems for courts, since it has proved to be a most difficult task to decide what, in a particular case, is a valid custom. Under the influence of English concepts of law, the rule that valid customs must have been observed 'for a long time' (see s.3 of the HMA quoted above) was interpreted very strictly, and new customs were denied judicial recognition. This led to many unjust and socially unacceptable decisions and prompted special legislation in Tamil Nadu.[5] A recent

[5] The *Hindu Marriages* (*Madras Amendment*) *Act*, 1967, inserts a section, 7A, behind s.7 of the HMA, to the effect that Hindu marriages in Tamil Nadu may be solemnised in less elaborate forms than seem stipulated by s.7 HMA; this was done in reaction to early cases that denied legal recognition to the so-called self-respect marriages. For details refer to Derrett, 1970, p.299.

case involving neo-Buddhists in Maharashtra has, however, given judicial recognition to newly-developed customary forms of marriage solemnisation (see note 2 above).

The confusion in this area of the law has been increased due to a one-sided interpretation of section 7(2) of the HMA (quoted above). That section has picked out one particular rite as more important than others, and is thus in line with the rule found at *Manusmrti* 8.227. Even though the wording of the section implies, clearly enough, that a *saptapadi* need not be performed in all Hindu marriage rituals, many Hindu law cases have ruled otherwise (Gupte, 1976, p.153) and have created problems for spouses who, after many years of marriage, found themselves deprived of status and, often, property rights (see, for example, *Bibbe* v. *Ram Kali; All India Reporter* 1982 Allahabad 248).

Now, what actually is a *saptapadi*, that crucial rite of seven steps? Our efforts to find an answer may serve to illustrate the gradual process of development and change in a fluid ritual field characterised by a plurality of rules and models. The most ancient forms of the *saptapadi* point to a dramatisation of friendship, not exclusively in the context of marriage rituals (for details see Menski, 1984, p.580ff.), but particularly between husband and wife (see the translation provided by Kanitkar and Jackson, 1982, p.18). Yet originally the seven steps of the ritual were not taken *around* the sacred fire; significantly the HMA stipulated 'before the sacred fire', that is, perhaps, in the presence of the holy fire. It is obvious that if one circumambulates a fire, more than seven steps may be needed, and seven circumambulations are not the same as seven steps! In some Hindu communities, the fire is circumambulated four times only, in others five times, but still one speaks of *saptapadi*. Most Hindus are unable to give us a clear answer, and the Hindu law books are confused too.

Some knowledge of Hindu ritual patterns helps to disentangle this confusion. The so-called *saptapadi* of our days is in reality the ancient Hindu ritual of circumambulation of the fire, called *agniparinayana* (leading around the fire), which, in Vedic times, was performed four times. This ritual appears now merged with the real ancient *saptapadi*, in which the bride (or both spouses) would take seven steps in one direction, either east or north (Menski, 1984, p.581-2). The latter ritual seems to have lost popularity and from my observations appears to be performed only in marriages involving very traditional and learned families in India. Such ritual niceties are, however, not widely known, and the general public is more concerned with the social and culinary aspects of marriage than with the ritual.

To summarise this section: by the time large numbers of Punjabis and Gujaratis left India for East Africa and Britain, redefined ancient customary traditions of Hindu marriage solemnisation with all their local and social variations were being observed. Hindu marriage had the definite aura of sacrament, at any rate for the higher castes, and the Hindu priests were in more or less full control of the ritual sequences to be followed,

Legal pluralism in Hindu marriage in Britain

It has already been indicated that, from a certain viewpoint, it may be disputed that one can talk of 'legal pluralism' with regard to Hindu marriages in the UK. Hindus domiciled in Britain are, like everybody else, subject to the *lex loci.* English law, as a uniform legal system with no special marriage rules for members of different religions (apart, however, from some special rules for Jews and Quakers), does not take notice of the fact that certain spouses may be Hindu. They are required to solemnise their marriages in a form that has legal validity in the eyes of, and according to, English law. Whilst we cannot dispute that Hindus in Britain are subject to English law, there is evidence that the individuals concerned also continue to be guided by Hindu law and have been put under pressure to work out compromises between conflicting legal demands. How this works in detail we shall see below. It is apparent that elements of Hindu law have almost imperceptibly been added into the fabric of English law, which is subtly changing under the influence of the multi-cultural population it is supposed to govern, because the alternative would be to allow a system of coexisting personal laws, as in modern Indian law. England does not seem ready for that, even though Muslims in particular would welcome such an arrangement.

On the other hand, the strong compulsive force of the uniform legal system makes itself felt in that it demands compliance with its rules or threatens with sanctions. This also means that the traditional sources of Hindu law, as outlined above, have no standing *vis-à-vis* English law: no form of Hindu marriage solemnised in the UK has legal validity under the *lex loci per se.*

It may be argued, and seems indeed the case, that the vast adaptive potential of Hindus, a consequence of the customary plurality of legal authorities outlined above, has made it comparatively easy for Hindus in Britain to follow the rules of English marriage law. For an English lawyer the matter may end there, and on a satisfactory note. But while we may now assume almost total compliance with the English law of marriage solemnisation among Hindus (there is much evidence that the picture was quite different ten years ago), it is certain that Hindus in Britain are also maintaining their customary forms of marriage solemnisation. I know of very few Hindu couples who simply had a registered wedding and no more. In those cases, the reason given for not celebrating a Hindu wedding as well was a financial one, the aim being apparently to avoid double expenses and extra costs related to the Hindu wedding. Public opinion among Hindus, however, is not in favour of such arrangements.

How, then, have the majority of British Hindus adapted to the new socio-legal environment? It is clear that a Hindu couple in Britain, whose marriage was solemnised in an elaborate ritual by a Hindu priest, in a hall hired for the purpose, or in a temple, and in the presence of many invited guests, is not valid under English law unless it was, or is subsequently, registered. Thus, if the couple enjoyed the 'first night' and consummated their marriage as Hindu husband and wife, and the next day the husband decided to abandon his spouse, the women and her relatives would have little remedy under English law. They could, at best, try to bring back the defaulting husband through community pressure. It must have been a tremendous shock for some Hindu parents and their daughters to discover that a purported husband could get out of marriage without any difficulties and without further liabilities under English law.[6] I have tried to trace court records of such instances, but have not been successful. It appears that Hindus, and Gujaratis in particular, have been very reluctant to go to court over such matters. The information I have is from individual cases that came to my notice, and in all those cases the girl's family has taken steps to look after her. The considerable element of shame involved seems to have contributed significantly to the rather rapid learning process among 'Asians' in this area of the law, because it was immediately and forcefully brought home to them that adjustment to, and compliance with, the new legal framework was necessary for their own protection. As a result, 'Asians' have become even more careful when it comes to arranging marriages, preoccupied as they are with female chastity and the reputation of their female family members.

What does a Hindu couple have to do in order to avoid pitfalls and to get validly married? Like everybody else they would have to apply for a certificate or licence from a Registrar. There are a number of different procedures with which we are not concerned here (for details see Bromley, 1981, pp.45ff.), but the choice of procedures is limited if either spouse has come from abroad, as is often the case. The solemnisation of marriage in an English Registrar's office does not make the marriage legally valid in the eyes of the Hindu spouses and their families. They will, therefore, make arrangements for a Hindu wedding, which could be held at any time up to several months later. Meanwhile the couple would continue to live in their respective homes, and the bride/wife would not consummate the marriage (see also Pearl, 1972-3, pp.71, 73). In the early stages of 'Asian' residence in the U.K. this was the only satisfactory and safe procedure, since celebrating the Hindu wedding

[6] Hindu law in India would put him under an obligation to maintain this wife, because she is a 'Hindu wife' under s.18 of the *Hindu Adoptions and Maintenance Act* of 1956.

first and subsequently registering the marriage could create considerable problems, as outlined above.

As the immigrant communities in Britain grew in size and began to establish themselves more firmly in certain areas during the 1970s, an option offered by the Marriage Acts 1949-70 became available to more and more Hindu couples, and is now exercised in many cases—though obviously there are tremendous local variations within Britain. Some sections of the Marriage Act 1949 provide the machinery for registering certain buildings for the solemnisation of marriages (see Bromley, 1981, p.48). A 'registered building' must fulfil certain criteria in order to qualify for this special status: it must be certified as a 'place of religious worship'; it must be a separate building; and at least 20 householders must support the application and certify that the building is used by them as their usual place of public religious worship.

David Pearl (1972-3, p.67) has complained that the above conditions 'are so restrictive that few immigrant communities would be able to obtain benefit from the provision'. He has outlined three difficulties facing applicants attempting to secure registration:

(a) The building in question must first have been certified under the Places of Religious Worship Registration Act 1955.
(b) It is necessary to prove that the building is a 'separate building' and that the whole building is used as a place of worship.
(c) The worship in the building must be public worship.

The first seems a mere administrative formality, but certification (which carried with it certain benefits) could be refused to buildings other than Hindu temples, for example Hindu community centres, on the ground that they were not places of worship. According to Pearl (1972-3, p.68), the second requirement has created 'a difficult stumbling-block to the immigrant communities seeking to register their religious buildings for the solemnisation of marriages'. In the early stages of 'Asian' immigration to Britain, these conditions must indeed have been difficult to fulfil; with regard to the situation before 1972 Pearl is certainly right. But matters have changed considerably since then. Hindu communities all over Britain have gained enough strength and financial support to establish their own, communal places of worship in the form of Hindu *mandirs* (temples). This process still continues, as smaller groups and sects beginning to assert their separate identity follow the older, established temples on this way. While a preference for the use of redundant church buildings may be noticeable, this need not be a general trend.

In some cases, it may still be difficult to satisfy the condition of 'separate building'. Most Hindu temples in Britain seem to comprise a large hall or some other form of accommodation which can be used for lectures and other public functions, and for marriages. The whole building may, therefore, not be used as a place of religious worship, and for that reason some Hindu temples appear to have met with difficulties in registering their building. What the picture is throughout the country would be very interesting to know. Pearl wrote that the rule requiring *public* worship posed no problems, and I have not heard of any. Moreover it should hardly be difficult for a temple committee to get 20 signatures of householders. But it must be noted that the above rules of law lead to, and presuppose, a somewhat distorted picture of the role of Hindu temples. The fact that Hindus traditionally worship in the home rather than at temples (most Hindu families in Britain have a *puja* corner in their home) is overlooked or ignored.

Here, then, are significant changes of Hindu socio-religious practice in this country: the temple in Britain has become more than a place of worship (on this see Jackson, 1981, p.65). It should also be noted that traditionally solemnisation of marriages did not take place in Hindu temples. Still, not all Hindu temples in Britain have the necessary accommodation to cater for weddings, and the pattern common in India—that is, hiring a suitable hall for the solemnisation of the marriage and subsequent celebrations—recurs in Britain. Hindu marriages in Britain are, then, often solemnised 'in the temple' because it is such a large, convenient hall. Otherwise there is little connection with the temple itself, though I have observed that some Hindu couples, *before* the solemnization of their marriage, enter the *mandir* to pray for blessings and good luck, and in one case a priest even performed some small ritual with the couple to the same effect.

What percentage of Hindu couples is actually using the facilities offered by 'registered buildings' would be interesting to know, but we appear to have no figures. It seems very common for Hindu couples to marry in a Registrar's office and then to have a Hindu wedding plus celebration in a hall, independent of any temple, but with the help of a Hindu priest. Here again, local circumstances will determine the range of options.

If a Hindu temple has been given the status of 'registered building', this means that Hindu couples can register their marriage there and undergo the Hindu rituals on the same day, a matter of some convenience, especially in view of the liminal state that follows a registered wedding. In the temple, there will be a Registrar present, or an 'authorised person' to ensure proper registration of the marriage. Apparently the English Law Commission in its Working Paper on Solemnisation of Marriages presumed that the Registrar and 'authorised person' would also be able to keep an eye on the Hindu marriage solemnisation. I find this somewhat pretentious, and indeed a common practice seems to be that a marriage between two Hindus in a 'registered building' is first solemnised by the Registrar, who then retires and leaves the couple to undergo whatever Hindu form of marriage they want. Thus, the picture that emerges is that the state's agents are concerned to ensure the proper registration of marriages (see in general terms, for English law, Bromley, 1981, p.39) and are not interested in 'ethnic' forms of marriage. We also have evidence that the formal requirements of the short secular ritual of registration (see Bromley, 1981, pp.47-8) have not been observed to the letter, since many Hindu spouses have not been able to make the stipulated declaration in English, but have still had their marriages registered.

While it could thus be said that the English law and its machinery are only interested in proper registration of the marriage, for the sake of evidence of the legal status of the parties, more recently some government agencies such as the Department of Social Security have begun to ask for proof of Hindu marriage solemnisaton in addition to the document of registration. This amounts to an implied recognition of the legal importance of the Hindu rituals of marriage in the UK. The communities themselves have maintained throughout that, for them, the Hindu form of marriage solemnisation is more significant than the English one.

A series of informal interviews and discussions with Hindu individuals and youth groups in 1982 and 1983 yielded some interesting insights into how Hindus in Britain have adjusted to the new socio-legal environment and how they have reconciled the two forms of marriage solemnisation expected of them.[7] To begin with, very few people we spoke to did not agree that both forms of marriage solemnisation were important. Overwhelmingly the Hindu marriage was thought to be of greater importance, but then many respondents had second thoughts and added that the registration of the marriage was just as important. Older people especially were aware of the crucial role of the latter: for tax purposes, all kinds of benefit, immigration, and travel abroad, and official paperwork. The most important aspect of the Hindu wedding, for the older generation, appeared to be that it helped to maintain Hindu culture in an alien environment. Young people, while readily agreeing that Hindu marriage solemnisation was necessary, were much less specific as to why this should be so and seemed to think that the social function connected with it was an important element. From this viewpoint seems to derive criticism of the Hindu marriage as too lengthy and too costly, as reported by Jackson (1981, p.65).

We also found that the registration of marriages preceded the Hindu form of solemnisation in almost all cases, that there was no consummation of the marriage until after the Hindu wedding, and that the registration was in effect looked upon as a form of engagement. The lesser importance attributed to the registered wedding is also shown by

[7] I am grateful to my student Ismail Mehta, now a barrister, who conducted most of this research for an undergraduate project.

the fact that fewer people are commonly invited to celebrate this form of marriage, indeed there may be no celebration at all: we have come across cases where a spouse went straight off to work after the ceremony in the Registrar's office. And lastly, it is significant that wedding anniversaries are counted from the day of the Hindu wedding—if indeed one celebrates such dates, as it is not a Hindu tradition to do so. The Hindu wedding of a couple, however, is most regularly accompanied by a big social function and it is then that public acknowledgement is made that the spouses have become husband and wife.

These findings left us somewhat unsatisfied. Even if the registration of the marriage preceded the Hindu solemnisation of marriage by only a few hours there were indications that the latter was considered crucial and was given more importance. Even then, not many guests would attend the short ceremony in the Registrar's chambers (numbers have often been restricted, anyway), while the Hindu ceremony was part of a big function. Was the Hindu marriage more important?

It took some time to realise that to discuss the matter in terms of relative importance was inappropriate. There are clearly two distinct forms of marriage solemnisation, supplementing each other and leading to a marital union that is fully legitimised from every viewpoint. Clearly, the two components of this complex process of solemnisation are not identical, either in form or in substance. A brief look at both of them should show what is meant here.

The ritual drama of a registered marriage comprises essentially an interaction between the Registrar as a representative of the state and the couple. This, at least, is how Hindus seem to view it. Even though at some point in the ritual the spouses have to make a declaration which refers to the other spouse, the Registrar's ceremony does not appear to establish a relationship of intimacy between the two spouses. The conclusion is inevitable that the couple here make a contract with the state, more or less reluctantly, because required to do so by law, and that the burden is now on the state to give the spouses a number of rights.

The ritual drama of the Hindu marriage, however, emphasises the polarity of the wife-giving and the wife-taking family, of husband and wife, male and female, and dramatises expectations in that framework. The major level of interaction is found between the two spouses who, step by step, approach the position of husband and wife through the performance of the marriage rituals which consist essentially of rites of separation and rites of incorporation. The end of the marriage rituals appears, in view of lack of public knowledge about the precise meaning of individual rites, to signify that groom and bride have become husband and wife. In this sequence of rituals the modern state is conspicuously absent, but the crucial element of community participation in the marriage is provided for by the more or less attentive crowd that attends the wedding. For Hindus in Britain, then, the registered marriage has indeed largely remained a 'legal formality' (see Ballard, 1978, p.189, for similar evidence for Sikhs), while only the Hindu wedding is taken to establish conjugal links between the spouses.

We do not have to look far to find out why this should be: Hindus are not content to consider the narrow, secular approach to marriage solemnisation, as taken by English law, as appropriate for themselves. Getting married, for them, is more than a matter of a contract between two individuals; it has, in the context of the Hindu notion of *dharma*, implications for the world at large. The requirements of the English law of marriage have thus been built into the British version of the Hindu world view without much friction: the added ritual of solemnisation in the Registrar's office has simply become a further element of the traditional, but constantly evolving and redeveloping legal pluralism. British Hindus, outwardly westernised, seem to continue to act in terms of *dharma*, even though much of what is done happens at the subconscious level.

It is quite a different matter to look at the Hindu marriage rituals themselves and to ask what changes may have occurred on the way from India to Britain, or via the East African sojourn. Some observations on this as yet largely uncultivated field of study may be added here.

It is quite well known, I think, that Hindu marriage rituals in this country, compared to India, are shorter and less complicated in ritual terms. In particular, many preliminary rituals contained in the traditional handbooks of marriage solemnisation are no longer performed. Hindu priests find themselves constantly under pressure to shorten rituals or to abandon some peripheral ones, so that we can already observe marriage rituals which consist of little more than the crucial *mangalpheras* or circumambulations of the holy fire. Generally, however, Hindu priests will insist that a more or less complete marriage ritual be performed. I have seen an old priest waiting patiently till everyone had had their meal and the spouses were ready for their departure to the new home, so that he could perform the send-off ritual without which, in his own opinion, his function was not satisfactorily completed. He was perfectly aware that, had he gone home, nobody would have cared to perform this little ritual, but he considered it his duty to ensure its performance,.

Considerable pressure is exercised on the priests to perform marriage rituals even on inauspicious days. In Britain, the weekends are the most convenient time for marriage functions, and so clients may insist that their priest perform the marriage rituals on a convenient day and in disregard of astrological factors. Priests who refuse to do this may suffer loss of remuneration, and many seem to adjust to the new situation by making it clear that their performance of auspicious rituals may well be fruitless on such a day and that they would not give any guarantee about the success of a marriage thus solemnised.

As far as the ritual substance is concerned, Hindu priests seem to exercise almost total control and face little supervision from participants in the marriage. Only once have I observed a priest interrupted in the middle of a ritual; this was so that he could repeat it in a form known to, and preferred by, some old ladies, the guardians of a particular local or caste tradition. In this case the priest was Gujarati, and the spouses were immigrants from Fiji, originating from Uttar Pradesh, and evidently subject to different traditions.

Priests have shown me how they select and compose their own variants of marriage rituals from a number of ritual handbooks, and how they vary the rituals depending on the caste status of the spouses and particular circumstances. Rarely would a family specify what rituals they wanted performed: the priest as ritual specialist is trusted. He has, after all, a certain reputation due to the fact that he acts for a number of local groups (rather than one particular caste only) which makes him experienced in the traditions of many people. In fact a versatile priest can considerably shape the customary forms of marriage solemnisation for different castes by introducing and maintaining ritual variants (see also Menski, 1984, p.875). I doubt whether this is even noticed by the lay Hindu who seems remarkably uninterested in the performance of marriage rituals.

Recently, however, as a reaction to frequent complaints by Hindu youngsters that the Hindu marriage rituals are cumbersome and 'meaningless', many Hindu priests have started to give a running commentary in English or one of the Indian languages on what they are doing and why certain rituals are performed. This often takes the form of sermon-like little speeches. Here is not the place to elaborate in detail on new interpretations introduced by contemporary priests. The trend seems to be to overlook the finer points of the Sanskritic ritual and to give a popularised version of what the rites are thought to express or to achieve. The phrase that a particular rite is performed for good luck appears, of course, rather often in this context.

I see two main problems for the future of Hindu marriage solemnisation in Britain. The first is that in the foreseeable future there will be a lack of committed and experienced Hindu priests, who alone could uphold the ancient traditions or their more recent variants in a sociocultural environment that seems unconducive to the perpetuation of notions of *dharma*. The currently active older generation of Hindu priests is going to die out over the next two decades. Few Hindu youngsters in Britain seem to envisage a career as *pandit*. The recent recruitment of a number of young priests from India has not been altogether successful, as some of those attracted did not possess the desired expertise and seem to have been more interested in the 'green pasture' overseas. Priestly activities are, after all, financially lucrative, but if, as I have heard in London, certain priests exploit their ritual monopoly by demanding excessive payment (a pound for every *om svaha*, of which plenty could be added at will in the course of a marriage ritual), it is understandable that there is a counter-reaction among those Hindus who are concerned to cut down the expenses connected with a wedding. As a result they may decide not to have any Hindu marriage rituals at all.

The second risk for the future of Hindu marriage solemnisation in Britain appears to be a growing ignorance of Hindu youngsters about their cultural traditions and the value of those traditions. While it would, perhaps, go too far to argue that it is crucial for Hindu spouses to know the exact meaning of the ritual elements making up a Hindu marriage, some basic knowledge about the function of these rituals would, I think, be very beneficial. After all the Hindu marriage rituals place the two individuals in a cosmic context as well as in a very real social context (the publicity of rituals), and dramatise the change of role experienced by the male and female spouse. The major concern is therefore not with the expectations of the individual *per se*, nor with those of a partially abstract legal entity like the modern state, but with the spouses as part of micro- and macro-cosmic constellations that force the individual to consider the needs and demands of others just as much as his or her own. In some forms of Hindu marriage rituals, the spouses' responsibility for each other, in particular, is beautifully expressed and dramatised in solemn vows. If spouses remain unaware of such basic Hindu notions, there may indeed be little need for elaborate Hindu marriage rituals. The price Hindus might have to pay could be the same degree of marital instability as currently experienced by those legal cultures that emphasise the needs of the individual above everything else. They might have to go as far as to accept the bitter pill of irretrievable breakdown of marital unions on the ground that one partner, for his or her own selfish reasons, has lost interest in the relationship.

Since Hindus in Britain are ideally placed to study the pros and cons of modern marriage laws at first hand, there is every likelihood that a trend not to abandon Hindu notions altogether will prevail. In view of this prognosis English lawyers might do well to reconsider their silent assumption that Hindus in Britain will, in the not too distant future, behave 'as the Romans do'. Hindu elements within modern English law deserve serious consideration and detailed study. Perhaps the fact that more 'Asians' are entering the legal profession will provide greater incentives for as yet largely-unsuccessful efforts to increase official awareness of the workings of elements of Hindu culture in the British context.

Further reading

Derrett, J. and M. Duncan, *An Introduction to Modern Hindu Law* (London and Bombay, 1963).

—, *A Critique of Modern Hindu Law* (Bombay, 1970).

Dhagamwar, Vasudha, *Towards the Uniform Civil Code* (Bombay, 1989).

Diwan, Paras, *Modern Hindu law* (4th ed., Allahabad, 1979).

Menski, Werner F., 'Solemnisation of Hindu marriages: the law and reality', *Kerala Law Times* journal section (1985), pp.1-10.

—, 'English family law and ethnic laws in Britain', *Kerala Law Times* journal section 1 (1988), pp.56-66.

—, 1991a, 'Marital expectations as dramatized in the Hindu marriage rituals of ancient India', in Julia Leslie (ed.), *Roles and Rituals for Hindu Women* (London, 1991), pp.47-67.

—, 1991b, 'Change and continuity in Hindu marriage rituals', in S.Y. Killingley (ed.), *Hindu Ritual and Society* (*The Sanskrit Tradition in the Modern World*, no.2; Newcastle, 1991), pp.32-51.

Pearl, David, 'South Asian immigrant communities and English family law: 1971-1987', *New Community* XIV, 1/2 (Autumn 1987), pp.161-9.

Poulter, Sebastian, *English Law and Ethnic Minority Customs* (London, 1986).

—, *Asian Traditions and English Law* (Stoke-on-Trent, 1990).

ISLAMIC LAW AND THE COLONIAL ENCOUNTER IN BRITISH INDIA[1]

Michael R. Anderson

In contemporary debates regarding Muslim identity in South Asia, no issue is as prominent or as hotly contested as the character and social role of Islamic law. Though the controversies are directly relevant to present-day concerns, the questions themselves are neither new nor innocent of colonial influence. The existing corpus of Islamic law in the subcontinent owes a great deal to the legacy of colonial jurists who systematised and gave shape to Anglo-Muhammadan law over many decades. In this essay, the history of Anglo-Muhammadan scholarship is considered in light of the colonial need for precise and reliable information about indigenous laws. In their preference for textual sources, the courts were inclined to endorse highly orthodox forms of Islamic law which were applied more widely and rigorously than in the pre-colonial period, ultimately contributing to a new politics of Muslim identity in the twentieth century.

British statesmanship determines from time to time how much of Oriental precept is to be treated as Law in the English sense, how much left to the consciences of those who acknowledge it as religiously binding, how much forcibly suppressed as noxious and immoral; and when this has been determined, European scholarship sifts and classifies the Oriental authorities, the mental habits of English and Scotch lawyers influence the methods of interpretation, and Procedure Codes of modern European manufacture regulate the ascertainment of the facts and the ultimate enforcement of the rule (Sir Roland Knyvet Wilson).[2]

As the tentacles of colonial rule stretched into the Indian subcontinent in the eighteenth century, the British had a minimal knowledge of Islamic legal arrangements. Yet in 1947, when the trunk of colonial power was formally chopped off, it left behind an elaborate system of administrative roots, including a working understanding of Islamic legal precepts. Since the same administrative roots have given succour to the post-colonial states of India, Pakistan, and Bangladesh, it is important to inquire into their provenance. The colonial courts charged with administering what had come to be called 'Anglo-Muhammadan law' were able to rely upon a legal scholarship that included transla-

[1] First published in Chibli Mallat and Jane Connors (eds.), *Islamic Family Law* (Graham and Trotman, London, 1990).

[2] R.K. Wilson, *An Introduction to the Study of Anglo-Muhammadan Law* (London, 1894), p.2. Footnotes omitted.

tions of Arabic and Persian texts, a handful of commentaries, as well as the precedent of hundreds of cases.

In some senses, the corpus of Anglo-Muhammadan law was simply the inevitable by-product of the colonial encounter. But its remarkable volume, produced at considerable cost and effort to successive colonial regimes, raises questions concerning the role of law in the establishment and maintenance of colonial power. If the genesis of Anglo-Muhammadan law lay in the quest to establish a definable and reliable relation between government and the governed, it entailed more than new legal institutions. It also demanded the formulation of a body of knowledge about the legal organisation of colonised peoples, including those professing adherence to Islam. Since the formidable amount of legal scholarship that accumulated under British rule was produced in an explicit complicity with colonialism, questions of its bias and validity are bound to be asked. What role did Anglo-Muhammadan scholarship assume in defining and mobilising colonial power? By what techniques was this scholarship created? How did the process of creating the Anglo-Muhammadan law affect its substantive content and application? In which ways did the substantive content mesh with understandings of identity and social order among the colonised peoples?

I. *Indigenous law and the early colonial state*

The imperatives of the Company's account-books required that administrators remain mindful of two broad goals: first, to extract economic surplus, in the form of revenue, from the agrarian economy, and second, to maintain effective political control with minimal military involvement.[3] For the most part, the various administrators of the East India Company (and later, the British Crown), followed the path of least resistance, relying upon co-opted indigenous intermediaries as well as military and police power to secure control. Throughout the subcontinent, the British exercised power by adapting themselves to the contours of pre-colonial political systems, including law. The result was that in many of its structural features, as well as its substantive policies, the colonial state sustained what were essentially pre-colonial political forms until well into the nineteenth century.[4] Although lacking in military and financial power, the edifice of the Mughal empire provided a source of *de jure* authority long after its *de facto* demise. Mughal administrative ranks, honours, rituals, and terminology persisted in muted although significant form even after Crown had supplanted Durbar in 1858. Yet while recent historiography has emphasised the conti-

[3] See D. Washbrook, 'Law, state, and agrarian society in colonial India', *Modern Asian Studies* 15, 3 (1981).

[4] See ibid., and R.E. Frykenberg, 'Company circari in the Carnatic, 1799-1859: the inner logic of political systems in India', in R.G. Fox (ed.), *Realm and Region in Traditional India* (New Delhi, 1978)

nuities between the *ancien régime* and the early colonial state,[5] it is clear that colonial rule brought a host of entirely new political institutions,[6] and that when indigenous mechanisms were adapted to colonial purposes, they were incorporated within new institutional fora.[7]

One of these new fora was the colonial law court. The Hastings Plan of 1772 established a hierarchy of civil and criminal courts, which were charged with the task of applying indigenous legal norms 'in all suits regarding inheritance, marriage, caste, and other religious usages or institutions'. Indigenous norms comprised 'the laws of the Koran with respect to Muhammadans', and the laws of the Brahmanic 'Shasters' with respect to Hindus.[8] Although the courts followed British models of procedure and adjudication, the plan provided for *maulavis* and *pandits* to advise the courts on matters of Islamic and Hindu law, respectively. By the early nineteenth century, the system of courts had been expanded, a new legal profession had been established,[9] and a growing body of statute and court practice extended the influence of the colonial state.

The actual social impact of the courts was constrained by the reluctance expressed by many colonial administrators to interfere in agrarian society unless presented with a compelling need. Moreover, the resilience of pre-colonial political systems meant that actual authority was shared among a number of entities, so that most disputes were settled at the local or community level.[10] In urban as well as rural areas, local bodies had acquired privileges of legal autonomy under Mughal rule that persisted during the colonial period. The autonomy of legal arrangements sheltered a diversity of legal norms, even among peoples professing a strict adherence to the same orthodoxy.

Nevertheless, British courts had a broad appeal to the landed gentry and other local notables. If colonial legal institutions appeared to have less impact at the lower levels of society, they did establish a new framework for disputes among the local and regional elite, who were

[5] See ibid., but also the work of C.A. Bayly, *Rulers, Townsmen and Bazaars: North Indian society in the age of British expansion, 1770-1780* (Cambridge, 1983); and *Indian Society and the Making of the British Empire* (Cambridge, 1988).

[6] D. Arnold, *Police Power and Colonial Rule: Madras 1859-1947* (Delhi, 1986).

[7] See the sensitive discussion by N.B. Dirks, 'From little king to landlord: property, law, and the gift under the Madras permanent settlement', *Comparative Studies in Society and History* 28, 2 (1986).

[8] Hastings' initial formulation reappeared, in modified form, in all the constitutive legal documents of the early colonial period.

[9] Bengal Regulation VII of 1793.

[10] B. Cohn, *An Anthropologist Among the Historians and Other Essays* (Delhi, 1987), chs.19, 22.

able to use courts to mediate disputes among themselves and to reinforce their dominance over agrarian producers. In British India, as elsewhere, individuals with superior economic and political resources often manipulated institutions to their advantage. Early district administrators in the North, for example, were frequently able to appropriate considerable amounts of land under their political control and then have themselves recorded as the proprietors under British legal authority.[11] Personages who had held political office in the pre-colonial regime often thrived under the law of private property, exercising political control by virtue of their new legal rights.[12] The prevalence of corruption and mini-despotisms allowed the well-heeled to use Company courts when it suited their purposes, but to exercise extra-judicial power when the law was inconvenient or contrary to their interests.[13]

Where the landed gentry and certain merchant groups were organised according to the dynastic principles of family and clan, the administration of family law played a role in broking wealth and power at the local level, ultimately underpinning the very intermediaries whose cooperation was essential to effective colonial rule. Property and labour were often regulated under the aegis of family law. The organisation of production in the family firm, including divisions of labour according to gender and age, presupposed the legal regulation of marriage, dissolution of marriage, inheritance, and endowments. For the Islamic gentry, material subsistence as well as political authority rested on the property grants of earlier rulers that were maintained under a variety of legal arrangements.[14]

In such circumstances, the administration of Anglo-Muhammadan law was more than a concession to 'native opinion'. Systems of personal law served to consolidate the authority of certain community groups, and thus incorporate community-based forms of surplus extraction into the colonial state.[15] The position of the landed gentry rested on pre-colonial patterns of family organisation. As much as it rankled the sensibilities of Macaulay and others who sought a uniform legal code.[16]

[11] E. Stokes, *The Peasant and the Raj* (Cambridge, 1978), p.84.

[12] See Dirks, 'From little king to landlord'.

[13] For a scathing indictment of the colonial courts, see J.B. Norton, *The Administration of Justice in South India* (Madras, 1953).

[14] For contrasting views on these processes, see Bayly, *Rulers, Townsmen, and Bazaars*, pp.129-3, 351, and G.C. Kozlowski, *Muslim Endowments and Society in British India* (Cambridge, 1985).

[15] Washbrook, 'Law, state and agrarian society', pp.654-70. For a more generalised discussion of this point, see P. Fitzpatrick, 'Law, plurality and underdevelopment' in D. Sugarman (ed.), *Legality, Ideology and the State* (London, 1983).

[16] E. Stokes, *The English Utilitarians and India* (Delhi, 1959), pp.184ff.; M.P. Jain, *Outlines of Indian Legal History* (2nd ed., Bombay, 1966), ch.24.

Anglo-Muhammadan law conserved and even strengthened aspects of community organisation on which colonial rule rested.

Yet at the same time, colonial administration of pre-colonial personal laws brought important changes. The autonomy of intermediaries operated in the context of state patronage and the ever-present threat of armed intervention. Moreover, the hierarchies of community and family grew more onerous as they were linked to an extractive state that could make unprecedented demands for economic surplus. If Company courts lacked the moral qualifications demanded by orthodox theories to interpret and enforce legal norms of Islamic inspiration, they carried the threat of a military power that, after the battles of 1818, could effectively put down any serious resistance.

Company administrators were increasingly able, as the nineteenth century wore on, to intervene in areas of Anglo-Muhammadan law that most threatened their authority. At the same time, they were less hesitant to prohibit practices which offended their sense of morality.[17] As the apparatus of the colonial state became more refined and administrators more capable of policing various forms of resistance, large portions of the Anglo-Muhammadan law were supplanted by laws of British origin. The earliest Anglicising trends were latent in the 1772 doctrine that in cases where indigenous laws seemed to provide no rule, the matter should be decided according to the Roman law formula of 'justice, equity, and good conscience',[18] which by 1887 was held 'to mean the rules of English law if found applicable to society and circumstances'.[19] Continual alterations of Islamic criminal law stepped up punishments for crimes against private property, while modifying other forms of punishments to conform with British preconceptions.[20] However, the most dramatic overturning of Anglo-Muhammadan law emerged by way of statute. Slavery was abolished in 1843; Islamic criminal law and procedure were replaced entirely by colonial codes in the early 1860s, and Islamic canons of evidence were supplanted by British-based rules in 1872.[21] By 1875, new colonial codes had displaced the Anglo-Muhammadan law in all subjects except family law and certain property transactions. The codes reflected a longstanding frustration

[17] B. Hjejle, 'The Social Policy of the East India Company with regard to Sati, Slavery, Thagi, and Infanticide, 1772-1858', unpublished D.Phil. dissertation, Oxford University, 1958.

[18] See J.D.M. Derrett, 'Justice, Equity and Good Conscience', in J.N.D. Anderson (ed.), *Changing Law in Developing Countries* (London, 1963).

[19] *Waghela* v. *Sheikh Masludin* (1887) 14 IA 89, at 96.

[20] J. Fisch, *Cheap Lives and Dear Limbs: the British transformation of the Bengal Criminal Law, 1769-1817* (Wiesbaden, 1983).

[21] Act V of 1843; *Code of Civil Procedure* (Act VIII of 1859), *Indian Penal Code* (Act XLV of 1860); *Criminal Procedure Code* (Act XXV of 1861); *Indian Evidence Act* (Act 1 of 1872).

with Islamic law, but they also furnished the state with a more precise and reliable legal apparatus to maintain and regulate its police power.

Nevertheless, as an administrative technique, the enforcement of separate systems of personal law was never eliminated entirely. If personal laws had been important to the early raj as a means of maintaining political control, they assumed a new significance in the emerging communal politics of the twentieth century. Throughout the colonial period, Anglo-Muhammadan law was taken seriously as a politically sensitive and technically complex subject for legal scholarship. But there was an irony in this, for what the Company courts applied as Islamic law was often more alien than familiar to putatively 'Muslim' groups. Anglo-Muhammadan scholarship often distorted its subject matter, frequently reflecting British preoccupations more accurately than indigenous norms. Indeed, colonial administrators may never have changed Islamic legal arrangements quite so profoundly as when they were trying to preserve them.

II. *Anglo-Muhammadan scholarship*

Following Hastings' plan, the limited bureaucratic machinery of the Company state found itself with an urgent need for a serviceable knowledge of indigenous legal arrangements. Apart from the language difficulties and the limitations of a small British administration juxtaposed with a substantial colonised population, the task was complicated by the fragmented and contingent quality of the sources of legal obligation.

Colonial scholars drew heavily upon pre-colonial legal scholarship. Adapted forms of the *shari'a* had been administered in South Asia for centuries, first by the various Sultanates, next under the authority of the strong Mughal empire, and finally by the successor states that arose during the eighteenth century.[22] Especially under the Mughals, the administration of *shari'a* formed an important part of the symbolisation of imperial legitimacy; its dispensation was viewed as a sacred duty. Legal scholarship thrived in these circumstances; the imperial court patronised the *'ulama,* or legal scholars, and Aurangzeb commissioned the influential *fatwa Alamgiri,* a collection of legal opinions in the *fiqh* tradition. On the administrative side, the *shari'a* was supplemented with a comprehensive set of imperial regulations as well as a cadre of officially sponsored *qadis* drawn primarily from the *'ulama.*[23]

Paradoxically, the decline of the Mughal empire appears to have stimulated a moral and cultural competition among successor powers that fuelled an increase in Islamic legal scholarship.[24] A sign of some

[22] A.A.A. Fyzee, 'Muhammadan law in India', *Comparative Studies in Society and History* 5 (1963).

[23] K.M. Yusuf, 'The judiciary in India under the Sultans of Delhi and the Mughal Emperors', *Indo-Iranica* 18 (1965).

[24] See B.D. Metcalfe, *Islamic Revival in British India: Deoband, 1860-1900*

status, legal study was widespread. Predominantly of the Hanafi school, orthodox legal specialists seem to have focused study on *al-Hidaya,* a twelfth-century text of Central Asian origin that primarily relied upon Abu-Yusuf and ash-Shaybani, the two pupils of Abu-Hanifa. Study of the Qur'an and the *hadith* seems to have been less important for the orthodox Hanafis.[25] But the cultural vitality of the period also gave rise to more innovative scholars, including Shah Wali Ullah (1703-62) who advocated an eclectic approach to the Sunni schools, insisting that the gates of *ijtihad,* or interpretive reasoning, had never closed.[26] Shi'i scholarship was also alive. In Bengal, for instance, two Nawab supported *madrasas* drew a wide range of legal students, some from as far away as Iran.[27]

There is no reason to doubt that pre-colonial legal scholarship was coupled with an earnest effort to enforce the *shari'a*. Unlike the 'Hindu' *dharmasastra* texts,[28] Islamic legal theory did not formally recognise custom as an independent source of law. So although *al-Hidaya* accorded custom a role in the absence of textual norms,[29] orthodoxy frowned on deviations. Yet the social impact of Mughal legal institutions remained limited to particular groups, especially the Islamic gentry and the urban merchants based in the *qasbah* towns. Many communities jealously guarded their autonomy, operating under the umbrella of imperial tolerance to retain localised institutions, practices, and norms which operated in derogation of a strict application of the *shari'a*.[30] Local leaders seem to have settled disputes with varying degrees of deference to textual norms.

The British confrontation with myriad forms of legal authority and variegated local practices highlighted one of the foremost problems of colonial control: how to obtain simple, reliable, and reasonably accurate understandings of indigenous social life without sacrificing great labour and capital.[31] Law and legal institutions provided a solution. Equipped

---

(Princeton, 1982), ch.2.

[25] Metcalfe, *Islamic Revival*, p.31.

[26] See Mohammad Daud Rahbar, 'Shah Wali Ullah and ijtihad', *Muslim World* 45 (1955), and more generally, Wael B. Hallaq, 'Was the gate of ijtihad closed?', *International Journal of Middle Eastern Studies* 16 (1984).

[27] P.J. Marshall, *Bengal: the British bridgehead* (Cambridge, 1988), p.31.

[28] Cf. J.D.M. Derrett, *Religion, Law and State in India* (London, 1968), chs.6, 7.

[29] T. Mahmood, 'Custom as a source of law in Islam', *Journal of the Indian Law Institute*, 7, (1965), p.104.

[30] For a more general treatment of this theme in South Asia, see K.I. Ewing (ed.), *Shari'at and Ambiguity in South Asian Islam* (Berkeley, 1988).

[31] The problem took various guises throughout colonial legal history. In 1856, Lord Harris viewed one of the main functions of the new police force as 'the procuring [of] continued accurate information on the state of the country

with indigenous advisers, colonial courts served as mechanisms of inquiry, while the classical religious-legal texts, whatever their genuine relevance, were taken as the key to understanding colonised cultures and societies. Most British intellectuals of the early colonial period stressed the importance of law in regulating social life. 'The rule of law' was a common piece of ideological baggage that linked law to public sentiments as well as political order. Law was more than an arm of sovereignty: it was employed as a proto-sociology that could guide policy. Accordingly, the first century of colonial rule witnessed the birth of an Anglo-Muhammadan jurisprudence comprising legal assumptions as well as law officers, translations, textbooks, codifications, and new legal technologies

Basic assumptions

The Hastings plan rested on the notion that indigenous norms could be plugged into British-based legal institutions without significantly compromising the integrity of either. Coming to understand that the *shari'a* was authoritative for Islamic legal scholars, many British administrators glossed over its internal contradictions and finely distinguished levels of moral approbation, and set about applying it as a set of more or less homogenous legal rules.

The presumption that a single set of legal rules could apply to all persons professing adherence to Islam violated both Islamic theory and South Asian practice. Hastings had subsumed all indigenous legal arrangements under two categories: Hindu (earlier, Gentoo), and Muslim (Muhammadan).[32] From the outset, this binary categorisation was inadequate to contain the diversity of legal life on the subcontinent. Not only did it fail to acknowledge the distinction between Shi'i and Sunni, and the differences among the schools within each; it also failed to address adequately the practices and beliefs of the many groups that adopted an eclectic approach to Islam and various forms of Hinduism. Backed by the literalist legalism of colonial administration, 'Hindu' and 'Muslim' became an important part of a new bureaucratic vocabulary of colonial control—a vocabulary that drew upon indigenous terms, but imbued them with a Procrustean quality as they were deployed in governance.'

Looking for a unified 'Muhammadan' law that could be slotted into

---

and the feelings and sentiments of the population'. Quoted in Arnold, *Police Power*, p.24. For a detailed twentieth-century account, see P. Mason, *Call the Next Witness* (London, 1945).

[32] It seems that in the formation of this plan, Hastings simply drew on the strategy that had been adopted during the Mughal period and remained in force in the successor states. What was new, however, was the rigid legalism that now accompanied the binary Hindu/Muslim divide. See Fyzee, 'Muhammadan law', p.402.

the Company court system, administrators made the much-celebrated mistake of treating certain classical Islamic texts as binding legal codes. To apply 'the laws of the Koran with respect to Mohamedans', was a project that mistook the Qur'an for a code of law. The Qur'an, and even more specifically legal texts such as *al-Hidaya* had never been directly applied as sources of legal precept. Their legal relevance had always derived from a properly authoritative *qadi* whose moral probity and knowledge of local arrangements could translate precept into practice. *Qadis* in the Mughal period had left much to what Bayly calls 'the sense of the neighbourhood'.[33] Even the most sophisticated textbound approach was subject to grave error, simply because texts were applied in ignorance of social circumstances.

Colonial judicial administration soon developed a more sophisticated treatment of textual sources. Nevertheless, it was accompanied by a basic prejudice that accorded primacy to text over interpretive practice.

'Native law officers'

Until Anglo-Muhammadan law was consolidated in textbook and precedent, court-appointed maulavis provided fatwa to guide the British judges. Collaborating with colonial rule in the most overt sense, these clerics drawn from indigenous centres of learning were charged with responding to the courts' questions on matters of Islamic law. When faced with a question of law, British judges would present the maulavi with a question formulated in an abstract, hypothetical manner, often shorn of relevant details. The resulting fatwa, necessarily in an abstract form, was then applied to the case at hand. This procedure resulted in a highly formalised and rigid application of legal rules. In 1935, Abur Hussain wrote of the early colonial judges that they applied the law 'mechanically to the causes before them, practically on third-hand information of the law from the Moulvis who sense of justice born and bred in the native social environment was not available to the Judges'.[34]

It is not surprising that the maulavis were mistrusted. British accusations of inconsistency stemmed partially from genuine questions of probity that may have been linked to a low official salary.[35] More importantly, suspicions arose from the diversity of opinion that any

[33] Bayly, *Merchants, Townsmen and Bazaars*, p.353.

[34] A. Hussain, *Muslim Law as Administered in British India* (Calcutta, 1935), p.14.

[35] Wilson, *Introduction*, pp.96-7. William Jones expressed a distrust typical of other British judges: 'I could not with an easy conscience concur in a decision merely on the written opinion of native lawyers in any cause in which they could have the remotest interest in misleading the court'. Quoted in Hussain, *Muslim Law*, p.30.

number of legal questions might generate. Islamic legal theories had always provided leeway for judicial discretion in applying *shari'a* principles.[36] Operating with their own preconceptions, British judges seemed unable to accept that there might be genuine differences of opinion on a point of law. When maulavis did disagree, their opinions often simply reflected the inherent inadequacies of the British text-based approach.

Together with pandits, the maulavis of the colonial courts were gradually eclipsed by the precedent of case law and the accrual of British expertise. In 1864, under Crown rule, the Court maulavis were dispensed with altogether,[37] so that the official administration of Anglo-Muhammadan law was severed completely from the judgment of men of distinguished moral authority. Yet *qadis* performed a wide variety of non-legal functions, acting as marriage registers and notaries as well as providing guidance on religious matters. In the vacuum created after 1864, conflicts arose as to the proper appointment of *qadis*, and pressure was put on the government to reinstate appointments for non-religious matters.[38] Despite the revival of a state-sponsored system of qadis in 1876, the laity took recourse in the private *'ulama* who increasingly were responsible for settling disputes at an informal level.[39]

Translations

Given the assumed centrality of legal text, and a persistent distrust of native law officers, it followed that legal administrators were eager to have Islamic texts in English translation so that indigenous laws could be applied directly by British judges. Sir William Jones, the great polymath of early Orientalism, proposed that Hastings should endeavour to compile 'a complete Digest of Hindu and Muhammad laws after the model of Justinian's inestimable Pandects'.[40] The model of the Roman legal system lent credence to the emphasis on a rule-based legality. At the insistence of Hastings, *al-Hidaya*, the influential compilation of Hanafi opinion, was translated by three maulavis from Arabic to Persian, and then into English by Charles Hamilton in 1791. But *al-Hidaya* lacked any treatment of inheritance, regarded by the British as the most intractable and politically important of Muhammadan law subjects. Accordingly, in 1792, *al-Sirajiyya*, a treatise on inheritance, was

[36] Cf. J. Makdisi, 'Legal logic and equity in Islamic law', *American Journal of Comparative Law* 33, 1985, and L. Rosen, 'Equity and discretion in a modern Islamic legal system', *Law and Society Review*, 15 (1980).

[37] Act XI of 1864.

[38] U. Yaduvansh, 'The decline of the role of the qadis in India, 1793-1876', *Studies in Islam*, 6, (1969).

[39] T. Mahmood, *Muslim Personal Law: role of the state in the sub-continent* (Delhi, 1977), pp.60-9.

[40] Quoted in Hussain, *Muslim Law*, pp.30-1.

translated direct from the Arabic by Jones personally.

The courts continued to rely upon advice from indigenous legal specialists for some time, so the translations made little impact on colonial administration until the early nineteenth century. Their primary significance lay in the understandings they engendered of an essentialist, static Islam incapable of change from within. They established, in the crucible of colonial rule, that a proper knowledge of India—and of the Orient more generally—could be had only through a detailed study of the classical legal texts.[41]

The translations had greater legal effect as judges began to rely upon them more directly. Although produced in haste, and with imperfect language skills, the unrevised eighteenth-century translations remained authoritative. A number of translating errors were discovered in *Al-Hidaya,* but corrections were made only to the Persian version in 1807. The English version remains uncorrected. The project of translating a broader range of texts, including non-Hanafi texts, never reached fruition, and was cancelled due to financial constraints in 1808. The nineteenth century saw only one additional major translation—an abbreviated version of the fatwa *Alamgiri* and a portion of an Itna 'Ashariya (Shi'a) text—translated by Neil Baillie and published in 1865 under the title of *A Digest of Mohummudan Law.*

Together, these three translations formed the textual basis of Anglo-Muhammadan law. Their inadequacies and blatant errors have been partially recorded in court cases and commentaries,[42] but sustained research on the ideological biases of their rendering remains to be pursued. Even a basic text on the *usul al-fiqh,* or roots of jurisprudence, that would be basic to any detailed understanding of Islamic law, did not appear until 1911.[43] It is not surprising that those few texts which were translated came to be treated as authoritative codes rather than as discrete statements within a larger spectrum of scholarly debate.

Textbooks

Increasingly, the textual basis of Anglo-Muhammadan law lay with compilations of materials ordered in a thematic way. In the earliest of these, W. H. MacNaghten compiled a number of *fatwa* produced by the

[41] The legal need for a settled universal rule that can be applied generally to a broad range of individuals may have given rise to a hypostasising trend in Orientalist scholarship. The institutional links between colonial legal institutions and Orientalist scholarship demand further exploration. In the meantime, for a suggestive discussion, see E.W. Said, *Orientalism* (London, 1978), pp.77-9.

[42] *Gobind Dayal* v. *Amir Muhammad* (1885) 7 All 775: *Jafri Begam* v. *Amir Muhammad* (1885) 7 All 822; see Hussain, *Muslim Law*, pp.45-52.

[43] A. Rahim, *The Principles of Muhammadan Jurisprudence* (reprint ed. Lahore, 1974).

court *qadis,* which he published in 1825 along with his own wide-ranging generalisations under the title *Principles and Precedents of Mohammadan Law.* He purported to present an authoritative distillation of opinion on various subjects. The effect was to gloss over areas of problematic interpretation and present a unified rule in place of genuine differences of doctrine. In the years that followed, colonial administration gave rise to a number of textbooks,[44] which treated their subject with varying degrees of sophistication, but nevertheless following MacNaghten's basic model. The device of the textbook organised knowledge in a way that made the most of a limited amount of understanding. It minimised doctrinal difference and presented the *shari'a* as something it had never been: a fixed body of immutable rules beyond the realm of interpretation and judicial discretion.

Codification of custom

Frustrated by the inadequacy of religious texts and native law officers, British administrators in the latter half of the nineteenth century began to focus upon custom as a source of law. After the Punjab Laws Act of 1872, revenue collectors in the Punjab were directed to conduct surveys with a view to ascertaining customary practices in each village. The emphasis on custom remained strongest in the Punjab, but it gave rise to a reconsideration of legal administration at the all-India level. The Punjab surveys reflect a preoccupation with landholding rights since their main function was to assist in the collection of revenue.[45]

Working with preconceived notions of custom as ancient and stable within a fairly static society, administrators took custom to be a fact in the world that could be ascertained and codified, glossing over the contingent and political nature of the arrangements that they sought to understand. In practice, custom was seldom fixed and permanent. Rather, to act according to custom necessarily entailed a reinterpretation of community standards and the interpreter's position within them. More than a simple rejection or affirmation of community standards, custom often involved very real struggle over what the standards were in the first place. If even a part of the recent anthropology of custom is to be believed, what the British called 'customary law' was inherently incompatible with the epistemological dictates of codification.[a]

Much codification operated by way of a search for precedent and underlying principle in what sometimes appeared to the British as the chaotic incoherence of village life. A kind of juridical homogenisation

[44] Nine major textbooks were published in the British period. In addition to MacNaghten, *Principles*; Wilson, *Introduction* and Hussain, *Muslim Law*; texts by W.H. Morley, S.G. Sircar, A. Ali, A. Rahim, A.F.M.A. Rahman, and Tyabji are of note.

[45] N. Bhattacharya, 'Custom and rights: a conflict of interpretations', paper presented at Oxford University Centre for Indian Studies, 13 November 1987.

took place, so that indigenous terms were adopted to describe a wide range of discrete practices.[46] Codification distorted social life by way of selecting and interpreting material. The issue of land tenure, for instance, was a complex matter involving reciprocal rights and duties in a number of relationships; it could never be contained adequately within the simple question that preoccupied many British administrators—that of who would inherit the land.[47] Nevertheless, codes of custom were used as guidelines for the collection of revenue and the formulation of state policy. The nineteenth century saw the compilation of both district-specific and regional texts that could be used by administrators and courts alike.[48]

At the level of legal administration, a number of tests were developed to establish the content, validity, and applicability of custom. In 1868, the Privy Council affirmed that in Hindu law, custom could outweigh the written text of the law.[49] A similar doctrine was established in limited areas of Muslim law only much later.[50] Nevertheless custom operated against the general presumption in favour of Anglo-Muhammadan law, so its applicability was strictly circumscribed. In accordance with British understandings of custom, a legally binding custom had to be enforceable, reasonable, and to have existed from time immemorial; scores of decisions recorded the fussy and detailed sifting of materials that courts used to establish the validity of custom.[51] Customs that were held to be immoral, illegal according to general legal principles, or contrary to public policy were unenforceable.[52]

The jurisprudence of customary law allowed the colonial state to recognise certain aspects of social practice that were important to particular classes or groups. But its recognition was never allowed to extend beyond a point that would be incompatible with the political and economic imperatives of colonial rule. Above all, the codification and

[46] See P. Robb, 'Law and agrarian society in India: the case of Bihar and the nineteenth-century tenancy debate', *Modern Asian Studies* 22, 2, (1988).

[47] Bhattacharya, 'Custom and Rights'.

[48] For the Punjab, see A. Gledhill, 'The compilation of customary laws in the Punjab in the nineteenth century', in J. Glissen (ed.), *La rédaction des coutumes dans le passé et dans le présent* (Brussels, 1962). More generally, see S. Roy, *Customs and Customary Law in British India* (Calcutta, 1911); A. Steele, *The Law and Custom of Hindoo Castes (within the Dekhun Provinces subject to the Presidency of Bombay)* (London, 1868).

[49] *Collector of Madura* v. *Moottoo Ramalinga* (1868) 12 MIA 397.

[50] See S. Roy, *Customs*, ch.10.

[51] *Abdul Hussain* v. *Bibi Sona Dero* (1917) 45 IA 10. See S. Roy, *Customs*, ch.18.

[52] For example, it was held that customary prostitution conducted as a family business was immoral and contrary to Islamic precepts. *Ghasiti* v. *Umrao Jan* (1893) 20 IA 193. See also the general discussion at S. Roy, *Customs*, ch.16.

judicial application of custom supplied administrators with a set of devices for incorporating diverse practices within the political recognition of the colonial state.[53]

New legal technologies

Colonial courts introduced a set of legal technologies, primarily bureaucratic procedure and methods of inquiry, that departed significantly form pre-colonial arrangements. Most of the new bureaucratic methods worked by way of categorising and systematising indigenous phenomena. Within a centralised bureaucratic framework, procedures were established for collecting information, making regular reports, and distilling data that could be used in Calcutta or London. A hallmark of the early nineteenth century was the increased use of standardised printed forms in district administration. After 1857, village records and district reports supplied detailed knowledge of the colonised society.[54] On the legal side of things, perhaps the most striking innovation was the use of documentation in matters of law and evidence.

Legal documents *per se* were not new. Mughal administrative manuals are testimony to the importance of documents in the political administration of the empire in the seventeenth century.[55] So too, written contracts provided a flexibility of financial arrangements that enabled merchants to share risks and accumulate capital for participation in pan-Asian trading networks.[56] But in matters of evidence, pre-colonial legal theory of Islamic inspiration seems to have placed a special emphasis upon oral testimony, and concomitantly, the probity of witnesses. In the evidentiary (and epistemological) theory of the *shari'a*, only the spoken testimony of a morally reliable witness was admissible as evidence before the court. Theoretically, a document such as a deed or contract could serve to remind witnesses of what had transpired, but its veracity rested on actual oral deposition.[57] Accordingly, *al-Hidaya* furnishes

[53] Before long codification of custom was contested politically; D. Gilmartin, *Empire and Islam: Punjab and the making of Pakistan* (Berkeley, 1988).

[54] R. Smith, 'Rule-by-records and rule-by-reports: complementary aspects of the British imperial rule of law', *Contributions to Indian Sociology* (n.s.) 19 (1985).

[55] J.F. Richards, *Document Forms for Official Orders of Appointment in the Mughal Empire* (Cambridge, 1986).

[56] See A.L. Udovitch, *Partnership and Profit in Medieval Islam* (Princeton, 1970), A. Das Gupta in D.S. Richards (ed.), *Islam and the Trade of Asia* (Oxford, 1970), and K.N. Chaudhuri, *Trade and Civilisation in the Indian Ocean: an economic history from the rise of Islam to 1750* (Oxford, 1985).

[57] For a discussion of this general principle in *shari'a* theory, see J. Wakin, *The Function of Documents in Islamic Law* (Albany, 1972). It is unclear how far the principle was applied in South Asia. For a comparative discussion, see B. Messick, 'Just writing: paradox and political economy in Yemeni legal documents', *Cultural Anthropology* 4, 1, (1989).

rules governing the admissibility of oral testimony, but makes no provision for documentary evidence. In practice, there is no reason to doubt that documents were important in Mughal and post-Mughal courts, reflecting their important role in politics and commerce. Nevertheless, it is clear that under British rule, the process of documentation and the role of the scribe were amplified.

Initially, colonial courts enforced the primacy of oral testimony over documentation, especially in criminal law.[58] The state slowly chipped away at the doctrine, by continually modifying the rules governing oral testimony[59] and introducing forms of writing into adjudication. Starting in 1793, all depositions and examinations of witnesses were to be transcribed into the language of the deponent. Once taken, depositions were then to be translated into Persian, checked for accuracy by the court officers, and then communicated in English to the Magistrate.[60] In 1797, the text of the deposition, rather than the oral testimony itself, was adopted as legally binding in the record of the court.[61] Gradually, the practice of formulating English summaries of the vernacular record was adopted, and English began to displace Persian as the official language of the court.[62] With the Criminal Procedure Code of 1861, and the Indian Evidence Act of 1872, adapted forms of the English law of procedure and evidence were introduced in systematised form.

The insistence on documentary evidence was 'unreal in the context of a largely illiterate society', serving to make legal institutions inaccessible to most of the population.[63] Other effects were subtle but pervasive. Standardised forms for business transactions, contracts, and government agreements became more widespread. Increasingly, the government ruled by way of administrative circular order. The growth of legal-administrative categories—inscribed into codes of custom, bureaucratic orders, mandates for investigation, and after 1871, into census forms—were symptomatic of a practical and ideological need for a stable knowledge of the colonised society.[64]

III. *Legal scholarship and state power*

The devices of Anglo-Muhammadan scholarship had this in common:

[58] T.K. Banerjee, *Background to Indian Criminal Law* (Bombay, 1963), p.249.

[59] The *shari'a* rules of evidence were modified so that Hindus could testify against Muslims and the strict evidentiary requirements for *hudud* offences were modified, although *hudud* punishments were also abolished gradually. See Fisch, *Cheap Limbs*, and Jain, *Outline*, ch.21.

[60] Regulation IX of 1793.

[61] Regulation IV of 1797.

[62] Banerjee, *Background*, p.284.

[63] Washbrook, 'Law, state, and agrarian society', p.658.

[64] Cf. Cohn, *An Anthropologist*, ch.10.

they served to fix the fluid practices of indigenous society in legal categories that could serve as a basis for political and legal decisions.[65] Even when colonial legal institutions had minimal impact on actual social practice, they did operate to provide information about the colonised society.[66] The reliance on texts over customary practices was a strategy that served to contain the contumacious complexities of indigenous mores. Colonial legal understandings were not strictly wrong, but they were arrested, frozen forms of representation. They often had more to do with a limited kind of textual accuracy than a genuine appreciation of the norms by which people actually lived. In simplifying indigenous legal arrangements to a form that could be administered by colonial courts, Anglo-Muhammadan scholarship reduced living norms to immutable concepts of purely divine inspiration.[67]

IV. *Colonial law and Muslim identity*

The apparatus of Anglo-Muhammadan scholarship bore the imprint of eighteenth-century assumptions—even as it was refined, in the twentieth century. What this meant for the detailed administration of the law deserves further study. In the meantime, one point warrants sustained attention: the Anglo-Muhammadan law seems to have contributed to an environment in which a new politics of Muslim identity could flourish.

Assertions concerning ethnic and national identity warrant caution; processes of identity formation are not well understood.[68] Nevertheless, some homologies between the administration of Anglo-Muhammadan law and the consolidation of Muslim identities in the late colonial period may be discerned.

Scripturalism

One of the most marked features of the late nineteenth and early twentieth centuries was the rise of a new kind of scripturalist Islam—a form of Islam that relied upon the textual sources of the Qur'an, *hadith* and *shari'a* commentaries as the only acceptable bases of religious author-

[65] See Robb, 'Law and agrarian society in India'.

[66] See M. Anderson, 'Law as knowledge, law as control: sati in colonial India, ca.1770-1840', forthcoming.

[67] For a more general discussion, see Homi K. Bhabha, 'The other question: difference, discrimination and the discourse of colonialism', in F. Barker et al. (eds.), *Literature, Politics and Theory* (London, 1986).

[68] For accounts that highlight the complexity of the topic, see S. Barnett, 'Identity choice and caste ideology in contemporary South India', in K. David (ed.), *The New Wind: changing identities in South Asia* (The Hague, 1977); and G.C. Bentley, 'Ethnicity and Practice', *Comparative Studies in Society and History* 29, 1 (1987).

ity.[69]

The administration of Anglo-Muhammadan law, as we have seen, proceeded on the basis of textual understanding. The focus on texts allowed administrators to ascertain general legal rules quickly, and it may have meshed with understandings of Islam found among sections of the indigenous elite, but it misunderstood the role of the *shari'a* in the life of most South Asian Muslims. The legalist ideology of colonial judges erred on the side of applying clear rules in a consistent manner, regardless of whether people genuinely treated them as binding.

Qur'anic precepts and the texts of classical legal scholars were not followed as strictly as colonial administrators had presumed. When harnessed to the centralised bureaucracy of the colonial state, shari'a principles were administered with a uniformity and rule-bound consistency that was unprecedented on the subcontinent. The orthodox rules of the Hanafi school spread beyond specific urban and gentry groups, as the colonial courts disseminated a unified 'Muhammadan law' to every part of British India.

But it would be a mistake to ascribe too much importance to the effects of colonial law. A number of indigenous processes were also at work. Islamic scholars in Deoband, Aligarh, and elsewhere engaged in a 'self-conscious reassessment of what was deemed authentic religion' based on a rereading of the classical texts.[70] Studies of the Qur'an and *hadith* gained a prominence that had been unknown during the Mughal period.[71] Popular understandings of Islam underwent profound changes during the late nineteenth and early twentieth centuries, so that a scripturalist approach to the *shari'a* spread from urban to rural areas, and from elite classes to middle classes.[72] Adherence to the *shari'a* became more widespread and was increasingly perceived to be central to the maintenance of Muslim identity.

Colonial categories

Under the colonial state, the category of 'Muslim', or often 'Muhammadan', took on a new fixity and certainty that had previously been uncommon. In theory, each individual was linked to a state-enforced religious category. Identities that were syncretic, ambiguous or localised gained only limited legal recognition; for the most part, litigants were forced to present themselves as 'Muhammadan' or 'Hindu'. Courts repeatedly faced the problem of accommodating the diversity of

[69] The term 'scripturalism' is drawn from Clifford Geertz, *Islam Observed* (New Haven, CT, 1967), p.65.

[70] Metcalfe, *Islamic Revival*, p.348.

[71] Ibid.

[72] See discussions in Metcalfe, *Islamic Revival*; Aziz Ahmad, *Islamic Modernism in India and Pakistan, 1857-1964* (London, 1967); and Rafiuddin Ahmed, *The Bengal Muslims, 1871-1906* (2nd ed., Delhi, 1988).

social groups within these two categories.[73]

For the purposes of applying the law, who was a Muslim? It was established at a fairly early stage that the courts would recognise the important legal differences between Shi'i and Sunni Islam,[74] but what of other more marginalised and syncretic groups? Could the Ahmadi and Wahhabi sects properly be classified as Muslims?[75] What to make of Khoja, Memon, and Mappilla groups who professed adherence to Islam but were customarily governed by personal laws of Hindu inspiration?[76] Finally, in 1922, the Madras High Court affirmed the principle that anyone who accepted the prophethood of Muhammad and the supreme authority of the Qur'an would be treated as a Muslim in the eyes of the law.[77] The erroneous belief that diverse personal law arrangements could be subsumed under the two great classes of 'Muslim' and 'Hindu' was a failing inherent in Hastings' judicial plan, but despite the problems it posed for colonial courts,[78] it did provide a framework; for legal rule. Many individuals and groups thus found themselves in a position of needing to operate within their state-defined social space in order to secure the economic, political, social, and religious patronage of the state. Previous to colonial rule, communities had been able to maintain a high level of autonomy within larger political agglomerations, but increasingly, local autonomy depended upon being able to influence matters of general policy at the all-India level. The search for political allies, both vertically and horizontally, fostered the formation of new coalitions based upon, among other things, Muslim identity.[79]

The politics of personal law

The administration of Muslim law by a non-Muslim colonial power transformed personal law into a ground for organised political struggle. Not that this was entirely new in South Asia; Islamic idioms had served

[73] And more marginally, the categories of Christian, Parsi, and Jews. In general, see *Abraham* v. *Abraham* (1863) 9 MIA 195.

[74] *Rajah Deedar Hossain* v. *Ranee Zuhoornussa* (1841) 2 MIA 441.

[75] See *Queen-Empress* v. *Ramzan* (1885) ILR 7 All 461; *Ata-Ullah* v. *Azim-Ullah* (1890) ILR 12 All 494; and *Hakim Khalil Ahmad* v. *Malik Israfi* (1917) 2 Patna LJ 108.

[76] See the famous Aga Khan case: *Advocate-General of Bombay* v. *Mohammad Husen Huseni* (1866) 12 Bom HCR 323.

[77] *Narantakath* v. *Parakkal* (1922) 45 Madras 986.

[78] Its legacy has continued to pose problems for post-colonial courts. See *Yagnapurushdasji* v. *Muldas*, AIR 1966 SC 1119; and comment by Derrett, 'The definition of a Hindu' (1966) 2 SCJ J 67. See also the more general discussion by M. Galanter, 'Hinduism, secularism and the Indian judiciary', *Philosophy East and West* 21, (1971).

[79] See P. Hardy, *Muslims in British India* (Cambridge, 1972); F. Robinson, *Separatism among Indian Muslims* (Cambridge, 1974).

to translate economic discontent into focused political action for centuries.[80] But in the late nineteenth century, various groups adopted a new approach to Islam, mobilising around Muslim identity in opposition to colonial rule.[81] In this process, a particular version of Islamic law came to be juxtaposed with colonial attacks upon it.

This was first evident in the law of *waqf*, or charitable endowment. Prior to colonial rule, the term '*waqf*' seems to have applied to a wide variety of royal and personal grant-giving arrangements operated among both 'Hindu' and 'Muslim' groups in South Asia. Mosques, Sufi shrines, and other religious institutions received income from the land-grants of the imperial nobility as well as the local gentry and prosperous merchants.[82] At the same time, a variety of legal techniques were used by Muslims in South Asia and elsewhere to transmit property from one generation to the next while protecting it from political appropriation.[83] However, under British administration the tools of Anglo-Muhammadan scholarship were used to craft a single, *shari'a*-based law of *waqf* used primarily for settling estates.[84]

In the last century of colonial rule, disputes over *waqf* properties were commonplace. Reflecting inter-personal and doctrinal disputes on specific endowments, a number of cases were heard by the colonial courts in the latter half of the nineteenth century.[85] They led up to the celebrated case of *Abul Fata* v. *Russomoy*, in which the Privy Council affirmed a High Court ruling that the *waqf* in question was not of the nature of a valid charitable endowment, but simply served to aggrandise the family.[86]

The decision was symptomatic of a broader colonial attack on *waqf* as a hindrance to economic growth in a market economy.[87] Despite genuine disagreements among Muslims concerning the merits of the case, the decision served as a rallying point for Muslim discontent. Following extensive agitation, Jinnah found his first major political victory in pressing for the Wakf Validating Act of 1913, that purported to overturn the Privy Council decision. But for all that Jinnah and others claimed that the Act would restore the purity of Islamic law, the Act

[80] See D. Arnold, 'Islam, the Mappilas and peasant revolt in Malabar', *Journal of Peasant Studies* 9, 4 (1982).

[81] Cf. C. Geertz, *Islam Observed*, p.65.

[82] Kozlowski, *Muslim Endowments*, ch.1.

[83] Ibid.; and D.S. Powers, 'The historical evolution of Islamic inheritance law' in Mallat and Connors (eds.), *Islamic Family Law*.

[84] Kozlowski, *Muslim Endowments*, ch.5.

[85] Ibid.

[86] (1894) 22 LR IA 76.

[87] See D. Powers, 'Orientalism, colonialism, and legal history: the attack on family endowments in Algeria and India', *Comparative Studies in Society and History* 31 (1989).

was closer to a political statement than a restoration. In a field where even the orthodox Hanafi *shari'a* was marked by internal contradictions, a single 'Muhammadan' law on the subject of *waqf* was pure chimera. The 1913 Act simultaneously affirmed a scripturalist version of Islam as it protected the economic interests of certain propertied classes.

The culmination of the scripturalist influence on law came with the Muslim Personal Law (Shariat) Application Act 1937. The act originated in the efforts, primarily among some of the *'ulama*, to secure statutory enforcement of the *shari'a*. Their successful lobbying resulted in an Act that abrogated what were seen as 'non-Islamic' customs. The Act affirmed, in the political arena, the equivalence of Muslim identity and a certain form of *shari'a*. It was an Act of indigenous instigation, but its form and purpose reflected a view of the *shari'a* that had been reshaped in the British administration of Anglo-Muhammadan law.

Conclusion

From the outset, a deference to indigenous family laws marked colonial administration, and as a general policy, it was never set aside. And yet, despite the effectiveness of this policy, it contained the latent contradictions of a non-Muslim government administering a Muslim law, which threw up repeated instances of misunderstanding and simplification. Company administrators encountered a variety of legal norms and institutions that varied according to the determinants of locality and community life. In their search for effective and inexpensive modalities of rule, the British came to rely upon the devices of translation, textbook, and codification, to adapt indigenous arrangements to the dictates of colonial control. Given the constraints of language, financing, and a limited tradition of scholarship, colonial administrators developed a legal system that could secure the allegiance of indigenous elites and collect revenue. In these circumstances, it is not surprising that colonial judges looked less for accuracy than for certainty and uniformity.

At the heart of Anglo-Muhammadan jurisprudence lay a conviction that Islam was a matter of religious rules, of a more or less inflexible nature, which were of equal relevance to all Muslims regardless of their cultures and histories.[88] The internal contradictions, genuine differences of interpretation, and nuanced instances of discretion that often accompanied *shari'a* norms were, in the main, displaced by a rule-bound legal system. If Anglo-Muhammadan scholarship endorsed a scripturalist version of Islam, that same vision was transformed into an

[88] A similar assumption seems to pervade much contemporary scholarship on Islamic law. See Enid Hill, 'Orientalism and liberal-legalism: the study of Islamic law in the modern Middle East', *Review of Middle East Studies* 2 (1976).

oppositional Islam that could be used in the anti-colonial struggle. It is one of the ironies of British rule that a jurisprudence which first served to implement colonial rule in the eighteenth century could give form to a part of the independence movement of the twentieth century. Meanwhile, the intimate interaction of legal administration and indigenous identity formation lent scripturalist Islam an enduring quality that has continued into the post-colonial period.

Further reading

Anderson, M.R., 'Classification and coercions: themes in South Asian legal studies in the 1980s', *South Asia Research* 10, 2 (1990), pp.158-77.

Al-Azmeh, A. (ed.), *Islamic Law: social and historical contexts* (London, 1988).

Coulson, N.J., *A History of Islamic Law* (Edinburgh, 1964).

Fyzee, A.A., *Outlines of Muhammadan Law* (London, 1964).

Hasan, M. (ed.), *Communal and Pan-Islamic Trends in Colonial India* (Delhi, 1985).

Hussain, A., *Muslim Law as Administered in British India* (Calcutta, 1935).

Jain, M.P., *Outlines of Indian Legal History* (5th ed., Bombay, 1990).

Kozlowski, G.C., *Muslim Endowments and Society in British India* (Cambridge, 1985).

Mahmood, T., *Islamic Law in Modern India* (Delhi, 1971).

—, *Muslim Personal Law: role of the state in the sub-continent* (Delhi, 1977).

Mallat, C. and J. Connors (eds.), *Islamic Family Law* (London, 1990).

Washbrook, D.A., 'Law, state, and agrarian society in colonial India', *Modern Asian Studies* 15, 3 (1981), pp.649-721.

NOTES ON 'PEASANT INSURGENCY' IN COLONIAL MYSORE: EVENT AND PROCESS[1]

Burton Stein

*This paper has two objectives. One is to describe a heretofore little-known event of peasant political mobilisation in Mysore during the 1830s, and therefore to provide a reporting and analysis of that extensive political moment. The second purpose is to present a critique of a recent book purporting to account for the phenomenon—*Elementary Aspects of Peasant Insurgency in Colonial India, *by Ranajit Guha—which, it is claimed, cannot encompass the complex processes displayed in the Mysore event.*

Peasant insurgency has been an awkward subject for the Indian scholar, and thus for comparativists—usually historical sociologists—who more often than South Asianists, have studied the matter. The awkwardness arises from the following paradoxes. India is one of the most ancient peasant societies in the world, and one in which it is possible to speak of a peasantry in many of its parts even when India is also one of the major industrial and advanced technical and scientific societies in the world. Yet, despite its provenance as an historical and contemporary peasant society, neither insurgency nor rebellion, much less 'wars' of the sort treated by Eric Wolf, have been events that have occupied the place in historiography that the subject has occupied in Europe (where the peasantry has passed from the scene for the most part) or in China where its peasantry ranks along with that of India as a major element of the present. Explanations of the absence of widespread peasant political mobilisations against established authority in India have seldom risen above those favourite residual explainers of all certainties (and most uncertainties), caste or religion.[2]

This paper discusses an event in early nineteenth-century Mysore which I cannot suppose was unique in colonial India, and which seems to raise complexities not explained in current accounts of the subject. The event is an uprising of rural people over much of the client Mysore

[1] First published in *South Asia Research* 5, 1 (May 1985), pp.11-27, in a version which more fully discussed some reservations about the approach of Ranajit Guha, *Elementary Aspects of Peasant Insurgency in Colonial India* (New Delhi, 1983). Herein, 'IOL' indicates 'India Office Library, London'.

[2] Guha, *Elementary Aspects*, brings peasant political mobilisations during the nineteenth century into history for the first time; his estimate is of some 110 events of this sort—'ranging from local riots to warlike campaigns' (p.1). Eric R. Wolf, *Peasant Wars of the Twentieth Century* (New York, 1969).

kingdom set up by the British in 1799, after the defeat and death of Tipu Sultan. This uprising began in 1830 in Nagar, the northernmost of the six 'faujdaris' of which the kingdom then consisted.[3]

In August of 1830, armed followers of a man calling himself the 'raja of Nagar' attacked but failed to seize a royal fortress in Shimoga district of Nagar in Mysore; shortly after, letters were circulated by the Nagar insurgents calling upon cultivating groups to protest against the government of the Mysore Raja's (Krishnaraja Wodeyar III, r.d. 1799-1831) by convening assembles of protest at government offices, by refusing to pay taxes, and by absconding from their villages.[4] In late September, cultivators in all parts of Nagar were following this course, and by December of 1830 the cultivators of Chittledrug, 100 miles from Nagar, and of Bangalore, 180 miles away, had risen in armed revolt against the Mysore government, refusing to pay taxes, assembling in violent protest, and clashing with arms against state authorities.[5] Early in 1831, the rebel tide rolled on, with the fortress in Nagar previously attacked now taken from one of the best commanders of the Mysore durbar, and successful defences mounted of other previously seized places. East India Company troops were introduced at this point, and by June 1831 Nagar was taken and the revolt broken, though anti-government opposition was not completely quelled until 1834. By then, the administration of Mysore had been taken over by the Company, and direct British administration was to obtain until 1881, during which time the state was ruled by Britons of the Mysore Commission.

The Governor-General, Lord William Bentinck, appointed a committee to investigate 'the recent disturbances in Mysore', and the report of that committee in December 1833, is the principal existing source of evidence about the event.[6] Since the uprising of 1830-31 was the ostensible cause for the assumption of direct administration over Mysore by the Company, the government of Krishnaraja III was severely criticised for having permitted 'corrupt' agents of the durbar to perpetrate such

[3] B. Lewis Rice, *Mysore: a gazetteer compiled for government* (London, 1897), vol.1, p.616.

[4] C. Hayavadana Rao (ed.), *Mysore gazetteer: compiled for government* (Bangalore, 1930), vol.2, pt.4, pp.2869ff.

[5] M.N. Gopal, *The Finances of the Mysore State, 1799-1831* (Calcutta, 1960), Appendix E, pp.250-1.

[6] 'The Origin, Progress and Suppression of the Recent Disturbances in Mysore, Submitted to His Excellency, the Right Honourable, Lord William Bentinck, Governor-General in Council' (Bangalore, 12 December 1833). Printed version of this report in 212 paragraphs and 77 pages consulted at the Mythic Society, Bangalore, accession number 12637 (hereafter cited as 1833 Committee Report.) In addition, there is a large volume of evidence taken by the investigating committee, but not the Report, which is contained in IOL, Home Miscellaneous Series (hereafter HMS), vol.709.

oppressions as to drive the Mysore peasantry into rebellion, and thereby to risk what was most vital to the British, a deficiency in revenue collections to meet the heavy subsidy payments due to the Company! As if to expunge retrospectively that criticism of the Mysore royal family, possibly in the service of contemporary Karnataka nationalism (another complexity that Guha ignores) a century and a half later, senior academics in Karnataka have discouraged most young scholars from writing about the event.[7]

In 1833, besides faulting the raja, the committee also laid a major portion of blame for the uprising upon adventurers, in Mysore and from elsewhere, who intimidated the placid peasantry of Mysore into its violence. Nowhere in the minutes of evidence taken by the committee was there any suggestion that those most actively involved in the rebellion, the people of Nagar, were ever interviewed nor their side of the story elicited, a good example of what Guha says of the official record in such matters. Still, even without that evidence, the main causes and the principal methods of organisation of the Mysore 'disturbances' are compellingly clear.

A principal cause of the Nagar uprising and its rapid spread to other parts of the Mysore state quite distant from Nagar was the pressure for increased revenue at a time of bad crop seasons and falling prices. Mysore was restored to an infant member of the ancient Wodeyar family of rulers in 1799, and a provision of the treaty that made the kingdom a client of the East India Company stipulated that 57 per cent of the presumed revenue of the kingdom was to be paid to the Company as a subsidy for maintaining a military force there. It was this force, of course, that prevented the dynasty from being swept aside in 1830-31. Additionally, the treaty stipulated that the kingdom was to contribute even more at times of war involving the Company, as occurred in the Maratha wars of 1802 to 1805, and 1817 to 1818.[8] It is true that the actual income of the state exceeded what it was supposed to be in 1799 (owing either to the duplicity or ignorance of Tipu Sultan before his death);[9] however, this does not alter things, because the excess of rev-

[7] One exception to this curiously protective view of the former royal family is the work of Sebastian Joseph, whose paper on the event is unique: 'A service elite against the peasants—encounter and collision (Mysore 1799-1831)', *Proceedings of the Indian History Congress, Bombay Session, 1980*, pp.670-81. Joseph's major focus was upon the rapacious activities of Maratha Brahman amildars at the time.

[8] This tribute from Mysore represented 50 per cent of the total imperial tribute from among 198 princely states in British India. Again, Sebastian Joseph's work is important: 'Mysore's tribute to the imperial treasury: a classic example of economic exploitation', *Quarterly Journal of the Mythic Society*, 70, 3 (1979), pp.154-63.

[9] 'Duplicity' involving fraudulent claims by Tipu Sultan about the revenue

enue collected for some years by the royal ward's celebrated dewan, Purnaiya, who also served Haidar Ali Khan and Tipu Sultan, was hoarded by him with the approval of British Residents in Mysore. That hoarded fortune, amounting to about five times the annual revenue of the country,[10] was rapidly spent by the raja after ridding himself of Purnaiya in 1810, and the kingdom was severely pressed to increase its revenue yields to meet the British subsidy with which it was yoked. Purnaiya's punctilious payment of the scheduled subsidy to the Company from 1799 to 1810 drew the widest encomiums from contemporary British observers and from most Indian commentators since that time.[11] With his departure, the accumulated surpluses of the kingdom were 'dissipated' in acts of royal largessse—gifts to Brahmans and court favourites, temples and mathas—in an obvious, even frenzied effort to establish his personal credentials as the ruler of the kingdom after his tutelage under and eclipse by Purnaiya. Another form that Krishnaraja III's royal assertions took was his attempt to hold the loyalty of Maratha Brahmans brought into royal service by Purnaiya, himself one, through financial rewards for their administrative services in his court and in the many localities of the kingdom. Maratha Brahmans were appointed to amildarships where it was known that they would enrich themselves, and so they indeed appeared to do. But one consequence of making rewards of such appointments was that these officials were moved about frequently to make room for deserving others. One village headman from Tumkur district on the eastern border of the kingdom, reported to the committee of investigation in 1833 that for the previous 15 years, there had been eight successive amildars posted in his taluk; other headmen reported similar alternations of officials in their taluks.[12] These were reports from powerful and wealthy village big-men who were rightly considered by the committee to have been victims, rather than perpetrators, of the 'outrages' of 1830-31, and their evidence was unanimous that the peripetetic amildars were all Brahmans, that most were Maratha Brahmans, and that all had become essentially tax-farmers rather than bureaucratic agents of the Mysore durbar.

As the financial crisis of the durbar deepened, amildari appointments were made on the basis of the notorious tax-farming contract called *shirti muchchilka*. From about 1814, most amildars secured their posts

---

collected in his territories as part of the 1792 treaty ending the third Mysore War; Gopal, *Finances*, p.4.

[10] Estimated to be about 73 lakhs of Kantaraya Pagodas by Sir Thomas Munro in his Minute on Mysore, 23 August 1825, in IOL, European Mss. F/89, Elphinstone Papers, Box 14, Bundle 4.

[11] See these, pp.2882ff. in Hayavadana Rao, *Mysore Gazetteer*.

[12] HMS, vol.709, pp.1116, 1133, 1360 and 1440.

by a written contract stipulating that the holder was to collect a larger revenue than that of the previous years, and that if that revenue could not be collected, the farmer was responsible for the deficiency. This system resembled the *mustagiri* system of Awadh at about the same time in the sense that the farmer was also vested with civil and criminal powers. It was also a system that had existed in Mysore before in Haidar Ali's time, though abandoned by Tipu Sultan.[13]

The growing revenue crisis of the Mysore durbar coincided with a secular decline in the prices of agricultural commodities that was also occurring in Madras. Behind this decline in agricultural and other prices was a reversal of bullion flows from large net imports into India during most of the eighteenth century to a net export of bullion and specie by the beginning of the nineteenth century. During the early nineteenth century this change in bullion movements was accompanied by a restructuring of the export trade as well, one that placed Indian merchants and bankers at a disadvantage in relation to European agency houses and bankers.[14] Hence, peasant producers, and especially those large producers who were also involved in grain-trading, were caught in a pincer of enhanced revenue demand and falling money income. Added to this monetary cause for falling prices were other, well-recognised factors that were again general in South India at the time: diminished court-related expenditures by chiefly families, disbandment of armies and diminished military spending as the hegemony of Company forces became firmly established, and the depressing effects of curtailed production by Indian weavers. For the neighbouring Madras Presidency as a whole, Sarada Raju calculated that the index of agricultural prices showed a decline from 100, based on 1801-11, to 72 in 1827-28, 74 in 1828-29, 83 in 1829-30, 72 in 1830-31, and 66 in 1831-32.[15]

The determination of the Mysore government to bring the more remote highland tracts of the kingdom (the *malnad*) into its fiscal net added a serious political dimension to the crisis of the period. Even if less crude fiscal means than the *shirti* system had been adopted, the increased demand for money revenue would have engendered opposition from local lordships and big-men in these areas as previously they had not contributed to the income of any regimes of the southern flatland (*maidan*) of Mysore. Resistance to political control exercised from this heartland of the Mysore state had been a problem even under the

[13] Gopal, *Finances*, pp.175-6.

[14] K.N. Chaudhuri, 'Foreign trade and balance of payments', in Dharma Kumar and Meghnad Desai (eds.), *The Cambridge Economic History of India* (Cambridge, 1983), vol.2, 'c.1757-c.1970', pp.813-26.

[15] A. Sarada Raju, *Economic Conditions in the Madras Presidency, 1800-1850* (Madras, 1941), pp.227-44. Between 1821 and 1831, Company exports of bullion and specie was Star Pagodas 60 lakhs, while Company imports were only 6 lakhs, p.236. Index of agricultural prices, p.229.

powerful Haidar Ali in the middle of the eighteenth century. Records of his reign refer to expeditions launched in the Shimoga upland against the ruling family of Nagar. The *Hydaru Charitra* of about 1797, records such an expedition in 1762 by Haidar Ali, and in 1772 Tipu Sultan led another.[16] There were several reasons for such expeditions to the *malnad*: to end the fiscal and military independence of local lordships there, to secure the northern boundary of the state against the Maratha country to the north, and to assure access to the commercially and agriculturally important area of Kanara which had been brought under the Muslim rulers of Mysore. The persistent independence of the raja of Nagar and the various *palegararu* ('poligars') of the large upland between the Western Ghats, where Nagar nestled, and the eastern upland portions of Karnataka adjoining the Ceded Districts of Madras, had hardened during the late eighteenth century.

Political interests were reinforced by others. Many of the chiefly families there were linked together by ethnic bonds in being *bedaru*, forest people, who had been brought into South Indian politics during the sixteenth-century Vijayanagara period for their war prowess; most too were Virasaivas and therefore linked by shared sectarian affinities as well as by institutional affiliations to various Lingayat matha centres.[17] Hostility by Lingayats to Mysore rule dated from at least the late seventeenth century. Then, the first of the Wodeyar kings to construct a fiscal system in order to sustain his ambitious military building (based on firearms), drove Virasaiva peasants to revolt. This was Chikkadevaraja Wodeyar (r.d. 1672-1704). In addition to his fiscal and other centralising reforms of the Mysore kingdom, it was widely alleged that he deceived and massacred Virasaiva *jangams* (priests) in the *maidan* in order to break Virasaiva political resistance there.[18]

In 1830 it was the reawakening of the earlier political opposition to *malnad* people to the domination of the Mysore durbar that appears to have become crystallised. This accounts for the version of the uprising that attributed major significance to an adventurist conspiracy rather than to spontaneous, mass rural resentment, though the two are linked in explanation of the events of 1830-31.

The central figure of conspiratorial evil is one Sarada Malla, a peasant from Kumsi in Shimoga. He transformed an unprepossessing criminal career (having served two gaol terms) into one of royal deliverer from the Mysore yoke. Sarada Malla became the acolyte of an aged

[16] *Hydaru Charitra* by Krishniah in about 1797. Madras Government Oriental Series, No.138, edited by N. Venkataramanayya (Madras, 1956), pp.93, 115-7.

[17] R.P. Ramachandra Rao, 'Poligars of Mysore and their civilization', *Quarterly Journal of the Mythic Society* 29 (1938), pp.150-66 and 310-25, and 30 (1939), pp.175ff.

[18] Hayavadana Rao, *Mysore Gazetteer*, p.2462.

jangam, allegedly the *purohita* of the last raja (or 'poligar') of Nagar, and still in possession of some of the royal emblems of that ruler. Under the name of Budi Basavappa, and armed with these royal insignia obtained from his *jangam* guru, Sarada Malla began to claim descent from the adopted son of the last Nagara raja, one Dodda Basavappa. He was fortified in this claim by obtaining a Company passport in the name of Budi Basavappa from the collector of Kanara in 1812 when he was released from gaol there, after serving a term for a robbery in Kanara. Later, in 1830, he was proclaimed 'raja of Nagar' by a group of village headmen and installed by them as ruler of the area; at the same time, an amildar in the Nagar region is said to have also accepted Budi Basavappa as 'raja of Nagar'.[19] Soon after, letters were sent to villages throughout Nagar by Budi Basavappa announcing his lordship and promising remissions of all revenue arrears and a reduction of land revenue to be demanded by his durbar. At several points there is evidence that these various moves were tacitly supported, perhaps inspired, by some Maratha Brahman officials seeking to embarrass a member of the Mysore royal family, one Viraraj Urs, who was belatedly appointed as amildar in Nagar under pressure from the British Resident in Mysore and the Madras governor, then Sir Thomas Munro, to end the corruption of the *shirti* amildars.[20]

Beginning in September 1830, first in Nagar and later in other parts of the *malnad*, 'cootums' or 'kutus' (*kuttam* in Tamil and other Dravidian languages),[21] or great popular assemblies began to be convened. The *kuttam* was an assembly of protest often against high revenue demands; it also often involved the withdrawal of peasants from cultivation and merchants from trade, the refusal to pay revenue, and finally the desertion of villages and bazaars. Such gatherings were reported in the Ceded Districts of Madras early in the nineteenth century, [22] and (as *gota*) in Maharashtra during the eighteenth century, according to Frank Perlin;[23] in addition, *kuttams* were reported in the early 1830s at Basavapatam and Dharwar in southern Maratha country, in Mangalore on the Kanara coast, and in Bangalore near the heart of the Mysore state according to the evidence of the sheristadar of the Resident's Bangalore office.[24] Large numbers were involved in these

[19] Summary is from Gopal, *Finances*, Appendix E, p.250. This conforms with the history as given in the 1833 Committee Reports, paras.51-6, pp.24-6.

[20] Gopal, *Finances*, p.250.

[21] T. Burrow and M. Emaneau, *A Dravidian Etymological Dictionary* (Oxford, 1961), p.128.

[22] IOL, European Mss., Munro Collection, F/151/12, Munro to Peter Bruce, 1 July 1806.

[23] 1833 Committee Report, para.57, and Perlin, personal communication, 1984.

[24] HMS, vol.709, pp.1603-4.

assemblies and many bore firearms and other weapons. One *kuttam* at Hole Honnur, near the *malnad* town of Shimoga, was composed of 3,000, and it was not dispersed before ten were killed and another hundred wounded.[25] In the opposite corner of the Mysore kingdom, modern Tumkur taluk a *kuttam* involved, 6,000.[26]

Dispersing the gatherings of even large gatherings of armed peasants and merchants in 1830 proved within the capabilities of many amildars in the central and southern parts of the kingdom by deployment of their armed revenue 'peons' (*kandachar*, the same as *sibundi* militia of revenue police in Company territories); if this was not sufficient, the troops of the Mysore durbar were used. Often these pacifications were accompanied by promises to investigate grievances and to end the *shirti* powers of tax-farmers.

However, in the upland zone of the Mysore state, anti-government military formations were more powerful, and resistance was backed ideologically and politically such as to pose more grave problems for the Mysore durbar. By late 1830, Budi Basavappa was joined by several powerful, local 'poligars', including the family of Tarikere,[27] and by armed Virasaivas from the southern Maratha country. The latter were recruited by Budi Basavappa shortly after armed resistance began. To these forces were added most *kandachar* militiamen of Nagar who, being Bedar like many of the core resistors, mutinied and joined the uprising. These forces were capable of seizing and holding many of the 80 fortresses of the *malnad*,[28] and were only driven from them by Company troops in March to May 1831.

Virasaiva solidarity was a major element of coherence of the uprising in the *malnad* and involved co-sectarians from across the border in southern Bombay. To that was added the solidarity among Bedars who, though constituting only 4 per cent of the *malnad* population, held many military and government posts there. Virasaivas (or, as they were enumerated then, 'Shivabhacts') comprised about 30 per cent of the Nagar population then, and were divided into three groupings: merchants (or Banijigars), hillmen of the western and central part of Nagar (Malavars), and men of the eastern part (Saradas). Some 75 per cent of all Nagar Virasaivas were cultivators.[29] Brahmans constituted 7 per cent

[25] 1833 Committee Report, paras.68-9.

[26] HMS, vol.709, p.1095.

[27] The history of this 'poligar' is found in Mark Wilks, *Historical Sketches of the South of India in an Attempt to Trace the History of Mysoor...* (Mysore, reprint of original 1810 work, 1930), vol.1, p.76.

[28] Listed in a ms. of 1789 from Bombay military records of garrisons of that time, entitled 'Castles and Fortresses in the Province of Bednore and Sounday', and found in European Ms.696, John Rylands Library of the University of Manchester.

[29] H. Stokes, 'Report of the Nuggur Division of Mysore, 19 May 1838', in

of the Nagar population, and were divided into Haviks and other local groups who were heavily engaged in Betel and other garden cultivation, and comprised about a third of the Brahman population; the rest of the Brahmans were outsiders and included Deshastha or Maratha Brahmans who monopolised higher public offices.

The mobilising abilities of the Virasaivas were evident throughout. In the mounting of a *kuttam*, letters were circulated among *jangams*, who were among the few literate ruralites, announcing the royalty of Budi Basavappa and exhorting villagers to join in protest assemblies against officials of the Mysore durbar. Failure to comply, it was threatened, would lead to individuals and whole villages being branded as apostates from Virasaivism. Repeatedly, members of the committee investigating the 1830 uprising were told by headmen of long-standing and proven reliability (and who were not from Nagar!) that such letters were read out or delegates arrived from other places saying that all should join the 'kutu', for if they did not, they would be humiliated and treated as polluted by having horns and bones of animals thrown into their houses and Margossa leaves affixed to their houses or to the gates of their villages.[30] The signification of Margossa, or *neem* leaves (*azadirachta indica*), appears to have been that of indicating a state of pollution from disease among Lingayats and others in South India. The idea that collective action was a social responsibility was reiterated by a number of witnesses to explain their own participation in some of the actions: 'That as union was the law or custom of their caste, they had taken part with the rest'.[31] Caste solidarity also enabled the rapid spread of protest assemblies according to witnesses who observed that it was the custom of merchants and cultivators in Mysore, when a major dispute arose, to call upon caste-fellows everywhere to join in support by closing shops, withdrawing from cultivation, and meeting in assemblies.[32]

The same appeals to primordial sentiment and social organisation—elaborately discussed by Guha—cannot explain the insurgency among even quite substantial peasants in those parts of the kingdom where there were few Virasaivas or Bedars. There was probably as little fellow-feeling between Hindu cultivating groups and Virasaivas in Mysore as in the adjoining Ceded Districts of Madras where it was

---

Selection from Records of the Mysore Commissioner's Office (Bangalore, 1864).

[30] HMS, vol.709, pp.1095 and 641. I am grateful to David Mosse of the University of Oxford for his suggestion about Margossa leaves; other references to the plant are found in H.V. Nanjundaya and L.K. Anantakrishna Iyer, *The Mysore Castes and Tribes* (Mysore, 1931), vol.4, p.85, and E. Thurston and K. Rangachari, *Castes and Tribes of Southern India* (Madras, 1909), vol.4, p.281.

[31] HMS, vol.709, p.679.

[32] Ibid., p.1616.

reported that Lingayats were denied the status of respectability enjoyed by 'kunbi' or 'kapu' castes there.[33] This animosity has continued to shape the contemporary politics of Karnataka. In non-Lingayat areas of Mysore, another set of forces seems to have been at work. These forces were leading to the serious protest and disobedience of the *kuttam* against the *shirti* system and extortionate amildars, but apparently required the catalyst of the armed opposition to the Mysore state elsewhere to flare into 'open revolt'.[34]

Information on this aspect of the insurgency is of two sorts. One was testimony from a set of wealthy rural men, usually of Hindu peasant castes (Vokkaliga), who were headmen of villages and for a long time village rentiers. They were, in effect, small tax-farmers. The other source was from high state officials, members of the royal family or Maratha Brahmans, serving as central administrators. Interviews with both groups by the investigating committee sitting in 1833 reveal a great deal about landholding in Karnataka at the time, and their evidence clarifies the motives of rural magnates for opposition to the Mysore durbar around 1830. To this record can be added the revenue accounts maintained by the Mysore state as well as reports on that matter from the Resident's office to the durbar.

Peasant big-men explained to the investigating committee that there were two general modes of land revenue collection. One was from lands bearing a money tax, called *kandayam*; the other, either called *waram* or *batayi*, was arable upon which a tax in kind was levied.[35] *Kandayam* lands were usually irrigated by wells or tanks, and these lands were treated as a species of the private property of cultivating families in all respects, except that they could not be sold. One form of this sort of tenure was *kandayamgutta*, a village tenure involving a fixed, money revenue; this was the preferred form of revenue-holding from the point of view of the state.[36] Though amildars were prohibited, by custom, from reallocating *kandayam* lands, some of it was granted to village servants (*balutadar*) for their services. For Mysore as a whole at the time, wet cultivation comprised 38 per cent of total cultivation, thus a wet holding was relatively scarce and valuable.[37] *Batayi* lands carried a nominal division of shares between cultivators and the state of half; however, the share to cultivators was often reduced by various fees to around 44 per cent.[38] Such lands held by public servants (and

[33] IOL, 'Atlas of the Company's Ceded Districts under the Presidency of Fort St. George', by Surveyor-General, Colin Mackenzie, 1 January 1820, Map W-IX-2.

[34] Gopal, *Finances*, p.251.

[35] HMS, vol.709, pp.1114-6.

[36] Rice, *Mysore*, vol.1, p.618.

[37] Ibid., p.615.

[38] HMS, vol.709, p.1154.

their families or dependants) paid no such additional fees, and the villages in which they held *batayi* were widely thought to be more lightly assessed than other, similar villages. In such cases, too, ordinary cultivators were employed as unpaid agricultural workers upon the lands of public officials presumably under some coercion.[39] Peasant big-men complained that *kandayam* lands, of which they were major holders, were being more heavily taxed by amildars,[40] and were passing under the control of the foreign, 'service elite' of Maratha Brahmans (as Sebastian Joseph has called them).[41] Another of their complaints was that amildars failed to meet their responsibilities to repair wells, tanks and anicuts, partly because 'they knew nothing of cultivation', and partly because they were interested only in the largest profits they could take on their brief tenure as amildars.[42] These factors, along with the series of bad seasons from 1825 on, contributed to the diminution of state revenues according to the evidence presented by witnesses in 1833. High state officials, on their part, complained that leading members of cultivating castes had entered into conspiracies with bad elements who were fomenting anti-state activities in order to avoid paying their rightful share of the revenue demand, and that far from being the protectors of ordinary village cultivators, as they claimed, these local big-men exploited the labour of their fellows for the profitability of their own holdings while permitting the revenues of the state to fall into arrears.[43]

From the welter of fact and accusation in the testimony collected by the committee of investigation in 1833, it would appear that one underlying cause of the revolt against the Mysore durbar was a conflict within rural classes. One class element, consisting of Maratha Brahmans, and perhaps other Brahmans, used connections in the Mysore court to obtain lucrative tax farms. *Shirti* contracts provided them with profits from high revenue appropriations, using the public powers that came with their revenue engagements, and the prospects of landlord super-profits from the appropriation of better fields and the coercion of labour in their tax domains. The other class element consisted of the older, established stratum of rural big-men, non-Brahman, cultivating caste leaders who had enjoyed smaller-scale tax-farming rights previously and who now resented the erosion of some of the profits and advantages they had long monopolised. Both groups exploited lower agrarian elements, and both combined office advantages with private entrepreneurship.

[39] Ibid., p.1155.
[40] Ibid., p.1605.
[41] Ibid., p.1653.
[42] Ibid., p.1132.
[43] Ibid., p.641.

Another cause of the insurrection of 1830-31, again general, was the increasing demand of the state. This was partly prompted by the high treaty schedule of subsidy payments to the Company, and partly by the determination of the durbar to establish central control over resources and territory previously exempt from most central demands. The crude method of *shirti* contracts from outsiders (Maratha Brahmans primarily) who, as strangers, would not contribute to the continuance of local autonomy from central control, is a manifestation of the relatively primitive character of the Mysore bureaucracy as compared to that of the contemporary Peshwa's regime in Maharashtra and that of the Company.

Nagar was subject to both of these kinds of conflict, which added to other factors (cultural and political) of solidarity and resistance to the Mysore durbar's thrusting centralisation. In Nagar, there had been no *kandayam* land, but only a flexible form of revenue collected in kind—generally designated as *amani*—in which the agrarian product was shared between the Nagar rajas or 'poligars' and cultivators. That system of 'shist', so-called, was set up around 1660, but in 1815 began to be altered by the Mysore durbar. Then a new set of money dues were imposed that doubled the tax burden on cultivated land and, in addition, lands on long and short fallows (called 'waste' by the British and in the committee report of 1833) previously not subject to taxes in Nagar were now made taxable.[44] Nagar also showed a lesser degree of differentiation within its peasantry, but still there was exploitation of lower peasants by superior ones called '*sattegadars*'.[45]

Conclusion

The Nagar 'disturbance', 'insurgency', or 'revolt' of 1830-31, was a peasant matter and something more. It was a major event in duration, in scope (most of northern, central and eastern Mysore), in numbers of persons involved, and in its consequences (the assumption there of direct British administration for half a century). It could not be explained without considering the variety of within-peasant differentiations of income, status and power that one would expect to find in most peasant populations in colonial India, nor without considering the complex levels of inter-involvement among different classes—landlord and merchant—also a part of most rural societies in India during the nineteenth century. These are the aspects which the schema of Guha, *Elementary Aspects*, seems incapable of considering. Perhaps it is because of the very involutional character of his scheme, one that is generated from postulated binary oppositions (elite versus subaltern, landlord versus dependent others, mature(?) versus 'incipient' capitalist social relations

[44] Rice, *Mysore*, vol.1, pp.614-5, and HMS, vol.709, p.640.
[45] Ibid., pp.1606-7.

of production, distorted official records versus his negational analyses of such records) that many of the elements—to my mind, equally 'elementary'—reach beyond his problematic. There appear to be levels of process involving peasants and their historical conditions and contexts that Guha's presentation of the question does not engage.

Among such processual and contextual issues which are raised by this accounting of the events in Nagar, are the following. Regarding the unrest and insurgency in Nagar itself, there is a long history to take into account that in many ways set the terms of the nineteenth-century conflict. Not all, nor perhaps most, peasantries in colonial India are so utterly without histories as Guha assumes for most of the cases he examines. Nagar had been a kingdom in its own right from the early seventeenth century. About the same time that the Wodeyar chief at Seringapatam seized that fortified place in defiance of the kings of Vijayanagara in 1610, Sivappa Nayaka of Ikkeri at Nagar, did the same.[46] Moreover, the rulers of the Ikkeri kingdom were Virasaivas who supported the institutions of that sect, and these rulers at Nagar long resisted inclusion in any *maidan* Karnatak authority, even including those of the powerful Haidar Ali Khan and Tipu Sultan. This history was called into support of the activities of the Mysore upland in 1830, and provided an ideological centring of the uprising there.

Another processual thread involving Nagara and the *malnad* portion of the revolt of 1830-31 was territorial. The border with Bombay Presidency in southern Maratha country and the border with Ceded Districts of Madras Presidency to the east were factors of importance. Armed supporters of Budi Basavappa reportedly crossed into Nagar from southern Maratha country after being recruited by him at the Virasaiva centre of Basavapatam (in modern Bijapur district). Across this same border not long before had come a family of Maratha Brahmans from the locality of Hangal (in modern Dharwar district) which was to supply many of the exploitative amildars in Nagar from about 1815 onwards. As Brahmans, probably of the Madhva sect of Vaishnavas,[47] as strangers, as creatures of the distant and distrusted Mysore court,[48] and as extortionate tax-farmers, these men were easy objects of suspicion and even hate by the general Nagar peasantry, and by Virasaivas in particular. On the other frontier of the Mysore state, the Madras Presidency tract known as the Ceded districts provided a sanctuary for many of the village headmen fleeing the oppression of the *shirti* system.

[46] Rice, *Mysore*, vol.1, p.356, and K.D. Swaminathan, *The Nayakas of Ikkeri* (Madras, 1957).

[47] Note the complex religious history of this area in David Lorenzen, *The Kapalikas and Kalamukhas: two lost Saivite sects* (New Delhi, 1972).

[48] There was a rotation of office of dewan from 1811 to 1831 between Maratha Brahmans and members of the royal family called Urs; Hayavadana Rao, *Mysore Gazetteer*, p.2851.

Since they had kinsmen on the Madras side of the border, in Bellary, these men could not only find shelter, but they were even encouraged to migrate by British collectors eager to swell the ranks of working cultivators. Many *maidan* cultivators, especially substantial ones, were therefore able to compare their increasing difficulties with the Mysore durbar with the successful efforts of the British administration in the Ceded Districts—following Munro's earlier strategy—of winning the rich peasantry over by protecting older privileges and even increasing them. Several witnesses before the investigating committee commented on this.[49]

Another historical process which the Nagar events uncover is that of the encroaching fiscal structure upon peripheral parts of many polities in the late, pre-colonial period and later. From about the middle of the seventeenth century, the core area of the Mysore kingdom had come under increasingly effective, centralised fiscal management by the state, but the extension to the upland peripheries and to the easternmost districts was more recent, and was substantially induced by the client status of the ruling regime after its restoration in 1799. The rapacious form of the state's fiscal net—the *shirti* system—was a manifestation of royal panic in Mysore as state expenditures increased, while income melted away as a result of the bad luck of weather and the bad choices and supervision of its fiscal agents. The Company ended this panic by taking over the Mysore administration for 50 years, thus relieving the rulers of that state of an impossible task. That is, the task, on the one hand, of impressing its royal subjects with the independence and traditionalism of the kingdom by conspicuous largesse (*dana*) when Krishnaraja III came of age and, on the other, of increasing the revenue to meet the costs of internal administration and colonial clienthood. The Mysore state system in the time of Tipu Sultan, as well as in the time of Krishnaraja III, was caught in the same contradiction between patrimonial forms that had characterised all late, pre-colonial regimes of India and their growing fiscal needs arising out of military and administrative developments. The conflict arising from that contradiction fed some significant part of the insurgency of 1830-31.[50]

A last process which is elicited by the events of 1830-31 is the complex differentiation of class interests on the Mysore countryside, a differentiation that mocks Guha's elite/subaltern dichotomy. Powerful local heads of cultivating groups—village headmen (petels) and supralocal headmen (shaikdars)—long in possession of minor tax-farming privileges and powers with which they levered their political control

[49] Evidence of the headman, Sidda Gowda of Sira taluk, who fled to Bellary, HMS, vol.709, pp.1104-5, 1108, and 1207-8.

[50] See Burton Stein, 'State formation and economy reconsidered', *Modern Asian Studies*, 19, 2 (1985), pp.299-325.

over localities as well as extending their personal wealth, were challenged and displaced by *shirti* agents appointed by the centre.[51] Beneath both powerful groups were allies and dependants (for example, *balutadars*, or village servants) in a complex order, all with special privileges and advantages over ordinary cultivators. Petels and their kinsmen could call upon ordinary cultivators for labour upon their lands; they bribed amildars to assess their own lands at a lower rate than these should have been, and passed any arrears they incurred on the revenue along to poorer peasants.[52] Hence, if we seek to identify *an* elite, we are placed in a difficulty. Moreover, differentiation did not only pertain to the various fiscal agents in complex and varying relations with agrarian production and producers, but to mercantile interests as well. To an extent, Karnatak merchant groups (*vartaka*) were separate from landed production, but some were centrally implicated in agrarian production through their trade in grain, through investments in the production of cash crops, through the provision to cultivators of irrigation improvements, seed, fertilisers, and even bullocks, and through providing for the circulation of tax proceeds of others, well placed in the chain of agrarian relations, into profitable commerce.[53]

Further reading

Desai, A.R., *Peasant Struggles in India* (New Delhi, 1979).

Dhanagare, D.N., *Peasant Movements in India 1920-50* (New Delhi, 1983).

Hardiman, David, (ed.), *Peasant Resistance in India, 1958-1914*; and Gyan Prakash, (ed.), *The World of the Rural Labourer in Colonial India* (Oxford in India Readings: Themes in Indian History; Delhi, 1992). These 'Themes in Indian History' volumes contain representative articles and descriptive bibliographies.

[51] HMS, vol.709, pp.1439 and 1447.

[52] Ibid., pp.113, 1473-6, and 1621-2.

[53] See Burton Stein, *Thomas Munro; the origins of the colonial state and his vision of empire* (New Delhi, 1989).

IDEAS IN AGRARIAN HISTORY: SOME OBSERVATIONS ON THE BRITISH AND NINETEENTH-CENTURY BIHAR[1]

Peter Robb

This paper looks at some aspects of land policy, one of the most important points of contact between British colonial rule and the mass of the population in British India (1765-1947). The paper argues that alongside more material factors the ways the rulers thought *about India was important in shaping British impact. The ideas were not monolithic or exclusively 'colonial'; they were both contested between state officials and others, and related to broader, international trends. The example taken here is the idea of* peasant proprietorship *(its supposed legitimacy from history, and its desirability in future). The background is the 'permanent settlement'—a fixed revenue demand—which gave property rights to* landlords *(not peasants) in the late eighteenth century. The discussion then broadens out to characterise colonial rule as influencing India by extending the role of the state in terms of categorisation and generalisation of Indian society. Ideas mattered, the paper suggests, because so much of the colonial influence derived from the British attempt to define and regulate India.*

As a precise study, British Indian officialdom is out of fashion. This is partly, I think, from a post-imperial suspicion that the British officials' own assessments of their influence on India were exaggerated, and from a feeling that we must not underestimate the force of Indian experience upon policy. The reply, on the first point, is that the state *must* be one of the most important objects of study, and, in regard to the second point, that there is more danger of forgetting to allow for British assumptions than of overplaying their importance. The fact that policy always accommodated itself to Indian realities, in no way reduces the importance of considering the theories and categorisations which also

[1] First published in the *Journal of the Royal Asiatic Society* 1 (1990), pp.17-43, being the 1989 Anniversary Memorial Lecture given in memory of Professor Eric Stokes, delivered at the Royal Asiatic Society on 11 May 1989. This version has been modified and abridged so as to exclude the discussion of Stokes' work and other historiographical comment. But see Eric Stokes, *The English Utilitarians and India* (Oxford, 1959), *The Peasant and the Raj. Studies in agrarian society and peasant rebellion in colonial India* (Cambridge, 1978), *The Peasant Armed. The Indian rebellion of 1857* (ed. C.A. Bayly; Oxford, 1986), and 'Agrarian relations I: northern and central India' in Dharma Kumar (ed.), *The Cambridge Economic History of India*, vol.2 (Cambridge, 1983), pp.36-86.

underlay it, and which continue to infest our own historical understanding. One of these long-living assumptions concerns the organic nature of Indian society, comprising a Brahmanical tyranny over the mind, a 'socialistic' village community suppressing the individual, and a consequent intellectual and economic stagnation. It was this stable world which British and Indian governments successively sought to protect and restore, as the fount of order and economic independence. An anti-'orientalist-indologist' critique has been made of this view,[2] but fails to detect the even more subversive assumptions implicit in terminology, indeed in language itself. I mean concepts which divide human behaviour according to certain, largely unconscious criteria, concepts such as 'social' or 'political', and terms which carry with them hidden norms and expectations, such as 'peasant' or 'landlord'.

I wrote ten years ago about the need to employ the idea of resources rather than structures in understanding Indian rural society.[3] I had discovered in nineteenth-century Bihar both the extreme variability of ranking year-by-year according to any one criterion (outside, that is, of very broad categories), and the conditionality and changing fortunes of particular advantages over time. Behind this idea—though I do not guarantee that I appreciated it fully at the time—lay others about the essential ambiguity and multiplicity of roles and functions in all societies. This is to assert that there is no such thing, in absolute terms, as, say, 'economics', and that different peoples have different pictures in their minds, and organise themselves according to varied principles and categories. The word 'peasant', for example, has spawned a vast academic industry, based on the premise that there is a kind of person or society common to many parts of the world and conforming more or less to certain characteristics. The peasant is an individual producer using family labour, concentrating on his subsistence, and (though subordinate to external elites) living among others of his kind. The problem with this definition occurs when researchers discover peasants who do not conform. In much of India, I believe, it is not true to say that the dominant mode is a peasant one. Though we all go on using the term in a more popular sense, we do not mean that we find everywhere family-farm production, homogeneity, and a lack of involvement in the market. On the contrary we find employment of labour, social differentiation, and the production of crops for sale.

My quarrel with the idea of the peasant is that the situation in many parts of India thus comes to be regarded, even subconsciously, as a variant, as something to be explained because it is not the norm. It

[2] Edward Said, *Orientalism* (London, 1978), and Ronald Inden, 'Orientalist constructions of India', *Modern Asian Studies* 20, 3 (1986).

[3] 'Hierarchy and resources: peasant stratification in late nineteenth-century Bihar', *Modern Asian Studies* 8, 1 (1979).

comes to be assumed too that social and economic change naturally takes a certain direction—away from 'true' peasant production towards market-orientation, away from the moral economy of a self-sufficient community towards that of international capitalism. On the contrary, it seems clear that the localities in India have long been deeply involved with the outside world. The old notion of isolated village republics was patently wrong. Moreover, on the other hand, in the nineteenth century, there remained village cultures which were distinct from that purveyed by the state or through long-distance exchange: that is to say that modern trade and government did not necessarily dissolve the old order.

II

In this lecture I want to tell just one story relating to the village community and British ideas. The example I will take centres on the Bengal Tenancy Act of 1885, arguably the most important single enactment of the nineteenth century. I will then go on to make some more, general points about the connection between British ideas and the course and impact of colonial rule.

The story centres upon a public row between two of the highest officers in Bengal—the Chief Secretary, Alexander Mackenzie, and the Chief Justice, Richard Garth—over the 1885 Act. Also involved was another judge, with experience on the revenue side, J. O'Kinealy.[4] One of the instructive features of the argument was the extent that the protagonists considered it a matter of public concern, in Britain as well as India; it was important, to their minds, both in politics and theoretically, at that happy time when the obscure details of Indian agrarian history were thought to raise significant intellectual issues. To understand the debate, therefore, one needs to know a little about the Tenancy Act. It was introduced after more than a decade of deliberations, which included earlier conflicts between government and High Court. The reasons for it included criticism of the existing state of the law mainly as consolidated in the Tenancy Act of 1859, and worries about landlord-tenant conflict in Bengal. The legal critique was embodied above all in a large digest of the law-as-it-stood, prepared under government orders by C.D. Field, a work which stood in a considerable tradition of nineteenth-century studies of tenancy. The conflict was instanced in rural violence which played an important part in persuading the government

[4] The memoranda discussed below may be found with the Government of India's Revenue and Agriculture Proceedings, Revenue Branch, A series, nos.16-46, July 1883. Some further references are included in my 'Law and agrarian society in India: the case of Bihar and the nineteenth-century tenancy debate', *Modern Asian Studies* 22, 2 (1988). This paper also discussed some other features of the Tenancy Act and the pro-raiyat school, for example the emphasis on the 'magic' of property and the arguments for state intervention (pp.322-6).

to take the tenancy question seriously.

But the key to the shape of the legislation was different: the hope of redressing the balance of power in favour of the tenants (or *raiyats*) in order to reduce oppression, ameliorate poverty, and unlock economic progress. Two influences were paramount in this regard: one was the rise in the credit of the Punjabi model of Indian government, associated partly with the overwhelming regard paid at this time to the ideas of Henry Maine and to the village community as the original or natural form of Indian society. The other was concern at the plight of the Indian poor and a belief in the need for government intervention, as argued by John and Richard Strachey and in the Famine Commission Report of 1881; in eastern India these suggestions referred particularly to conditions in Bihar, as revealed in various studies and reports during the 1870s. Lieutenant-Governors' visits to Bihar had featured in shifting the emphasis towards the questions of poverty and underproduction, in the mid and late 1870s, in the time of Richard Temple and Ashley Eden, and away from the problem of rent and rent-collection (as raised in the early 1870s under George Campbell). The two main influences were combined when Charles Tupper, who in the 1870s had helped increase Punjabi influence in the Revenue and Agriculture Department of the Government of India, was placed on special duty in connection with the Bengal rent bill, and in the early 1880s produced an important report on Bihar. Thus the bill over which Garth and Mackenzie clashed introduced a special set of provisions for that area, regarded as needing more and different measures from the remainder of the province.

Officers who had served in Bihar were also crucial to the formulation of the new tenancy policy. Mackenzie began his service in Shahabad district in 1863, and also served briefly in Bihar a decade later on famine duty; apart from a stint of a few months as a magistrate and collector in Murshidabad, Mackenzie was pre-eminently a secretariat man, beginning early as an under-secretary and occupying various positions in the Board of Revenue and other provincial offices before becoming a departmental secretary in 1877—his three or four years in Bihar constituted almost the whole of his experience of the *mufassil*. O'Kinealy, his almost exact contemporary, began his judicial career, after transfer from the revenue branch, in 1874 in Bhagalpur district, a time when discussions were going on among Bihari officers about the condition of the poor and the oppressions of the zamindari system. Other officials too, who were crucial in the tenancy debates, had served in Bihar in posts relating to famine or agrarian conditions—men such as Anthony Macdonnell and Michael Finucane. They will not concern us today, except to remind us of the importance to the formulation of agrarian policy in India at this time of one final factor, the Irish (and Irish land questions).

Mackenzie set out the aims of his legislation, on behalf of Ashley Eden and his government, in a letter written in 1880, at the high-point of the government's reforming zeal, just after the report of the Rent Law Commission on which both Mackenzie and O'Kinealy had served. Sir Ashley Eden wanted, wrote Mackenzie, 'to define and strengthen the position of the great mass of cultivators, while giving landlords a reasonably cheap and effective procedure for regulating and revising rents'. In particular, the raiyats, 'as a class, should be secured in the enjoyment of those rights which the ancient land law and customs of the country intended them to have, protected against arbitrary eviction, left in the enjoyment of a reasonable proportion of the profits of cultivation, and, in short, placed in a position of substantial comfort, calculated to resist successfully the occasional pressure of bad times.' Thus the diagnosis was that the province's agrarian problems derived from the insufficient margin left to the actual cultivator by the landlord (or *zamindar*). The remedy was for the state, under the guise of providing 'effective procedure', to regulate rents and agrarian relations. The justification for this interference was the restoration of ancient rights and the promise of future comfort.

The details of the Tenancy Act need not concern us; briefly it provided for a presumption that tenants had a right of occupancy in their land, with certain other privileges in regard to rent, unless it could be shown that they had only held land in the village for less than twelve years. This turned the 1859 Act on its head, both in regard to the presumption of occupancy, and in deriving rights more or less from residence in a village, rather than from the long possession of specified plots of land. None the less, in the Act as passed, the reformers abandoned their earlier attempts to associate occupancy rights with all raiyati land and not with the occupant, though they retained the important but poorly defined and as yet unmeasured distinction between zamindari land and tenants' land: no occupancy rights accrued in respect of the so-called home-farms of the landlords, and such land was recognised in effect as any land thus specified, supposedly by custom, even if it was held by tenants, plus any land that was untenanted. A result of the Act was to encourage the already-extensive claims over such land (identified as a special problem in Bihar); another result was that, in law, as one set of distinctions between tenants was removed, room was left for the development of others. There was no longer any effective difference between 'original', 'full' or 'resident' raiyats on the one hand and other, less privileged villagers on the other; anyone who had held or inherited any land in a village—unless they were patently newcomers—could claim occupancy rights in regard to all the land which they held there. Moreover, the unit under consideration was not the estate (the lands of one owner or set of owners under one revenue head); it was the village, as defined by government surveys (or historically by Maine). Hence rights gained under one landlord could be transferred to land held from another. Indeed it was because the reformers held in their minds this picture of a stable Indian village made up of largely undifferentiated tenant-cultivators, that it seemed not to matter if the right accrued to occupants rather than being vested in all land. But this left open several possibilities: transfers of land from weaker to stronger occupancy raiyats, the further creation of under-tenancies, and the loss of presumed tenant rights by legal or other manoeuvres.

For several years, during all these discussions, Bengal's Chief Justice held aloof. He was on leave abroad, or he was ill, or (as he said, when he broke his silence in 1882) he was unwilling to oppose the strong pro-raiyat views of Eden until they had taken definite shape. But, finally, after the Rent Law Commissions' report had been turned into a draft bill, and that draft had been amended by the local government and further changed by the Government of India, and yet another version had been prepared to meet the objections of the Secretary of State, Sir Richard Garth did put pen to paper. His previous silence did not prevent him from complaining that the High Court had not been properly consulted. But he saved his venom for those whom he called the extremists of the Rent Law Commission, two of the younger members who were responsible, as he saw it, for 'revolutionary provisions' which, 'unjustly and unnecessarily', would dispossess the landlords of rights they had enjoyed for nearly a century, and relegate them to a position 'far inferior to that which they occupied before the Permanent Settlement'—that is before the foundation in 1793 of the Bengal system of revenue, land law and administration. Garth objected above all to the extension of the occupancy right and to limits on rent enhancement. The young men in question were Mackenzie and O'Kinealy, both of whom at that time had had some twenty years' service in India. The interference they proposed was justified by them, Garth complained, on a ground '(if it is worth to be called by that name)' which was as 'transparent a pretext as ever was presented'. Their extreme views, he wrote, were supported by no one, and by nothing save their own 'constructions' of previous legislation, and indeed were contradicted by all the eminent men who had expounded the law since the permanent settlement—men who were, it was true, 'unfortunate enough to have differed in opinion with Mr. Mackenzie'. Loftily, the Chief Justice trusted that 'even Mr. O'Kinealy' would learn 'some little respect for authority and precedent' when he became 'a *permanent* member of the High Court'; Garth hoped he would before long. Garth then published his memorandum in the newspapers; it was seized upon eagerly by the well-organised opponents of the Tenancy Act, and was also translated into Bengali and Hindi and circulated widely in the province. There followed various correspondence, including letters to

The Times in London. Some of the readers must have been glad of Garth's assurance that, as he was 'happy to say', O'Kinealy and Mackenzie were two gentlemen who were 'both very good friends' of his.

At one level this was just another round in the long rivalry between Court and executive in Bengal. Garth complained that measures passed by one Lieutenant-Governor and confirmed by another, should not be lightly set aside; otherwise the public would have no security that in another ten years another Lieutenant-Governor might not arise who would take another view and cause another general revolution. This was a doctrine to limit state power, while presenting the courts as the defenders of higher principles. According to Garth, legislation, if it interfered with rights, was justifiable only in a real emergency; and rights, though they might derive from legislation, rested ultimately upon the common law. Thus any occupancy right for the tenants must have depended, before 1793, upon prescription; that is, it was a common law presumption of legal title on the basis of possession from time immemorial, a provision recognised in Roman law and given legislative form in England (with a thirty-year limit) in 1832. Boldly, Garth accommodated this precedent to Indian experience by supposing that 'prescription' was really the same as what Indians meant by 'custom': these 'poor people', the raiyats, he explained sadly, knew no difference between the two, and in fact probably had no word in their language to signify 'prescription'. In short, he supposed that the underlying principles of law were universal. Fundamentally he was convinced that property was a natural state of man, that it was regulated by contract, and that, though either might evolve, neither should be overturned by governments. Nor should the courts be required to intervene in transforming or denying them: Garth was concerned that the rent law would create a 'frightful amount of ill-feeling and litigation'. On the other hand he recognised also that practice differed, and that enactments could alter things: he imagined that the period of prescription required for tenant rights had varied from place to place before 1793, and that afterwards the zamindars 'took advantage of the liberty of contract which they acquired' in order to 'break in upon existing customs' by requiring written agreements from their tenants, setting out rents and the duration of tenancies. But he argued both that such changes had produced new rights which could not now be overturned, and that the consequences of extending similar rights to tenants would be to create in the occupancy right a valuable property, a prize for land speculators: the more valuable it was, the less likely the cultivating classes would be to acquire it; indeed the condition of the actual cultivator would probably decline.

This last was a shrewd thrust at the advocates of tenant-rights, but generally Garth was a man of narrow imagination: the law had a concrete reality for him to an extent with which the revenue officers had little patience. It was far from the case that agrarian relations were being regulated by law-courts to the degree that Garth believed, though the laws of property had undoubtedly made an impact on the situation of zamindars; on the matter of contract for example it was known that very few formal leases were issued between landlords and tenants. It was not until somewhat later that the courts did intervene to an increasing extent—the ten-year averages of rent suits almost doubled between 1890 and 1903—and the increase was in large part attributable to the Bengal Tenancy Act (as Garth had predicted), and to the greater access provided by Small Cause Courts (with jurisdiction in cases worth up to Rs.500 for subordinate judges) and by an expansion in the number of munsiff's courts (competent in civil cases worth up to Rs.1,000).

The replies to Garth concentrated upon the legal arguments. It was pointed out that proprietary rights in Bengal were very concentrated and very lightly taxed, and that rental incomes had increased vastly since the permanent settlement; but the reformers were convinced that there was no need to justify change on such arguments of public policy. What was now proposed—the words come from H.S. Cunningham, another High Court judge—was not a subversion but a re-establishment of the law, exercising a right reserved in 1793 for the state to intervene to prevent the 'raiyats being improperly disturbed in their possessions'. According to this view the great mass of resident raiyats had commonly possessed occupancy rights throughout India. There is an interesting confusion or conflation here. Mackenzie and his fellows believed the usual cultivator was a resident; they thought that 'resident cultivator' was a fair translation of *khudkashta* (original or proprietary) raiyat, and that the privileges of such raiyats were well-established. Therefore, the usual cultivator had (or should have) the same rights, which only the previous errors of government and the courts had obscured. It now seems clear that not all residents, not even all resident cultivators, were *khudkashta* raiyats; and indeed that not all *khudkashta* raiyats were true cultivators or even necessarily resident. Rather there were categories of privileged proprietary tenants; there were village residents who inherited tenancies and other obligations or benefits, but without such privileged status; there were resident cultivators who had little or no land directly from a zamindar, or who were otherwise not regarded as full members of the community; there were *khudkashta* raiyats in one village who occupied fields in another, as *pahikashta* (non-privileged) tenants; and so on: the picture, as will already be plain enough, is of a very great complexity. There was no pair of categories neatly covering all the possibilities, and available for Western legislators.

O'Kinealy wrote along similar lines to his colleague, Cunningham, and with rather less circumspection than might have been expected from one yet to receive his 'permanent' appointment to the High Court. He had been a reluctant recruit to the Rent Law Commission, he explained, and returned to the subject only to meet Garth's 'rather personal attack'—one written, moreover, calmly in England and not in India or in the heat of discussion; one then published in the Indian newspapers. Reluctant or not, O'Kinealy was unable to refrain from citing what he regarded as factual and legal errors in Garth's submission. There was rather a long list of these, for some of which O'Kinealy drew on his twelve years of experience as a revenue officer. This gave him a different view of the intellectual capacities of the average raiyat—as for their not understanding 'prescription', for example, he could only say that since becoming Government Legal Remembrancer, supervising the drafting of government pleadings, he had seen hundreds of documents making just that plea. But, as a former revenue officer, the main difference was in his approach to the legal record. Garth interpreted the current state of the law mainly from the perspective of universal legal principles. O'Kinealy scanned the many authorities from Cornwallis onwards to reveal general support for the idea that, in India, 'no tenant could be ejected except for non-payment of rent, nor could his rent be enhanced beyond the customary rate'. Thus armed he suggested that it was the Chief Justice and not he who should learn to respect authorities, and that 'It is not by mere general statements in regard to us or our motives that our arguments can be set aside'.

It must be said, however, that this was to take a rather sanguine view of the history of enactments, legal statements and judgements by the British in Eastern India over the preceding hundred years. Indeed had O'Kinealy been correct, the need for a new tenancy law would not have seemed as obvious as he otherwise claimed it to be. What O'Kinealy was doing was interpreting a diverse series of statements of principle which purported to describe *what the existing situation in India was in regard to tenant rights*. In other words, just as Garth's ultimate authorities were the analytical principles of the law, those of O'Kinealy were the customs of India: each of them supposed that their authorities had a unique validity. In detail, however, O'Kinealy derived his understanding of custom from the statements of British administrators, whom he therefore had to assume had an accurate knowledge of Indian realities. He declared that the permanent settlement and subsequent regulations did not give the zamindars freedom of contract; therefore he assumed they had previously been bound by custom. He argued that rents were not, as Garth thought, customarily a share of produce, but expressed as a money rate; he believed therefore in the reality of a district or *pargana* rate, moderated by the state, and which zamindars were bound to apply. He found that *khudkashta* raiyats were not regarded as 'settled' in the meaning of English law, and that regulations in 1793 specified periods of prescription; he concluded that such rules reflected actual rights generally held in eighteenth-century Bengal.

Mackenzie's reply was similar. 'The situation is no doubt serious', he commented, 'when the Chief Justice of the Province thinks it his duty to use language like this of any Government measure, and when he not only makes these charges in general terms, but, in the face of the public, he impeaches two officers of Government by name as the authors and instigators of all the mischief.' Mackenzie denied the last point vehemently, giving details of the votes on the Rent Law Commission: the views he and O'Kinealy put forward were not original to them and mostly were not opposed on material grounds, and indeed were supported by the Indian judicial member (now the first Bengali district judge), a man 'deeply read in Indian law and well acquainted with Indian custom'. If there had been a radical among them, on tenant rights, it had been H.L. Harrison, the secretary to the Board of Revenue, cited by Garth as if he supported his views; Harrison had wanted to 'protect the actual cultivator whoever he might be'. This Board-of-Revenue view view (for it received some support from the Commission's chairman, H.L. Dampier, a member of the Board) represented the pure voice of pragmatism, interpreted in the way then current: that is, the revenue officer's appreciation that the real problem was to find some way of protecting the agricultural producer from those whose rights in land (or for that matter over capital) enabled them to batten on his output. It was this thinking—the conclusions drawn from the evidence of starvation and agrarian riots—which Mackenzie described as the 'stern logic of facts' which had forced reform upon a reluctant government. But Mackenzie also revealed the rather different remedy which they had in mind.

He started from the premise, similar to that advanced by O'Kinealy, that the 'old law and custom of Bengal made no practical distinction between resident and non-resident ryots, and that all ryots without distinction of class (not being mere casuals or nomads) were entitled to hold their lands without disturbance, so long as they paid rents not less than the established rates.' Moreover the British laws had not turned these raiyats into 'mere contract tenants'. This was the basis of the local government's reply to some objections from the Secretary of State; but it was a remarkable claim, considerably beyond anything contained explicitly in the much-vaunted authorities. Its origin was theoretical; we can recognise in it not the ghost but the living presence of the Indian village community. India was divided, as Baden-Powell put it, into groups of holdings called villages, in which a collective ownership derived from the bond of union among the original tribe or settlers. This was the primary form of landholding in India. By contrast, the zamindar was an intermediary who owed his position to his having swallowed up some of these communal rights in land.[5] Mackenzie did not conclude from this that it was possible to return to the pristine condition of the village in Bengal, but he did conclude that the government's goal was to secure an occupancy right for settled cultivators, so as to exclude 'land jobbers and mahajans' and to create 'a well-to-do peasant class, able to resist the vicissitudes of seasons and to pay a fair rent'. He was concerned at any further decay in the primary rights of the village land-holders at the hands of outside speculators or moneylenders—his view of the village community was that it was a sealed unit, distinct from the world surrounding it—but he did not take Garth's point that their depredations would be increased as a consequence of vesting valuable property in the tenants. On the contrary, he believed that property would enable the raiyat to defend himself. In short, his aim was to support a 'class'—his word—of proprietary peasants. In his book on *The Indian Economy*, Pramit Chaudhuri refers to the idea of a 'kulak state', seeking economic growth rather than redistribution.[6] Clearly, if it existed, it was not an invention of independent India.

Thus Mackenzie betrayed some characteristics of the tenancy reformers' approach. I shall only list them, but I consider them highly relevant to the nature and impact of the state's intervention. First, the reformers were social rather than economic in their theoretical emphasis (and followers of Richard Jones rather than of Ricardo). Secondly, they took an historical rather than a functional view of rights. Thirdly, in their attempts at examining and regulation, they concentrated on property and not the management of production, a quite different question. Fourthly, they were gradualist rather than radical in their programme, seeking Indian improvement rather than the transformation of India.

The final point to be made about this debate is that, to all appearances, Mackenzie and O'Kinealy won. Mackenzie concluded his minute by submitting that Garth had failed 'on many important points to exhibit that accuracy of statement, weight of argument, and insight into the Bengal Rent Question, which would warrant the Government and the public in accepting his conclusions'. Later Mackenzie's note was described by the Calcutta correspondent of *The Times* as an 'unwarrantable public attack' on the Chief Justice. In Calcutta the *Englishman* newspaper called it scurrilous. Mackenzie remarked that, unlike Garth, he had refused to publish; had he intended to do so, he would have written with more decorum, removing a few passages that would then have seemed 'unbecoming'. But he had circulated a few copies privately, and, as one person was rash enough to part with his, it had fallen into

[5] See B.H. Baden-Powell, *The Indian Village Community* (London, 1896), ch.1.

[6] Pramit Chaudhuri, *The Indian Economy. Poverty and development* (London, 1978), ch.9.

the hands of others who had had it reprinted. The Government of India concluded that, by and large, Mackenzie had acted quite properly. As finally passed, the 1885 Act included several compromises, but in its main features it endorsed the reformers' case. Personally they were honoured and promoted; professionally their view of Bengal tenancy prevailed, with influence to this day.

Why had there been such a fuss? The quarrel was merely the hottest point in a cauldron of argument, a flurry of letters rising over a war of pamphlets.[7] Were there really such vast interests at stake, such great principles? The strangest part of the story is the extent to which the whole affair was conducted well away from what might be called the political issues. I take these to be as follows. Were the British in Bihar and Bengal going to divert their hopes for political support and public welfare, under Punjabi influence, away from the landlords and towards peasant proprietors? Were they going to abandon their construction of an aristocracy supported by principles of English law, in favour of the refurbishment of supposedly more appropriate village communities dominated by landed raiyats and custom? More generally, were they going to rule India by absolute, 'British' principles, or by accommodating themselves to Indian custom? And was their purpose efficiency or equity? The short answer is that they were not going to come down firmly on either side of these questions, but that in shaking up the existing system they generated a great deal of heat from interests that seemed to be threatened—a grand alliance of land (based almost equally on the privileges of property and professional employment), of capital (in support of landlords as a means of controlling commercial agriculture), and of law (defending analytical principles and comprehensive or residual jurisdiction).

The question, in Eden's or Mackenzie's terms, was how to benefit the actual cultivator. But such categories as were employed in the Act were incapable of encompassing the complexities of rural society, or of achieving the economic and political ambitions of the government. Nothing the reformers could do would differentiate precisely between those they wanted to encourage and those they did not. Instead they made an artificial equation of cultivator and tenant, a similar lack of fit to that which bedevilled the Punjab Alienation of Land Act of 1900

[7] There are dozens of such pamphlets preserved in the India Office Library, London, several of them being reprints from newspapers, others reports of the proceedings of public meetings, for example of the East India Association or of the London Committee formed to oppose the Bengal Tenancy Bill, and yet others studies commissioned by interested parties such as the Central Committee of Landholders. Leading pamphleteers included Ashutosh Mookerjea, Henry Bell, Roper Lethbridge and W.S. Seton-Kerr. Extremely full government papers were also published, in reports or as supplements to the Calcutta *Gazette*.

with its artificial distinction between cultivator and moneylender.[8] This artificiality arose in part out of the need to generalise an immense complexity (a problem which remains for students of Indian agrarian society) but also from assumptions made *a priori* about the nature of India, the meaning of the mass of contradictory observations. Thus the zamindari supporters referred to inherited aristocratic rights like the lords of an *ancien régime*, but equally had to burrow into the small print of regulations and judgements. The pro-tenant school chose a different interpretation of India, on theoretical grounds, which coloured their observations, but which also had to be supported legalistically. The advocacy and understanding were partial in both senses of the word, and thus it was that, to a larger extent than usual, the prescriptions for agrarian society always failed to have quite the effect that was intended. Essential parts were omitted from remedies because the need for them was obscured. Thus the permanent settlement in 1793 had contained no legal means of preventing the devotion of agricultural surplus to leisure (through the creation of under-tenures or rent-farming) rather than to improving productivity; it relied, I suppose, upon the 'invisible hand'. In a similar fashion, in 1885, for tenants, there was no effective bar to the creation of sub-tenancies; the Act relied in this case on the alleged special appropriateness and efficiency of the sturdy peasant proprietor. As Garth had pointed out, some landlords and some tenants were able to use the new laws in unintended ways, to amass wealth and oppress the poor. These errors were additional to the failure to attend to productivity by intervening in the way agricultural decisions were made.

III

One of the morals of the story is that ideas are important to agrarian history partly because they help explain what happened. We are used to historical explanations which emphasise pragmatism and self-interest; but often we have to enter the realm of ideas and discover how problems and solutions were perceived, in order to understand why particular actions were taken, and their results. The impact of the permanent settlement of 1793, of the Bengal Tenancy Act, and indeed of zamindari abolition in the 1950s differed in each case from what the promoters intended, and in each case this owed much to the imperfections or distortions of their theories and perceptions. The permanent settlement sought property rights under the physiocratic assumption that Bengali zamindars were or could become improving landlords. The result in law was the replacement by a single legal identity, the landed proprietor, of

[8] The work of Clive Dewey is most important here, and a notable continuation of Stokes's: see his 'The official mind and the problem of agrarian indebtedness in India 1870-1910' (PhD, Cambridge, 1972), and 'Images of the village community: a study in Anglo-Indian ideology', *Modern Asian Studies* 6,.3 (1972).

a multitude of roles associated with local power and with representing the state, especially in revenue collection. The nineteenth-century tenancy laws were supposed to safeguard the 'actual cultivator', and zamindari abolition was intended to provide an equitable redistribution of land to tenants; but arguably both benefited middle-level landholders and agricultural entrepreneurs, people already rich in resources. Consistently the aim was missed because of a mixture of erroneous assumptions about how the society worked, or what it was which was being tackled: in particular there was a continuing insistence upon private property, and at the same time, paradoxically, from the early nineteenth century, upon the Indian village community.

The hidden premise in this kind of argument is that what happened in India was influenced chiefly by British rule and its laws. Yet it will not do merely to assume the British role, as the officials did at the time. We need a working model of the nature of British impact on India, and hence of the role of the state. I do not suppose that we will ever reach an agreed view on these questions. But assessing ideas offers a way of describing a mechanism for influence and indeed for longer trends within South Asia. Ideas—like words themselves—establish categories; they provide boundaries. For the remainder of my time today, I wish to emphasise the usefulness of this concept of the 'boundary' or 'frontier'. It seems to me the most important lesson which can be drawn from the example I have been describing: beneath the personalities lay an intellectual dispute which (like the Tenancy Act itself) was about the drawing of lines, the definition of sets or categories.

To understand British rule in India, one has to think in terms of social multiplicity on the one hand and of standardisation on the other, as ideal types. I am anxious not to be thought to be attributing the one to India and the other to the West; my interpretation does not depend upon any notion of an unchanging India rooted in caste and thus antipathetic to a broader polity. It does depend, however, at one level upon the old, 'orientalist' idea of India's diversity. My point is that this is in no way a peculiarly Indian phenomenon, though it took some special forms in India. There the power and diversity of localities were very great: resting on a religion in which place was crucial. But also these several communities had been subject to external influences over the millennia—from beliefs, government and trade. Thus the British greatly exaggerated when they supposed nothing much had changed in India before their arrival. I reject too the suggestion that India was a conglomeration of isolated, unchanging cells, until unified by an external agent, British rule or international capitalism. Indeed, there has been no even transition from structure to culture in India, to adopt Ernst Gellner's terms; on the contrary, elements of 'structure' have been strengthened, even while shared cultures also spread. We have had a false image in our minds, of a journey from one point to another, when we needed instead to picture various kinds of identity co-existing, in varying degrees, with the possibility of several being intensified simultaneously.

I propose an alternative view of Indian society made up of three components. The first is the mass of local communities which, because they were hierarchical, may be pictured as small triangles. Secondly, there were horizontal groupings, either cutting through some of these triangles or ranged above them, but in the main of a similarly circumscribed character; I have in mind merchant communities in various towns, and family and clan ties across regions. Thirdly there were networks, linking parts of different components: I refer for example to the structures of administration, ritual and trade stretching between localities and over space and time. Processes of change could influence any or all of these components. The British tried at times to protect the local communities and to restrict the expansion of some horizontal identities and networks. It was in that kind of enterprise that O'Kinealy and Mackenzie were united. But on the whole such attempts failed: networks were strengthened, and larger and more objective identities facilitated. In that different sense, Garth won after all, though ironically he did so partly because of his opponents' reforms.

Subject to this qualified view of India, then, one can make a distinction similar to that between dialects and language, between little and great traditions. There are many such dichotomies: between wild and tame, private and public, and so on, all of which are in some degree analogous. My argument, in short, is that, in the midst of the particularities of Indian society, the British were extending or introducing categories and connections. The institutions which the British set up or which developed in their time were able to reach further and further into the localities, and to extend the reach of the one order over the many. This intensified a process of the *longue durée*; in so far as it resulted from British rule, it was more a matter of capacity—through technology, communications and bureaucracy—than of will. As the boundaries of the general were extended, so the armies of the particular were overrun.

Quite a lot of Indian history used to be about such frontiers in the literal sense: how empires rose and fell; how the British extended their territory. The borders were supposed to be definite and precise, capable of measurement; there were to be no blurred zones of indeterminate control—not in this view of India—no buffers between one territory and another. Indeed though they never achieved this ideal over the entire land frontier of the Indian empire, the British spent much time and energy in the attempt. No doubt it shortened lives. Even one British province would argue fiercely with another, when, say, a boundary-river changed course; and the administrative revolution of the nineteenth century consisted in the establishment of definite spheres of authority. This idea of the nation—which is what at one level it was—obviously conflicted with that other idea of India as an inchoate multitude. Thus, though the attack on diversity is very far from complete anywhere, and certainly not in India, there was a British assault upon it. It was spearheaded by an emphasis upon binary oppositions: the officials admitted ambiguities and admixtures, but they preferred 'either-or'. Indeed, despite recent interest in uncertainty or randomness, the great weight of our reasoning depends upon definitive categories: that which is *x* cannot also be *y*, when *x* does not equal *y*. This is the origin of categorisation, in which essentialism is a kind of pathology. It is the logical basis of our notions of time, of change, and hence of cause and effect. It lay behind the British view of Indian history, of territory and sovereignty, and of the very divisions of Indian society. British ideas about communities referred to supposedly 'natural' units; but there are histories of community, many and various reconstructions of identity. Inevitably a British definition of Indian territories coincided with a British identification of Indian peoples, and indeed of Indian-ness. Boundaries were being set on the land, but also within it; between peoples, and within them too. Moreover the British assault on internal or local frontiers, driving them back, and the setting up of firm borders around categories new and old, were two sides of the same coin.

I am suggesting that much of British rule concerned demarcation, surveillance, and incorporation. It was, above all, a policing of zones. The Bengal tenancy debate was about how to define the zones in regard to property and agrarian structure, and over the manner in which they should be controlled. Thus the idea of the frontier is useful not just as a metaphor for the expansion of British power and influence, and for the longer-term growth of the state, but also for describing simultaneously the hardening of divisions and the broadening of categories to which I referred a moment ago. The central task which the British thus imposed on themselves was to give India a single form. As the British ruler was king of all-India and not of all the Indians, he laid claim to an ultimate authority: this was his dominion; that is, his jurisdiction was undivided in all functions, within the compass of his sovereignty. Given the realities in India, this implied a continual assault against internal frontiers, extensions of rule other than the topographical. Perhaps all states have sought this kind of sovereignty; until recent times few achieved it.

Let me now apply this argument generally to policy, the context for the Bengal tenancy debates. The process of state regulation developed in stages. In regard to property, the land settlements and resumption proceedings between the 1770s and 1830s and '40s dominated one phase. Refinements of knowledge and techniques and a multiplication of the areas of concern occupied the second phase, which lasted until the 1870s. This was a time of administrative reform, legal codifications and educational development. It was also the great age of the survey. Each of these efforts in its fashion applied definitions and established categories, thus extending and ordering knowledge in the same Benthamite way as the codes which sought to rationalise the laws. And then, in the later nineteenth century, such efforts merged into a so-called 'science' of government. The compass of the rulers had changed from a willingness to deal through landed intermediaries and to concentrate on revenue collection, in the first phase, into a gradually increasing desire to examine and regulate the society as a whole. In the Bihar countryside, the attention avowedly shifted first from zamindar to tenant (notably in the 1859 and 1885 Acts), and then, in the closing years of the century, towards the well-being of the general public, for example in the Famine Code, sanitation reports, investigations into prices, incomes and health, and even schemes to secure the economic fortunes of the region. From concern too with certain excrescences of religious practice, such as *sati*, the British moved on, over the same period, to record status and custom for whole communities, as is well-known in regard to the proto-anthropological work of the classics of settlement literature, the census reports, and various ethno-linguistic surveys. By this time, the motto was 'completeness'—equally in lists of castes or of economic products or of types of tenancy. Thus the British provided a new dimension not so much in the ambitions as in the actions of government India.

This development in the nature and intrusiveness of the state may be illustrated in that central question of agrarian policy, the revenue. Centralising states seek, when they can, to achieve three things in this regard: to widen the fiscal base, to contact and control the real payers (the producers of wealth), and to relate demand to an objective standard such as income. In Britain, it has recently been argued, these goals were barely achieved even in the eighteenth century. The peripheries of the nation, geographically and socially, were hardly taxed; collection was carried out largely through intermediaries; and the levels of taxation did not relate to any actual measurements. This implied limits on direct taxation, which was liable to meet with resistance—the notion of consent having been introduced—while indirect taxation represented a fairly small proportion of the total. The term 'feudal' may loosely be applied to these conditions.[9] In India too, in the situation which the East India Company inherited, the land tax, which constituted the great bulk of revenue, was not collected in the main from producers, and, for all the bureaucratic forms, the central states' access to them had actually declined in many areas during the eighteenth century, with the growth

[9] This view of British taxation was suggested in a lecture given by P.K. O'Brien to the Economic History Society in 1989.

of hereditary zamindaris, revenue-free land and revenue-farming. The amount and basis of the demand supposedly rested upon objective measurement in the past, and there were elaborate manuals relating to assessment, crop estimation and so on. But in practice the payments were decided mainly by negotiation and coercion. Thus they were uneven across territory and inequitable between payers. North Bihar, for example, was much more lightly taxed than South Bihar, partly because of its large proportion of revenue-free holdings; and everywhere high castes usually paid less than low.

The permanent settlement of Bengal was thus to an extent just another quasi-feudal response by a weak state. The settlement deliberately refrained from seeking a relationship between the state and the cultivator; it effectively dismantled the local revenue administration; it had none of the eagerness of some later revenue surveys to base demand on the capacity rather than the output of soils, in order to discourage sloth. But it also marked the beginnings of a transformation in the revenue-base of the state. First, it abandoned for ever the decentralised auctions of the farming system, and fixed the liability to pay upon the land itself, and hence upon its owners, known persons whose identity the state recorded and controlled. Second, though it deliberately refrained from relating payments to capacity, except in the broadest terms and at one moment, and indeed often set the amounts with regard to previous 'treaties', it none the less made them quite definite and permanent, thus removing almost all of the previous element of negotiation: there were arrears under the Bengal system but few remissions. Third, it allowed for some evening-out of the incidence of the demand, not at the outset, but through the subsequent resumption of a large proportion of revenue-free holdings on to the revenue rolls. In taxation therefore the British—in so far as they could give real effect to the system they instituted—had already in 1793 regulated the payers (meaning the zamindars) and fixed the demand, and were soon to extend the revenue-base through resumptions. The boundaries of state control had thus been extended.

Of course it would be ridiculous to present the settlement as a blueprint for an interventionist state. But it contained elements of this possibility, in substance, and also in form, considering that it was a body of regulations enforceable in courts. It sowed the seed also for later capacity, in that it was partly designed to educate and control the employees of the state. The British had recognised from the first the importance of information: a lack of it had inconvenienced Clive, but this began to be remedied under Warren Hastings, and the process continued more or less throughout the nineteenth century, reaching its apogee in the settlement reports, finally introduced to Bengal districts from the 1890s. The permanent settlement forestalled too, in Bengal, the probable initial revolt against increasing taxation, already felt in some senses during the eighteenth century, by establishing a countervailing interest in property. By contrast, later attempts to tax the landed interest further, for supposedly local purposes such as roads or police, were strongly resented in the countryside, and contributed to the undermining of the compact between zamindar and raj. But the revenue-base did not remain unchanged, in the face of such late nineteenth-century expansions, quite apart from the increase in the numbers of payers through the partition of estates. The new local taxes from the 1870s were claimed avowedly from tenants as well as from landlords, an extension of the net which was further augmented by the hesitant introduction of forms of income tax, initially on a far from objective basis, and then of course by the eventual shift towards indirect taxes: in that context the history and significance of Indian excise may not be as dull a subject as it sounds. Meanwhile, elsewhere in India, because of the rejection of the zamindari settlement at the time of the Fifth Report in 1812, a similar widening of the revenue-payers had occurred much earlier, within the land-revenue systems themselves, and there settlement work was precisely intended, at least from the 1840s, to relate demand to the capacity to pay. However there is good evidence for believing that in these cases too, as of course during the twentieth century, resistance to British rule was fuelled by attempts to extend the amounts and scope of taxation.

Thus revenue gives one illustration of state intervention, of the pushing back of the frontier between public and private. It does not tell us why the process accelerated. It was a curiosity that a Westernising state should to a large extent have privileged what it perceived to be indigenous. The first question is: why did this not slow down the encroachments of law and policy? The British tenancy debate suggests one reason. The indigenous was favoured, but by various sleights of hand. Consider the idea of 'restoring rights'. The notion of rights-as-property is inherently conservative, but in this case the garb of history was put on so as to conceal a reform; it was a pretence of tradition while espousing change. When Mackenzie or Eden talked of 'ancient rights' they were at the same time according a special status to Indianness, *and* attempting to modify it. The expression sought to establish, retrospectively, a British view of sovereignty and law, of the public and private, and of the nature of rights. But according to the idea of India which these officials also accepted, 'ancient' and 'rights' were contradictory or mutually exclusive. It was thought that only Western law could so confine the arbitrary and personal exercise of power as to permit the growth of individual property. Now, in practice, before British rule, there do seem to have been general concepts of law and localised notions of propriety which restricted the absolutism of states and overlords. And yet the 'ancient rights' of 1885 were indeed new: they were encapsulated in statute and interpreted by courts. Thus there was a divide between the English jurist and the pro-peasant official which could be seen as a struggle between absolutism and relativism, but it was an ambiguous one. In the end, two sides occupied the same house, intellectually speaking, and were in favour of change.

For that reason a desire to preserve the past did not necessarily impede the state's interventions to alter the present. And I believe it was in the nature of these interventions to grow. The process of British government was partly one of measurement, and measurement implies definite margins. Such mapping, whether literal or metaphorical, has to choose categories, and to confront others. Now, India was not a void to which the British gave form. Of course in another sense the term 'India' itself is just such a category as those which I am describing, but, taking 'India' as a necessary short-hand at this stage of the argument, I mean that it already contained jurisdictions, norms and processes. Little by little the British set out their own, state's view of arenas, conduct and values. For some of the time they thought they were respecting custom, and they were always restricted by practicalities. But in declaring, say, one matter to be criminal and another to be lawful, they established or formalised boundaries which were inevitably different from those which existed already, ideas for example about where and on what basis a particular dispute should be adjudicated. Sometimes Indians declined to accept the standards of behaviour or the role for the state which their rulers advanced; such quarrels over jurisdiction helped inflame the uprisings of 1857. Indians engaged too in controversies over the standing of general, secular law in regard to marriage or women's rights. In such cases, the state's opponent was a transgressor who took upon himself the role (in the practice and mythology of British rule) of the tiger or the Pathan:he risked reprisals for violating the supposedly 'civilised' arena established by rule. Thus, the same pattern was followed in social and religious life, as over territory—where border disputes or supposed violations of Western-style treaties had encouraged further annexations. Above all, an incompatibility of opposing standards—British crossings of an Indian boundary, or Indian of a British—could lead to further state interventions, *even when the rulers sought to preserve or make use of the indigenous*, in the manner of recruiting the Pathans or the Gurkhas for the army: this was because the attempt to recover ground for Indian practice was accomplished by further, if different state regulation, as in the Bengal Tenancy Act. Old institutions were restored but for new purposes: peasant proprietors in order to spearhead capitalist agriculture, or the village community as the agent of the state. Thus is explained that odd circumstance that British interventions really began to bite in India at the very time when historicist caution was at its height, and relativism was beginning to spread. Equally, in some cases, Indians readily colonised the institutions and frameworks provided to them, as in the use of the courts in a wide range of conflicts; I have not emphasised this factor, but I do not underestimate it. In these ways Indians too admitted extensions of the areas which the state defined.

What were the consequences? Land was most obviously subject to this process. British surveyors placed marking stones and prepared maps, and British laws defined categories of land and tenure. These definitions, however resisted or subverted in practice, acquired a special authority, and over time they inevitably influenced behaviour. Designated forest lands were *used* differently; in a number of ways *khas* or state land *was* distinct from private, and a zamindari from a raiyati holding. I do not mean that these state-based categories were the only ones or even the most important; nor that categories of this type were peculiar to British rule. I mean that the extent and effectiveness of such categories were markedly extended during British rule. And the process was by no means confined to land. The same normative definitions were applied, with varying impact, to peoples, castes, customs, crops, resources, canals, taxes. Moreover the British were not neutral. They had preferences in regard to behaviour, expectations about acceptable occupations; especially they favoured the settled agriculturalist, and at some points, as we have seen, the peasant proprietor. Thus a single ideological line connects the campaigns against *thagi*, characterising and suppressing semi-nomadic criminal gangs, and the Punjab Alienation of Land Act, defining and protecting peasant proprietors against 'outside' moneylenders.

The impact of such measures lies in the reduction of allowable alternatives and variants. Because, as I say, Indian society was not wholly hierarchical and not, in that picturesque phrase, 'religion-soaked', but because it was also not composed in entirety of horizontal classes, it had (as we know) a supreme ability to *react*: it did so to power-changes, seasons, economic conditions; it could do so because there were solidarities as well as divisions of region and occupation, but also flexibility and ambiguities in land use or status. The British did not remove these uncertainties, but they were rather effective at increasing the generality and thus the exclusiveness of categories. Take the case of common land. There is a great difference between that which is freely available for use, that which is open to the members of a community, and that which (though still common) is owned by a collective institution, whether community or state. In India, all three kinds existed in 1800: there were unclaimed lands available for settlement, lands used at will by villagers, and lands whose use was regulated by village or other elites—though in all cases access was complicated by considerations relating to the status of the user. The British at least pretended formally to ignore these social and ritual distinctions, but their law certainly recognised no waste land and no land which was not owned; in default of valid claimants land belonged to the state. Thus they lumped common land into a single category, and also of course went much further and encouraged private ownership in the lands controlled by the elites.

In a similar vein, the measurement of landed property and the resumption of revenue-free lands removed yet more elements of choice in agricultural practice. The more fixed and pervasive ownership became, the more difficult it was, for example, to use land as part-payment for services or labour, something which continued throughout the nineteenth century at many different social levels; the danger of ownership was that it rigidified these arrangements, with varied consequences for rich and poor. Incidentally, payment in land was one of the features which mixed the categories in India, as between landlord and official, or peasant and labourer; British policy generally was tending slowly to disentangle these complexities. Thus too the identification of 'criminal' or 'agricultural' castes, for legal purposes, reinforced the character and restricted the mobility of all groups.

Nor did such measures act singly: their impact was cumulative. What then was happening? We may go back to the analogy of dialects and languages. Generalisation, as in standard speech which contains parts of the variant forms, implies assimilation or suppression of alternatives; each definition, by stipulating like and unlike, encroaches on the space of the 'other'. The incorporations which the British inspired thus represented a management of ideas; many were adopted by Indians (or resulted independently from indigenous processes) and still have credence. Now, large elements of knowledge in any society are like dialects; they are decentralised; they are not available for general use. The British, by extending their internal margins, tried also to extend the range of ordered and manageable knowledge. They did so of course because they wished to maintain control and to improve and exploit the environment. The process was not confined to the state; it was extended equally in regard to the economy (market awareness for example) and religion (the spread of both orthodoxy and reform). In addition, knowledge may be sought either to establish how something should be done, or to investigate how it might be done better. British rules were often claimed to be merely describing the present, but they were designed ultimately to subvert it, along a linear concept of time. Again this was not an exclusively Western phenomenon, but in India the British raised the odds by regarding it as the basis and justification for their empire. They claimed to rule so as to civilise, and tried to civilise through rules. Vernacular practices—the folk arts, if you like—tend to repeat themselves; their purpose is partly to preserve themselves in the memory, each enactment forming an equal link in a circular chain. Once such decentralised knowledge is recorded, it becomes fixed; once it is fixed, it is communicable objectively, subject to analysis. It becomes history: what was, distinct from what is or might be. The British set to in India, to record, borrow, assimilate, generalise and learn from localised experiences. Thus they contributed to processes of change and new roles for the state, as illustrated in a very small way in the example I have discussed today, the intervention in agrarian relations and the definition of tenant rights.

Further reading

Baden-Powell, B.H., *The Land Systems of British India* (Oxford, 1892), 3 vols.

Bayly, C.A., *Rulers, Townsmen and Bazaars. North Indian society in the age of British expansion, 1770-1880* (Cambridge, 1983).

Beames, J., *Memoirs of a Bengal Civilian* (London, 1961).

Breman, J., *The Shattered Image: construction and deconstruction of the village in colonial Asia* (Amsterdam, 1988).

Bose, S., *Agrarian Bengal: economy, society and politics, 1919-1947* (Cambridge, 1986).

Chaudhuri, B., *Growth of Commercial Agriculture in Bengal (1757-1900)* (Calcutta, 1964), and 'Rural power structure and agricultural productivity in eastern India, 1757-1947' in M. Desai *et al.*, eds., *Agrarian Power and Agricultural Productivity in South Asia* (Berkeley, 1984), pp.100-170.

Das, A., 'Changel: three centuries of an Indian village', *Journal of Peasant Studies* 15, 1 (1987), pp.3-60.

Kling, B.B., *The Blue Mutiny: the indigo disturbances in Bengal, 1859-1862* (Philadelphia, 1966).

Metcalf, T.R., *Land, Lordlords and the British Raj. Northern India in the nineteenth century* (Berkeley, 1979).

Pouchepadass, J., *Paysans de la plaine du Gange: le district de Champaran 1860-1950* (Paris, 1989).

Ray, Ratnalekha , *Change in Bengal Agrarian Society* (New Delhi, 1979).

Robb, P. (ed.), *Rural India. Land, power and society under British rule* (London 1983; 2nd ed. Delhi, 1992).

Rothermund, D., *Government, Landlord and Peasant in India: agrarian relations under British rule, 1865-1935* (Wiesbaden, 1978).

Sen, A., P. Chatterjee and S. Mukherji, *Perspectives in Social Sciences* 2. *Three studies on the agrarian structure in Bengal* (Calcutta, 1982).

Spangenburg, B., *British Bureaucracy in India* (New Delhi, 1976).

Washbrook, D., 'Law, state and agrarian society in colonial India', *Modern Asian Studies* 15, 3 (1981), pp.649-721.

Yang, A., *The Limited Raj. Agrarian relations in colonial India, Saran district, 1793-1920* (Berkeley, 1989).

SMALLPOX AND COLONIAL MEDICINE IN NINETEENTH-CENTURY INDIA[1]

David Arnold

The history of medicine and disease provides valuable insights into the nature of cultural practices, social identities and state institutions in modern South Asia. In this essay David Arnold uses the example of smallpox to contrast Indian and colonial attitudes to disease and its prevention. Smallpox is a particularly striking case: not only was the disease widely prevalent in nineteenth-century India, it was also identified with the Hindu goddess Sitala, whose propitiation and worship formed an important part of popular religious belief in many parts of India. In addition, the practice known as variolation was a remarkably widespread example of indigenous disease control and a form of prophylaxis that was sufficiently popular and effective to defy its Western replacement, vaccination, for nearly a century. Although the British sought to extend their authority in India through medical science, their attempts to supplant variolation and its practitioners in fact reveal the technical and political limitations of colonial authority in India and the enduring problem of finding an appropriate agency.

To many nineteenth-century British medical officers smallpox was 'the scourge of India'. Reputedly 'one of the most violent and severe diseases to which the human race is liable', smallpox was held responsible for 'more victims than all other diseases combined', outstripping even cholera and plague in its 'tenacity and malignity'.[2] Several million deaths in the late nineteenth century alone were attributed to its destructive powers. Fatal in a third of all cases, smallpox also resulted in the permanent scarring and disfigurement of many of its survivors: one estimate blamed the disease for three-quarters of the blindness in India.[3]

But high mortality and lasting disability were not all that marked out smallpox as a disease of exceptional significance in nineteenth-century India. Smallpox occupied a distinctive place in both Indian and British attitudes to disease, curing and prevention. One of the most readily

[1] First published in David Arnold (ed.), *Imperial Medicine and Indigenous Societies* (Manchester and New York, 1988), pp.45-65.

[2] *Annual Report upon Vaccination in the North-Western Provinces, 1866-7* (hereafter cited as *NWP VR, 1866-7)*, p.4; T.E. Charles, *Popular Information on Smallpox, Inoculation and Vaccination* (Calcutta, 1870), p.1; S.P. James, (Calcutta, 1909), p.1.

[3] James, *Smallpox*, p.50.

identifiable as well as one of the most virulent of India's epidemic diseases, smallpox was widely represented in religious belief and ritual, with smallpox deities worshipped throughout virtually the whole of India. The disease was also uniquely subject to human intervention. Jennerian vaccination, introduced to India in 1802, encouraged the British to regard smallpox as a preventable disease. At a time when the concerns of colonial physicians remained narrowly focused on European needs, vaccination represented a rare attempt to carry Western medicine to the people. Indeed, it entailed a degree of state medical intervention unparalleled until the anti-plague campaigns of the late 1890s.[4] But, despite what the British saw as the indisputable benefits of vaccination, the practice was slow to gain general acceptance. One factor in this was the attitude of the colonial administration itself, especially with regard to carrying the costs entailed. There were practical difficulties to be overcome, too. But, in addition, vaccination was faced with the challenge of a rival prophylactic practice in inoculation and a rival agency in the indigenous variolators. Through a combination of these factors, it took a hundred years for vaccination to become an effective form of mass prophylaxis in India, and a further seventy years before the dread disease was finally eradicated.[5]

Partly because smallpox figured so prominently in British and Indian ideas about medicine and disease (and partly, too, because it was so extensively discussed in the medical literature of the time) smallpox offers valuable insights into the nature, purposes and impact of colonial medicine in India, and also, by reflection, into the interventionist capacities and practical limitations of colonial state power in India.

Disease and ritual in India

References to a pustular disease called masurika in Sanskrit medical texts dating back over two thousand years suggest that smallpox was an ancient affliction among the peoples of South Asia.[6] It is probable, however, that the virulence of the disease was not constant but fluctu-

[4] David Arnold, 'Touching the body: perspectives on the Indian plague, 1896-1900', in Ranajit Guha (ed.), *Subaltern Studies*, V (Delhi, 1987), pp.55-90.

[5] It has sometimes been argued that smallpox vaccination was responsible for a massive population increase in the Dutch colony of Java during the nineteenth century. Scholars are now sceptical both that such a large increase actually occurred and that vaccination was sufficiently widespread and effective before the late nineteenth century to have had much demographic effect. See Bram Peper, 'Population growth in Java in the nineteenth century: a new interpretation', *Population Studies*, XXIV (1970), pp.71-84. The parallels with Indian seem close.

[6] Ralph W. Nicholas, 'The goddess Sitala and epidemic smallpox in Bengal', *Journal of Asian Studies*, XLI (1981), pp.25-6.

ated with differing viral strains and with changing human susceptibility. Ralph Nicholas has argued, mainly on the basis of literary sources, that smallpox was relatively mild in Bengal until, in the eighteenth century, Maratha raiding and British conquest disrupted rural society and caused the famines and population movements that favoured the dissemination of smallpox. He argues, too, that in these circumstances inoculation would have been neglected, thus removing a hitherto important check on its spread.[7] There is certainly evidence from more recent times of a close correlation between smallpox epidemicity on the one hand and famine and political dislocation on the other.[8]

Smallpox also followed a shorter and more predictable cycle. Endemic throughout most of India, the disease returned in epidemic strength every four to eight years with the creation of a pool of susceptible children born since the previous epidemic. In India the disease also showed a striking seasonality. It was so prevalent between February and May that it was widely known in eastern India as basantaroga, the 'spring disease'.[9] With the onset of the monsoon season the disease declined, reaching its lowest annual ebb in October and November. Atmospheric conditions (the smallpox virus was more active and more readily transmissible in dry weather than in wet) offer a partial explanation for this pattern of occurrence. But social and cultural influences were important, too. In India the spring months were traditionally a time for congregation and travel. Pilgrimages to major shrines, popular religious fairs and marriage festivities were all most common during the dry part of the year when travel was easiest and little work was needed on the land. These activities provided the social mobility and contact necessary for smallpox transmission. Famines, in addition to weakening human resistance to infection, had a comparable effect: the famine-struck wandered in search of food or congregated in relief camps and towns where smallpox and other diseases were easily communicated.[10]

In the absence of detailed statistics before the 1880s, it is difficult to gauge the full extent of smallpox mortality in British India. It is possible that early estimates were greatly exaggerated. Because smallpox was a familiar disease and one greatly feared in Europe itself mortality may have been mistakenly attributed to it rather than to diseases that were then largely unknown. In Calcutta, for which some data exist,

[7] Nicholas, 'Sitala', pp.32-4.

[8] E.G., *Review of the Madras Famine 1876-78* (Madras, 1881), p.150; A.B. Christie, 'Smallpox' in G. Melvyn Howe (ed.), *A World Geography of Human Diseases* (London, 1977), p.267.

[9] Nicholas, 'Sitala', p.39.

[10] Leonard Rogers, *Smallpox and Climate in India* (London, 1926); *Annual Report of the Sanitary Commissioner of the North-Western Provinces,* (hereafter *NWP SCR*), 1886, p.26.

smallpox deaths averaged 734 a year between 1837 and 1865; but many fatal cases probably passed unrecorded in these early years. In the first five months of 1850, an epidemic year, there were 3,329 known deaths among the city's estimated 387,398 Indian inhabitants.[11] R. Pringle, writing in the Lancet in 1869, speculated that in the populous Doab tract of northern India as many as 95 per cent of the population may have been exposed to smallpox at some stage in their life. So prevalent was the disease, he added, that 'it has become quite a saying among the agricultural and even wealthier classes never to count children as permanent members of the family...until they have been attacked with and recovered from smallpox'.[12]

By the 1880s more reliable mortality statistics were being compiled in India, though recording procedures were still clearly deficient. By this date, too, vaccination may also have begun to have had some effect on reducing mortality from the disease. From 1.44 million deaths in the decade 1868-77 and 1.46 million in the decade 1878-87, smallpox mortality fell to 0.96 million in 1888-97 and 0.83 million in 1898-1907.[13]

A major cause of Indian mortality, smallpox was also greatly feared among Europeans in India. Before 1800 British residents had some recourse to variolation (inoculation with smallpox matter), perhaps in emulation of current European rather than Indian practice. Otherwise they fled 'in terror' from their homes until the epidemic had passed.[14] With the rapid adoption of vaccination after 1802 Europeans became less vulnerable to smallpox than many other diseases encountered in India, such as cholera. But in the 1849-50 epidemic in Calcutta, 76 Europeans were taken to the city's General Hospital suffering from the disease and there were 20 fatalities. Most of the victims were 'poor Europeans', especially soldiers and sailors. Wealthier Europeans were thought to be protected not only by vaccination but also by the spaciousness of their houses and gardens and by the absence of close contact with Indians.[15]

Diminished susceptibility to the disease did not, however, mean that smallpox ceased to be a matter of European concern. Vaccination was sometimes so poorly performed as to be almost 'worthless' and until revaccination was introduced in the second half of the century immunity could be shortlived. Children were felt to be particularly at risk from Indian servants who might transmit the disease from their

[11] *Report of the Smallpox Commissioners* (Calcutta, 1850), p.3; *Bengal VR, 1872*, p.7.

[12] Quoted in James, *Smallpox*, p.49.

[13] James, *Smallpox*, pp.76-7.

[14] J.Z. Holwell, *An Account of the Manner of Inoculating for the Smallpox in the East Indies* (London, 1767), p.4.

[15] *Smallpox Commissioners*, pp.20-2.

'obscure homes in the bazaar'.[16] As late as 1893 one of the arguments used for compulsory vaccination in Pune (Poona) was 'in consideration of the proximity of the city to the large European population of the cantonment and the constant intercommunication which exists between the city and the cantonment'.[17] Since some degree of contact with the Indian population was unavoidable, one of the priorities of Western medicine in India was to build a cordon sanitaire around the white community, with those Indian closest to it—domestic servants, soldiers, even plantation labourers—among the first to be singled out for vaccination. Demands that inoculation be prohibited and vaccination made compulsory were prompted first by a desire to protect European, rather than Indian, lives. Latterly, however, wider commercial and administrative considerations were involved, with European planters and factory owners seeing practical advantages in a vaccinated workforce.[18]

Most Europeans in nineteenth-century India held a secular view of smallpox and, in the later decades, took readily to the germ theory of disease causation. For the majority of Indians, however, smallpox bore a strong religious signification. Across a wide belt of India, from Bengal in the east to Maharashtra and Gujarat in the west, the goddess Sitala was identified as the deity responsible for bringing or preventing the disease. In southern India the goddess Mariyamma shared some of the same attributes. Although many diseases and afflictions found representation in the pantheon of popular Hinduism, Sitala enjoyed prominence as a deity of exceptional potency. If humoured and honoured through prayers, offerings and devotional acts, she could give protection from the disease or modify its effects. Angered or neglected, however, her wrath took the form of the violent fever that raged through her victims' bodies and resulted in lasting disfigurement or death. Since Sitala was understood to be intrinsically the 'Cool One', she was offered cooling foods and her victims were plied with cold drinks and balms. A patient who died of smallpox was not cremated—the customary practice among many castes in India—for fear of scorching the goddess and further provoking her.[19]

Because the disease followed so familiar a cycle, annual ceremonies were held in the deity's honour in many parts of eastern and northern

[16] *Smallpox Commissioners*, p.24.

[17] Deputy Sanitary Commissioner, Central District, to Sanitary Commssioner, Bombay, 17 July 1893, Bombay General 1, 706, Maharashtra State Archives, Bombay.

[18] Assam Vaccination Report, 1881-2, Home (Sanitary), 115, September 1882, National Archives of India, New Delhi (hereafter NAI), *Bengal VR, 1915-16*, p.2.

[19] Nicholas, 'Sitala'; Susan Wadley, 'Sitala: the Cool One', *Asian Folklore Studies* XXXIX (1980), pp.33-62; Lawrence Babb, *The Divine Hierarchy: Popular Hinduism in Central India* (New York, 1975), pp.126-32.

India during the spring (and smallpox) season. At this time, too, there were Sitala fairs and pilgrimages (especially by women and children) to major shrines to the goddess (such as at Gurgaon, southwest of Delhi).[20]

For most Hindus (and indeed for the many Muslims who shared this aspect of folk culture with Hindus) belief in Sitala and Mariyamma was an integral part of their wider understanding of disease and of benevolent and malevolent forces. As the 'Cool One', Sitala's worship embodied popular beliefs in the antithetical concepts of cooling and heating in ritual and diet. Some of these ideas were not far removed from notions of disease that had been common in Europe in earlier centuries. But to nineteenth-century British doctors, missionaries and administrators such beliefs were rank superstition, evidence only of Indian apathy and ignorance. The duality of the smallpox goddess (protector as well as persecutor) was lost to them. She appeared only as a demon, part of the dark side of Hinduism which, along with sati, thugi, and female infanticide, Europeans found deeply repugnant.[21] From a position of such hostility and contempt, the British were ill-placed to understand the tenacity with which Indians clung to their faith in Sitala and hence one of the reasons for the popular antipathy to godless vaccination.

Variolation

If familiarity with a dreaded disease prompted its ritualisation, it also encouraged attempts at medical control. Smallpox was uniquely favourable for this purpose, producing variolous matter from skin eruptions and scabs that could be transferred and absorbed by the recipient through subcutaneous injection, through swallowing, or by inhaling the powdered crusts. The virus itself remained active for at least a year in carefully preserved crusts and, if effectively inoculated, conferred lifelong immunity. Transmission required no complex vector relationships and a basic understanding of how the disease passed from one individual to another did not have to await the scientific discoveries of the late nineteenth century. For these reasons the practice variolation or smallpox inoculation may have developed independently in different parts of Eurasia and Africa rather than being diffused from a single source as is generally assumed. In India it appears to have been long established in the east, in Bengal especially, while in the west, particularly in Sind, its introduction was sometimes attributed to the Muslim invasions.[22] In the nineteenth century variolation was widely practised in Bengal, Bihar and the eastern half of the North-Western Provinces

[20] William Crooke, *The Popular Religion and Folklore of Northern India*, 1 (1896, reprinted Delhi, 1968), p.126; *NWP SCR, 1881*, p.25.

[21] *Missionary Register for 1836* (London, 1836), p.465; R. Caldwell, 'On demonolatry in southern India', *Journal of the Anthropological Society of Bombay*, I (1887), pp.91-105.

[22] *Bombay VR, 1874-5*, p.30.

(today's Uttar Pradesh), but seems to have been uncommon west of Allahabad. It was to be found in parts of the Himalayan region and the Punjab hills, further west in Sind, Gujarat, and Maharashtra, and as far south as Goa (where it was practised by the Portuguese clergy). In Dravidian south India, in the area where Mariyamma replaced Sitala, inoculation, though not unknown, appears to have been far less common. As late as 1801, five years after Jenner's discovery of the prophylactic effects of cowpox, the British in the Madras Presidency were still trying to persuade Indians to adopt inoculation.[23]

As practised in India, variolation had a number of distinctive features. Firstly, it was seen to be sanctioned by religion. Although some Hindus relied upon worship of Sitala alone, for many inoculation was itself a religious ritual. In Bengal it as commonly performed by Brahmans (India's leading ritual specialists) and accompanied by songs and prayers invoking the protective benevolence of the goddess. Further offerings were made to Sitala on the child's recovery from the ordeal of immunisation.[24] Secondly, variolation had its own special practitioners, known as tikadars or 'mark-makers' in eastern India. According to J.Z. Holwell's account of variolation in Bengal, published in 1767, the most celebrated of these came from Banaras, Allahabad and Vrindaban.[25] But by the mid nineteenth century many other castes were also involved, including Malis (a caste of gardeners and agriculturalists) and Sindurias (vermillion-sellers) in northern India and Napits (barbers) in Dhaka (Dacca).[26] Thirdly, variolation was a form of medical treatment sought after and paid for by the people themselves: unlike vaccination, it was not dependent upon state patronage and intervention. Individual tikadars had long-standing relations with client villages which they visited every year or two, inoculating large numbers of children at a time.[27]

In a situation where smallpox was almost universal, variolation was practised on a scale the British were unable to match until late in the nineteenth century. In 1871 there may have been twenty times as many variolators as vaccinators in northern Bengal. In 1873 it was reckoned that in one district of Orissa alone a hundred tikadars were at work, carrying out 25,000 inoculations in a single season.[28] A 'vaccine census' conducted by the Government of Bengal in 1872-3 revealed that out of 113,015 people examined, 57 per cent had been inoculated,

[23] Madras Board of Revenue Proceedings, 20 January 1801, Board's Collections, F/4/96/1953, India Office Records, London (IOR).

[24] *NWP VR, 1872-3*, p.31.

[25] Holwell, *Account*, p.8.

[26] *NWP VR, 1869-70*, pp.20-3; *Bengal VR, 1867-8*, pp.3-4; *Bengal VR, 1872*, p.56.

[27] *NWP VR, 1872-3*, p.31; Holwell, *Account*, pp.18-20.

[28] *Bengal VR, 1871*, p.14; Home (Public), 156, March 1873, NAI.

15.35 per cent had survived an attack of smallpox and so had acquired natural immunity, 10.42 per cent remained unprotected, but only 17.23 per cent had been vaccinated.[29] Other estimates placed the proportion inoculated even higher—at 70 per cent or more of the population of mid-century Bengal.[30] Variolation was certainly not so widespread elsewhere in India, but the figures give some indication of the size of the task that colonial medicine faced in trying to oust an indigenous rival.

The efficacy of variolation has been a matter of some dispute in recent years. Peter Razzell has argued that in eighteenth-century Britain variolation was employed on a sufficiently large scale and with enough care to check smallpox mortality and cause a downturn in the overall death rate.[31] Conventional medical opinion, now as in the nineteenth century, is highly sceptical of such claims and maintains that variolation is doubly dangerous. Inoculating with live smallpox virus exposes patients to the risk of a severe, possibly fatal, attack. In addition, the disease thus transmitted remains as virulent as that contracted in the normal way and is equally capable of spreading smallpox in epidemic form.[32]

In his description of variolation in Bengal, Holwell detailed the careful procedures followed by the tikadars and suggested that they were fully aware of the contagious nature of the disease. The tikadars, he said, used variolous matter collected the previous year: 'they never inoculated with fresh matter, nor with matter from the disease caught in the natural way, however distinct and mild and species'.[33] This implies that they deliberately propagated an attenuated form of the virus in order to induce a moderate reaction. Holwell claimed that inoculation seldom resulted in the appearance of more than 200 pustules and sometimes produced as few as 50. He stressed that variolation did not give rise to epidemics 'as is commonly imagined in Europe'.[34]

After 1802, however, with the introduction of vaccination into India, European physicians took a far more critical view of variolation. John Shoolbred, Bengal's second Superintendent-General of Vaccination,

[29] *Bengal VR, 1873*, pp.110-1.

[30] *Smallpox Commissioners*, p.28; James, *Smallpox*, p.6. Variolation declined sharply in the late nineteenth century, but lingered on in some remoter areas well into the following century, e.g. in Sind: *Bombay VR, 1920-1*, p.3.

[31] Peter Razzell, *The Conquest of Smallpox: The Impact of Inoculation on Smallpox Mortality in Eighteenth-Century Britain* (Firle, 1977); cf. Paul R. Greenough, 'Variolation and vaccination in South Asia, c.1700-1865: a preliminary note', *Social Science and Medicine*, XIV (1980), pp.345-7.

[32] Thomas McKeown, *The Modern Rise of Population* (London, 1976), pp.11-12, 107-9.

[33] Holwell, *Account*, p.17.

[34] Holwell, *Account*, pp.4, 30.

reported Brahman tikadars as admitting to one death in every 200 clients inoculated, which he compared to a figure of one fatality in 300 cases in Europe. But, without offering any evidence for his assertion, Shoolbred claimed that the practice was 'certainly much less favourable here than in Europe' and probably caused the death of one in every 60 or 70 of those inoculated.[35] Such was the intensity of British hostility that in 1831, W. Cameron, the Superintendent-General of the day, dubbed variolation a 'murderous trade' and called its suppression 'indispensable to the interests of humanity'.[36]

But British medical officers in India were not entirely unanimous on this point, though there was never any doubt in their minds that vaccination was a superior and a safer practice. Some felt, however, that it would be reckless to ban variolation before vaccination was freely available. T.E. Charles, Bengal's Superintendent-General of Vaccination in 1869, believed that prohibiting variolation would 'constitute a great hardship' to the people unless vaccination could be provided as an 'efficient substitute'. Like J. Wise, Civil Surgeon at Dhaka, Charles doubted whether variolation caused anything like the number of deaths attributed to it by current medical opinion in Britain. Both placed the likely mortality at around one per cent and were sceptical, too, of the view that variolation often sparked off epidemics.[37] Charles went so far as to suggest to the Government of Bengal that variolators should be allowed to continue their work under licence in areas where vaccination was not yet available or widely accepted. His proposal was rejected as giving encouragement to an undesirable practice. The most the government would permit was the recruitment and training of tikadars as vaccinators.[38]

Vaccination

The arrival of vaccination marked a new and critical stage in the development of Western medicine in India. Hitherto, European practitioners had confined themselves almost exclusively to ministering to the needs of their own community and to the British and Indian soldiers employed by the East India Company. Not only had there been no serious attempt to take medicine to the masses: there existed a profound ignorance about the diseases prevalent in India and the state of health of the bulk of the population. Vaccination was introduced into India at a

[35] John Shoolbred, *Report on the Progress of Vaccine Inoculation in Bengal, 1802-3* (Calcutta, 1804), pp.27-8.

[36] *Smallpox Commissioners*, p.54.

[37] T.E. Charles, 'Report on the necessity for regulating the practice of smallpox inoculation in Bengal', in *Bengal VR, 1869*, pp.1-11; J. Wise to Commissioner, Dhaka Division, 14 September 1871, Home (Public), 366, February 1872, NAI.

[38] *Bengal VR, 1871*, p.v.

momentous time. As a result of the rapid expansion of British dominion in South Asia, India's new rulers were beginning to appreciate a need for a more detailed knowledge of the society and the country over which they governed. This included greater knowledge of the causes of mortality and the nature of India's disease environment, factors likely to have a direct bearing on the economic life and even the political security of the new regime. At a time when Western medicine could offer few cures or prophylactics, smallpox stood almost alone as a 'preventable disease'. Without sophisticated medical knowledge and at seemingly little expense, smallpox could, it was hoped, be conquered. More could be achieved by vaccination, it was sometimes said, than by any other known sanitary or medical measure.[39]

An appreciative European community, quick to send Jenner £7,000 in thanks for its own delivery from smallpox, confidently anticipated that Indians would take up with 'equal gratitude' a discovery which Europe had already found to confer 'such inestimable benefits'.[40] There was an ill-informed expectation, too, that Hindus, with their famed reverence for the cow and its products, would seize 'with the greatest ardour' this latest bovine boon to man.[41] There were also more practical considerations in view. For a regime but recently established by force of arms and with the struggle against the Marathas still unconcluded, vaccination offered a welcome opportunity to win 'good will from the people' and give 'fresh proof' of Britain's 'humane and benevolent' intentions.[42] In approving expenditure on vaccination in 1805, Lord Bentinck, Governor of Madras, declared himself 'happy in the reflection that no expense was ever made for objects of greater individual happiness or of public advantage'. But he added, more pragmatically, that in a country where the state derived so great a share of its income from the land 'every life saved is additional revenue and an increase to the population and to the prosperity of the Company's territories in an incalculable ratio'.[43]

But expectations of the ready and appreciative acceptance of vaccination were soon dashed. Indians from the outset proved reluctant to submit to vaccination or take up the practice for themselves. Some, as in the villages of Madras, suspecting the government of a 'sinister intention', gathered in crowds to drive away the vaccinators sent to

[39] *NWP VR, 1873-4*, p.13; *NWP SCR, 1886*, pp.26-7.

[40] James, *Smallpox*, p.20; Madras Public Consultations, 19 January 1803, Board's Collections, F/4/153/2613, IOR.

[41] Shoolbred, *Report*, p.82.

[42] John Z. Bowers, 'The odyssey of smallpox vaccination', *Bulletin of the History of Medicine*, LV, 1981, p.24; Archibald Seton, Agent, to Magistrate, Bareilly, 7 June 1805, Bengal Public Consultations, 4 October 1805, Board's Collections, F/4/198/4452, IOR.

[43] Minute, 18 June 1805, Board's Collections, F/14/201/4544, IOR.

'diffuse the benefits of vaccination among them'.[44] Such a negative response confirmed many Europeans in an unfavourable view of Indians. Shoolbred in Bengal in 1804 called Hindus 'naturally averse to all innovation' and denounced the labouring classes as 'stupid and insensible' for failing to recognise vaccination's 'inestimable value'.[45] Duncan Stewart, Superintendent-General of Vaccination for the province in the early 1840s, likewise blamed Hindu ingratitude and ignorance, especially 'the trammels of a degrading religion, by which their thoughts are chained, their reasoning faculties hoodwinked and their mutual affections thwarted'. Even 'the most simple, obvious and unquestionable temporal advantage' was, he claimed, unacceptable to Hindus if it entailed 'the slightest deviation from ancient usage'.[46] Such sentiments persisted well into the second half of the century. In 1878, for instance, the North-Western Provinces' Sanitary Commissioner attributed the limited impact of vaccination to the 'natural apathy of the people, their disinclination to accept a new thing, and their unreasonable religious beliefs or caste prejudices'.[47]

Opinions such as these show the ease and frequency with which racial and cultural antipathy clouded British medical and administrative judgment. That vaccination also encountered considerable opposition in Britain was general ignored: India's religion, social practices and customs were instead singled out for blame. In fact, although cultural resistance was undoubtedly an important contributor to vaccination's slow progress in India, it was only one of the inhibiting factors.

Despite the claims often made for the simplicity and effectiveness of vaccination, many technical difficulties stood in the way of its success in India. Commentators who contrast variolation with vaccination are apt to forget how crude and ineffective the latter often was, during the early nineteenth century especially. In India there was, first of all, a problem of supply. Cowpox was rare, possibly unknown, in the country, and until the 1890s much of the vaccine was imported from Britain. The first vaccine reached India in June 1802 through a relay of children vaccinated from arm to arm from Baghdad to Bombay.[48] Subsequently, vaccine crusts or sealed tubes of lymph were sent by sea or brought overland from Britain: India's medical dependency thus replicated its political and economic ties. By the time the lymph came to be used, however, it was often inert, and this was one reason for the high rate of

[44] A. McKenzie, Superintendent-General of Vaccine Inoculation, to Secretary, Madras, 5 September 1806, Judicial Proceedings, 31 October 1806, Board's Collections, F/4/268/5891, IOR.

[45] Shoolbred, *Report*, pp.20, 26.

[46] Duncan Stewart, *Report on Smallpox in Calcutta, 1833-34, 1837-38, 1843-44* (Calcutta, 1844), p.9.

[47] *NWP SCR, 1878*, p.30.

[48] Shoolbred, *Report*, pp.2-4.

unsuccessful vaccinations in India.[49] Once established, the vaccine was maintained (as in Britain) by the arm-to-arm method. But here, too, there were difficulties. The vaccine was often 'lost' in transmission and during the wet and humid monsoon months vaccination could be ineffective or produced 'foul, sloughing sores'. In consequence, in northern and eastern India the 'vaccination season' was confined to the cooler, drier months between September and March.[50]

For as long as vaccination relied on imported lymph and the arm-to-arm process the scale of operations in India was very limited. In Bombay, the province where vaccination was most enthusiastically pursued, there were only 446,000 vaccinations between 1846 and 1850, with a further 849,000 between 1851 and 1855.[51] From the middle of the century, however, significant advances were made. In the North-Western Provinces depots were established in the hills of Kumaon to collect vaccine crusts and lymph to supply to the plains: some 20,000 crusts were despatched in 1867-8 alone.[52] In the 1850s the Bombay Vaccination Department began experimenting with the production of calf lymph, though it was 20 years before this technique was sufficiently reliable for general use. Arm-to-arm vaccination persisted in parts of Bengal until the First World War, but by that date calf lymph, preserved with glycerine, was being produced in sufficient quantity to end dependence on imported supplies. The Vaccine Institute at Belgaum was manufacturing 600,000 doses of calf vaccine a year by 1911.[53]

As a result of these changes, the scale of vaccination could be substantially increased in the late nineteenth century. From 4.5 million operations a year in the late 1870s, the total for British India rose to 6.5 million a decade later, and touched 9 million in the early years of the twentieth century.[54] There were important advances in technique, too: the lancet was replaced in the 1870s by the vaccinating needle, and fewer punctures were made. This reduced the inconvenience to the labouring classes and the risk of infection. By 1900 vaccination was a far more efficient and reliable operation than it had been 30 or 40 years earlier.

The persistence of the arm-to-arm method of vaccination also highlights one of the reasons for vaccination's early unpopularity. Unlike variolation, where old crusts were used (sanctified with a sprinkling of

49 James, *Smallpox*, p.37; *Bombay VR, 1867*, p.xxi.

50 *Smallpox Commissioners*, pp.50-1; *NWP SCR, 1876*, p.28; *NWP VR, 1895-6*, p.14.

51 *Report on Measures adopted for Sanitary Improvements in India during the year 1868* (London, 1869), p.137. At this date vaccination reached only an estimated 1.5 per cent of the population in the Bombay Presidency.

52 James, *Smallpox*, pp.37-8.

53 *Bombay VR, 1908-11*; *Bengal VR, 1915-16*, p.3.

54 James, *Smallpox*, p.76.

Ganges water), vaccination transferred body fluids directly from one individual to another. For most Hindus this was ritually very polluting, especially since low-caste or untouchable children were usually the only vaccinifers: higher-caste parents went to great trouble to ensure that their children were not used in this way.[55] The extraction of lymph from a child's arm could be alarmingly painful. According to Surgeon-Captain H.J. Dyson, Sanitary Commissioner for Bengal in 1893:

> The child, attended by its weeping mother, is taken round the town or village, and sometimes from one village to another, and after all the lymph has been extracted from the vesicles on its arms, it is a common practice for the vaccinators to squeeze the inflamed base of the vaccine pustules further in order to obtain serum for more vaccinations.

In his experience, the 'agony caused to the child was often intense'. Vaccination could result in long periods of suffering caused by 'severe and deep ulcers', and sometimes there were fatal complications. Dyson urged that calf lymph should replace arm-to-arm vaccination as quickly as possible, even though the expense was considerably greater.[56]

Substituting calf lymph, however, created problems of its own. Many Hindus believed that taking lymph from calves involved the animals in unacceptable suffering. Opposition to the practice was particularly strong in western India in the 1870s and 1880s: some municipalities refused to grant funds for the purpose and individual contractors were subjected to such pressure that they declined to supply heifers for vaccination purposes.[57] With time, however, opposition died away and many Indians clearly preferred the use of calf vaccine to the old arm-to-arm method. There was some revival of opposition during the Non-Co-operation Movement in the early 1920s, and Gandhi expressed his personal distaste for vaccination which he described as a 'filthy process' and 'little short of taking beef'.[58] But Gandhi's views on this matter did not command much public support and by the 1930s vaccination had won a wide degree of acceptance in India.

Vaccination was disliked for other reasons, too. Unlike variolation, usually performed on children over five, vaccination was primarily directed at infants under one year old, an age at which many mothers felt them to be too young for such an operation.[59] The mildness of the

[55] *Bengal VR, 1867-8*, p.13; *NWP VR, 1869-70*, p.2; *Bengal VR, 1896-9*, p.10.

[56] H.J. Dyson to Secretary, Bengal, 30 June 1893, Bengal, Municipal (Sanitation), 3, July 1894, West Bengal State Archives, Calcutta (WBSA).

[57] *Bombay VR, 1870-71*, p.89; *Bombay VR, 1874-5*, p.19; *Bombay VR, 1890-91*, p.5.

[58] D.G. Tendulkar, *Mahatma: Life of Mohandas Karamchand Gandhi*, III (Delhi, 1961), p.4.

[59] 'The prejudice in Hindustan against doing anything to or even looking at

reaction produced by vaccination—one of its virtues in British eyes—was often taken as an indication of its ineffectiveness compared to inoculation. Scepticism was increased by the high failure rate from vaccination compared to the lifelong immunity acquired through variolation.[60] This was also an obstacle to revaccination: another was that it involved exposing girls of post-pubertal age to the touch of a male vaccinator.[61]

But one of the greatest objections to vaccination was its secularity. There was no dietary or ritual preparation as in variolation; no invocation of Sitala; no priestly ministrations to provide reassurance during and after the operation. Such an 'irreligious' act was thought to be offensive to the goddess and was certainly out of keeping with the religious conceptualisation of disease and medicine among Hindus and Muslims alike.[62] There was, however, some room for compromise. Despite the disapproval of their superintendents, some Indian vaccinators (especially those who had formerly been tikadars) diluted the raw secularity of their work with a few Sitala prayers and rituals. Parents also took the initiative, delaying vaccination until an auspicious day or hour and employing priests to seek Sitala's blessing.[63] In many respects rivals, variolation and vaccination were at least comparable forms of medical intervention: vaccination could be offered as a superior form of an existing prophylaxis. Resistance to it was often greatest among tribal communities with no prior experience of variolation or among religious sects, like the Faraizis, Muslim fundamentalists of eastern Bengal, for whom variolation and vaccination were equally unacceptable forms of interference with 'God's will'.[64]

In striking contrast with the colonial image of Western medicine as the benevolent gift of a superior civilisation, vaccination aroused in many Indians a deep suspicion of the nature and purposes of British rule. Why, it was wondered, were the British so keen to put their mark (*tika*) upon the people? The explanations provided by popular rumour perceived a basic malevolence or self-interest on the part of the British at Indians' expense. Vaccination was said to be a deliberate attempt to violate caste and religion and so make converts to Christianity. Those

young children is a great obstacle to successful vaccination': Oudh (Awadh) Vaccination Report, 1872-3, Home (Public), 495, July 1873, NAI.

[60] *Smallpox Commissioners*, pp.lxviii, lxxii; *Bombay VR, 1867*, p.10; *NWP VR, 1872-3*, p.29.

[61] *Bombay VR, 1905-6*, p.1.

[62] A. Christison, *Report on the Vaccine Operations in the Agra Division, 1858-59* (no publication data), p.9.

[63] Medical, 75, February 1867, WBSA; *Bengal VR, 1872*, p.45; *NWP VR, 1872-3*, p.32.

[64] *Bengal VR, 1877*, p.7; *Bengal VR, 1873*, p.18; *Bengal VR, 1878*, p.25; *Bengal VR, 1893-6*, pp.xxiv-xxviii.

marked by vaccination would later die in agony or be sacrificed to ensure the successful completion of a bridge or railway embankment. Vaccination was feared as the prelude to new taxation or forced labour. One of the commonest beliefs was that the British were searching for a child with white blood or milk in his veins: this would be the saviour (the Mahdi of the Muslims) who would drive out the foreigners unless first caught and destroyed.[65] To British medical officers and administrators such tales were further evidence of Indian ingratitude and ignorance. Viewed more sympathetically, however, they testify to a deep distrust of British rule and show how readily state medical intervention was identified with other coercive and alien aspects of the colonial regime.

A question of agency

Confident that vaccination would gain rapid acceptance in India, the British at first gave little thought to the need for a permanent vaccination agency. It was assumed that once the practice became popular Indians would take it up for themselves at minimal cost to the state. It was not long, however, before this early optimism evaporated and the state's financial commitment to vaccination was viewed with growing concern. As early as 1808 the Government of India was advising caution over expenditure on vaccination and further directives in 1811 urged reductions as soon as the practice became general among the Indian population. In 1829 the Government of Bengal decided that the expense of running thirty vaccination centres was unjustified by the results and all but six were abolished.[66]

Bombay, however, developed a more ambitious vaccination programme. Under the direction of the Governor, Lord Elphinstone, a scheme was devised in 1827 to carry vaccination to the rural population. The province was divided into circles, each with its own team of itinerant vaccinators. These were to visit each village at least once a year and provide free vaccination to as many children as possible. The vaccinators were to be Indians, but, following an administrative pattern common in colonial India, they were placed under European inspectors, who were to examine their returns and check on their work. The Bombay system was said to have two 'great merits': 'it brought vaccination to the doors of the people—too lazy, too poor, or too ignorant to seek it', and 'it ensured the examination by the European medical officer of

[65] *Bengal VR, 1867-8*, p.2; *Bengal VR, 1869*, pp.xix, xliv; *Bengal VR, 1877*, p.10; *Bengal VR, 1893-6*, p.xxvi; *Bombay VR, 1858-9*, p.25; *Bombay VR, 1865*, p.2; *NWP VR, 1870-1*, p.11; *NWP VR, 1873-4*, p.21.

[66] *Bengal VR,* 1867-8, p.5; Public to Bengal, 6 April 1808, Board's Collections, F/4/297/6889; Public to Bengal, 3 September 1813, Board's Collections, F/4/446/10749, IOR.

every case attended upon'.[67] Seen to be successful in Bombay, the scheme was introduced into several other provinces (though not Bengal) in the 1850s and 1860s.

But the Bombay system had its limitations. There were frequent reports of vaccinators submitting false returns, exaggerating the number of vaccinations actually performed, or being too illiterate to fill in the forms correctly. Low-caste vaccinators were thought to command little public respect, and in general much was seen to rest upon a rather unreliable subordinate agency. In the words of the Madras Sanitary Commissioner in 1884, 'nothing tends more to injure the cause of vaccination than incompetent and untrustworthy agency'.[68]

The creation of a special vaccination staff and the setting up of provincial vaccination departments were not in themselves sufficient, therefore, to ensure the success of vaccination. In Bengal, where the challenge from variolation was strongest, the government adopted a series of expedients to try to supplant the rival practice. Soon after vaccination was first introduced into the province attempts were made to recruit some of the leading tikadars as government vaccinators and persuade Brahman pandits to issue public declarations that there was nothing in the Hindu sastras or sacred texts that prohibited vaccination or made variolation a religious duty.[69] This ploy had little effect, however, and in Calcutta, the principal seat of British power in India, the number of variolators appears actually to have increased during the early nineteenth century.[70]

Further attempts at co-opting variolators were made in Bengal and the North-Western Provinces in 1870s. In 1873 Bengal alone counted 472 ex-tikadars among its vaccinators and five years later there were nearly 1,000 of them. It was hoped that by allowing them to charge for their services vaccination would in time become independent of state subsidy.[71] But the scheme met with little success. Villagers would not pay for a vaccination they did not want and vaccinators could collect their fees only with difficulty. In the past variolators had earned substantial sums—one in Banaras division boasted of receiving Rs.80 to 90 a month—and few were willing to forgo the profit and prestige of a tikadar to become a despised state vaccinator on Rs.10 to 18 a month. In fact, a number of ex-variolators quickly reverted to their former calling.[72] European medical officers also had strong prejudices against

[67] James, *Smallpox*, p.21.

[68] *Madras SCR, 1884*, p.113.

[69] Board's Collections, F/4/186/3906, IOR; *Smallpox Commissioners*, pp.28-9, xxii; *Bengal VR, 1870*, p.3.

[70] *Smallpox Commissioners*, p.35.

[71] *Bengal VR, 1873*, p.1; James, *Smallpox*, p.31.

[72] *NWP VR, 1869-70*, p.23; *NWP VR, 1871-2*, p.24; *Bengal VR, 1872*, pp.45-6.

recruiting such men, seeing them (the lower caste variolators especially) to be shabby, untrustworthy and an offence to their own professionalism.[73]

One alternative strategy was to look beyond the formal vaccination agency to leading Indians in the hope that these might use their influence and authority to encourage vaccination among their families, followers and dependants. This was a strategy much favoured in the North-Western Provinces where British power rested heavily upon the 'chiefs and landlords of the people'. Among those whose 'wisdom and philanthropy' were successfully invoked in the late nineteenth century were the rajas of Banaras, Balrampur and Tehri.[74] In western India, however, the strategy brought less success and it was only with difficulty that the rulers of princely states could be persuaded to allow vaccinators to operate in their territories.[75] In the cities, government servants, newspaper editors, lawyers and educationalists were also enrolled in the cause of vaccination; but some of India's most influential urban residents, the Marwari and Bania merchants, traders and moneylenders, were among the most resolute opponents of vaccination—partly from religious scruple, but also because they were generally resistant to most Westernising influences.[76]

Attempts to shift a large share of the financial burden and administrative responsibility for vaccination onto the newly-created municipal and local boards was also no more than a qualified success. Indian councillors were often personally unenthusiastic about vaccination and reluctant to divert scarce funds to so unpopular a cause. Even when compulsory vaccination was introduced by law, many municipalities in practice dragged their feet and failed to perform the number of vaccinations required.[77]

Frustration at the slow progress of vaccination, at continuing high levels of smallpox mortality, and the persistence of variolation, produced strong pressure from the medical profession for legislative action. The first move in this direction—Lord Wellesley's ban on variolation in Calcutta in 1804—was so ineffectual that it was soon abandoned, and for several decades no further moves were made. Fifty years after Wellesley, another Governor-General, Lord Dalhousie, declared that it was as impossible to prohibit variolation as it was to 'make the

[73] *NWPFR, 1872-3*, pp.13, 32; *Bengal VR, 1872*, p.21.

[74] *NWP VR, 1872-3*, p.11; *NWP SCR, 1878*, p.30; *NWP SCR, 1879*, pp.35, 39.

[75] *Bombay VR,, 1868*, p.xvii.

[76] *Bombay VR, 1867*, p.19; *NWP VR, 1872-3*, pp.14, 27; *Bengal VR, 1873*, p.4; *Administration Report of the Commissioner of Calcutta for 1898-99* (Calcutta, 1899), part 2, pp.39-40.

[77] *Madras VR, 1890-91*, p.7.

monsoon penal'.[78] In 1872 Sir John Strachey of the Viceroy's Council opposed a draft vaccination bill prepared by the Bombay government on the grounds that any attempt to impose vaccination by force would provoke resistance and make it even more unpopular than at present. He argued that the 'prejudices of the people' could only be overcome by gradual persuasion and example.[79] The virtues of 'patience and time' were again urged on the Bombay government when it submitted a revised bill five years later.[80]

But, for all the Government of India's prevarication, the provincial administrations were coming to see the need for some form of legislation. Recent enactments in Britain, outlawing variolation and making vaccination compulsory, provided influential precedents. In 1865 variolation was banned in Calcutta and its suburbs, and in 1866 the prohibition was extended to surrounding villages as well.[81] Faced with repeated epidemics, and confident that it now had sufficient vaccine for the purpose, in 1877 the Government of Bombay finally passed its own Vaccination Act. This made vaccination compulsory within the city of Bombay for all infants under six months old, and for all children under fourteen brought into the city from outside, on penalty of six months' imprisonment or Rs.1,000 fine for the parent or guardian. Inoculation was prohibited and no recently inoculated person was to enter the city.[82] A similar act was passed for Karachi in 1879, and the Bombay legislation became the basis for the Government of India's own Vaccination Act in 1880.

The dramatic decline in the number of deaths due to smallpox in Bombay and Karachi following the introduction of compulsory vaccination provided an argument for the further extension of legal measures. The voluntary system had been 'ineffectual', the Bombay government reasoned, not so much because of religious objections as from public 'indifference, indolence or ignorance'.[83] But the colonial authorities remained wary. Quite apart from financial considerations, the administration (especially in the North-Western Provinces and Punjab) remained nervous of a public backlash against coercive medical intervention. The mere rumour of compulsory vaccination was enough to set off a scare and threaten disturbances in Delhi in 1870-

[78] James, *Smallpox*, p.14; *Papers on Vaccination in India* (Calcutta, 1851); Home (Public), 156, March 1873, NAI.

[79] Strachey, 3 October 1872, Home (Public), 151-3, notes, November 1872, NAI.

[80] *Bombay VR, 1875-6*, p.1.

[81] James, *Smallpox*, p.14.

[82] R.D. Dalal, *Manual of Vaccination for the Bombay Presidency* (Bombay, 1980), part 2, pp.69-77.

[83] Home (Judicial), 89, February 1890, NAI.

71.[84] The intensity of the public reaction against compulsory anti-plague measures (again mostly in northern India) in 1898-1900 further hinted at the political risks medical interventionism might entail for an alien government.[85] In consequence the Government of India allowed only a gradual extension of the 1880 Vaccination Act: by 1906 it had been introduced in 441 towns and cantonments, representing only 7 per cent of British India's total population. Very few small towns and rural areas were included before the 1930s. Even in 1950, three years after India's independence, vaccination was compulsory in no more than 732 of the country's 842 municipalities and barely half of its 408,000 villages.[86]

The Vaccination Act was also notoriously difficult to enforce. Registration of births, begun in the 1870s, remained so defective that vaccination staff had no clear idea of the number of infants requiring vaccination. In major cities like Bombay there was the further complication of high rates of immigration from the countryside with many babies and children arriving unvaccinated and unregistered. Prosecutions were few, partly from lack of interest by the police, magistracy and municipal authorities. In some municipalities in the 1880s and 1890s the Vaccination Act was frankly admitted to be a 'dead letter'.[87]

As a result, upwards of 20 per cent of infants even in the best vaccinated urban areas escaped vaccination. Although immunisation significantly reduced the number of susceptibles, there remained a substantial pool of children and adults among whom smallpox could continue to circulate. Epidemics were becoming less frequent in the early twentieth century, but they numbered an increasing percentage of adults among their victims.[88] The nineteenth-century assumption that vaccination made smallpox a 'preventable disease' was thus only partly valid. The need also to isolate smallpox cases and their contacts was urged from time to time during the century, but was always rejected as entailing too great an interference in the lives of the people and requiring an army of medical subordinates for its enforcement.[89] Again, the experience of the early plague years, 1896-1900, showed the practical and political snares such measures were likely to encounter. In consequence, smallpox was not even made a notifiable disease in colonial India, and it was not until the international smallpox eradication campaign of the 1960s and 1970s that the disease was finally tackled in a sufficiently comprehensive way to ensure its final

[84] Home (Public), 246, April 1872, NAI.

[85] Arnold, 'Touching the body'.

[86] James, *Smallpox*, p.22; *Statistical Appendices to Annual Report of the Director-General of Health Services, 1950* (Delhi, 1955), p.53.

[87] *Bombay VR, 1895-6*, p.22; *Madras VR, 1893-4*, p.5.

[88] *Madras VR, 1898-9*, p.2; James, *Smallpox*, p.100.

[89] *Bengal VR, 1869*, p.xiii and p.i of government review.

extinction in India.

Conclusion

Medical intervention against smallpox in nineteenth-century India was only partly constrained by a lack of appropriate epidemiological knowledge and immunisation technology. Smallpox was a disease as familiar to Europe as to South Asia; its basic mode of transmission was well understood; and there existed in vaccination an at least potentially effective prophylaxis. To some extent the problems vaccination encountered in India mirrored European experience—the reluctance of people to seek vaccination (except during epidemics), the low level of immunity conferred (until the introduction of revaccination and improved vaccine preservation methods), and the difficulty of creating a suitable mass immunisation agency. But in many respects the history of smallpox and vaccination in India is expressive of a colonial situation in which the administration was culturally and politically remote from the lives of its subjects.

Belief in a smallpox deity provided an alternative, religious, explanation for the incidence of the disease and prescribed ritual observances than ran counter to Western medical secularism. In variolation, too, vaccination found a formidable rival, sustained by a specialised agency of its own. It enjoyed the confidence of the people and (until late in the nineteenth century) was more readily available in many parts of the country than state vaccination. Disdainful of indigenous belief and folk practice, the British medical establishment was as loath to compromise with Sitala as it was with variolation. But while there could be no question of outlawing disease deities, the British saw the supplanting of variolation as essential to the success of their own medical system. As far as vaccination was concerned, medical monopoly, not cultural pluralism, was the desired goal. Finding persuasion, co-option, and the enlistment of leading Indians, inadequate for the purpose, the colonial authorities eventually turned to legislation to ban variolation and hasten public acceptance of vaccination. An exotic, without root on Indian soil, vaccination long remained closely identified with foreign rule, attracting suspicions and fears that ranged far beyond doubts about its medical efficacy. The negative character of British attitudes to Sitala and variolation was thus matched by Indian antipathy to vaccination and the coercive, unheeding system of colonialism it was taken to represent.

To perhaps a greater degree than in Britain, vaccination in India was inhibited by technical difficulties—there were problems of climate, for example, and of obtaining sufficient pure lymph. But it was constrained, too, by the nature of the colonial regime itself. Disposed to see the health of its European subjects and servants as a first priority, the colonial state was reluctant to make the financial and administrative commitment necessary for an effective assault on smallpox. The sheer size and expense of such an undertaking was always a deterrent. But there was an inhibiting ambivalence in British attitudes as well. Vaccination was welcomed as a demonstration of the superiority of West over East, science over superstition. And yet, from an abiding sense of political insecurity, heightened by the Mutiny and Rebellion of 1857-8 and by rumbling discontent over other forms of medical intervention, the state shied away from a vaccination programme that might provoke resistance and revolt. A fear of the consequences of compulsion was thus an important check on the state and on the medical profession's interventionist ambitions. It encouraged greater reliance, in this field of colonial activity as in many others, on persuasion, on Indian intermediaries, and upon a gradualist approach to the prospect of social change.

Further reading

Arnold, David, *Colonizing the Body: state medicine and epidemic disease in nineteenth-century India* (Berkeley, 1993).

Babb, Lawrence A., *The Divine Hierarchy: popular Hinduism in Central India* (New York, 1975).

Crooke, William, *The Religion and Folklore of Northern India* (London, 1926).

Dyson, Tim (ed.), *India's Historical Demography: studies in famine, disease and society* (London, 1989).

Klein, Ira, 'Death in India, 1871-1921', *Journal of Asian Studies* 32 (1973), pp.639-59.

Nicholas, Ralph W., 'The goddess Sitala and epidemic smallpox in Bengal', *Journal of Asian Studies* 41 (1981), pp.21-44.

Ranger, Terence and Paul Slack (eds.), *Epidemics and Ideas: essays on the historical perception of pestilence* (Cambridge, 1992).

Wadley, Susan S.,'Sitala: the Cool One', *Asian Folklore Studies* 39 (1980), pp.33-62.

THE INDIAN NATIONAL CONGRESS: A HUNDRED-YEAR PERSPECTIVE[1]

David Taylor

India's pre- and post-independence political experience are linked primarily through the institution of the Indian National Congress, which celebrated its centenary in 1985. Starting life as an organisation of the professional middle classes, it provided a platform for a variety of critiques of British rule in India. After 1919, under Gandhi's leadership, the Congress became an increasingly activist organisation and led several national campaigns of resistance to colonial rule. The success of these campaigns played a crucial role in the achievement of independence. While the Congress widened its social and geographical range during this period, it failed to prevent the growth of Muslim separatism. In the last 30 years there has been a flowering of historical scholarship on the Congress. Earlier assessments have been restated in sophisticated and subtle ways, while other writers have emphasised the importance of looking separately at the individuals and groups who participated in the Congress movement. This essay, prepared originally as a lecture to the Royal Asiatic Society on 10 April 1986 to mark the centenary, attempts a synoptic account of the Congress in the light of the wide range of recent findings and interpretations.

India, it is often pointed out both by Indians and by others, is the world's largest democracy, not simply in terms of the sheer number of people who participate in elections but also because of the continuous stream of open political activity. Democracy is not just a label that has been applied to the country at the whim of an individual or clique but is manifestly something that is alive and well. In the last decade alone, there have been two changes of government at the national level, and the government in New Delhi currently coexists, more or less willingly, with non-Congress ministries in several major states. There have indeed been voices to suggest that India in its present economic circumstances cannot afford the luxury of uncontrolled political activity. One of the arguments, for example, put forward for a presidential system has been that the level of 'unproductive' political activity would be reduced. It could certainly be argued that the relatively sluggish rate of economic growth that has been maintained over the past four decades is linked to

[1] First published in the *Journal of the Royal Asiatic Society* 2 (1987), pp.287-305. The original text benefited greatly from some incisive and stimulating comments from Peter Robb.

political constraints. That question, however, is not the theme of this article. For better or worse, India's democracy is here to stay, and one of the most important tasks for the historian or the political scientist, is to try to identify the factors that have given it its apparent staying power.

At the most general level of analysis I suspect the answer lies in the dynamic interaction between the social diversity of the country and the sense among a large part of the population that national identity is as important as regional or sectional distinctions. This is a delicate balance to maintain both at the ideological and practical levels and on many occasions, especially in the past decade, it has appeared to be on the verge of collapse. In the Punjab especially the centre has had, indeed is continuing to have, considerable difficulty in containing terrorist-backed demands for regional autonomy or independence, but it could also be said that one of the precipitating factors in the Punjab and elsewhere has been that overcentralisation of power in New Delhi has threatened to stifle the urge for self-determination at the local level which is an essential element in the functioning of a healthy democracy.

The framework within which this dynamic interaction was established was of course the Indian struggle for independence which, however one measures it, lasted for well over half a century. During that time the British were gradually placed in such a position that eventually they decided that in their weakened state after the Second World War there was no point in trying to reconstruct a system of imperial control, thus avoiding the mistakes of the Dutch and French. In the course of the struggle the nationalist leadership grew in size and sophistication so that it could incorporate in its thinking traditional, revivalist and Western ideas of politics and society.

The vehicle for much of this incorporation was the Indian National Congress, the centenary of whose foundation fell in December 1985, but before considering the significance of Congress to Indian history I should sound a note of caution. The thrust of much recent writing on Indian history has been to emphasise that the Congress cannot be equated *tout court* with the nationalist movement, nor the nationalist movement with the totality of political activity during the colonial period. For the so-called Cambridge school, associated with the late Professor Gallagher and Dr Anil Seal, the thrust has been to 'deconstruct' the Congress and to see it not as a free-floating all-India entity but as a shifting alliance of local groups. From a very different perspective, the 'subaltern' school (the name derives from Antonio Gramsci's usage) based in Calcutta, Canberra and elsewhere has emphasised that outside that realm of organised Congress activity, indeed outside the realm of all organised political activity, there were important developments which both influenced the course of nationalist politics and also posed an actual or potential challenge to the way in which the middle and upper classes defined social and political reality. Professor Sumit Sarkar in his *Modern India* refers to 'elemental forces' which regularly surfaced during the nationalist movement and which frightened the government at least as much as anything that Gandhi and the Congress did. Whatever position one occupies *vis-à-vis* Cambridge and Calcutta, however, no one today would wish to argue that the history of the nationalist movement is to be equated with that of Congress or that the initiative within Congress always rested with Gandhi, Nehru or Patel. Although space will not allow me to mention, except in passing, movements and events outside Congress, I do not consider them to be unimportant or secondary.

In this article I will be looking at both the ideological and the institutional aspects of Congress. I will try to trace the genesis of such ideas as democracy, secularism, and planned economic development which have played a major role in India's political history before and after independence, even if often they have been no more than convenient slogans. Debates within Congress reverberated outside the party and set the agenda for wider intellectual debate. At times, of course, other, more exclusive outlooks influenced the thinking of many members of the party. As Nehru once said in the 1930s, many Congressmen were communalists under their secular cloaks. At the institutional level, I will be arguing, as Judith Brown has in her own *Modern India*, that forms matter. During the period after 1920 especially, the top leadership of the Congress at national and provincial levels, used the mechanism of the party to organise mass campaigns against the government as well as to fight elections. Having won the 1937 elections over much of the country, they then succeeded in co-ordinating the work of up to eight provincial ministries so as to achieve both administrative and political goals. That experience carried the party through into the post-independence period, although from the very earliest days it was clear that the final decision-making would rest with the Prime Minister. The rules of the political game in India have changed very significantly since 1947, and Congress, especially under Mrs. Gandhi, was foremost in altering them, but there has always been continuity as well as change.

The idea behind that first meeting in Bombay, that Indians had aspirations and interests in common, had already begun to emerge in the previous decade of intense political activity. The sharp swings of policy from Lytton, the romantic imperialist in love with princely India, to Ripon the Gladstonian liberal, had provided much to provoke and encourage the members of the new political associations which had been founded in the 1860s and 1870s, the East India Association, the Indian Association, the Poona Sarvajanik Sabha and so on. Those who were thus provoked and encouraged were men who had time to reflect on the nature and consequences of British rule in India. In the quarter century since the Great Rebellion of 1857 had signalled the irretrievable breakdown of the old order, what had hitherto been individual and scattered alien elements in India had been brought together into a single structure of government. Physically they had been joined together by the railway, introduced into India only a few years after it had similarly begun to transform the face of Europe, and by the introduction of regular postal and telegraph services. The railways and the post office between them provided the means for contact between different parts of India which cut across the traditional avenues of communication which had tended to be limited to specific groups and used for specific purposes such as trade. Just as important were the changes that were occurring in the form of government. All in a rush in the 1850s and 1860s had come the codification of law and judicial procedure, the establishment of the universities, the introduction of recruitment through examinations for some sections of the civil service and the introduction of a non-official element into the Governors' and Governor-General's legislative councils. All this physical and institutional construction created in the minds of the British, or at least of some of them, what one historian has called 'the illusion of permanence'. On the Indian side, too, there were those who in the nineteenth century would have found it difficult to imagine India without the British connection in some form or other, but they also drew the conclusion that the government was not simply to be equated with the racially defined elite that monopolised its senior positions at the time and that the government had responsibilities for the welfare of the country and its social and economic advancement. From a more self-interested perspective, government was something that was plastic and manipulable, an edifice within which individual careers could be made and whose resources could be used both for group and for national ends.

In the course of time, these ideas were to be brought into a more direct relation with economic interests, especially but not only those of the industrial bourgeoisie. At this point, however, although the first cotton mills had already been established in Bombay and the first Marwari merchants and bankers had moved to Calcutta and begun to compete directly with the British in the jute industry and in other fields, Indian industry was still in its infancy and its leaders, whatever their private views, anxious to remain on good terms with the government. Merchants by and large were also content to remain at a safe distance from political activity, although in some cities the leading merchant families acted as patrons to the politicians. In the countryside the Deccan riots of 1875 and the Pabna disturbances of 1873 had demonstrated the strains that new forms of land ownership combined with commercialisation of agriculture might bring about, but they were easily contained by government action. There was no continuing peasant organisation in search of a political voice, although from the very beginning peasant issues were on the political agenda.

In the first instance, then, the possibility of political action in pursuit of *national* goals was explored by the intelligentsia which had taken shape in the schools and colleges and later on in the bar libraries, reading-rooms and associations of the big cities. Although there were no doubt unemployed graduates and rootless scribblers among them, the lead was taken by the successful, by lawyers such as Pherozeshah Mehta, whose income and lifestyle were every bit as magnificent as that of his European peers, by Justice Ranade, whose career in public service made him one of the first Indians to become a high court judge, by W.C. Bonnerjea, the first president of Congress and another highly successful barrister, and so on. Although few of them had escaped some personal slight or obstruction to their careers from British arrogance, it could hardly be said that they saw political activity as their only means to personal achievement. Even those like Shishir Kumar Ghose and Anand Mohan Bose who devoted their lives to political organisation and journalism clearly had the abilities and opportunities which would have enabled them to make successful careers elsewhere.

These early pioneers of the Congress had had time to reflect on the transformation of Indian society that appeared to be under way and to consider how best to channel it. In many cases, their concern with social and political change went together with an interest in one or other of the religious reform and revival movements of the period. The interrelationship of religious fervour, intellectual rationalism, which in Bengal as in contemporary Europe was often given quasi-religious status, and social orthodoxy, however, was extraordinarily complex. Depending on their intellectual orientations and personal positions, the early pioneers explored different aspects of this transformation, both in writing and through personal involvement. Among the most powerful ideas that were developed at this initial stage were those that had to do with the economic impact of British rule, its strengths and its weaknesses. In 1867 Dadabhai Naoroji had in his lecture 'England's debt to India' formulated for the first time in public the most important theme in nationalist critiques of British rule in India, namely the notion of the drain of wealth from India to Britain. Although it has subsequently been refined and modified, its basic approach was enormously influential throughout the nationalist movement and up to the present day. But the important point about Naoroji, Ranade, R.C. Dutt and others is that they recognised the irreversible changes that contact with the West had brought about and sought to harness the potentiality of the industrial revolution to the elimination of the grinding poverty that perhaps they had come to see with new eyes through their knowledge of progress in Europe and America. As Professor Bipan Chandra, the leading historian of this aspect of Indian nationalism, has written:

> Their criticism was never merely or even mainly that the traditional social order was disintegrated by British rule but that the structuring and construction of the new was delayed, frustrated and obstructed (*Nationalism and Colonialism in Modern India*, p.43).

From this perspective, writers like Ranade advocated a positive role for the state which would begin to propel India along the path that European countries were already following. In the rural sector the dominant view was that if the burden of taxation could be lifted from the peasantry through fixing once and for all the level of the revenue demand, and if the discretionary powers of the bureaucracy could be reduced, then production would increase, a market be provided for new industries, and so on. Looking back from the experience of development in the twentieth century, in India itself and elsewhere, one can see that this was too simple a view of how the process can be set in motion. It ignores, as British officials at the time were very ready to point out, the possible clashes of interest between the landed and the landless in the rural areas, although the early political associations were far from being unconcerned about the rights of tenants and cultivators against the demands of landlords and moneylenders, and on occasion actively campaigned for them

Simultaneously, many of the early nationalists were involved with schemes for social reform. Many of them saw the key to progress in education and became heavily involved in running schools and colleges within the new framework of university affiliation and officially sponsored and recognised examinations. Within, for example, the institutions run by the Deccan Education Society or, a little later on, by the 'College' wing of the Arya Samaj, students could be taught that Western education was not incompatible with a proper respect for Indian traditions and with a desire for national service. Efforts were made by a few individuals, Karve in Maharashtra for example, to extend the scope of education for women. Education is a permissive process, which brings the young person to the position where he or she can make an informed choice in his or her own life. For some early nationalists, however, this was not enough and they sought to use the power of the government to impose changes in key areas of Indian life, most notably in marriage customs. B.M. Malabari was able in 1891 to cajole sufficient support to persuade the government to pass the Age of Consent Act, but the opposition that his actions aroused demonstrated the limits beyond which such activities could not be taken.

Some of the people I have mentioned were politically highly active in their own cities and provinces, particularly in Bengal where the lines seemed more sharply drawn between rulers and ruled. Others, however, either through choice, or, in the case of officials like Ranade, out of necessity, were inclined to a more quietist position. In its earliest years, though, Congress was able to bring together most shades of opinion among the educated middle class. It is sometimes suggested that Congress at this time spoke only for the selfish interest of that class in its apparent overriding concern for access to jobs and places, but this is, I think, to misunderstand its nature and purpose. The delegates to the early Congress meetings saw themselves as delegates to a national convention which had of necessity to move slowly and to concentrate on problems that had to be tackled at that level and where a consensus existed. At least in some cases, however, they represented local bodies which were active, as we have already seen, in many different fields. One must not forget, as well, that until 1895 the Social Reform Conference was held in conjunction with the annual sessions of Congress, just as a little later there would be industrial exhibitions to educate and inform the delegates of the progress that India was making in this field.

The early Congress thus encompassed a significant diversity of interests and outlook, despite its domination by men with legal training and experience who had made their base in the cities of nineteenth-century India and despite the overpowering sense of Victorian earnestness that one gets reading early Congress reports or looking at group photographs of the delegates. In the earliest years of the Congress the diversity was also masked by the fact that those who occupied the most prominent positions in it, the chairmen of the reception committees and the presidents of the annual sessions, were prosperous, secure, on easy terms as far as that was possible under the raj, with the British. In the 1890s, however, it became clear that there were in fact quite marked differences of opinion on many issues. Initially historians tried to make sense of these differences by making use of a neat distinction, which followed of course the labels used at the time, between the 'moderates' who dominated the early Congress and pursued the 'politics of mendicancy' and the 'extremists' who, in a Whiggish progression and emerging from a somewhat different social matrix, put forward a purer view of nationalism and in their political activity remained unremittingly hostile to the government. One of the most decisive achievements of more recent historical research, however, has been to show how difficult it is to draw any clear line between groups except in specific contexts and at very precise points in time. It was not just that, as the greatest 'extremist' of them all, Tilak, said, the extremists of today are the moderates of tomorrow, prophetic as that statement was to be concerning his own followers, but equally that there was no necessary correlation between radical or conservative views in the political fields and similar views in other areas. It would in any case be impossible to find value-neutral definitions of radical, moderate, conservative or whatever that would enable us to make comparisons. Reflection on Tagore's writings on nationalism would be a useful exercise for anyone who thinks otherwise. At this early stage of the development of Congress, in fact, it was those with a more 'reformist' mentality who probably found it easier to think in terms of an all-India political movement, while those who found the compromises that such a stance involved too much to take may at the same time have been unsure of their position concerning the appropriate base on which to build a mass movement, and therefore in some cases less able to sustain a campaign beyond their regional or linguistic community.

Before proceeding further something should be said concerning Allan Octavian Hume and the other British sympathisers with the early Congress. Although Hume's part in the actual foundation of Congress has perhaps been exaggerated in the past, what he did for Congress, as he had already done for causes as diverse as Indian ornithology and theosophy, was to act as a gadfly working away both at officials and at the various provincial leaders to encourage them to take each other seriously and to see Congress as a vehicle through which a dialogue could be developed. In his attempts to popularise the idea of Congress among the rural population he anticipated later developments, but his views were always somewhat idiosyncratic and when he finally left for England in 1892 there must have been some discreet sighs of relief. Apart from Hume there were other British sympathisers, some with direct Indian experience as officials or businessmen, others with commitments in British politics which they saw as correlating directly with Indian interests. Both categories tended to perform true to type. Those with links to the Gladstonian wing of the Liberals looked to the introduction of representative institutions as the way to stimulate responsible political activity in India, but stuck staunchly to the tenets of free trade, regardless of the comparative strengths of the two economies. The radicals within British politics, including some of the Irish nationalists, were more prepared to back the Congress line without reservation but only one or two were prepared to put very much effort into actually publicising and working for the cause.

II

For the first 30 years or so of its existence Congress remained almost entirely an apex organisation sitting on top of a pyramid of local and provincial organisations which were themselves of very disparate character and level of activity. Although its individual leaders were men of some substance in national affairs and taken seriously by the government, Congress as a body had little *locus standi*. Up to the First World War, in fact, the British Committee of the Congress and its publication *India*, acted as the main focus of Congress activity outside the annual sessions. It also took, to the increasing irritation of many Congressmen, the bulk of whatever funds were available at the national level. Outside Congress itself, however, with the participation of many Congressmen, there had been major developments in the idea of nationalism and in forms of political agitation. Some of these had been foreshadowed by Tilak in Maharashtra where he had succeeded, in the urban areas at least, in using religious festivals and religious symbolism for political purposes. They came to fruition in the course of the agitation against the partition of Bengal, during which some of the ideas associated with the extremist school of thought were put together in new and more powerful ways. Although the emotional focus of the movement remained firmly rooted in Bengal, the earlier inspiration of Vivekananda and the direct leadership of men like Aurobindo enabled a wider meaning to be given to the association of religion and political action. The motto of 'swadeshi' became both the inspiration of new ventures in a variety of fields, even if few of them lasted very long, and also the basis of a programme of action that followed the Irish example in attempting to strike at the economic foundations of British rule. The agitation against the partition eventually died down, although it was only during the First World War that the revolutionary societies or terrorist groups were finally repressed, but it had changed the terms on which the nationalist movement and thereby Congress saw the task ahead. The agitation had also, however, exposed for the first time some of the practical obstacles that would lie in the way of those who sought to implement the nationalist dream. As has been pointed out often enough, the means by which the agitation's leaders sought to mobilise support alienated as many as it recruited. Above all, the Muslim population of Bengal, the majority of the population, although they were concentrated in the vast rural backwater of East Bengal, soon found themselves out of sympathy with what was going on, both because of the translation of Bengali nationalism into an overtly Hindu idiom and also because of the feeling that the leaders of the agitation had no intention of changing the basic order of things whereby the rural areas supported the middle class of Calcutta in their cultured pursuits.

The attitude of the Congress leaders in other parts of India was only coolly sympathetic to the plight of the Bengalis, and even at the height of the agitation the December 1906 session of Congress only endorsed the boycott programme within Bengal itself. A year later the tensions between the Bombay-based leadership of Mehta, Gokhale and their colleagues in the 'moderate' wing and the 'extremists' came to a head with the split at the Surat Congress session, in which the moderates won the day. Apart from wishing in general terms to maintain their hold on Congress, the moderates were particularly anxious to do so at a time when the British were about to introduce the first major instalment of constitutional reforms in the shape of the 1909 Councils Act. Yet even though Tilak was shortly to be sentenced to six years' imprisonment in Mandalay, and Aurobindo was to flee to Pondicherry and there to begin an entirely new phase of his life, the 'extremist' view of the world, because it was not in fact exclusively associated with a specific group of individuals, made its own very definite contribution to the corpus of Indian nationalist ideas. The partition agitation itself, despite its confinement to Bengal, was equally important in that it was the first prolonged confrontation between the British in India and a politically organised movement with a far-reaching programme of demands.

The methods of the partition agitation were to be adopted in 1919 and 1920 by Mahatma Gandhi in the Rowlatt satyagraha and the non-co-operation movement, but none of those who had led that agitation were to join him in these latter movements. Between, let us say, the Surat split at the end of 1907 and the special Congress session in Calcutta in September 1920, enormous changes had taken place within Congress, even though the links with the past were far from broken.

The first change was, as I have indicated, one of leadership. Of the old leaders, some had died, Gokhale and Mehta most notably. Others had taken part in the setting up of the National Liberal Federation in 1918 with the intention of responding positively to the new reforms promised by the British after the Montagu Declaration of 1917. This event, it should be noted, took place well before Gandhi began to take an active part in Congress affairs. In their place had come first of all young men recruited either directly by Gandhi through his early local campaigns or through the Home Rule Leagues, particularly the one led by Mrs. Besant. Such figures as Vallabhbhai Patel, Rajendra Prasad, and of course Jawaharlal Nehru, all became involved in nationalist activity at this stage, as well as such less well-known but equally energetic figures as Indulal Yajnik in Gujarat. But there were others as well who had been involved with Congress at an earlier stage but not centrally so who now moved forward to take a more prominent position. Motilal Nehru and C.R. Das fall into this category. Alongside this shift in leadership went a move from the old centres of Congress activity, which by and large had coincided with the main centres of colonial government and economic penetration, to new areas. Gandhi's home region of Gujarat was now to become the most committed of all to Congress activity, while Bihar, Karnataka, the Andhra region of Madras and other areas also provided theatres in which the nationalist struggle could be carried on. Most significant of all, in the north Indian heartland of U.P., the then United Provinces, Congress began to acquire a solid base. This expansion in part reflected the shock waves set up by the Jallianwala Bagh massacre and by subsequent related events in India and Britain. It was also however a consequence of more generalised economic and political changes. Increased commercialisation of agriculture had brought a greater proportion of the rural population within reach of economic forces over which they had little control, for example the wide fluctuations in prices during and just after the First World War. At the same time the industrialists of Bombay and Ahmedabad, who had done well during the wartime boom, were beginning to be conscious of their potential power, although their attitude to direct involvement in Congress activity was still very ambivalent. Politically, and here the work of the Cambridge historians has been important in increasing our understanding, the transfer of control over real, if very limited resources, at the provincial level from British to Indian hands had led to a rethinking by many of how political action could best be utilised for group interest. In some cases this led men to sever their formal connections with the Congress so as to contest the first elections for the new 'Montford' councils which took place at the end of 1920, and during the decade more were to follow. In other cases, however, depending both on the position of the individual and on the balance of forces within the province, it could lead to decisions to join Congress or to take a more prominent part in its activities. In general Congress was, whether it liked it or not, becoming transformed from an organisation primarily of the intelligentsia into a movement that, however much it succeeded in the short term in transcending them, had to develop the ability to cope with the diversity and contradictions of Indian society. It had also to develop an organisation and structure which would give it the capacity to function effectively even in the face of government hostility. This it duly acquired after the Gandhians' final victory at the Nagpur Congress session of December 1920. Thereafter Working Committee and AICC became part of the everyday vocabulary of Indian politics, as did the idea of Congress having a mass membership paying either a four-anna subscription or, later on, a prescribed amount of homespun yarn.

During the non-co-operation movement Congress under Gandhi's leadership and inspiration established the basic *modus operandi* through which it was able to develop its ability to confront the raj on equal terms. In this first campaign the emphasis was on tactics that had already been tried in Bengal, namely boycott both of British goods and of government institutions of all kinds, schools, law courts, ceremonies, elections to the new councils. In many ways, however, the non-co-operation movement was a failure. Gandhi had failed to achieve any of the major objectives that he had set out, and towards the end he was beginning to lose support from some of his business supporters, while from his personal point of view there was beginning to be an unacceptable level of violence in Bombay city and then in the village of Chauri Chaura. Above all, the alliance that he had been able to make with the Muslim community had broken down when he failed to fulfil his promise to resolve the Khilafat issue. It was over the Muslim question that the tension referred to above between the ideals of Congress and the manifest divisions within society, whether these were endogenous or in some way the product of British 'divide and rule' policies, was felt most acutely. There had always been Muslims in Congress, men like Badruddin Tyabji with similar professional and intellectual interests to the other early Congressmen, but they had never been more than a small minority and with the rise among some Congressmen of Hindu revivalist themes their role diminished further. Gandhi, however, by his use of the Khilafat issue had been able to bring in both the Muslim equivalent of the Hindu intelligentsia and some of the most prominent *ulama*. Basic differences had, however, only been papered over, and after the failure of the Khilafat campaign Hindu-Muslim relations degenerated.

III

Despite the apparent set back caused by the end of non-co-operation, Congress during the 1920s continued to develop along a number of fronts. In the legislative councils the Swarajists, the more politically oriented members of the movement, or in some cases the more opportunist, succeeded in destroying the credibility of the Montford reforms and with them the possibility that the British could put together a viable coalition of moderate and conservative forces. Gandhi and his small band of immediate followers spent the 1920s developing what became known as the 'constructive programme', looking for ways in which immediate changes could be made to rural life and, where necessary, using the satyagraha weapon for internal reform, as in the case of the Vykom temple satyagraha in 1924. Many, however, found the 1920s a difficult time. Nehru used the period to extent his range of international contacts and generally to widen his knowledge of India and the world. Others, Patel for example, dabbled in municipal government.

The mass struggle was renewed in 1930 in the form of the civil disobedience movement, which began with what is probably the best known of Gandhi's experiments in political action and certainly the most fully worked out, the Dandi salt march, and lasted, with one longish break, until 1934, although in reality the movement had lost its momentum by the end of 1932. Unlike the non-co-operation movement, there was from the beginning an attack not just on the moral legitimacy of the raj but on the institutions of government through various forms of civil disobedience, including non-payment of taxes. Even before civil disobedience began, events showed how Congress was moving closer to a position of equality with the government. On the one hand, Lord Irwin was prepared to talk directly to Gandhi, discussions which provoked Churchill to his notorious gibe about Gandhi as a half-naked faqir. On the other hand, the proceedings of the All-Parties Conference which was held in 1928 as a counter to the all-British Simon Commission, whose appointment in 1927 by Lord Birkenhead had served as a catalyst for renewed political action, were clearly dominated by Congress. But I must emphasise that the Congress which dominated the proceedings of the conference was not entirely Gandhi's. Many of the voices that were heard were of those who had joined it long before Gandhi had arrived on the Congress scene and whose interests lay more in their own provinces and communities than anywhere else. The final report was as much the work of the doyen of the Liberals who had left Congress in 1918, Tej Bahadur Sapru, as of Motilal Nehru, the conference's chairman.

The All-Parties Conference report, which recommended what was then seen as the half-way house of dominion status, was, like the Simon Commission itself, overtaken by events. At the Lahore Congress at the end of 1929 the goal of complete independence, for which the younger Nehru and others had been pressing for some time, was made part of the official Congress programme, and 26 January 1930 was celebrated as Independence Day. Gandhi's failure to obtain adequate concessions in his talks with Irwin led him to embark once again on mass mobilisation as a means to bring pressure on the government. With the notable exception in most parts of India of the Muslims, his call evoked a response across a remarkably wide social spectrum. This response can be explained in various ways. Although the British strategy of co-opting princes, landlords and others as junior partners in the raj had worked to a point, the cracks were beginning to show and some of the more far-sighted of those who had been recruited were beginning to hedge their bets, non-Brahman landlords and professionals in Madras and Maharashtra for example. The work that had been done by Gandhi himself and by his lieutenants like Patel in the Bardoli satyagraha was bearing fruit. Another generation of students had come of age since the non-co-operation movement and was inclined towards radical action. This period was in fact the high point of revolutionary terrorism with figures like Bhagat Singh and the Hindustan Republican Army. The consequences of the Great Depression, which disrupted the whole basis of the rural economy, must also be taken into account. With all this to work with, Congress was thus able to extend the basis of its support and to make it clear both to the British and to its supporters that it intended to press on until ultimately it secured untrammelled power. But, as I said at the beginning, we must take heed of the findings of recent research. These really only confirm what one would have expected from a movement as organically linked to Indian society as Congress was. In the first place, Gandhi and his associates were as concerned to prevent the agrarian unrest they were harnessing to the nationalist cause from spilling over into an attack on the social order, as to confront the British. It was no coincidence that the Gandhian campaigns were centred in areas such as Gujarat where discontent could easily be focused on the government, whereas in U.P. or Bihar peasant leadership was either outside the Congress altogether or linked to the radical wing that was emerging at this time. Secondly, some of those who joined the Congress undoubtedly did so for opportunist reasons, although the great influx here was to come a little later.

Perhaps the greatest problem of the civil disobedience movement, however, was the almost total failure to involve the Muslim community, except in the North-West Frontier. The Khilafat issue was dead and buried, while many of those who had joined hands with Congress during it were now positively hostile. Although a small group of intellectuals in U.P. continued to participate actively in Congress affairs, many others had felt that the spirit of the Lucknow pact had been jettisoned at the time of the All-Parties Conference in 1928. They were not in fact far wrong, but from Congress's point of view separate electorates and the whole paraphernalia of special protection had been outmoded by its commitment to adult franchise and complete independence. One can see too how the prospect, however remote, of real power made it difficult to build in institutional curbs on its exercise. Even with hindsight it is difficult to see exactly the combination that would have brought together the right sections of the Muslim and Hindu communities under the Congress umbrella in such a way as to defeat the communalists on both sides. Each section of the former, the *ulama*, the radical peasant leaders of Bengal and elsewhere, the aspirant salariat and bourgeoisie, especially in U.P., the provincial landlord politicians of Punjab, could all have been induced to enter into an alliance, but would the terms of such an alliance have generated sufficient support to confront the raj in such a way as to dislodge it, and would an alliance with one section have fatally alienated another? After the experience of the non-co-operation movement, the attitude of the party managers, men like Patel, appears to have been to give the Muslim issue lower priority and to concentrate on the big battalions of support that could be generated by concentrating on the potential areas of Congress support in Gujarat and elsewhere. Thus the All-Parties Conference gave priority to a strong centre which would rally the Hindi heartland over making what would have seemed to many both in and out of Congress unwarranted concessions.

With the end of the civil disobedience movement the final phase of Congress's development during the nationalist period began. Whereas the national leadership had been ambivalent towards the Swarajist programme of council entry, there were few such qualms about holding office, let alone contesting elections under the 1935 Act, among the mainstream Gandhian leaders, although Nehru was less sure about the results of such actions. To do so would consolidate the advantage gained during the civil disobedience period and Patel and others felt confident about their ability to control local factionalism and particularist tendencies. It was indeed essential that they do so in order to give a framework of authority to the Congress to replace the essentially temporary authority it enjoyed during the height of the civil disobedience battle. Thus in 1934 the Congress constitution was redrafted in such a way as to give greater authority to the central leadership. Without such a framework of authority and focus of activity there was the risk that the Congress body would be wagged by the rapidly growing radical tail which had announced its presence through the formation in 1934 of the Congress Socialist Party and in 1936 of the All-India Kisan Sabha. As I shall suggest later on, the existence of this pluralism within Congress was essential for the health of post-independence democracy but from the point of view of the leadership it was a force that had to be curbed and controlled. By and large the task was achieved pretty well. From the point of view of the right wing within the party they retained effective control without having to make any significant concessions to the left. The ability of the right to handle Nehru when he was president of the Congress twice running in 1936 and 1937 reminds one in many ways of the 'Yes Minister' approach, the careful 'redrafting' of resolutions for example to retain the letter but lose the spirit. In June 1936 the differences had to be made public when the Gandhian majority on Nehru's Working Committee resigned en bloc, but it was in many ways a staged affair, for it was already clear that effective power lay with the right.

The events of the Second World War are too complex to be easily summarised, and in any case they belong more to a consideration of the transfer of power than to a discussion of Congress. The Quit India movement in August 1942, which the British had thought to abort by the pre-emptive arrest of the whole leadership, showed how deeply the nationalist message had reached, but by and large the nation was prepared to wait for the end of the war and for the final push, a push which in any case, although this only gradually became apparent, would be at a half-open door. One must not overlook, as the Attenborough film of Gandhi succeeded in doing so remarkably, the importance of Bose and the Indian National Army, but as things fell out, their direct impact on events was very limited. As far as the Muslims were concerned, the Congress had to face the fact by 1939 that it had missed the bus as far as generating significant Muslim support was concerned. This realisation, however, dawned only rather slowly. Like the British at an earlier time dealing with Congress itself, the Congress leadership thought that somehow it could outflank the Muslim League by dealing with provincial leaders whose political standing was being remorselessly eroded by the tide of Muslim League support. Nehru, who had seen the divisive potential of Muslim demands, had tried to deal with the problem by going straight to the Muslim masses, but this too was unrealistic.

IV

In 1947 the Congress was forced to accept the loss of the Muslim-majority provinces. For some, this was the vivisection of Bharat-mata, for others, notably of course Nehru, it was the denial of the composite culture that had been built up over the centuries. Hindu and Muslim communalism were two sides of the same coin and free, secular India would have to live with the consequences of both. Apart from partition, however, if that is not like asking Mrs. Lincoln how she enjoyed the play, Congress leaders could feel satisfied with what had been achieved since 1885. Starting from scratch, and with no precedents apart from nationalist movements in Europe to guide them, they had built up a mass movement which transcended some, although, as recent research has emphasised and the first elections after independence were to demonstrate, by no means all, the divisions within Indian society. The Congress outlook on Indian development and the world was more closely in tune with articulated Indian opinion than at any time before or since. Unlike the situation in Pakistan, there was no difficulty in framing a constitution that embodied the major themes that Congress had emphasised over the years. India was to be a federation, but with so many qualifications and reservations that in matters of national interest the constituent states would be unable to offer more than passive resistance. Secularism was embodied in the constitution, but gestures were made in the directive principles to such Hindu concerns as cow protection. The advancement of what are euphemistically called the weaker sections of society was ensured by the essentially secular device of positive discrimination, while at the same time the practice of untouchability, even in religious contexts, was outlawed. Despite the occasional doubts that had been expressed in the past by members of the Indian elite, there was no doubt either that India would be a parliamentary democracy, with adult franchise for both sexes. It is worth noting here that, as with the Nehru report of 1928, much of the work on the constitution was done by someone who was not a Congressman, in this case had never been a Congressman, B.R. Ambedkar. His willingness to be associated with the work of the constituent assembly, even though both before and after he was a vigorous opponent of the Congress as a political party, shows how widely accepted were the basic tenets that Congress had worked for since 1885. It was Nehru's ability to project himself in these terms that gave him his unique command of the Indian political system in the 1950s. We can see a similar process at work in the way in which the idea of a planned economy was swiftly accepted by almost all of India's elite. During the last phase of the nationalist movement, when Indian industry was growing in confidence, the Congress leadership and those sympathetic to it were able to put together a consensus in favour of a planned economy. There were of course sound economic reasons in the context of the Indian economy for the adoption of a planned approach, with all its implications of protection for Indian industry and, in India at least, a guaranteed role for the private sector, but the willingness of the leaders of Indian industry to put together the Bombay plan in 1944 sprang from the close links men like Birla and Thakurdas had established with Congressmen on both left and right.

The values that I am suggesting had accumulated during the nationalist movement and which served as a charter for the elites of new India, senior civil servants, professionals, industrial managers, as much as, perhaps more than, politicians, had nevertheless to face a series of interrelated challenges to their relevance and their robustness. Were they in fact appropriate to the task of development of the whole country, rural as well as urban, poor as well as middle class? Were they capable of providing an adequate basis, ideologically and otherwise, to resist the pressures on government from self-seeking and parochial interest groups, some of them already inside the charmed circle of power, others clamouring at the gates to be let in and quite capable of using the nationalist movement's weapons against it? Or to put it in rather different terms, if the dominant social force behind Congress in 1947 was in fact a growing bourgeoisie, was this class capable, through Congress, of achieving the thoroughgoing modernisation required for economic development? And would these values succeed in attracting to membership or active support of the party those large sections of the population who had only been lightly touched by the nationalist movement? As 1947 receded into the past and with it direct memories of the freedom struggle, this problem became more acute. How was Congress as a party to function as an organisation after the immediate question of political freedom had been resolved? The crises that have beset the Indian polity in the past few years indicate that these challenges remain in large part unresolved, even though under their impact major changes have already come about in Congress itself and in many other institutions of the political system.

To deal adequately with these questions is beyond the scope of a single article, so that I will limit myself to some rather brief comments. Challenges to the relevance of Congress have come from a number of quarters. The Gandhians who discovered in 1947 that Gandhi's charisma was one thing, effective influence another, dispersed in different directions. Some were content to continue as social workers, but with the JP movement of the mid 1970s, however, there was heard an authentic voice of protest not just against the abuse of power but against the whole system of Western-style competitive democracy. Claims that the political system of which Congress was the centre was irrelevant to India's needs have come of course from the left, including those who were once members. Our attention has been drawn to the many ways in which the system either represses protest from below directly or deals with it through co-option. There have also been those who claim that the present system is bound up with a bureaucratic culture that is incapable of generating new ideas in tune with India's drive for modernity, and that therefore the whole notion of democracy should be scrapped or at least replaced by some sort of 'guided' alternative.

Congress has continued nevertheless to dominate the political scene, largely because of the way in which the relationship between government and society was handled under Nehru. New claimants for a share in the benefits of power, and there were many, were accommodated through skilful use of the federal system. This applied particularly to the rise of groups and individuals who represented the dominant forces at the village level, so that during the 1950s there were many changes of leadership in state governments. Secondly, the planning process which was initiated in the early 1950s was designed to give ample scope to the private sector provided it was prepared to accept the government's terms. On the whole, Indian industry showed itself willing to do so. Taken together, these techniques enabled the construction of what was described in the 1960s by Rajni Kothari and W.H. Morris-Jones as the 'Congress system'. And yet these adaptations imposed costs that were perhaps not fully realised at the time. Although Nehru was able by and large to maintain the autonomy of the centre, after his death in 1964 the men who had gained power at the state level began to demand control of New Delhi as well. The stage was set for the many bruising battles that Mrs. Gandhi had to fight to keep control of affairs. In so doing she used to the full all the resources that were available to her, including the Congress organisation and name, but she tended to put them to uses that they were not designed for. By the time she returned to power after the Janata government in 1980 she had split the party twice and taken in effect direct control of the organisation at every level, so that there was little opportunity for the party to function independently. At the very least this meant blocking off a useful safety valve. In general, Congress as an organisation went through a period of steady decline, and it would I think be true to say that the Congress values of the past were to be found elsewhere than in the Congress party. During the emergency it was widely believed that plans were being made for a switch to a presidential form of government. It is also suggested by many observers that in the post-1980 period Mrs. Gandhi began to look more to support from the majority Hindu community, especially in the Hindi-speaking states of north India, than to the minorities who had since Independence been staunch supporters of the party. This, however, was only the current version of a dilemma that had always faced the Congress, and all other parties within plural democracies, namely what should the proper relationship be between majority and minority. There were costs also in the economic field. The 'licence-permit raj' generated by the planning process had allowed inefficient and outdated units to survive behind artificial barriers against competition both from abroad and from newcomers at home. The way was also opened for large-scale corruption, often involving members of the Congress, who after all depended on business for the larger part of their election funds.

In his first months in office, Rajiv Gandhi made it clear that he was looking for a major overhaul of India's institutions, including the Congress. It is too early to say exactly what this will mean, although the internal party elections that were promised for the middle of 1986 and would have been the first for many years did not take place, indicating a relatively lower priority for party matters compared to more immediate problems. Mr. Gandhi has also talked of his vision of a modern, scientifically oriented India in terms that, allowing for the difference of period, would be recognisable by his Congress predecessors. Yet, just as much as they, he faces the continuing task of welding a vision of the future together with the political organisation of the party into an effective instrument for the achievement of national goals.

Further reading

A. *General surveys*

The works of Brown and Sarkar present synoptic surveys of the subject from somewhat different perspectives. These may be defined as liberal and radical respectively, although these terms may not adequately pin down the range of material presented and discussed. The edited volumes by Gallagher, Johnson and Seal and by Guha represent the 'Cambridge' and 'subaltern' approaches.

Brown, Judith, *Modern India: the origins of an Asian democracy* (London, 1985).
Chandra, Bipan, *Nationalism and Colonialism in Modern India* (New Delhi, 1979).
Gallagher, John, Gordon Johnson and Anil Seal (eds.), *Locality, Province and Nation: essays on Indian politics 1870-1940* (Cambridge, 1973).
Guha, Ranajit (ed.), *Subaltern Studies: writings on South Asian history and society* (New Delhi, 1982-).
Sarkar, Sumit, *Modern India, 1885-1947* (New Delhi, 1983).

B. *Works on specific themes or individuals*

Brown, Judith, *Gandhi: prisoner of hope* (New Haven, 1989).
Cashman, R., *The Myth of the 'Lokamanya': Tilak and mass politics in Maharashtra* (Berkeley, 1975).
Gopal, S., *Jawaharlal Nehru: a biography* (3 vols., London, 1975-84).
Hardy, P., *The Muslims of British India* (Cambridge, 1972).
Heimsath, C., *Indian Nationalism and Hindu Social Reform* (Princeton, 1964).
Kumar, Ravinder, *The Making of a Nation: essays in Indian history and politics* (New Delhi, 1989).
Low, D.A. (ed.), *Congress and the Raj: facets of the Indian struggle, 1917-1947* (London, 1978).
Markovits, Claude, *Indian Business and Nationalist Politics, 1931-1939* (Cambridge, 1974).
Nanda, B.R., *Gokhale, Gandhi and the Nehrus: studies in Indian nationalism* (London, 1974).
Pandey, Gyanendra, *The Construction of Communalism in Colonial North India* (New Delhi, 1990).
—, (ed.), *The Indian Nation in 1942* (Calcutta, 1988).
Pantham, Thomas and Kenneth L. Deutsch (eds.), *Political Thought in Modern India* (New Delhi, 1986).
Parekh, Bhikhu, *Gandhi's Political Philosophy: acritical examination* (London, 1989).
Singh, Anita Inder, *The Origins of the Partition of India, 1936-1947* (Delhi, 1987).
Wolpert, S., *Tilak and Gokhale: revolution and reform in the making of modern India* (new ed., Berkeley, 1977).

CHARAN SINGH, 1902-87: AN ASSESSMENT[1]

Terence J. Byres

Charan Singh (1902-87) is frequently identified as 'champion of India's peasants'. That description refers to his long career as an active politician. Less well known is his written work. That is rarely mentioned, and when it is, the tone (especially that of urban intellectuals) is dismissive. It is argued here, firstly, that Charan Singh was, indeed, an accomplished politician, but one who successfully represented the interests not of the whole peasantry, but of its rich and middle strata. It is suggested, secondly, that his published work is of greater significance than is generally acknowledged; that it falls squarely into the broad tradition of neo-populism; and that he was, unusually, a true 'organic' intellectual of the rich and middle peasantry. Both his political career and his ideas merit more serious attention than they have attracted hitherto; and such attention needs an adequate class perspective.

I. *Origins, social background and early influences*

Charan Singh was born on 23 December 1902, in the village of Noorpur, in Meerut district of western UP (then the United Provinces of British India). He tells us, through an anonymous interlocutor, that 'a man's ways, views and attitudes owe their origins, to a large extent, to his social background. So do those of Charan Singh'. One can accept both the general proposition and the particular application in Charan Singh's case. There may, however, be dispute over the relevant, determining constituents of social background. Charan Singh chose to emphasise that he was born: 'in a peasant's home under a thatched roof supported by kachcha mud walls, with a kachcha well in front of the residential compound of the family, used for drinking water as well as for irrigation' (Singh, 1986:1). That, no doubt, is so. Other aspects of his 'social background' may, however, have had equal, or greater, significance in moulding his 'ways, views, and attitudes'. In this respect, one may consider both certain generic characteristics of the community into which he was born and the particular circumstances of Charan Singh's family. The reality of Charan Singh was altogether more complex than that rendered by the image of son of a simple peasant family, reared in humble surroundings.

Certainly, his peasant origins are impeccable. He was born into a family of Hindu Jats. The Jats are a cultivating, or peasant, caste. In

[1] First published in *Journal of Peasant Studies* (Frank Cass & Co.) 15, 2 (January 1988), pp.139-89, and abridged for this volume.

northern India they are either Sikhs or Hindus, with Sikh Jats concentrated in the Punjab and Hindu Jats numerous in western UP and Haryana. Such 'cultivating communities' in India vary in their approach to physical labour. All, in principle, are willing to work the soil themselves. Among some, however, that willingness diminishes among those of their number whose material circumstances improve. Thus, for example, 'the Sagdope cultivator in West Bengal or the Vellala in Tamil Nadu rarely does all or even most of the work himself once he comes to own more than three or four acres of land'. Not so the Jat. The Jats are the archetypal working peasantry of northern India. Thus, 'the Jat cultivator in Western Uttar Pradesh or Haryana himself performs most of the operations of his farm even when he is moderately well-to-do' (Beteille, 1974a, p.191). Moreover, unlike other so-called peasant, the tradition is for his women to work with him in the fields (Beteille, 1974b, p.53). Charan Singh drew upon a genuine peasant tradition.

One notes, indeed, the variety of material circumstances among Jats, as among other peasant castes. Clearly, the Jat community—the Jat peasantry—is not, and was not at the beginning of the twentieth century, homogeneous. The Jat peasantry of that time was a distinctly differentiated one. That does not preclude their being joined by 'primordial ties', such as those of kinship and caste (see Alavi, 1973, for a general treatment, not related to Jats), and ideologically. But it does suggest the need to be alert to class relationships, processes of class formation and class action, all of which may be mystified or concealed by particular ideological formulations and constant ideological appeals. Charan Singh was to become a master of such formulations and appeals.

The Jat *kisan* tends to be a peasant proprietor. Not all Jats are, or were, in the early twentieth century, proprietors. Indeed, at the time of Charan Singh's birth 'his father was the youngest of the five brothers who held the land under their plough as tenants of the big zamindar or landlord of a nearby village Kuchesar' (Singh, 1986, p.1). Certainly, however, there is, among Jats, a fierce commitment to the ideal of proprietorship. That is important. It may yield a deep antagonism towards the landlord class: and especially the class of large landlords, of the kind which rented out land to Charan Singh's family at the time of his birth. Such an antagonism may be as bitter among rich and middle peasants—whether or not they are tenants—as among poor.[2] Certainly, Charan Singh possessed it.

In fact, within six months of his birth Charan Singh's family had become proprietors, in the village of Jani Khurd, 25 miles from his birthplace, and also in Meerut district. The family bought ten acres of land, perhaps using money earned by two of his uncles who served as

[2] For a discussion of peasant stratification see Appendix A, p.300.

soldiers in the British Indian Army (Singh, 1986, p.1). Those ten acres seem, later, to have grown to around 15 acres (six hectares) (Naik, 1979, p.31), and that would have placed Charan Singh's family in the lower reaches of the rich peasant stratum. He disliked intensely the description *kulak*, which was frequently attached to him, and lost no opportunity to reject it vehemently. But those origins among an industrious and well-to-do peasantry in western UP were of great significance. His sympathy for and appeal to the rich and middle peasantry of northern India were deep and powerful.

If, for Jats, peasant proprietorship is the ideal condition, while participation in physical labour is commonplace, the agricultural labourer's lot is anathema,. As has been observed: 'the Jats of Northern India... would accept the role of sharecroppers but not that of agricultural labourers, however destitute their condition' (Beteille, 1974a, p.84). To be a landless labourer and to labour directly for others as a means of survival is to be demeaned. Here is another important constituent of Charan Singh's 'social background', which was deeply entrenched in his 'ways, views and attitudes'.

Charan Singh would have grown up, too, with a hostility towards moneylenders, especially when they were large landlords.[3] Whitcombe, indeed, draws one's attention to 'the common phenomenon of the combination, in one person, of moneylender and grain dealer...[which] prevented the borrowing ryot, a similarly common phenomenon, from getting a fair price for his produce (Whitcombe, 1972, p.188). Rich peasants would experience this far less than other strata of the peasantry. Charan Singh, however, came from a rich peasantry which was not of the Russian *kulak* variety, inasmuch as it did not indulge significantly in moneylending or in trading. It was a rich peasantry, moreover, likely to be in conflict with usurer's and merchant's capital. These dislikes would ultimately yield attempted political action from Charan Singh.

In the Indian context, class antagonisms and class attitudes of the kind identified may be compounded and deepened by considerations of caste. The result may be a particularly potent mixture. Here we have a contentious issue, on which disagreement is considerable both generally and with respect to Charan Singh and those he represented. We note the following.

If, as was common in UP, in the late nineteenth and early twentieth centuries, the zamindar was also a Brahman, antagonism was given an extra edge. Whitcombe draws one's attention to the existence, a few years before Charan Singh's birth, in Aligarh, a district in UP not far from Meerut district, of Brahman zamindars 'whose holdings were com-

[3] On this, for the United Provinces up to the time of Charan Singh's birth, see Whitcombe, 1972, ch.4, particularly pp.163-4 and 167-8; and, for traders, pp.180-91, 195-6.

monly found in amongst collections of Jat villages...[and who] exploited the moneylending trade' (Whitcombe, 1972, p.276). It is not clear whether the zamindar in Kuchesar village was a Brahman. Certainly, however, it could be said of Charan Singh that he 'does hate the Brahmans and our Brahmanic social order' (Naik, 1979, p.31). Charan Singh did not conceal his hatred of Brahmans. Whatever its precise origins, he never lost that hatred.

Considerations of class and caste interpenetrate and commingle at the other end of the class spectrum. The vast bulk of landless labourers in northern India—and in other parts of India—at the turn of the century, as now, were untouchables (see Beteille, 1972, pp.414-6; Mahar, 1972, pp.18-9, 30; Mencher, 1972, pp.38-42, 46-7; Neale, 1972, p.57). If Jats nurse a hatred for Brahmans, they bear no less deep a contempt for untouchables.

Such are some of the influences which contributed to the cultural, emotional, intellectual and political formation of Charan Singh. Before considering first his political practice and then his intellectual/ideological formulations, it is useful to provide a brief sketch of his political career.

II. *Charan Singh's political practice*

Representative of rich and middle peasantry: before and after 1947

Charan Singh awaits the serious scholarly treatment which is his due. Among those few scholars who have given him attention, there does, at least, seem to be a consensus that he represented not all peasants but a section, or sections, of the peasantry. But which section or sections? That is not always sufficiently clear. Baxter tells us that he was a 'spokesman for the middle farmer and individual ownership' (Baxter, 1975, p.118). As we shall see, he was certainly a powerful advocate of peasant proprietorship. Quite what to make of the notion of 'middle farmer' is not, however, very clear. It does not capture the nature of those class interests represented by Charan Singh. Duncan, who has given him close attention, describes him as 'the most prominent spokesman and champion [in UP]...of the more prosperous sections of the peasantry' (Duncan, 1979, p.2). That takes one nearer to an accurate identification, but lacks precision. Brass, a knowledgeable and sympathetic observer, is somewhat more precise in identifying him as the 'leading spokesman for the interests of the middle-level and rich peasant proprietors' (Brass, 1980b, p.4). Brass's identification seems to me to be accurate in relation to the results of Charan Singh's political action. Both rich and middle peasants have been the beneficiaries, and Charan Singh received support from both strata. Of these, however, the rich peasantry have been the major gainers.

Charan Singh's significance, moreover, lies in the contribution he made to the emergence and consolidation of rich peasants as a class in north-west India. In so doing, he cleared some of the way for an agrarian capitalism from below in western UP We shall see that Charan Singh argued a neo-populist case against capitalism. That is not inconsistent with his reducing some of the barriers to agrarian capitalism: with his helping to unleash forces whose full power he underestimated and whose ultimate implications he disliked. Charan Singh's major achievements, on behalf of rich and middle peasants, were secured after 1947. Already, however, before Independence, he was finding his way, encountering the powerful obstacles constituted by the organised class power of existing dominant classes, and learning the necessary political skills.

An early target, 1938: 'the rapacity of the trader'

If one were to identify obstacles to the development of capitalism from below, among them would be the entrenched power of merchant's capital: of traders. In the UP in which Charan Singh grew up, and in which he was politically active in the 1930s, all strata of the peasantry confronted traders as a class hostile to their interests. Poor peasants, perhaps under powerful compulsions to market a 'distress surplus', were especially vulnerable (see Narain, 1961, pp.36-8, and Byres, 1974, pp.237-40, on the notion of a 'distress surplus'). But middle and rich peasants were by no means exempt from the power of traders. That power acted to constrain the capacity of rich peasants to accumulate.

Charan Singh's first attempted legislative act on behalf of his agrarian constituents had as its target traders. This was in 1938. He had published, in the *Hindustan Times*, in March and April of 1938, an article on 'Agricultural Marketing' (Singh, 1938). Later in that year he introduced into the UP Legislative Assembly, as a private member, an Agricultural Produce Markets Bill which sought 'to safeguard the interests of the producer against the rapacity of the trader' (Singh, 1986, p.2). He later recalled that his legislation 'did not envisage any control on price or quantity of the commodity sold or purchased, but only on malpractices indulged in by the cleverer of the two parties [that is, the trader in relation to the producer]' (loc.cit.). He made no mention of obstacles to capitalism, of course. That was not part of his agenda. But his description of the aims of his legislation could have been inspired by Adam Smith.

Nor did he single out particular strata of the peasantry. All agricultural producers, he implied, suffered, and all would benefit from action to curb the power of traders. In fact, those most likely to be able to take advantage of such action would undoubtedly have been rich peasants, with their greater holding power; and, to a lesser degree, middle peasants. Poor peasants, caught in a powerful web of exploitation, would have needed action on a far wider front, if they were to derive benefit.

In this, his initial legislative effort on behalf of 'peasants', he was not successful. But he was serving his political apprenticeship and acquiring rare expertise. He tells us that it was not until 1964 that such a bill was passed in UP (Singh, 1986, p.2).

There is some significance in Charan Singh's later memory of his unsuccessful bill and in his account of subsequent attempts to act on this front. He states that between 1938 and 1964, 'he was foiled...by representatives of vested interests who were entrenched in high places both in the Congress and its Government' (Singh, 1986, p.2). That, surely, cannot be in dispute. Traders to this day are powerfully organised and effectively represented. In 1938, and in the quarter century which followed, they were so *a fortiori*. Charan Singh describes the response to his efforts on this front of his old adversary in Congress, C.B. Gupta: who 'argued...that as the farmers had become rich and educated and could, therefore, hold their own against the traders...the Agricultural Produce Markets Bill was...unnecessary' (loc.cit.). Charan Singh, perfectly accurately, saw the fallacy in this. It might be true of some large 'farmers'. It was not, however, true of the mass of the peasantry. Nor could the power of traders be so lightly dismissed *vis-à-vis* even rich peasants, at that juncture.

A second target, 1939: moneylenders

Like merchant's capital, but an even greater degree, usurer's capital enters the pores of a pre-capitalist agriculture. Like merchant's capital it bears more heavily on the poor peasantry than on middle or rich peasants, but is significant, nevertheless, for rich peasants, where they are in its thrall, in placing a curb upon their ability to accumulate.

Charan Singh was prominent, in 1939, in formulating and introducing the Debt Redemption Bill. Again, he tells us of opposition from the 'moneylenders' lobby', and of his 'great disillusionment that some leading lights of the Congress Socialist Party, including, for example, Acharya Narendra Dev, who professed such great solicitude for peasants and workers from the public platform, took up a strong creditor attitude' (loc.cit.). This time he was successful, and he tells us that the bill 'brought great relief to the peasantry' (Singh, 1986, p.3). In practice, it must have been of particular advantage to rich and middle peasants. Poor peasants were too weak and too vulnerable to take advantage of its provisions.

Further action before 1947: focus upon landlordism

Other of his actions before 1947, which he draws to our attention, are worthy of note. They are none of them spectacular, or particularly successful. But they carry the seeds of future political action of considerable significance.

On 5 April 1939, he brought before the Executive Committee of the Congress Legislature Party a resolution calling for the reservation of a minimum of 50 per cent of public employment 'for the sons and dependants of the cultivators or agriculturists who formed the mass of our people' (Singh, 1986, p.2). That was not considered, since the party resigned from the legislature in October 1939. His persistence on behalf of agrarian interests was becoming obvious, however. In April 1939, he drafted a Land Utilisation Bill, whose aim was to 'transfer...the proprietary interest in agricultural holdings of UP to such of the tenants or actual tillers of the soil who chose to deposit an amount equivalent to ten times the annual rent in the Government treasury to the account of the landlord' (Singh, 1986, p.3). His war against the hated landlord class had begun. In June, he published a newspaper article (Singh, 1939), which contained the embryo of the land reform he would pursue relentlessly after Independence. That land reform had at its core the abolition of landlordism in UP By 1945, he had prepared a draft Congress Manifesto on Land and Agriculture, which provided for that abolition, and it was approved by the All-India Congress Working Committee at its meeting in Calcutta in December 1945 (Singh, 1986, pp.3-4).

Charan Singh was preparing himself politically and ideologically as the *kisan* champion. It was after 1947, however, that the fruits of that preparation ripened, and the middle and rich peasantry found in him a representative of power, political skill and effectiveness. It was the landlord class that would first feel the full impact.

The assault upon landlordism

(i) *Enactment and provisions of the Zamindari Abolition Act*

In UP, as in other parts of India, the *kisans*, and most notably the rich peasantry, on their own behalf, had for long waged a war against the landlord class. That war had started in the nineteenth century. The peasantry had made some gains, and the rich peasantry was emerging more clearly as a distinct class. Still, in 1947, landlords remained masters of the Indian countryside, in UP as elsewhere.

The most important battle in that war was about to be fought. The preliminary skirmishing had, in fact, started before 1947. Now the fighting began in deadly earnest. It was a long, drawn-out affair, brilliantly managed by Charan Singh. It was also decisive, at least on Charan Singh's home ground, western UP Charan Singh's role was crucial. A long-time opponent of landlordism, he designed the UP land reform legislation, whose aim was to strike a mortal blow at the landlord class: the Zamindari Abolition Act (Brass, 1980b, p.4; Duncan, 1979, p.2). That, in itself, was an achievement.

The Zamindari Abolition Act's gestation as legislation, quite apart from its implementation, was prolonged. The entrenched power of landlords ensured that. Daniel Thorner refers to 'the preliminaries to, and the stately legislative progress of, zamindari abolition' (Thorner, 1956, p.48). That, surely, is an accurate description. The legislative process—its preparation, which reached back to the late 1930s, and its successful conclusion—spread over more than a decade. Charan Singh, successful lawyer and practised politician, bided his time and saw the legislation through to a successful conclusion in terms of enactment. As Parliamentary Secretary of the UP Congress Government from 1946 to 1951, and as a powerful member of the State cabinet from 1951 to 1967, holding posts crucial in the sphere of agrarian relations, he masterminded the Act and took it to its final enacted form.

In a nutshell, the Act's progress and major provisions were as follows:

> The Zamindari Abolition Committee in Uttar Pradesh appointed in 1946 presented its report in 1948. The Bill based on that report was referred to a Select Committee and was passed by the State Legislature in 1950 and signed by the President in 1951. Its became effective only from July 1952... The Uttar Pradesh Zamindari Abolition and Land Reform Act, as enacted in 1950, and modified subsequently by amending Acts in 1952, 1954, 1956 and 1958 lays down the following main provisions:
>
> (i) All zamindari estates situated in Uttar Pradesh were transferred to and vested in the State free from all encumbrances. All rights, titles and interests of the intermediaries (all proprietors between the State and the tenant) passed to the State.
>
> (ii) Holdings of zamindars classified as *sir* and *khudkasht* land, not leased out to any occupancy tenant, were recognised as their personal property and did not vest in the State... All zamindars were vested with *Bhumidari* right in respect of their *sir* and *khudkasht* lands without any payment to the State. *Bhumidari* right meant the right to full proprietorship with the right to inherit, transfer, mortgage etc. (Government of India, 1976, p.92).

It now had to be implemented, in the teeth of fierce opposition.

(ii) *Reorganisation of the patwari system*

The *enactment* of agrarian legislation, in the face of the determined and organised opposition of powerful dominant classes, is, in all conscience, difficult enough. Its *implementation*, however, faces yet more demanding obstacles.

In this instance, a key figure was the village *patwari*: the keeper of the village records or, to describe him somewhat anachronistically, the village accountant (Thorner, 1956, p.47; Neale, 1962, pp.201, 315; Whitcombe, 1972, pp.20, 42-3, 236, 246-7; Duncan, 1979, p.2). There was, in UP, a veritable army of *patwaris*—some 27,000 of them (Singh, 1986, pp.42, 44, 47). The *patwari* had existed since long before the arrival of the British; he normally had three to four villages in his charge; and his function in keeping village maps, and records of boundary changes, of tenancies, of levels of rent and changes therein, and of who was in possession of what land, was critical (Neale, 1962, pp.201-2, citing Walsh, 1929, pp.149-51).

The *patwari* had for long had an apparently dual position. On the one hand, he was the servant of the landlord, who kept 'records of transactions between his master, the zamindar, and the cultivators—under his master's aegis—records, that is, of all claims, arrears, advances and debts in which the zamindar's interests were involved' (Whitcombe, 1972, pp.42-3). On the other, he had an allegiance to the state. We are told that 'precedent from time immemorial bequeathed him to Government as the keeper of the records, meaning those records which were in fact kept, being mostly zamindars' tax records' (Whitcombe, 1972, p.20). The British, as their power was consolidated, sought to establish his independence. They did not wish, however, to disturb the *patwari's* position in the 'village community' (Whitcombe, 1972, p.247). The *patwari's* low official salary and dependence upon the zamindar for payment (Whitcombe, 1972, pp.20, 250-1) constituted powerful reasons for his true allegiance never being in doubt. That was so in the late nineteenth century. It was still so in 1947.

The *patwari* was enmeshed in the local network of power, and subject to the overwhelming authority of the local dominant class. According to one writer, the *patwari* occupied what was 'usually [an] hereditary post' (Neale, 1962, p.315). That is no doubt so. Thorner, however, qualifies that description appropriately: to the effect that when the post fell vacant the landlords had the 'powers of nomination' of the successor (Thorner, 1956;47, citing the *Report of the UP Zamindari Abolition Committee*: Government of United Provinces, 1948, pp.176-7); the same point is made by Whitcombe (Whitcombe, 1972, p.43). That, of course, is not inconsistent with the power being, in fact, hereditary. But it serves to underline the landlord's long-standing coercive hold over the *patwari*. The *patwari* was the landlord's nominee and representative in the village. He would not lightly oppose him or undermine his position.

It was upon the *patwari's* records that the enforcement of land law depended (Neale, 1962, p.201). The *patwari* system was an established source of considerable discontent for the UP peasantry (Duncan, 1979, p.2), and not least for Charan Singh's essential constituents, the rich and middle peasants. It was the rising class, rich peasants, and, to a lesser extent, middle peasants, who found the activities of the *patwari* most irksome as they struggled to assert their rights, newly enshrined in legislation, and to secure dominance. Poor peasants and landless labourers were too weak to be capable of deriving substantial benefit from the Act. At this critical juncture, however, the Zamindari Abolition Act was threatening to founder on the rock of the *patwari* system.

The central issue was 'precisely which portions of a zamindar's holdings were to be classified as *sir* and *khudkasht* (Thorner, 1956, p.47). Various criteria were advanced by which one might judge whether or not land fell into this crucial category, but it was in this respect 'that the *patwari* could work the greatest mischief'. Upon his entries in the village records hinged the determination, in this regard, of the respective rights of cultivators and landlords; while the slow progress of the legislation 'gave to the *patwaris* of the UP an opportunity such as had never before occurred to them, even in their fondest dreams'. As Thorner drily observes: 'They did not fail to avail themselves of it'. Their behaviour, in this respect, was open and 'notorious' (Thorner, 1956, p.47).

At this point, Charan Singh stepped in decisively. He had become Congress Minister for Revenue and Agriculture in 1952, and was acutely aware of the activities of *patwaris* in falsifying village records. In 1953, they went too far 'when they struck for higher wages' (Thorner, 1956, p.48). Charan Singh acted. It was at his prompting that 'the UP Government incurred no popular displeasure by dismissing thousands of them at one stroke' (loc.cit.); and it was he who, at this juncture, 'was responsible for the reorganization of the *patwari*... system' (Duncan, 1979, p.2). That was a significant achievement.

Certainly 'the mischief which the *patwaris* perpetrated was not only great, it was also irreparable' (Thorner, 1956, p.48), inasmuch as they were responsible, through their falsification, for much land to which tenants should have acquired permanent rights remaining 'in the hands of the zamindar-turned-bhumidar' (loc.cit.). But, we note, it was *poor* peasants who were the major losers in this respect.

Moreover, it is true that those who succeeded the patwaris, the so-called *lekhpals*, 'the new title for village record-keepers and panchayat secretaries', were 'as venal as their predecessors...[and] as disliked and mistrusted as the old *patwaris*' (Neale, 1962, p.245). In that sense, 'the efforts to "clean up" the servants of the local governments failed' (loc.cit.). That, however, is to judge the outcome by an impossibly demanding criterion. Charan Singh's intervention served to push the implementation of the Act substantially the way of a sizeable number of rich and middle peasants, who were the undoubted beneficiaries of the UP land reform. If the *lekhpals* (or the *patwaris*, as they were still called, Neale, 1962, p.245) continued in the venal way of their predecessors, it was increasingly at the behest of rich peasants, who had previously found their activities irksome and constraining. Rich and middle peasants themselves would now use the *patwari* in their own interests.

The legislation, once it had been enacted and implemented, to the extent that it was implemented, did not abolish landlordism in UP (Brass, 1980a, pp.396-7), and especially not in its stronghold in eastern UP. Nor did it bestow advantage upon landless labourers, or poor peasants. It did, however, benefit considerably rich and middle peasants, particularly in western UP: Charan Singh's home territory, where they existed as a more powerful force than in the eastern part of the state (on the greater significance of rich and middle peasants in western UP see Clift, 1982). this was a notable accomplishment. It could not have taken place, of course, had there not been a long prior struggle against landlords, and had not the large landlords been, at least in post-1947 India, a weakened class and one on the defensive. Nevertheless, Charan Singh had proved himself to be a formidable adversary, on behalf of those he represented, in circumstances that were far from easy (for his own account, see Singh, 1986, pp.41-50).

Land consolidation and the rich and middle peasantry

At this period, too, Charan Singh was largely responsible for another important piece of legislation (Duncan, 1979, p.2), which smoothed the way for rich and middle peasants in particular, and especially the former (Brass, 1980a, p.398). This was the Uttar Pradesh Consolidation of Holdings Act of 1953, which represented 'a programme of land consolidation for individual peasant holdings' (Duncan, 1979, p.2).

Fragmentation of holdings, or the existence of operational holdings in more than one plot—often significantly more than one plot—was rife in UP, as in other parts of India. It is still pervasive in most of

Table: *Fragmentation of Holdings in Uttar Pradesh, 1954-5*

Size Group	Cost Accounting Sample			Survey Sample		
(acres)	Number of Fragments		Average size of fragments	Number of Fragments		Average size of fragments
	Per Farm	Per Acre		Per Farm	Per Acre	
Below 2.5	2.79	1.62	0.62	3.41	2.20	0.45
2.5 - 5.0	5.98	1.55	0.65	6.46	1.70	0.59
5.0-7.5	9.04	1.43	0.70	9.26	1.51	0.66
7.5-10.0	10.54	1.21	0.83	11.91	1.39	0.72
10.0-15.0	12.28	1.02	0.98	14.57	1.22	0.82
15.0-20.0	16.66	0.99	1.01	10.39	1.21	0.83
20.0-25.0	15.52	0.70	1.43	21.67	1.10	0.91
25.& above	19.59	0.61	1.65	24.36	0.70	1.43

Notes: (1) The region represented lies in western Uttar Pradesh: that is, the two districts of Meerut and Muzaffarnagar. (2) The study was conducted for the three agricultural years from June 1954 to May 1957. (3) The cost-accounting and survey methods were being tested, to see if the latter could yield as satisfactory results as the former. The cost-accounting method involved a prolonged stay by the fieldworker in the selected village and the intensive study of a small number of cultivators; while the survey method consisted of periodic visits by the investigator to gather data from a larger number of respondents. The cost accounting method was more expensive, but more reliable.

Source: Government of India, 1963, p.26.

India. Fragmented holdings existed for rich and middle peasants as for poor peasants. This is clearly shown for UP in Table 1, where figures for western UP (the two districts of Meerut and Muzaffarnagar) are given for 1954-57: operational holdings of up to five acres had between three and six fragments per holding; those from five to 15 acres, between nine and 15; and those with 15 acres and above, between 16 and 24. We take this is have been the situation, very crudely, for poor, middle and rich peasants, respectively.

Whatever the origins of fragmentation (and these remain to be examined properly) and whatever the attempts (not infrequent) to rationalise or justify its existence, there can be little doubt that fragmentation represented a significant barrier to the efficient working of the land: a barrier felt most keenly by rich peasants, especially those who were proto-capitalists, and who, perfectly accurately, saw consolidation as a necessary prerequisite for the most effective use of their land. Extensive fragmentation, on the scale indicated, represents a most powerful obstacle to accumulation in agriculture.[4] Charan Singh himself observed of the situation in the early 1950s that: 'consolidation of land-holdings is a condition precedent to all and any development in the countryside' (Singh, 1986, p.102).[5] He was hardly exaggerating. Later, from the mid 1960s, when the 'new technology' became available, the case for consolidation took on added force for the rich peasantry, and this was especially so in relation to mechanisation (Brass, (1980a, p.398), which was more or less non-existent in UP agriculture in the early 1950s. For the moment, the consolidation made possible by the Act of 1953 represented a significant step forward, and for that Charan Singh must take much of the credit.

It was a step that was taken far more confidently and more pervasively in western UP—where the rich and middle peasantry were an important force—and which had particular 'significance for the middle and larger landholders. That it should have started a process which, by the end of the Fourth Plan (that is, by 1971), 'had encompassed more than half the cultivated area of the state' was no mean achievement (Brass, 1980a, p.398).

It was an achievement secured elsewhere in India only in the Punjab and Haryana (Government of India, 1976, pp.184, 188, 233-4; on the Punjab see, for example Chadha, 1986, pp.66-8; Randhawa, 1974, pp.38-44). The Punjab, Haryana and western UP are the heartland of agrarian capitalism ('capitalism from below') in India—the regions of most rapid agricultural growth. It is no accident that they are also the

[4] For a discussion of aspects of fragmentation see Appendix B, p.301.

[5] For Charan Singh's own account of the 'disadvantages' of fragmentation see Singh (1986, pp.100-1). In short compass, he covers most of the issues identified in note 4.

areas where consolidation has progressed furthest.

Such changes do not take place without organised class action, and intervention by the state on behalf of emerging classes struggling for dominance. Opposition is likely to be deeply rooted and considerable. Thus, as one authority points out:

> Persons with vested interests like having possession in joint holdings or on common land of the village in excess of their share and enjoying adverse possession of land of others would resist the voluntary introduction of the consolidation scheme and, if introduced, they would retard its progress by opposing it at every stage. The experience has shown that differences do arise when land is actually parcelled out and men with conflicting interests from opposition groups and the dominating ones tend to harm the interests of the weaker groups and would attempt at making the scheme fail (Government of India, 1976, p.197).

Even among possible beneficiaries, there is natural reluctance to part with land seen as 'one's own'. There is, moreover, considerable suspicion that, where exchange of fragments is to take place, good land may be exchanged for bad.

Charan Singh directed the intervention that took place in UP, and which overcame much of the existing opposition, reluctance and suspicion.[6] He fought off a variety of opposition to the Act of 1953, both within Congress and outside (Singh, 1986, p.103). He tells us, further:

> of the various schemes and measures which [he]...had to handle in performance of his public duties, consolidation of holdings was the one most susceptible to corruption. The varying quality of land held by the various owners and the attachment to their plots that farmers develop everywhere, were the two main causes of corruption. These two factors gave ample opportunity to the consolidation staff to make illegal gains. But...Charan Singh kept a strict vigil on this aspect of the scheme. This fact was acknowledged by the Opposition on the floor of three Legislative Assembly in the year, 1958 (Singh, 1986, p.104).

There is no reason to doubt this account, at one level. His vigilance in seeing through consolidation is beyond dispute. Whether it can be seen as an example of his 'understanding of...[the] problems of the masses' (Singh, 1986, p.103) is another matter. That is in the nature of populist rhetoric. The major beneficiaries were the rich and middle peasantry of western UP.

Resistance to land taxation

In the 1960s, the rich peasantry emerged ever more strongly as a force to be reckoned with in north-west India. Charan Singh continued to rep-

[6] Included in the literature on consolidation in Uttar Pradesh, the following are enlightening: Agarwal, 1971; Elder, 1962; Sreeraman, 1966; Trivedi and Trivedi, 1973; Vajpeyi, 1964; Ladejinsky, 1965, pp.17, section 11.

resent their interests, along with those of middle peasants, forcefully, cleverly, and successfully. So far, our account has centred on struggle within the countryside. Now that struggle extended to a confrontation with urban interests and the central state. This was clearly so on two important fronts: taxation and food procurement.

A critical issue in the political economy of post-1947 India has been the inability of the Indian state to tax agriculture adequately, and in particular, within agriculture, rich peasants, along with the other dominant landed classes, most notably, landlords. It is an issue which has attracted considerable attention (for a brief account of the evidence up to the mid 1970s see Byres, 1979, pp.224-71). It is one which remains unresolved. As a recent authoritative commentator observes:

> the chronic resource difficulty of the states has a major source in their unwillingness to *tap the agricultural sector* to raise resources... Distributionally, benefits tend to accrue largely to the richer farmers (Chakravarty, 1987, p.49, emphasis in original).

The 'unwillingness' of the Indian states so to proceed might better be described as 'inability'; and that present inability derives from the able resistance led in the past by such as Charan Singh.

It has been pointed out that in 1962, when Congress Minister for Agriculture, 'he played an important part in the opposition to the increase in land taxation which Congress had attempted to introduce' (Duncan, 1979, p.2) (on the attempted land taxation see also Brass 1980a, pp.398 and 422; Brass, 1968, p.112; Brass, 1984, pp.309-12). More accurately, his part may be described as having been crucial.

In that year, Charan Singh tells us, retrospectively: 'the then [Congress] Chief Minister [of UP], Shri C.B. Gupta sought to increase...[land taxation] by 50 per cent' (Singh, 1986, p.151). Charan Singh moved quickly and decisively. He recalls the episode briefly, but pointedly, thus:

> Charan Singh opposed the move vehemently and provided the intellectual opposition to it in a long confidential note or memorandum submitted to the Chief Minister, dated 29 September 1962... The matter went up to the Planning Commission and Congress Leadership in New Delhi; ultimately the proposal was dropped (loc.cit.).

Charan Singh had won a signal victory, on behalf, especially, of the rich and middle peasantry.

The opposition to increased land taxation was successful both because of Charan Singh's skilful advocacy and because of adroit political manoeuvring. The case which he argued in a lengthy memorandum to C.B. Gupta (reproduced in detail in Singh, 1986, pp.151-94) is a clever mustering of evidence, a deployment of special pleading and, not least, an open political warning.

It includes a treatment of taxation figures and data relating to the intersectoral terms of trade, interpreted to show 'agriculture's' inherited and continuing disadvantage. The peasantry, it is held, is already taxed sufficiently, and could not bear a heavier burden of taxation. Moreover, it is argued, the land tax is a regressive tax, which bears hard upon the less well-off; and agricultural income tax would be preferable. It warns of the disincentive effects of such increased taxation and the consequent negative impact upon agricultural output. It suggests possibilities for raising extra revenue, other than increased taxation: for example, the abolition of prohibition of alcohol, which deprived the state of valuable revenue. It points to the special problems of agriculture, brought by its being subject to recurring natural disaster, and not least the indebtedness that this inevitably brings. It stresses the pervasiveness of rural poverty. It makes comparisons with other Indian states, in particular the Punjab, showing a more advantageous position for the peasantry than in UP

Charan Singh ignores the differentiation which existed in the UP countryside and the advantages accruing to rich and middle peasants; concentrating, instead, on the difficulties being experienced by poor peasants and landless labourers. His supposed favouring of an agricultural income tax fails to mention that if that had been a real possibility his opposition would have been no less vehement. He raises the spectre of what would later be termed 'urban bias' (see Lipton, 1977) and for a critique (Byres, 1979). It is an impressive piece of special pleading. These were ploys at which he was adept.

All the foregoing is persuasively argued. But it must have been the political reasoning, bluntly stated by Charan Singh in his memorandum, that was most convincing to Congress politicians. He pointed out:

> The cultivators in Uttar Pradesh form the largest percentage of any state in India, viz. 67.45 and constitute 77 per cent of the rural electorate, and not only 50 per cent as the sponsors of the Bill imagine (Singh, 1986, p.179).

Nothing could be clearer than that. He continued:

> The proposed increase in the land taxation will affect the mind of the peasantry unfavourably towards the Congress organization in as large a degree as the (Zamindari Abolition and Land Reforms Act had affected it favourably. Arguments here may not appear convincing to friends who hold the opposite view, but it cannot be disputed that the measure will affect the political fortunes of the Congress beyond repair... The enactment of this measure amounts to committing...political *hara-kiri* (Singh, 1986, pp.178-9).

He said menacingly, for the first time focusing upon his natural constituents: 'It is holders of more than 12.5 acres or so that enjoy political influence in the countryside. This influence, in future, will be exercised to our disadvantage (Singh, 1986, p.188). No more telling argument could have been made. The rest his fellow Congress politicians might ignore. This must have concentrated their minds wonderfully.

The increase was not introduced. A careful study published in 1973, which examined agricultural taxation in Uttar Pradesh up to 1966, concluded:

> there is...vast scope for additional taxation of the agricultural sector in this state. To this may be added that more than 50 per cent of the total taxable capacity lies with farmers having holdings above 20 acres (Dwivedi, 1973, p.148).

Charan Singh had been instrumental in fighting off an attempt to tap some of that taxable capacity and reach the better-off farmers. To this day, the rich peasantry of UP, and the prosperous capitalist farmers who have emerged from their ranks, escape effective direct taxation.

Food procurement

When, in 1967, Charan Singh took over as Chief Minister in the non-Congress coalition government, he faced the determination of the central government to impose a food procurement scheme upon him; and not only that, but one of a kind which was especially unwelcome. In the event, he did initiate such a scheme. He did so with his customary skill.

Again, the interests of rich peasants, and to a lesser degree middle peasants, were at stake. Now, however, it was more difficult to conceal representation of these under the cloak of action on behalf of the whole 'peasantry'. The rapidly proceeding process of social differentiation was yielding widening fissures within the UP peasantry, and especially in western UP Differential class interests appeared more nakedly than previously.

From the early 1950s India had relied increasingly on imports of food and on U.S. foreign aid to supply urban demand. Net imports as a percentage of net production rose steadily, and reached crisis proportions in 1965-66.[7] After record foodgrain production in 1964-65, the monsoons failed in 1965-66 and 1966-67. Output fell drastically, with devastating results. India became heavily dependent on the United States for food aid. The Indian state was determined both to raise dramatically the rate at which agricultural output was growing and to increase the quantum of domestic food surplus under its control. Both required immediate action. The former, which gave rise to the so-called 'green revolution

[7] Net imports as a percentage of net production had stood at 1.3 in 1953-54 and fallen to 0.8 in the following year. It then rose in each year until 1959-60, fell in 1960-61, and rose steadily thereafter, until it reached a crisis level of 16.3 in 1965-66 (Vyas and Bandyopadhyay, 1975, pp.A3, Table 1).

strategy', would take some time to bear fruit. The latter, our concern here, called for results at once. The central government was adamant.

The marketed surplus of Indian agriculture was in overwhelmingly private hands. Private traders purchased that surplus directly from producers and, through the wholesale trade, distributed it to urban and rural consumers. They attracted widespread opprobrium: as 'exploiters' of both the direct producer and of urban and rural consumers; as creators of artificial shortages and exacerbators of natural shortages; as the source of a powerful upward bias to agricultural prices. Such traders constituted, throughout India, a powerful class.

Acquisition of a food surplus, under the control of the central state, via action in the individual states, had for long been the subject of discussion. A variety of piecemeal action had been generated. A number of possibilities existed.

One solution was the nationalisation of the grain trade. The major recommendation of the Foodgrains Enquiry Committee of 1957 (the Mehta Committee) (Government of India, 1957) had been that the trade in foodgrains be progressively 'socialised', that is, taken out of the hands of private traders. The Indian state appeared to have embraced that goal. It faced the organised power of the All-India Foodgrain Dealers' Association, but it seemed to be attempting to move in that direction. A long prior history of efforts at procurement existed. Then, in January 1965, the Food Corporation of India had been established, to undertake the purchase, sale and distribution of foodgrains in India. At the same time, the Agricultural Prices Commission was founded, to advise on appropriate pricing policy.

If the state were, through the Corporation, to procure food, it could do so through compulsory levies or through competing directly with traders. If the former, it could, in principle, acquire a grain surplus either from the wholesale trade or directly from the producer. The latter had been attempted in the past, but the predominant emphasis was on striking at the wholesale trade and the generally detested speculative and 'hoarding' trader. By the mid 1960s, however, there had been a shift of view. Traders, and the wholesale trade, were not exempted from culpability. But attention now shifted from the trader as the only culprit. The previous policy, indeed, had yielded limited success: as was observed at the time, the available figures 'hardly indicate progress towards socialisation of the grain surplus' (Krishna, 1967, p.1697).[8] It was decided

[8] Over the 16 years 1951 to 1966, inclusive, the government managed to purchase only 2.4 per cent of total output of foodgrains in India, which represented a mere 8 per cent of the marketed surplus. In the second and third five-year plan periods (1956-61 and 1961-66) respectively, the government purchased a mere 1.1 and 1.8 per cent of the total output of foodgrains, or 3.5 and 6 per cent of the foodgrain marketed surplus. In 1965 and 1966, the figures were: in the former year, 4.6 per cent of output or 15.2 per cent of

that procurement at the wholesale market level could not now be effective, and that it was those producers with a large marketable surplus and holding capacity who had to be the direct target of procurement. It was against this background, in a situation of national crisis, that Charan Singh acted.[9]

There had, in fact, been pressure on the UP government to improve procurement operations since 1964. UP's dependence on central supplies of imported wheat meant that her government was susceptible to insistence that the state's procurement performance be improved. In March 1966, the Congress UP Food Minister gave notice of a procurement scheme involving a direct levy from wholesalers. The central government, intent on procurement directly from the producer, ensured that the scheme was abandoned. In the early months of 1967 a serious shortage of foodgrains had emerged. No scheme for procurement directly from the producer had been introduced in UP in 1966. Now, in March 1967, a newly-elected Congress state government announced that a levy on producers would be initiated.[10]

The Congress government fell on 1 April, and Charan Singh took over as Chief Minister. His concern of the 1930s with the exploitative activities of traders had long since gone. This was a reflection, no doubt, of the radically altered circumstances, in which rich peasants could now look after their own interests. Poor peasants, heavily indebted and without storage capacity, remained desperately weak and subject to what Charan Singh had earlier called 'the rapacity of the trader' (see Duncan 1979, p.4). Middle peasants, too, were vulnerable. But not so rich peasants With access to cheap government credit, and supplied with subsidised inputs, many of them 'had developed a storage capacity and an experience of the market which enabled them to engage in speculative practices' (Duncan, 1979, p.5).

Charan Singh faced a dilemma. He would have preferred no policy of procurement. He had, in recent years, stated his opposition to government interference. But the pressures upon him to adopt such a policy could not be resisted. He had no obvious concern to defend the interests of traders. If a procurement scheme were to be forced upon him he would have preferred one that looked to the wholesale trade. He had given voice to a 'preference for the free market and for freedom of the peasant to exploit market conditions to the best of his ability' (Duncan, 1979, p.7). That operation involved a levy on holdings of eight acres

---

the marketed surplus; in the latter, 5.5 per cent of output or 18.5 per cent of the marketed surplus. These figures are derived from Krishna (1967, pp.1697, 1705, 1706). They indicate clearly that anything approaching socialisation of the grain surplus had not been achieved.

[9] For some of the details in this paragraph, see Duncan, 1979, pp.4-5.

[10] Ibid., pp.6-7..

and above, progressively graded up to 25 acres, and the setting up of government purchasing centres throughout UP (loc.cit.). Great play was made of the fact that only holdings of more than eight acres were subject to procurement: that is, 'a minority of "well-to-do" *kisans*' (Duncan, 1979, p.8). That, on the face of it, was hardly calculated to please the rich peasantry. Other aspects of the scheme meant that it was a compromise which, in practice, was not disadvantageous to rich peasants.

From the very beginning, the scheme's operation was hedged round with a variety of concessions: for example, areas hit by drought were to be exempt; a reduction was allowed for those cultivators who had sown less than their full acreage; and there was a generous time limit for registering objections to the amount levied. In addition, 'the government...issued supplies of cement, sugar and galvanised iron sheets to be made available to peasants coming forward with their produce' (Duncan, 1979, p.8).

Charan Singh further emphasised two aspects of the scheme: first, that only a small fraction of any holding's marketable surplus was being procured compulsorily; and second, that the price paid of between Rs.80 and 85 per quintal was a high one (Duncan, 1979, pp.7-8). That is so, and, indeed, 'for many peasants, with a modest surplus to sell, the government purchasing centres provided far better terms of sale than those normally offered by traders in the foodgrains market' (Duncan, 1979, p.8).

In the short tun, Charan Singh, 'by controlling the terms of the implementation of the policy' (Duncan, 1979, p.8) was able both to argue that he was looking after the interests of 'the vast majority of the peasants in the state' (loc.cit.) and to placate rich peasants. More than that, the scheme actually steered resources the way of rich peasants.

In fact, he was initiating a scheme which, in the longer run, would be of great advantage to rich peasants. Over the next decade, the operation of a system of administered prices for agriculture, especially in areas like western UP through the medium of both minimum support prices and procurement prices, gave a significant upward bias to agricultural prices (Mitra, 1977, p.110-11). The procurement scheme introduced by Charan Singh, under pressure from the central government, created machinery and procedures which would be used to secure an outcome quite the opposite of that originally intended: a strengthened capacity to hold surpluses and an upward bias to prices.[11] It is doubtful

[11] As has been observed, each price twist 'in favour of farm products contributes to the holding power of surplus farmers and traders, enabling them to bid for still higher prices in the subsequent season. The fact that the tax burden, in particular the burden of direct taxes, is as good as negligible for the relatively affluent agriculturists, has further contributed to the progressive strengthening of their capability to hold back stocks; the policy

if Charan Singh intended such an outcome. On the contrary, he was using his political skills to defuse a potentially dangerous situation. He did that successfully. He also contributed to an outcome that would be of great, ultimate benefit to rich peasants.

The national state: the kisan *rally and the* kulak *budget*

The 1970s found Charan Singh on the national stage. He had been Minister of Home Affairs in the Janata government, in 1977-78, and been forced to resign. After his 'expulsion from the cabinet' (Ping, 1979a, p.53) he used his large peasant support—overwhelmingly from northern India, but with the strong possibility of its spreading to other parts of the country—as a sword of Damocles in the political struggle then being waged. In the seven months after his enforced resignation, in his national political manoeuvrings, he used the intimidating prospect of considerable peasant mobilisation, via a mass peasant rally, in his dealings with Morarji Desai and other of the Janata leaders from whom he was estranged.

In the 'carefully orchestrated' campaign leading up to the rally, Charan Singh's lieutenants suggested that as many as a *crore* (ten million) of *kisans* would participate in it (*Hindu*, 17 October 1978). Charan Singh himself, in a speech on 7 July 1978, 'told the audience—many among it were sturdy peasants from areas adjoining Delhi—that the proposed rally had evoked great enthusiasm among people in all parts of the country, from Tamil Nadu in the south, to Bengal and Orissa in the east' (*Hindu*, 8 July 1978). It is unlikely that anyone could have taken seriously the possibility of ten million peasants descending on Delhi. Equally, widespread national support for Charan Singh had obviously not materialised. Yet, there was an undeniable frisson of apprehension around at that time: a feeling of what might yet come to pass.

In the event, the *kisan* rally did take place, in Delhi, on 23 December 1978, Charan Singh's 76th birthday. The threatened *crore* of *kisans* did not foregather. But, according to one estimate, one million did, in 'the largest rally in the history of the capital' (Ping, 1979a, p.53). There were, it seems, no particularly large contingents from outside northern India. But addressing the rally, along with Charan Singh, as well as the Chief Ministers of the Punjab (P.S. Badal), UP (Ram Naresh Yadav), and Haryana (Devi Lal), was the Chief Minister of Bihar (Karpoori Thakur); while a message of support arrived from the Chief Minister of Karnataka (Devaraj Urs) (*Hindu*, 24 December 1978).

The *kisan* rally's slogan drew upon populist imagery, invoking the

---

of liberal monetary advances made to this section of the farming community...has imparted an additional bullishness, year after year to market prices for farm products, so that even a larger-sized crop has not led to a decline in prices, but its opposite' (Mitra, 1977, pp.110-11).

'urban bias' notion, of which Charan Singh had been a powerful exponent for many years (although he did not use that expression): 'Today, India's villages are the colony of the city' (Ping, 1979a, p.53). It was observed by one commentator, with some accuracy, that the rally 'symbolised the coming of age of the *kulak* class as a formidable political force' (Ping, 1979a, p.53). In that coming of age, Charan Singh had played an influential part. He was now the rich peasantry's leading political representative and major ideologue: a formidable adversary and skilled politician.

Urban intellectuals were puzzled as to what quite was to be made of him. There he was, posturing on the national stage, and threatening urban India with an army of peasants. Romesh Thapar, for example, observed that: 'Charan Singh is not a very reliable factor in any national assessment. He is too mercurial and given to unbalanced generalisation on economic and political theory' (Thapar, 1979, p.175). Thapar was inclined to take the then Minister for Industry, George Fernandes, more seriously. Charan Singh may, indeed, have struck those who were unfamiliar with his writing as 'mercurial' and 'unbalanced'. In fact, as we shall see in the next section, it is the consistency and the coherence of his arguments, stated over 40 years, that are remarkable. Charan Singh was no unstable rural buffoon.

About one thing Romesh Thapar was absolutely correct, however, and that was that 'Charan Singh [would] settle down to budget for his kisans' (Thapar, 1979, p.175). Perhaps that was not too difficult a prediction to get right.

Charan Singh buckled to the task and produced his budget in March 1979. One of his associates described that budget as having about it 'the breath of the people and the smell of the soil' (Ping, 1979c, p.76). Again, the populist imagery is significant. More realistically, the budget was reported in some parts of the Indian press as a 'kulak budget'. It merits that description. The duty on chemical fertilisers was cut by half; taxes on mechanical tillers, light diesel oil (for electric water pumps), plastic PVC pipes (for irrigation) were either reduced or abolished; the Agricultural Refinance and Development Corporation was exempted from income tax, with the intention that the saving would be passed on to borrowers in the shape of lower interest rates; commercial banks were given concessions with respect to rural lending; the subsidy on minor irrigation to larger farms was extended; outlays for dairy farms, rural electrification and grain storage facilities were raised (Ping, 1979c, p.76). These were all benefits which would accrue very substantially to the rich peasantry and the emerging capitalist farmers. It might be dressed up in populist garb. Its reality, however, was clear enough.

Charan Singh and the extremes of the class and caste spectrum

Before turning to a consideration of Charan Singh's intellectual practice, it is worth noting certain features of his politics which surfaced at the time of the *kisan* rally and thereafter. These relate to the manner in which class and caste interpenetrate.

I have noted above his hatred of 'Brahmans and the Brahmanic social order'. At the time he was prominent on the national political stage, a former colleague suggested that: 'His dislike of the leftists, I suspected, was partly due to the fact that a vast majority of them were Brahmans' (loc.cit.), while 'his hatred of Nehru and Indira Gandhi was partly due to the fact that they came from an aristocratic, Brahman, background' (Naik, 1979, p.32). Charan Singh did not conceal his hatred of Brahmans. Whatever its precise origins, he never lost that hatred.

Considerations of class and caste interpenetrate and commingle at the other end of the class spectrum. Charan Singh made much of his concern for the 'farming community' and for the 'rural poor'. Yet, as was observed at the time of the *kisan* rally, he 'apparently does not even recognise the existence of the largest segment of the rural poor—the landless agricultural labourer' (Anonymous, 1978, p.2053). That is, in one sense, true, inasmuch as landless labourers are simply not mentioned in his writing, his speeches, his political programmes. But, at another level, he assuredly did recognise their existence: as a large and growing class, antagonistic to the 'farming community' which he represented.

When pushed on landless labourers, and on very poor peasants (often sharecroppers), he sometimes lost his reticence. When asked, 'What about those with no land at all, the landless peasants?', the reply was chilling and uncompromising:

> Well, landless—if a man is landless he cannot be called a farmer, peasant. Then he's a labourer. If you want to give land to the labourer—well there is no land for giving to the labourer (Ping, 1979b, p.81).

That logic extended to the poor peasant, also. If there was no land to be 'given away', the poor peasant was no more likely to be favoured. The *Kisan Sammelan* which organised the *kisan* rally, and which represented Charan Singh's ideology, resolutely opposed any land redistribution at all (Ping, 1979a, p.55). In none of his activities was Charan Singh less mercurial or more uncompromising.

As already pointed out, the vast bulk of landless labourers are untouchables. When, in October 1978, Charan Singh was preparing for the *kisan* rally it was reported that

> two senior Haryana dissident leaders, Mr. Rizak Ram and Swami Agnivesh...disapproved of the way the rally was being organized. They said: 'If the kisans hold a rally to air their grievances against the Government, it is understandable. But the proposed kisan rally had assumed the colour of a fight between kisans and Harijans (*Hindu*, 17 October 1978).

That, of course was denied. It would have been disastrous to acknowledge openly such a reality.

At the *kisan* rally itself, Charan Singh is reported to have 'rebutted the allegation made against him and the kisan sammelan that they were "anti-Harijan"' (*Hindu*, loc.cit.). The rebuttal, as reported, was hardly strenuous or convincing: 'He said he had the same concern for the Harijans, if not more, than those who accused him of being "anti-Harijan"' (loc.cit.; for another 'denial', which is no more convincing see Naik, 1979, pp.31-21). The gloss he put on the rebuttal was pure mystification: 'Their problems—the age-old discrimination and poverty—were identical to those of the suffering farming community' (*Hindu*, 24 December 1978). What is left unsaid is that in Charan Singh's universe the vast majority of *Harijans* are not members of the 'farming community' at all. They are, for the most part, landless agricultural labourers, or very poor peasants (often grossly disadvantaged sharecroppers), whose interests are very much at variance with those of the 'farming community': especially rich peasants who hire agricultural labour and are hungry for more land, but also middle peasants.

The bitter antagonism of interests inherent in a compound of caste and class has explosive potential. Indeed, it is often suggested that Charan Singh's *Lok Dal* has been 'associate[d]...with various atrocities committed against the poor and landless [that is, *Harijans*] in the countryside' (Brass, 1984, p.330). Against this, it has been argued:

> Close scrutiny of incidents of alleged atrocities against the low castes [that is, *Harijans*], the poor and the landless in UP...does not indicate any clear pattern of association of such incidents with the middle castes [such as Jats] or the Lok Dal. Such incidents tend to be more complex and diverse in origin and are not even necessarily tied to class struggles in the countryside (Brass, 1984, p.330).

It would be foolish, indeed, to deny the complexity of such 'incidents'. That they are unrelated to the peculiarly potent mixture of caste and class which exists in contemporary India, or to influences unleashed by Charan Singh's brand of politics remains unproven, however. No assessment of Charan Singh can ignore the issue. Perhaps future, careful research will cast more searching light upon it.

III. *Charan Singh's intellectual practice*

An Indian variant of neo-populism

Those acquainted with currents of thought and of political practice that have run, often with great force, outside of India, will recognise that Charan Singh fits squarely into a long-established tradition of populist and neo-populist ideas. In this case, we encounter an Indian variant of neo-populism.

In a previous paper (Byres, 1979), I considered the ideas of Michael

Lipton (Lipton, 1977), which I categorised as a modern example, devised in his own very personal style by a western intellectual, of neo-populism. I there indicated the content of Lipton's ideas and defined what I mean by populism and neo-populism (others, of course, have different definitions, and still others may deny that anything that might usefully be described as populism or neo-populism even exists, but that is not my present concern). I will not repeat those definitions. What I would stress, however, is that so to place Charan Singh in the tradition of populism/neo-populism is more than a gratuitous observation of merely passing interest. It is a consideration which gives perspective to Charan Singh's writing and which helps place his ideological and political significance.

Charan Singh himself favoured and claimed kindred interest in Lipton's ideas and prescriptions. In his last substantial work he cites both Lipton's book and an earlier article (Lipton, 1968; Lipton, 1977) at length in support of his own position (Singh, 1981, p.164, 182, 186-8, 192, 224-5, 233, 512-3). There is a certain irony in this, inasmuch as Charan Singh had been expounding his arguments *in extenso*, with skill and with passion, for some 40 years before this. Indeed, I have already had occasion to note Charan Singh's long-standing espousal of a variant of the 'urban bias' notion. Lipton nowhere quotes Charan Singh. He might well have done so, in detail and with favour.

In fact, the genus of ideas to which Charan Singh's writing belongs, populism/neo-populism, has been most sharply defined, most powerfully formulated, and most influential, when it has grown spontaneously in indigenous soil: when it has been the specific response to particular national and/or local objective circumstances. Charan Singh's ideas fall precisely into that category. They are, in this respect and in others, to be compared with the populism and neo-populism that flourished in Russia in the second half of the nineteenth century and the first two decades of the twentieth century, and with the populism that flowered in the USA. in the last decade of the nineteenth century.

This tradition, then, to which Charan Singh belongs, has included—perhaps most significantly, in terms of coherence, power of formulation and influence—the great Russian populists (the *Narodnik* writers, who were Lenin's intellectual and ideological adversaries, in, for example, his *Development of Capitalism in Russia*) and the remarkable Russian neo-populist, Chayanov, with his formidable output of work and his large and prolific school, the Organisation and Production School. That particular variant was *sui generis*: a product fashioned by the individual genius of such as Chayanov, but unmistakably the response to Russian objective circumstances.

Equally, the North American variant was unambiguously the result of American objective circumstances. Far less powerful than the Russian form, of far shorter duration, unproductive of any comparable scholarly tradition, yet coherent enough, politically important and worthy of the closest attention: and not fully comprehensible outside of the modalities of rural America, and the particularities of American capitalism of that era.

Both the Russian and the American variants are populism/neo-populism in the high tradition, and each grew out of its own local circumstances: whatever strength it possessed deriving from the powerful tensions of those circumstances. So, too, with Charan Singh's ideas. They are recognisably in that high tradition, and have emerged from the soil of north-west India. Indeed, their power and their significance derive, in part, from this latter aspect. They are characteristically indigenous. Their roots lie deep in Charan Singh's native Uttar Pradesh. They are insistently specific, and all the more powerful for that. They are tied closely to Charan Singh's own class origins and own class allegiance, and emerged in actual and bitter political and class struggle. In Charan Singh, ideas/ideology and political practice are inextricably intertwined.

Indeed, in the variants noted, and in Charan Singh's case too, the relevant circumstances have been those of a burgeoning capitalism in its early phases: before it is necessarily obvious, or even likely, that it will finally sweep all before it. Capitalism, with its immanent contradictions, its disruptive (and potentially more disruptive) change, and its rich variety of local circumstance and differing trajectories or paths, is confronted. So it is that populism/neo-populism is likely to have a strongly anti-capitalist content: and anti-urban, too, since capitalism, in its undesirable manifestations, is likely to be identified with its apparent source, the city. So it is, too, that it may romanticise past relations in the countryside, invoking golden ages and agrarian idylls that never existed. This is the case even where, as with neo-populism, it serves the interests of those emerging classes which are likely, if capitalism develops adequately, to become fully capitalist (that is, rich peasants and some middle peasants).

Neo-populism has been, in other places at other times, and was, in Charan Singh's case, a carefully articulated ideology, whose roots lie in actual and strong class interests and class aspirations, as class formation has proceeded in the countryside: those of rich and middle peasants, before they have been transformed into capitalist farmers in the full sense. What it does, objectively, is to create space within which, under the banner of an undifferentiated and supposedly exploited countryside (exploited by exogenous influences), rich and middle peasants can appropriate whatever gains are going.

Neo-populism is an ideology which, in its concrete and differing manifestations, has been shaped in response to objective class-in-itself changes in the countryside, as yet incompletely worked out (and with no guarantee that they will be worked out completely); and which provides a rationale for class-for-itself action on behalf of those sections of the peasantry (or the 'farming community', as it is frequently described) which are clearly better-off. This is so in Charan Singh's case.

Elements of Charan Singh's ideological/analytical discourse

Aspects of Charan Singh's ideological/analytical discourse have already emerged: a version of 'urban bias'; stress on widespread rural poverty; a vision of an undifferentiated peasantry, upon which the forces perpetuating poverty bear equally and within which advantage is distributed evenly. These are clearly features of a neo-populist position. We may now deal with his discourse more systematically.

(i) *Anti-landlordism*

Charan Singh's hatred of the class of large and powerful landlords, or *zamindars*, ran deep, and he never faltered in his uncompromising and scathing denunciation of landlordism. Agricultural production did not depend upon the existence of the landlord class, 'who render no service to the land or the tenants' (Singh, 1947b, p.15). Rent was 'a wholly unnecessary payment', made to 'a class of persons who simply live upon the labour of others, who take absolutely no part in any enterprise and whose profession is idleness' (loc.cit). Landlordism 'reduces the toiling masses to the starkest poverty and degradation' (loc.cit.); it 'has cramped both men and crops...[and] has stood for economic inequality and political reaction' (Singh, 1947b, p.iii); it is 'positively injurious and mischievous' (Singh, 1947b, p.6). He argues a powerful and passionate case against landlordism (see Singh, 1947b, ch.i, especially pp.14-19).

In such circumstances, one might advocate the reform of tenancy: with the state intervening to ensure security of tenure; the abolition of undesirable tenancy forms, like sharecropping; and 'fair' rents. Charan Singh would have no truck with that. Landlordism had to go.

Charan Singh has always claimed Gandhi as his mentor (his 1978 book, *India's Economic Policy*, is subtitled *The Gandhian Blueprint*). There was one feature of Gandhi's thinking which might have embarrassed him, however. That was Gandhi's notion of 'trusteeship': the idea that landlordism need not be abolished, since landlords might be regarded as 'trustees' for those who are their tenants, and could be persuaded to behave reasonably. He quoted Louis Fischer's interview with Gandhi, in June 1942, and concluded: 'According to his [Gandhi's] theory, the trustees have misbehaved and are therefore liable to removal' (Singh, 1974b, p.164, citing Fischer, 1943, p.54).

The eradication of landlordism was necessary. But what was the ideal system of working the land? In another terminology (and one with which Charan Singh was perfectly familiar), the agrarian question might be resolved broadly either via an attempted socialist path, that is, collectivisation; or through capitalism, that is, the development of thoroughgoing capitalist agriculture. He was acutely aware of both of these possibilities, with a clarity that one rarely encounters among academic specialists on agriculture. He was, in the breadth of the possibilities he contemplated, an unusual intellectual. He provided a reasoned and vehement rejection of the former. He had more sympathy with a capitalist solution, but resisted the full-scale development of capitalism in the countryside. Rather, his proposals amounted to a third path: a path that was emphatically not socialist, but one that was not capitalist either (see Singh, 1978, p.117). His was the classic populist solution, based on a strong peasantry. Its fundamental prerequisite was peasant proprietorship.

(ii) *Peasant proprietorship*

From the outset of the exposition of his position, in his first major work, published in 1947, *Abolition of Zamindari: two alternatives* (Singh, 1947), pre-eminent in his prescriptions was 'the system of land tenure...pleaded by the well-known French social philosopher, Proudhon, a century ago, viz., peasant proprietorship, that is, ownership of the land by the man who actually tills it' (Singh, 1947b, p.22). That remained a constant in his discourse (see, for example, Singh, 1959, pp.v-vi, 1-3; Singh, 1964, pp.v-vi, 3-6; Singh, 1978, pp.11-12, 16, 25, 119; Singh, 1981, pp.122-3).

A detailed case is argued (Singh, 1947b, ch.v, pp.127-61), which we cannot pursue here. Prominent in that case, however, were two arguments, in which the apparent virtues of 'decentralisation' were extolled: a political and an economic one. Thus: 'just as decentralisation in the field of politics is our aim, so in the sphere of economic activities decentralisation happens to be the correct ideal' (Singh, 1947b, p.iv). That decentralisation, and its accompanying benefits, could be achieved only with peasant proprietorship.

First, argued Charan Singh: 'peasant proprietorship develops a democratic rural society' (Singh, 1947b, p.135). He was careful to stress that property rights should not be abused, and that 'if the owner or holder does not fulfil the social and economic duties incumbent upon property, he must be treated as a speculator or a defaulter and be divested' (Singh, 1947b, p.127). In view of his stress upon democracy, it was hardly reassuring, however, to find him, in 1947, noting approvingly that 'these principles were adopted by the German Nazi Party also in their official manifesto dated 6th March 1930, issued from Munich on the position of the Party with regard to the farming population and agriculture' (loc.cit.).

The second argument was the powerful incentive inherent in

proprietorship. Charan Singh does not actually cite Arthur Young, but there are clear echoes of Young's famous aphorism: 'The magic of *property* turns sand to gold'.[12] In Charan Singh's words: 'a peasant owner has been known to work harder and for longer hours than a tenant or a wage-labourer.... [T]he reward that he gets lies more in mental satisfaction and less in pecuniary grain' (Singh, 1947b, p.132). There is silence on those who, in the Indian countryside, could not be endowed with the full magic of property: poor peasants, who are insufficiently endowed with land; and landless labourers, who have no land at all.

In support of his advocacy of peasant proprietorship, he invokes the authority of India's past: another common populist trait. Thus, he said, 'panchayat of ancient memory shows us the way on the political or administrative side' (Singh, 1947b, p.iv). A mythical Indian past is invoked, in which the virtues of the ancient Hindu land system reigned supreme, a past when India 'was a country of small holders or peasant proprietors' (Singh, 1947b, p.9). Quotations from ancient texts, such as the *Artha-Shastra* of Kautilya are learnedly reproduced; references to the Indian 'village community', of apparent equals are made; and there is an evocation of a benevolent state intervening, it seems, only when the peasant proprietor failed to cultivate the land properly, or let it out to another (the principle, apparently, which the German National Socialist Party enshrined in its agrarian programme of 1930) (Singh, 1947b, pp.5-9). There is no word of the possible emergence of differentiation among this Arcadian brotherhood of independent peasant producers. Presumably, the benevolent state intervened to stop it. Presumably, too, the modern state might have to do likewise. The implicit theory of the state is nothing if not simplistic.

(iii) *The case against collectivisation and co-operative agriculture*

Charan Singh developed a detailed and passionate argument against collectivisation, the socialist solution to the agrarian question, and a deadly threat to his ideal of peasant proprietorship. Collectivisation was anathema.

In his first book, whose Preface is dated October 1946, socialism is rejected via detailed examination of the only example he had before him, that of the Soviet Union (Singh, 1947b, chs.ii, iii, iv, pp.23-126). He would refer often, in subsequent works, to the Soviet Union; and post-1949 China, too, attracted his attention. It is in that first book, however, that he develops his case against collectivisation, with care and in

[12] From Arthur Young's *Travels in France*, vol.1, cited approvingly by John Stuart Mill in his chapter 'Of Peasant Proprietors' (Mill, 1891, pp.169). In the same vein, Young wrote: 'Give a man the secure possession of a bleak rock, and he will turn it into a garden; give him a nine years lease of a garden, and he will convert it into a desert' (cited by Mill, loc.cit.). Charan Singh was squarely within that tradition.

detail. I cannot here attempt to convey the full scope of his argument. Certain features of it are, however, worthy of note.

His case is made partly via lucid and cogent exposition of Russian agrarian history in the years before and including collectivisation (Singh, 1947b, ch.ii, pp.23-50), in which, *inter alia*, Stolypin's land reform law of 1906, which attempted to introduce peasant proprietorship, is singled out for praise (pp.27-8). It was, said Charan Singh, Stolypin's great achievement that 'ten years after the initiation of the land reforms of 1906 and immediately before the Revolution, a class of relatively prosperous independent peasant farmers had been created' (p.27). This was the path that Russia should have continued along, and the one that India must follow.

He refers sympathetically to the rich peasantry. He comments, of the collectivisation period: 'those who a short time before had been called useful citizens and the foundation of Russian agriculture, were to their surprise and despair suddenly restigmatized as Kulaks' (pp.43-4). 'Kulak' was a word which he detested. In subsequent years, he would be driven to fury when it was used of himself or of those whom he represented (see Naik, 1979, p.31).

Charan Singh's thorough grasp of the possible paths away from poverty, via socialism and capitalism, is clear. His understanding of the importance of the town-country relationship, and of the significance of the inter-sectoral terms of trade emerges (see, for example, pp.41-2). He shows an acute awareness of the divisions inherent in Russian rural society: of the differentiation of the Russian peasantry into rich, middle and poor strata. He may have chosen, both here and in his later works, to ignore this with respect to India, but he was well aware of it in the context of Russia.

The actual rejection of collectivisation has several strands. We note the following. First, he stresses the absence of rights among workers on the collective: the 'erstwhile peasants...have even less rights in relation to their employer—the state—than [do workers or tenants in relation] to the private capitalist, millowner or landlord' (p.80); collectivisation deprives the peasant of those most cherished of freedoms, 'that freedom of conduct or the opportunity to live by one's own direction and individual initiative which are the pride and the peculiar characteristics of agriculture everywhere as practised hitherto' (p.88). Second, the mechanisation that is, apparently, an inevitable concomitant of collectivisation is thoroughly undesirable, in that it makes 'man a mere appendage of the machine' (p.87). Third, and very important, collectivisation in the Soviet Union has not raised the average yield of arable land (pp.99-103). There are several reasons for this, but pre-eminent among them is the simple fact that without material incentives people will not work (pp.107-8): a fact demonstrated in the Soviet Union by the great diversion of energy and resources to the private plot (pp.108-10).

The arguments are familiar ones. What is striking is the thoroughness and the cogency with which they are presented by Charan Singh. There is nowhere in the Indian literature that the case against collectivisation is better presented.

Later, that early attack upon collectivisation became a detailed assault upon co-operative agriculture (Singh, 1959; Singh, 1964). In the late 1950s, he saw the introduction of co-operative agriculture, in the sense of co-operative working of the fields rather than service co-operatives, as a true threat. He supported the latter, but opposed the former, with no less intensity than he did collectivisation. Indeed, co-operative agriculture was regarded at worst as synonymous with collectivisation, and at best as a prelude to it.

It would create a new class of intermediaries, as bad as the hated *zamindars*, and 'prepare the ground for authoritarian control' (Singh, 1964, p.vii); it would undermine and destroy peasant proprietorship; and reduce the farmer to a mere farm hand (Singh, 1964, p.vi). The increase in the size of the operational unit would lead, inexorably, to a fall in output per acre; and the disadvantage of size would be compounded several times over by widespread mechanisation and its attendant evils, of pervasive unemployment, and a heavy import bill for machinery, which India could ill afford (Singh, 1964, pp.vi-viii). The case against co-operatives, indeed, ushered in a new concern and included a new argument against mechanisation:

> It is not generally realised that with the replacement of the bullock by the tractor, farm-yard manure will become scarce and increasing use will be made of chemical fertilizers...the use of inorganic fertilizers reduces soil fertility, even though the immediate results may be striking. Organic manure, on the other hand, maintains soil fertility and makes the soil an inexhaustible source of food supply (Singh, 1964, p.viii).

This he argued in some detail.

A large amount of evidence was mustered in support of the various strands in his case against co-operative agriculture. He was an assiduous supplier of data. In fact, some of the arguments adduced by Charan Singh against collectivisation and against co-operative agriculture are arguments, too, against large-scale capitalist agriculture. What, then, of his attitude towards the development of capitalism in agriculture?

(iv) *The attitude towards capitalism*

Charan Singh, in true neo-populist style, displayed a less passionate, although firm, anti-capitalist stance, which was clearly stated in 1947. It would be repeated, in somewhat different form, in the 1950s and 1960s (Singh, 1959; Singh, 1964), in the 1970s (Singh, 1978), and in the 1980s (Singh, 1981). The early statement is of particular interest.

Several issues were raised.

First, there was the relationship of 'peasant proprietary' to capitalism, and here Charan Singh conducted a dialogue with Marxism. He confronted and rejected two arguments. On the one hand, there was the 'hackneyed objection...that this system envisages a pre-capitalist society out of which Capitalism has emerged, and that its establishment or re-establishment would mean turning back of the wheel of progress (Singh, 1947b, p.140). This he denied, arguing that 'small private property in land...instead of being a "fetter on production" is rather an encouragement to higher production' (Singh, 1947b, p.141). We have glimpsed some of his reasoning on this, in terms of incentives. This was bolstered by evidence to which he returned again and again in his various writings, on the superior productivity of small holdings. This I discuss briefly below.

On the other hand, he opposed the argument that peasant farming had a pronounced capitalist tendency, and would inevitably 'engender capitalism' and 'develop into a system of large farms' (Singh, 1947b, pp.151-2). He insisted resolutely that with the appropriate 'checks and balances', the system of peasant ownership need never so develop. The peasant proprietor was an ideal, non-capitalist being:

> To call the peasant a capitalist is a perversion of facts since the capitalist's job of accumulating capital was never performed by the peasant. A peasant proprietor is neither a capitalist nor a labourer... Although he may occasionally employ others, he is both his own master and his own servant... He does not exploit others, nor is he exploited by others; for he labours for himself and his children alone and he does not look for remuneration of his hard work at the farm in the way that a factory worker does.... He is not inspired by economic motives alone (Singh, 1947b, p.152).

He insisted that for India, peasant ownership was 'the ideal economy'. In 1947, it was 'the next step'. There was no reason why it should not be 'the final step' (Singh, 1947b, p.154). Capitalism, indeed, threatened peasant proprietorship, and the continued existence of the peasantry. But capitalism in agriculture was far from inevitable.

Capitalism brought with it a number of undesirable consequences, which could be avoided under peasant proprietorship. These included, indeed, widespread use of wage labour (which involved a loss of freedom, though less, perhaps, than under collectivisation) and highly undesirable mechanisation of agriculture. This argument concerning mechanisation, as developed by Charan Singh, straddles both socialist and capitalist economies (Singh, 1947b, pp.115-26), but is clearly seen as applicable to capitalist agriculture. It would drive people from the land and create devastating unemployment. His case against mechanisation in agriculture was developed and was to be repeated in his later books: tractorisation is uneconomical and does not increase yields per acre (Singh, 1964, pp.79-88, 108-14; Singh, 1978, pp.104-5; Singh, 1981, pp.119-20, 134-5). The argument was not always pursued in the context of consideration of capitalist agriculture. But that was the unspoken premise, which did become explicit on occasions (for example, Singh, 1964, p.vii; Singh, 1981, p.135).

What Charan Singh would never admit was that the peasant proprietorship which he advocated so strongly, and the political action which he took so effectively, might clear the ground for the development of a 'capitalism from below': a capitalism from within the ranks of the peasantry. Yet that is precisely what the outcome has been in his native western Uttar Pradesh, as well as in the Punjab and in Haryana. The rich peasants among his constituents, whose emergence and consolidation as a class he has helped greatly, have moved recognisably towards capitalism. They do accumulate; they do exploit the labour of others; they are clearly motivated by considerations of profit; and they have mechanised. He encountered, in his political practice from the early 1960s onwards, the powerful contradictions so engendered. In the last decade of his life, he must have been abundantly aware of this: surrounded, as he was in western UP, by tractors and other of the outer trappings of capitalist transformation. But barely a hint is explicit in his intellectual practice—his ideology.

(v) *Charan Singh and the inverse relationship*

We may briefly consider Charan Singh's use of a body of evidence which plays an important part in his discourse. This is the evidence which reveals the superior productivity (the greater output per acre) of small over large holdings: the famous inverse relationship, which, when it became known in India, gave rise to a prolonged, extensive and continuing debate among Indian economists, starting in 1962. He refers to that evidence throughout his writing, and from it he draws strong conclusions.

That celebrated debate among academic economists was initiated in 1962 by Amartya Sen, when he published an elegant article which offered an explanation of the inverse relationship (Sen, 1962). Sen would later comment that he 'had the unenviable role of doing the initial poking at what has turned out to be a beehive' (Sen, 1975, p.148). But Charan Singh had been poking around since at least 1947, although he disturbed no angry academic bees. What he did, however, was use the inverse relationship for very clear political purposes. He saw its ideological significance with great clarity and came back to it again and again. Charan Singh, in fact, drew attention to the likelihood of an inverse relationship before any evidence for India had become available, and was among the first to seize upon and consider the systematic data for India. He receives no credit for that in the Indian debate. His name appears nowhere in it. In turn, he himself makes no mention of the debate.

In 1947, Charan Singh cited an early book of David Mitrany, where Mitrany quotes data showing the inverse relationship in Swiss agriculture (Singh, 1947b, pp.95-6) citing Mitrany (1930-254): data gathered by Ernest Laur, the same Laur quoted by Chayanov, when he drew attention to the inverse relationship (Chayanov, 1966, p.236). Charan Singh also quoted data for Denmark and claimed the authority of a German professor writing in the 1920s (Singh, 1947b, p.96). What held in agriculture elsewhere, Charan Singh inferred, must hold in Indian agriculture.

In 1959, and again in 1964, he cites inverse relationship data extensively, in his argument against co-operative agriculture (Singh, 1959, ch.vi, pp.21-75; and Singh, 1964, ch.vi, pp.35-105, which was a second edition of the 1959 book).He gave figures for England, Denmark, Norway, Sweden, Switzerland, and the U.S.A. Now, however, at least by 1964, he had Indian data to cite, which clearly and systematically showed the inverse relationship: the Farm Management data for Madras, Punjab, West Bengal, Bombay, and his own state of Uttar Pradesh (Singh, 1964, pp.48-50: these were not available at the time when the 1959 book was written). It was those very data, indeed, which gave rise to the inverse relationship debate, which proceeded in complete isolation from Charan Singh. He returns to the inverse relationship in the 1970s (Singh, 1978, pp.14-6) and the 1980s (Singh, 1981, pp.115-9, 147).

A fascinating range of issues are raised, which we have no space to consider here. There are aspects of Charan Singh's use of the inverse relationship which are, however, worthy of mention: partly because they reveal a relatively sophisticated treatment by him of this matter; and partly because they highlight contradictions inherent in his ideological discourse, which he was scarcely able to contain. He used the inverse relationship, with some skill, in his case against collectives, co-operatives and capitalist agriculture. As he summed it up himself: 'given the same resource facilities, soil content and climate...a small farm produces, acre for acre, more than a large one, howsoever organised, whether co-operatively, collectively or on a capitalist basis' (Singh, 1981, p.115).

In pursuit of this, he considered, in a relatively sophisticated discussion, the reasons for the inverse relationship (Singh, 1959, pp.23-7; Singh, 1964, pp.38-43): a discussion, indeed, which anticipated many of the explanations given in the academic debate: and which suggested an explanation not unlike Sen's—though without Sen's elegance and rigour, of course. He confronted, in his 1947 book, the question of whether this might be an historically specific phenomenon, which could be swept away either by the development of capitalism or that of socialism (see, for example, Singh, 1947b, pp.96-7). His answer was that it is not. He may be quite wrong on that. I believe that he is. But in addressing that question he showed an awareness of the essential political economy issues at stake which is relatively rare in the academic debate on the inverse relationship. Moreover, the comparative framework which he consistently maintained on this suggested questions about the Indian inverse relationship result which the academic debate seldom grasped. It is, in many ways, a remarkable performance.

Consideration of the inverse relationship raised some serious political problems, however. Charan Singh consistently opposed radical redistributive land reform. But, did not the existence of the inverse relationship constitute strong evidence in favour of such redistribution? In principle, it did, of course. He was faced with a dilemma. The logic he was deploying could be used in a way harmful to the interests of his natural constituents, rich and middle peasants. There was a partial escape route open. How far down the line of holding size did the inverse logic—whatever that was—hold? If it operated down as far as one acre, or even less, should one not be contemplating redistribution in such units? He suggested, in fact, that beneath about 2.5 acres: 'Mother Earth refuses to yield to human coaxing any further—when there are no additional returns due to additional application of human labour' (Singh, 1981, p.119); (see also Singh, 1964, p.46, where the same words are reproduced).

But Charan Singh never allowed the full implications of the inverse relationship logic, as he represented it, to conflict with his class allegiance. The 2.5 acre lower limit was used to suggest a floor, and not an ideal ceiling target, as one might have expected. He suggested a ceiling of 27.5 acres per adult worker, and a floor of 2.5 acres (Singh, 1978, p.20; Singh, 1981, p.147). Rich and middle peasants were not to be adversely affected by any rash application of the inverse relationship logic.

(vi) *Further elements in brief*

There are many other elements in Charan Singh's discourse, which a full treatment would consider in detail: elements that bear the features of a neo-populist vision. There are also those that are conspicuous by their absence. We may briefly identify examples of both.

An almost Physiocratic insistence upon agricultural primacy, which sometimes borders on the mystical, recurs throughout his writing. Thus, he insisted, 'at the basis of all arts and industries lies agriculture, the art of producing raw materials from land, without which neither life nor civilization is possible'; so that 'the prosperity of a nation must largely, if not solely depend on the use that it makes of this free gift of nature, on the way that land is utilized; (Singh, 1947b, pp.3-4).

He did not deny the need for some form of industrial development: to that extent he was a neo-populist rather than a populist. But it had to be industry with a strong 'correlation to agriculture' (Singh, 1947b, p.iii), of low capital intensity, and capable of absorbing labour. Heavy industry, for a country like India, was 'economically wasteful' (Singh, 1981, p.398). Rather, what is called for is 'an economy in which hand-operated industries or handicrafts and cottage industries will predominate' (Singh, 1978, p.92). Heavy industry, and large-scale mechanised industries, may come 'in the course of time', but that stage 'will take a very long time to come', or to be justified (Singh, 1978, p.93). It will come, moreover, only after an agricultural revolution has taken place, which will create the necessary base: of an adequate 'surplus of food and raw materials' and a broadly-based 'demand for manufactured goods' (Singh, 1978, pp.92-3). For that to happen resources had to be directed towards agriculture, rather than be pumped out of it.

He opposed large-scale mechanisation in agriculture, as we have seen, and favoured an agriculture based on human and animal power. But he did not oppose all mechanisation. He advocated 'only small machines…as in Japan, which will supplement and not supplant human labour' (Singh, 1978, p.116). He was strongly in favour of new agricultural inputs, so long as they were predominantly bio-chemical—with the exception of artificial fertilisers, his opposition to which we have noted above (see, for example, Singh, 1964, p.434 et passim).

Anti-urban sentiments consistent with the rural idyll invoked abound: the evils of the city are deprecated and are to be avoided. He observes: 'City life has a charm, but in the long run it is fatal to a people' (Singh, 1947b, p.88).

An urban bias thesis runs through his writing. Part of his case against collectivisation was that 'it means correspondingly so much less liberty to the worker on the land and his subordination to the urban industrial worker' (Singh, 1947b, p.iv).That was an argument that could be extended to capitalist industrialisation and capitalist agriculture. Contemporary India is rife with an urban bias that pillages agriculture (see Singh, 1981, chs.6-8, pp.161-236, for his final detailed statement of existing urban bias—where the chapter headings are 'Capital Starvation of Agriculture', 'Exploitation of the Farmer', and 'Deprivation of the Village').

That great line of division in Indian society, caste, is discussed (see, for example, Singh, 1964, pp.329-34, 350-2; Singh, 1981, pp.535-48), and the reasonable position taken that it is an 'institution that is out of date' (Singh, 1964, p.329) and should be abolished. Caste, however, hardly features prominently in his published writing.

Throughout his work there is a consistent ignoring of any possible social differentiation, along class lines, that might exist among the Indian peasantry. That other line of deep division, class, is resolutely overlooked. On this, as on so much else, he and the great Russian neo-populist, Chayanov, see eye to eye. Chayanov was a distinguished academic: that common phenomenon, an ideologist *for* the rich and middle peasantry. Contemporary academia is full of them, although not all with Chayanov's gifts. Charan Singh was a consummate politician: and rare, indeed, an 'organic' intellectual *of* the rich and middle peasantry. Contemporary academia, it seems, has preferred to treat him with condescension.

Appendix A

In this essay frequent reference has been made to the division between rich, middle and poor peasants. Such a categorisation, I believe, is essential to any adequate understanding of the political economy of Charan Singh. These strata of the peasantry, or classes, need to be identified with great care, in concrete historical situations. Their precise characteristics will vary with time, place and circumstance, and according to the degree of capitalist penetration of the countryside. Thus, in 1902, in western UP, at the time of Charan Singh's birth, they had features and relationships *inter se* significantly different to those of 40 years later, in 1947, when Charan Singh was launched upon his career of representing 'agrarian interests'; while four decades further on still in 1987, when he died, qualitative change of a substantive kind had wrought yet greater differences.

With the foregoing in mind, one may cautiously hazard the following. (a) *Rich peasants* may be part-owners and part-tenants, whose land may be fragmented, and who obtain lower output per acre than either middle or poor peasants. They will, however, where they are tenants, be able to secure better tenancy terms than poor peasants. They will accumulate 'traditional' forms of capital to a certain extent; they will be market-oriented, marketing a genuine 'commercial' surplus; and they will hire wage labour, on balance, as net hirers-in of labour. They may have some vulnerability to usurer's capital (moneylenders) and merchant's capital (traders), although to nothing like the extent of poor peasants. (b) *Middle peasants* may also be part-owners/part-tenants, and may have fragmented operational holdings. They are less market-oriented than rich peasants, and may market a smaller proportion of their output than poor peasants (since they are not subject to the compulsions which induce a 'distress' surplus). Their operational holding will be smaller; and they employ only small amounts of labour at peak seasons, family labour being their predominant source of labour input. They may not be immune from the operations of moneylenders and traders, especially in circumstances of weather failure, price collapse, etc. (c) *Poor peasants* are far more likely to be tenants than either rich or middle peasants, and will be tenants to a greater degree, with a far greater likelihood of being sharecroppers. Their small, fragmented holdings will produce, because of the intense application of labour, higher output per acre than those of either of the other two strata; they are likely to market a 'distress' surplus; and, in order to survive, they will be forced to sell their labour to others (they will be het hirers-out of labour). They are especially vulnerable to the activities of moneylenders and traders. (On all of this see Byres, 1974, pp.232-7, and Byres, 1981, pp.420-4). Much of it has been touched upon in the course of the essay here.

Size of holding may be a useful, if imperfect, stratifying variable. Thus, I suggest that, crudely, in western Uttar Pradesh, in the early and mid 1950s, those with operational holdings of up to five acres were probably mostly poor peasants; those with between five and 15 acres were probably, for the most part, middle peasants; while those with 15 acres or above were probably rich peasants.

A further thorny issue arises. Rich peasants have to be distinguished from capitalist farmers. Great caution is necessary, but among the criteria by which one might identify the latter are the following. Rich peasants will tend to use elements of the productive forces which are not qualitatively different from other sections of the peasantry. A capitalist farmer, however, will be quite distinct in this respect. He will be in a wage relationship with free wage labour, extracting surplus value via that wage relation and re-investing it productively in agriculture on an increasing scale. That capital intensification will involve mechanisation of farm operations, and especially tractorisation. A capitalist farmer will be able to hold and control his markatable surplus. On some of the complexities of capitalist transformation in north-west India see Byres, 1972 and 1981.

Appendix B

So far as I know, the origins, development and regional variety of fragmentation in India have never been properly explored. A common explanation runs in terms of inheritance practices, or 'the system of private law and custom' (Government of India, 1976, p.185). Thus, the Report of the National Commission on Agriculture tells us: 'The sub-division of holdings is chiefly due to the law of inheritance, customary among Hindus and Muslims, which except where the Hindu joint family system is in operation, enjoins the succession to an immovable property by all the heirs. The custom of dividing private property amongst heirs is to give each heir a proportionate share in all good or bad lands and not the whole equivalent of his share in a compact block. In the result, the successive generations descending from a common ancestor inherited not only smaller and smaller shares of his land but also broken up into smaller and still smaller plots. The fragmentation refers to the manner in which the land held by an individual or undivided family is scattered throughout the village/area in plots separated by land in possession of others' (Government of India, 1976, p.193). There is a certain plausibility, not to say inexorability, about this: 'once the process of fragmentation begins, it is accentuated with each succeeding generation' (op.cit., p184). But the issue needs far closer and more careful investigation than it has received so far.

Such an explanation is, on its own, insufficient. As the National Commission Report suggests, 'excessive fragmentation is the result of the influence of the social structure that creates too great a demand for the limited area of land by population largely dependent on it' (op.cit., p.184). We have a second, necessary hypothesis: pressure of population on land. Presumably, there should be regional variation in degree and extent of fragmentation, on the basis of varied population pressure,.

The second hypothesis may be given greater precision. For example, it has been suggested that 'better irrigated regions may be subject to a higher degree of fragmentation and subdivision of farms due to the population pressure that generally exists in such regions' (Bharadwaj, 1974, p.42).

Such explanations ignore the relations of production: assuming ownership of the land and a common set of influences throughout the peasantry. But what of those large number of peasants who are tenants? Obviously, if those who rent in land also own some land, the operational holding will be fragmented. Not only that, but, it has been suggested, where a big landlord rents out irrigated land, say to a sharecropper, he may prefer to parcel it out to very small tenants, in very small plots, in order 'to maximise his returns (as a share of total *gross* output on his entire land) (Bharadwaj, 1974, p.42). This is because 'while his bargaining position remains strong *vis-à-vis* the petty tenant, the latter may also have to resort to very intensive cultivation in order to eke a subsistence out of the small plot leased to him' (loc.cit.). The matter awaits adequate investigation. For a brief and inconclusive discussion in the context of UP see Neale (1962, pp.261-2).

Neale, with UP as his focus, rehearses some of the attempts so to locate advantage in fragmentation, telling us that 'the process is not without benefits, however meagre' (Neale, 1962, p.154). He locates some of those supposed 'benefits', although he does come out strongly against fragmentation. Thus he cites 'witnesses before the Royal Commission on Indian Agriculture [of 1926]...[who] were sometimes inclined to minimise the evils of fragmentation by mentioning security resulting from the variety of crops a cultivator could grow on different plots' (loc.cit.). This position Neale rejects, using the argument of the UP Banking Enquiry Committee (whose report was published in 1930), which, he says, 'pointed out that a single good crop should keep the cultivator fed, and cited a case where consolidation resulted in almost all the land being planted to rice while the tenantry was remarkably well-to-do' (loc.cit.). Another argument dismissed by the Banking Enquiry Committee, according to Neale, was that 'fragmentation provided some protection against the random incident of hail'. The committee felt that 'the "preventive" was worse than the disease' (loc.cit.).

The Banking Enquiry Committee, however, did think 'that there was "much force" to the argument that consolidation would require separate homesteads and thus separate drinking wells and separate threshing floors and would involve increased risk of dacoity and burglary'. This, too, Neale dismissed, quite rightly, on the grounds that 'it is a little hard to see why, for villages and their fields together averaging about a square mile, so there could not be any overriding reason to break up the village site' (loc.cit.).

Other writers, at other times and for other places, have also attempted to give rational justification for fragmentation: in terms of growing varieties which mature at different times, and so saving on labour; of a capacity to grow crops on both high and low ground (where high and low ground exist), and so securing risk dispersal, where, say, flooding is endemic; and so on (see Muscat (1966, pp.148-9) on Thailand. It has also been argued, against consolidation, where irrigation is important, that the cost of creating complex new waterways may be prohibitively large. But none of this is at all convincing: especially when one confronts the needs of a capitalist or proto-capitalist agriculture. It is possible, apparently, to find rationality in almost anything. The inherent, powerful disadvantages of fragmentation were discussed in the famous United Nations report, *Land Reform: Defects in Agrarian Structure as Obstacles to Economic Development*, when it wrote of 'the evils of fragmentation' (United Nations, 1951, p.11) summed up a whole tradition of thought on the subject. One finds it echoed, for example, in the Indian Farm Management Repoprts, such as the one on UP (Government of India, 1963, p.26), and in writers like Neale (1962, p.154). In both cases, the same phrase is used. For useful brief statements of the inefficiencies associated with fragmentation see Government of India, 1976, p.195 (for India); Neale, 1962, pp.152, 154, 262 (in the UP context); and Parsons, Penn and Raup (eds.), 1963, p.206, more generally.

The United Nations Report went on (loc.cit.) to refer to the 'waste of time and effort, the impossibility of rational cultivation' which fragmentation entailed. The National Commission on Agriculture points to the impossibility of 'full and proper land utilization', for a variety of reasons: 'useless expenditure and waste of time in moving labour, cattle, seed, manure and irrigation water from one plot to another, and in bringing the harvested crop to a single threshing floor'; the associated difficulties of 'supervision of farm operations'; increased 'expenses on irrigation, farming, drainage etc.'; 'loss of land on boundaries' (Government of India, 1976, p.195). In addition: 'access to scattered fields becomes difficult during the crop season and leads to disputes and tensions over trespass etc.' (loc.cit.). Neale (loc.cit.) also touches upon some of this.

Such disadvantages apply to all strata of the peasantry who work fragmented land. For rich peasants, who may be proto-capitalists, fragmentation is likely to constitute a significant barrier to accumulation. Development of the productive forces faces a powerful constraint: whether that development takes a purely bio-chemical or a mechanised form (that is, on the one hand, for example, new seeds, the application of inorganic fertilisers, new forms of non-mechanised irrigation; on the other, tractors, tube-wells, etc.). Fragmentation poses especially difficult problems for mechanisation.

References and further reading

Agarwal, S.K. (1971), *Economics of Land Consolidation in India* (Delhi).

Alavi, Hamza (1973), 'Peasant classes and primordial loyalties', *Journal of Peasant Studies* 1, 1 (October).

Anonymous (1978), 'The great disorder', *Economic and Political Weekly* XIII, 51 and 52 (23 and 30 December).

Baxter, Craig (1975), 'The rise and fall of the BKD in Uttar Pradesh', in Myron Weiner and John Osgood Fields (eds.), *Electoral Politics in the Indian States*, vol. IV (Delhi).

Beteille, Andre (1972), 'Pollution and poverty' in J. Michael Mahar (ed.), *The Untouchables in Contemporary India* (Tucson, AR).

—, (1974a), *Studies in Agriculture* (Delhi).

—, (1974b), *Six Essays in Comparative Sociology* (Delhi).

Bhambri, C.P.(1980), *The Janata Party: a profile* (Delhi).

Bharadwaj, Krishna (1974), *Production Conditions in Indian Agriculture. A study based on farm management surveys* (London).

Bose, Ajoy (1987), 'Champion of India's peasants is dead', *Guardian* (30 May).

Bottomore, Tom (ed.) (1983), with an editorial board of Laurence Harris, V.G. Kiernan and Ralph Miliband, *A Dictionary of Marxist Thought* (Oxford).

Brass, Paul R. (1965), *Factional Politics in an Indian State: the Congress party in Uttar Pradesh* (Berkeley and Los Angeles, CA).

—, (1968), 'Uttar Pradesh' in Weiner (ed.) (1968).

—, (1980a), 'The politicisation of the peasantry in a North Indian state: Part I', *Journal of Peasant Studies*, 8, 4 (July).

—, (1980b), 'The politicisation of the peasantry in a North Indian state: Part II', *Journal of Peasant Studies*, 8, 1 (October).

—, (1984), *Caste, Faction and Party in Indian Politics*, vol. 1, *Faction and Party* (Delhi).

Byres, T.J. (1972), 'The dialectic of India's Green Revolution', *South Asian Review* 5, 2 (January).

—, (1974), 'Land reform, industrialization and the marketed surplus in India: an essay on the power of rural bias', in David Lehmann (ed.), *Agrarian Reform and Agrarian Reformism* (London).

—, (1979), 'Of neo-populist pipe-dreams: Daedalus in the Third World and the myth of urban bias', *Journal of Peasant Studies* 6, 2 (January).

—, (1981), 'The new technology, class formation and class action in the Indian countryside', *Journal of Peasant Studies* 8, 4 (July).

Chadha, G.K. (1986), *The State and Rural Economic Transformation: the case of Punjab, 1950-85* (New Delhi).

Chakravarty, Sukhamoy (1987), *Development Planning: the Indian experience* (Oxford).

Chaudhuri, Pramit (ed.) (1972), *Readings in Indian Agricultural Development* (London).

Chayanov, A.V. (1966), edited by Daniel Thorner, Basile Kerblay and R.E.F. Smith, *The Theory of Peasant Economy* (Homewood, IL).

Clift, F. Charles (1982), 'The Evolution of Rural Disparities in Agricultural Development in Uttar Pradesh, India', unpublished D.Phil thesis, University of Sussex.

Duncan, Ian (1979), 'The politics of foodgrain procurement: a case study from Northern India', paper presented to the Peasants Seminar of the Centre of International and Area Studies, University of London, 29 June (pp.78-9, 118).

Dwivedi, D.N. (1973), *Problems and Prospects of Agricultural Taxation in*

Uttar Pradesh (New Delhi).
Elder, Joseph (1962), 'Land consolidation in an Indian village: a case study of the Consolidation of Holdings Act in Uttar Pradesh', *Economic Development and Cultural Change* XI, 1 (October).
Fischer, Louis (1943), *A Week with Gandhi* (London).
Government of India, Ministry of Food and Agriculture (Department of Food), (1957), *Report of the Foodgrains Enquiry Committee* (New Delhi).
—, Ministry of Food and Agriculture (1963), *Studies in the Economics of Farm Management in UP Combined Report for the Years 1954-55 and 1956-57* (Delhi).
—, Ministry of Agriculture and Irrigation (1976), *Report of the National Commission of Agriculture*, Part XV, *Agrarian Reforms* (Delhi).
Government of United Provinces (1948), *Report of the United Provinces Zamindari Abolition Committee*, vol.1 (Allahabad).
Gramsci, Antonio (1971), *Selections from the Prison Notebooks*, edited and translated by Quintin Hoare and Geoffrey Nowell Smith (London).
India's Who's Who, 1971 (New Delhi).
Kiernan, V.G. 'Intellectuals' in Bottomore (ed.) (1983).
Krishna, Raj (1967), 'Government operations in foodgrains', *Economic and Political Weekly* II, 37 (September). This is reprinted in Chaudhuri (ed.) (1972).
Ladejinsky, Wolf (1965), 'The Ladejinsky Report. Tenurial conditions and the package programme. Part III (Ludhiana and Aligarh)', *Mainstream* II, 30 (27 March).
Lehman, David (ed.) (1974), *Agrarian Reform and Agrarian Reformism* (London).
Lipton, Michael (1968), 'Strategy for agriculture: urban bias and rural planning' in Streeten and Lipton (eds.) (1968).
—, (1977), *Why Poor People Stay Poor: a study of urban bias in world development* (London).
Mahar, J. Michael (1972), 'Agents of dharma in a North Indian village' in Mahar (ed.) (1972).
—, (ed.) (1972), *The Untouchables in Contemporary India* (Tucson, AR).
Marx (1961), Karl, *Capital*, vol.1 (Moscow).
Mencher, Joan P. (1972), 'Continuity and change in an ex-Untouchable community of South India', in Mahar (ed.) (1972).
Mill, John Stuart (1891), *Principles of Political Economy* (London).
Mitra, Ashok (1977), *Terms of Trade and Class Relations* (London).
Mitrany, David (1930), *The Land and the Peasant in Rumania* (New Haven, CT. and London).
Muscat, Robert J. (1966), *Development Strategy in Thailand. A study of economic growth* (New York).
Naik, J.A. (1979), *From Total Revolution to Total Failure* (New Delhi).
Narain, Dharm (1961), *Distribution of the Marketed Surplus of Agricultural Produce by Size-Level of Holding in India, 1950-51* (Bombay).
Neale, Walter C. (1962), *Economic Change in Rural India: land tenure and reform in Uttar Pradesh, 1800-1955* (New Haven, CT. and London).
—, (1972), 'The marginal laborer and the harijan in rural India', in Mahar

(ed.) (1972).
Parsons, Kenneth H., Raymond J. Penn and Philip M. Raup (eds.) (1963), *Land Tenure* (Madison, WI).
Parthasarathy, G. (1978), 'Proletarianisation in Indian agriculture: rapporteur's paper', *Indian Journal of Labour Economics* XXI, 1 and 2, April-July.
Ping, Ho Kwon (1979a), 'Revolt of the landless peasants', *Far Eastern Economic Review* 103, 2 (12 January).
—, (1979b), 'The rise of the aging sun', *Far Eastern Economic Review* 103, 11 (23 March).
—, (1979c), 'Singh takes the first step to capitalism', *Far Eastern Economic Review* 103, 12 (12 March).
Randhawa, M.S.(1974), *Green Revolution: a case study of Punjab* (Delhi).
Sen, Amartya (1962), 'An aspect of Indian agriculture', *Economic Weekly*, Annual Number, 14, 4-5-6, February.
—, (1975), *Employment, Technology and Development* (London).
Shils, Edward (1968), 'Intellectuals' in Sills (ed.) (1968, vol.8).
Sills, David L. (ed.) (1968), *International Encyclopaedia of the Social Sciences* (17 volumes) (New York and London).
Singh, Charan (1938), 'Agricultural marketing', *Hindustan Times*, Delhi (31 March and 1 April).
—, (1939), 'Peasant proprietorship or land to the worker', *National Herald*, Lucknow (13 June).
—, (1947a), *How to Abolish Zamindari: which alternative system to adopt* (Allahabad).
—, (1947b), *Abolition of Zamindari: two alternatives* (Allahabad).
—, (1949), *Abolition of Zamindari in UP Critics Answered* (Allahabad). Originally published with the same title in the *National Herald*, Lucknow, on 16 August 1949, this is reprinted as 'Criticism answered' in Singh (1986).
—, (1956), *Whither Co-operative Farming?* (Allahabad).
—, (1958), *Agrarian Revolution in Uttar Pradesh* (Lucknow).
—, (1959), *Joint Farming X-Rayed: the problem and its solution* (Allahabad). Later published in a new, revised edition; see Singh (1964).
—, (1964), *India's Poverty and Its Solution* (London). See Singh (1959).
—, (1970), *The Story of New Congress-BKD Relations: how new Congress broke the UP coalition* (Lucknow).
—, (1981), *Economic Policy: the Gandhian blueprint* (New Delhi).
—, (1981), *Economic Nighmare of India: its cause and cure* (New Delhi).
—, (1984), *Shishtachar* (Delhi).
—, (1986), *Land Reforms in UP and the Kulaks* (New Delhi), as told to an anonymous author by Charan Singh.
Sreeraman, N. (1966), 'A note on consolidation of holdings in Uttar Pradesh—a field survey', *Indian Journal of Economics* 46.
Streeten, Paul and Michael Lipton (eds.) (1968), *The Crisis of Indian Planning. Economic policy in the 1960s* (London).
Thapar, Romesh (1979), 'Charan-ing the Finance Ministry', *Economic and Political Weekly* XIV, 5 and 6 (3 and 10 February).
Thorner, Daniel (1956), *The Agrarian Prospect in India* (Delhi). A second

edition, with a new introduction, was published in 1976 and reprinted in 1981 (New Delhi).

Trivedi, K.D. and Kamala Trivedi (1973), 'Consolidation of holdings in Uttar Pradesh: a study of policy implementation', *Journal of Administration Overseas* 12.

United Nations (1951), *Land Reform: defects in agrarian structure as obstacles to economic development* (New York).

Vajpeyi, Dhirendra Kumar (1964), 'Some problems in land consolidation work in Uttar Pradesh', *Public Administration* 2.

Vyas, V.S. and S.C. Bandyopadhyay (1975), 'National food policy in the framework of a national food budget', *Economic and Political Weekly* X, 13 (29 March).

Walsh, Sir Cecil (1929), *Indian Village Crimes* (London).

Weiner, Myron (ed.) (1968), *State Politics in India* (Princeton, NJ).

—, and John Osgood Fields (eds.) (1975), *Electoral Politics in the Indian States*, vol.IV (Delhi).

Whitcombe, E. (1972), *Agrarian Conditions in Northern India*. Vol.1. *The United Provinces under British rule* (Berkeley, CA).

Williams, Raymond (1976), *Keywords: a vocabulary of culture and society* (London).

INDEX

Agrarian relations, 205, 208, 223.
Ahmedabad, 134, 255.
Akbar, 19, 46, 139.
All-India Kisan Sabha, 259.
Allahabad, 66, 230.
Ambedkar, B.R., 260.
Amritsar, 72.
Andhra Pradesh, 28, 30, 254.
Animists, 10.
Arabic, 13-14, 17, 27, 78, 89, 166, 174-5.
Artha Shastra, 39, 292.
Aryans, 10-12.
Arya Samaj, 71, 250.
Asiatic Society of Bengal, 140.
Asoka, 16-17.
Aurangzeb, 19, 170.
Awadh, 190.

Bangladesh, viii, x, 5-6, 10, 14, 25-28, 31, 67, 165.
Baroda, 132, 134.
Benares, 66, 94, 230, 239-40.
Bengali, 6, 8, 13-14, 19, 23-28, 32, 41, 46, 64, 67, 105-6, 116, 171, 203, 206-8, 210-13, 216, 218, 220, 226, 228-31, 234-5, 237-9, 249-50, 253, 255, 258, 266, 284, 297.
Bernier, E., 2.
Besant, Annie, 254.
Bhutan, viii, 6.
Bihar, 8, 16, 202, 204-5, 212, 218, 229, 254, 258, 284.
Bombay, 21, 68, 97, 132, 134, 193, 198, 234-5, 238-9, 242, 247-8, 255, 261, 297.
Bose, S.C., 259.
Boycott, 253, 255.
Brahmans, 12-13, 23, 46, 49, 57-8, 189, 193-8, 230, 232, 239, 267-8, 286.
Braj, 65-6, 69.
British rule, x, 126, 166, 179, 185, 214-5, 219, 221, 238, 248-9, 253.
Buddhism, Buddhist, viii, 10, 15, 17, 38, 41, 64, 154.
Burma, 7, 96.

Calcutta, 21, 24, 26-7, 79, 68, 178, 211, 226-7, 239-40, 246-8, 253-4, 271.
Caste, 12-14, 18, 29-30, 150-2, 162, 167, 186, 194-6, 214, 221-2, 228, 230, 234, 236-7, 239-40, 265-8, 286-7, 299.
Chisholm, R.F., 123, 132, 134.
Cholera, 224, 227.
Christianity, viii, 3, 10, 13-14, 18, 110, 114, 119, 237.
Civil disobedience, 256, 258-9.
Colonial state, 166-9, 177-8, 181.
Commonwealth, 22.
Communalism, vii, 2, 5-6, 18-19, 22-3, 28, 170, 247, 258, 260.
Congress Socialist Party, 259, 270.

Dacca, 27, 232.
Datta, Madhusudan, 104ff.
Daniell, Thomas and William, 120-6.
Deccan, 7-8, 14-15, 17, 19, 248.
Delhi (New), 13, 28, 66, 82, 229, 245-6, 262, 284.
Democracy, 6, 21-2, 28, 245-7, 259-60, 262-3, 291.
Dev, Acharya Narendra , 270.

Dharma, 38-41, 53, 150-1, 161-2.
Dharmaśātṛa, Dharma Sastra, 39, 53, 58, 151, 171.
Dutt, R.C., 249.

East India Company, 92, 166, 187-8, 217, 232.
'Extremists', 251, 253-4.

CENTRE OF SOUTH ASIAN STUDIES, SCHOOL OF ORIENTAL AND AFRICAN STUDIES, UNIVERSITY OF LONDON

COLLECTED PAPERS ON SOUTH ASIA

1. Peter Robb and David Taylor (eds), *Rule Protest Identity: aspects of modern South Asia*
2. David Taylor and Malcolm Yapp (eds), *Political Identity in South Asia*
3. Kenneth Ballhatchet and John Harrison (eds), *The City in South Asia: pre-modern and modern*
4. Philip Denwood and Alexander Piatigorsky (eds), *Buddhist Studies: ancient and modern*
5. Peter Robb (ed.), *Rural South Asia: linkages, change and development*
6. Peter Robb (ed.), *Rural India: land, power and society under British rule*
7. Richard Burghart and Audrey Cantlie (eds), *Indian Religion*
8. Tim Dyson (ed.), *India's Historical Demography: studies in famine, disease and society*
9. John L. Hill (ed.), *The Congress and Indian Nationalism: historical perspectives*

LONDON STUDIES ON SOUTH ASIA

1. Duncan B. Forrester, *Caste and Christianity. Attitudes and policies on caste of Anglo-Saxon Protestant missions in India*
2. S.R. Ashton, *British Policy towards the Indian States, 1905-1939*
3. Audrey Cantlie, *The Assamese. Religion, caste and sect in an Indian village*
4. Sharif Uddin Ahmed, *Dacca: a study in urban history and development*
5. John D. Rogers, *Crime, Justice and Society in Colonial Sri Lanka*
6. Geoffrey A. Oddie, *Hindu and Christian in South East India*
7. Avril A. Powell, *Muslims and Missionaries in pre-Mutiny India*

For Product Safety Concerns and Information please contact our EU representative GPSR@taylorandfrancis.com
Taylor & Francis Verlag GmbH, Kaufingerstraße 24, 80331 München, Germany

www.ingramcontent.com/pod-product-compliance
Lightning Source LLC
Chambersburg PA
CBHW070558270326
41926CB00013B/2357
* 9 7 8 0 7 0 0 7 0 2 8 4 8 *